ArtScroll History Series®

Rabbi Nosson Scherman / Rabbi Meir Zlotowitz

General Editors

THE REBBES

Published by

Mesorah Publications, ltd

OF CHORTKOV

By RABBI YISROEL FRIEDMAN

FIRST EDITION
First Impression ... November 2003

Published and Distributed by
MESORAH PUBLICATIONS, LTD.
4401 Second Avenue / Brooklyn, N.Y 11232

Distributed in Europe by
LEHMANNS
Unit E, Viking Industrial Park
Rolling Mill Road
Jarow, Tyne & Wear, NE32 3DP
England

Distributed in Australia and New Zealand by
GOLDS WORLDS OF JUDAICA
3-13 William Street
Balaclava, Melbourne 3183
Victoria, Australia

Distributed in Israel by
SIFRIATI / A. GITLER
6 Hayarkon Street
Bnei Brak 51127

Distributed in South Africa by
KOLLEL BOOKSHOP
Shop 8A Norwood Hypermarket
Norwood 2196, Johannesburg, South Africa

REQUEST
The author would be grateful to receive any stories, photos or documents
pertaining to the Chortkover Dynasty that are not mentioned in this book.
He may be contacted by writing to him at:
12 Newhall Avenue, Manchester M 7 4 JU, England

ISBN:
1-57819-098-3 (hard cover)

Typography by CompuScribe at ArtScroll Studios, Ltd.

Printed in the United States of America by Noble Book Press Corp.
Bound by Sefercraft, Quality Bookbinders, Ltd., Brooklyn N.Y. 11232

לזכרון עולם
נשמת הרב החסיד המפואר מחשובי חסידי טשארטקוב

רבי שמואל יצחק בקנרוט
נפטר כ"ד מנחם אב תשל"ה
הונצח על ידי בניו שיחיו

הרה"ח ר' גילי ור' אברהם בקנרוט הי"ו

~

לזכרון עולם
נשמת הרב החסיד המפואר מחשובי חסידי טשארטקוב

רבי נחום יואל היילפרין זצ"ל
נפטר ה' כסלו תשמ"ז
הונצח על ידי בניו שיחיו

~

לזכרון עולם
נשמת הרב החסיד המפואר מחשובי חסידי טשארטקוב

רבי יוסף היילפרין זצ"ל
נפטר ח"י תמוז תשנ"ט

וזווגתו החשובה מרת פריידא ע"ה
נפטרה ה' מנחם אב תש"ס
הונצחו על ידי נכדיהם

הרה"ח ר' יהושע עוזר ור' שמואל היילפרין הי"ו

~

לזכרון עולם
נשמת הרב החסיד

רבי יוסף דוב בן הרב חיים שלום שניידר ז"ל
נפטר ב' אלול תשמ"ב
הונצח על ידי נכדו

הרה"ח ר' הרשל קופר הי"ו

Table of Contents

Part 1 Mezeritch to Rizhin

Chapter 1: The Maggid Of Mezeritch   16
The Family Tree / Traveling Maggid / Meeting the Baal Shem Tov / The Maggid Is Crowned Successor / Gaining Support of the Masses / The Derech of Chassidus / Reb Avrohom HaMalach / Reb Sholom Prohibishter

Chapter 2: The Rebbe of Rizhin   35
The Young Tzaddik / The Drunkard and the Royal Crown / Admiration of the Gedolim / Glory and Humility / Eisav's Clothes / Helping Yidden in Eretz Yisroel / Prison / His Legacy

Part 2 R' Dovid Moshe of Chortkov

Chapter 3: In the Shadow of the Rizhiner   52
Reb Dovid Moshe Is Born / Marriage / Dividing the Inheritance / The Brothers Part Ways / Remaining in Potik / In Service of Hashem

Chapter 4: The Move to Chortkov   64
Leaving Potik / Moving to Chortkov / The Rebbe's Palace / Chortkov Becomes a Center / A Changed Environment / Munish Chazzan

Chapter 5: A Shabbos in Chortkov   74
Preparation / Meeting the Rebbe / Kiddush / The Rebbe's Tisch / A Chassidishe "Sitz" / Old Chassidim Remember

Chapter 6: A Life of Kedushah   88

Daily Schedule / Reading a Kvittel / Between the Lines / A Faithful Servant / All Is for the Best / Eating L'Shem Shamayim / Night Program

Chapter 7: Showing the Way   102

Ignoring Provocation / A Bad Deal / Emunah and Bitachon / Serving Hashem With Joy / False Tzaddikim / Every Action for a Higher Cause

Chapter 8: Leader of His People   116

Leader of Leaders / Responsible for the Nation / Which Shul to Daven in / Oblivious to Worldly Matters / Only the Pure Truth / Eiffel Tower / Ruach HaKodesh

Chapter 9: Giving to Tzedakah   130

Helping the Poor / Hated money / An Accusation in the Heavenly Court / To Have an Honest job / Owned All the Money

Chapter 10: The Last Days   137

Moving to Eretz Yisroel / The Final Months / Reunited With the Shechinah / The Last Day / Crowning a New Rebbe / Hespedim

Part 3   R' Yisroel of Chortkov

Chapter 11: The New Rebbe   148

A Changing World / The First Years / My Job Is to Daven / At His Father's Side / I Am Not My Father

Chapter 12: His Marriage and Family   163

Marriage / The Sadigerer Rebbe / Prison / A Human Korban / The Worst Person / Captivated His Chassidim / A Living Mussar Sefer / Venerated by the Goyim / The Bright Star

Chapter 13: Founding Yeshivos   179

Concern for the Youth / The First Yeshivah / History of
Yeshivos in Poland / Learning in the Shteibel / Volozhin
Yeshivah / Bradoshin Yeshivah / Stanislov Yeshivah /
Catering to the Youth / Keren HaTorah

Chapter 14: In Support of Work   196

Pioneering New Ideas / Recognizing a Person's Mission in
This World / Combating the Despair / Agudas HaChareidim /
The General Cheder / In Face of Opposition

Chapter 15: The Royal City of Vienna   212

The First World War / Vienna / A Broad Ahavas Yisroel /
Helping Refugees / True Wisdom / Rescuing Those by the
Wayside / False Tears / Refusal to Forsake Viennese Jewry /
In the Field of Medicine

Chapter 16: On the Go   228

Keeping in Contact / On the Go / Lemberg / Lublin / The Wet
Pillow / Chortkover Communities / Blood Libel / America

Chapter 17: Guiding His Chassidim   245

Individual Care / A Spiritual Doctor / D'veikus / Pure
Intentions / Sincere Actions / In Pursuit of Peace / Humble
as Hillel / Tefillah / The True Tzaddik / Helping the Poor /
Unclean money

Chapter 18: In Agudas Yisroel   270

Kattowitz / Under the Rebbe's Aura / Expansion / The
Knessia Gedolah / Like a Gramophone / With the Chofetz
Chaim / Resolutions / Daf Yomi

Chapter 19: The Second Knessia Gedolah   288

Just a Regular Member / Rav Shach's Fast / Melech Yisroel /

Martyrs of Chevron / Time for action / Bais Yaakov /
Lasting Impressions

Chapter 20: Toward Eretz Yisroel   298
Supporting Aliyah / Rejecting Zionist Offers / The Balance of
Power / Not a Second Paris / Responsibility for the Yidden in
Eretz Yisroel / No Time to Lose / Who May Ascend / The
Gerrer Rebbe's Support / Chortkover Settlements

Chapter 21: The Rebbe and His Faithful Chassid,
Reb Meir Shapiro   293
A Magnet for Gedolei Yisroel / My Urim VeTumim / Near
Lemberg / President of Agudah / Daf Yomi / A Person's
Mission in This World / An Inner Connection / Building Starts /
The Yeshivah Is Opened / Yeshivas Chachmei Lublin / On the
Way to Chortkov / To Prepare the Way / Only With Joy

Chapter 22: The Last Months   349
The Nazi Rise to Power / Black Clouds in Europe / May
Hashem Help the Survivors / The Last Seudah in Berlin /
The Last Succos / Thanking Hashem for the Bad / The
Levayah / The Kever as a Makom Tefillah / Revelations After
His Petirah

Part 4   The Continuation of a Dynasty
Chapter 23: Joint Leadership   372
Reb Nuchem Mordechai and Reb Dov Ber / Refusal to Be
Anointed Rebbes / Brotherly Love / Reb Dov Ber's Life and
Service / His Premature Passing and Loss

Chapter 24: In the Shadow of War   385
A True Servant of Hashem / In His Father's Footsteps /
Under Nazi Tyranny / Escape to Eretz Yisroel / The
Destruction of Chortkov / The Enemy's Mistake / Reb
Nuchem Mordechai's Last Years

Chapter 25: Fourth Generation of the Dynasty 400

The New Flag Bearer / The Chortkover Yeshivah / The Rizhiner Yeshivah / Chinuch Atzmai / Sins of the Righteous / An Early Demise / Reb Hershele Zlatipoler

Chapter 26: A Rebbe in Disguise 417

Reb Dovid Moshe Friedman Crowned as Rebbe / A Hidden Tzaddik / Under His Zeide's Direction / The War Years / Hidden From the Public / Unworthy to be Rebbe / Our Signatures Bear Witness Forever / Only the Truth / Lofty Kavanos / His Last Years / A Sleepless Night

Glossary 437

Preface

THE PUBLISHING OF EVERY BOOK ABOUT *GEDOLIM* and *tzaddikim* is an important milestone and contribution to *Klal Yisroel*. Understanding and analyzing the lives of *tzaddikim* whose every breath was according to Torah leaves an indelible imprint on those who thirst to know — and to conduct themselves according to — true Torah values. Thus we find that *gedolim* of the caliber of Reb Yaakov Emden and the Chida (Reb Yosef Chaim Dovid Azulai) spent much time painstakingly recording the lives and actions of other *gedolim*.

The Malbim stresses (in his foreword to the *sefer "Shem HaGedolim"*) another aspect of the importance of recording the lives of *gedolim*. Just as it would be insensitive for a guest who enjoyed the hospitality of an anonymous host not to inquire about the identity of his benefactor, so, explains the Malbim, would it be insensitive for us not to be inquisitive about the lives and actions of our *gedolim*.

In the Chortkover Dynasty, special emphasis was placed on the importance of relating stories about *tzaddikim*. The Rebbes would often relate incidents about how their fathers and *zeides* had acted and how their actions should act as a guide for us. Not all stories, however, can be used nowadays as a practical guide. There are many stories about the *kedushah* and *tzidkus* of *gedolim* which are beyond our grasp and have no application for us in our lowly decadent world. Nevertheless, such stories do have a value for us, even if we are far removed from such heights. We must at least be aware of what heights previous generations were capable of reaching. The rapid decline of morals and values in modern society lent an extra urgency to the importance of reminding future generations of the ways of our *gedolim* in the past.

Indeed, it is those people who aim high that achieve great results. Even if they end up falling short of their original goals, nevertheless they are still left with considerable gains. If, however, one is happy to aim just for the basic minimum, then, if one falls short of that, he is left with nothing. Thus our sages exhorted us (*Shabbos* 112b): "If we regard the earlier *tzaddikim* as being *malachim*, then by comparison we will be humans. If, however, we only aspire to be humans, for this is how we regard previous *tzaddikim*, by comparison we will be like mules!"

It was the wish of the Rebbes of Chortkov that their lives and teachings be recorded for future generations. This fact is plainly clear from a *haskamah* that Reb Yisroel of Chortkov gave in 1929 to the *sefer "Kerem Yisroel"* detailing the lives of the Rebbe's father and *zeides*. In the introduction to this *sefer*, the author, who was a prominent Rav in Galicia, mentions that it had not been his own idea to compose such a *sefer*. Rather, it was the Rebbe himself who had actually approached him and instructed him to transcribe the life and history of his family, so that later generations should know of past *tzaddikim*.

In his *haskamah*, the Rebbe wrote to the author:

> His undertaking and his work are extremely pleasing and important in my eyes and I offer him my thanks. I was always envious of those families who have recorded their family lineage. Our holy family lineage traces back to Dovid HaMelech. Yet, until now no one has exerted himself to record in a *sefer* the deeds of our holy fathers who were famed *tzaddikim*, to compile their achievements and the stories of their ways, that they remain for future generations.

Thus, it is with heartfelt gratitude to Hashem that I present here the biography of the Rebbes of Chortkov. I do not pretend for a moment that the book gives a full and complete picture of their lives and achievements. To truly do justice to the *tzaddikim* mentioned, it would be necessary to devote several volumes to each one of them. This book serves therefore to give the reader a glimpse into the life and ways of these great men, a short appreciation of their great contribution to our lives.

Many years of hard work went into compiling this book: first, gathering the information and material; then, many long hours of research; and finally the actual writing. Great care has been taken to present the stories and incidents as they took place without embellishment or exaggeration. To this end, the only sources used were those whose authors were known for their honesty and integrity and could be relied upon not to distort the truth. It is not just a duty but also a privilege to be able to thank those who helped me along the way.

First I would like to thank my mother, Mrs. Leah Friedman of Edgware London, who raised me in the path of the Torah and invested much time and energy in my education. Her total dedication and constant guidance accompany me in all my endeavors. In addition, I am also indebted to her for the many long hours she spent correcting the grammar and proofreading the text. May she have much *nachas* from all her children and grandchildren and many happy healthy years to come.

Also I would like to thank my father-in-law, Reb Nuchem Mordechai Halpern of Manchester, and my mother-in-law, for their constant encouragement and support in all my endeavors.

I am especially indebted to my wife Esther Chana for always being there at my side. Since I know she would not want me to say any more, let it suffice just to mention that the ראשי תיבות of אסתר חנה are the same as אשת חיל!

The publication of this book was only possible through the generous help of the following people to whom I am very grateful: Reb Avrohom and Reb Gili Backenrot, Reb Moshe Binyomin Brenig, Reb Mendy Bude, Reb Hershel Cooper, Reb Moshe Binyomin Doppelt, Reb Avrohom and Reb Yossi Halpern, Reb Yehoshua Oizer and Reb Shmuel Halpern, Reb Yehoshua Prever and Reb Dovid Shechter. Thanks are given to Reb Avrohom Chaim Spiegel, who provided many photos, documents and stories.

My thanks are also extended to Rabbi Nosson Scherman, editor of Artscroll Publishing, and to Rabbi Avrohom Biderman, as well as to the staff of Mesorah publications for their dedication and commitment in producing this book and making it a work of beauty. A number of individuals deserve special mention: Reb Eli Kroen, who designed the striking and appealing cover; Mrs. Mindy Stern, who read and commented on the manuscript and then proofread the book; Devorah Scheiner, who had the challenging task of typesetting this work; and Chava Esther Ehrlich, who helped coordinate much of the work. I am grateful for their many efforts.

The publication of the book should be *l'ilui nishmas* my father, Reb Dovid Moshe Friedman, of Edgware London, who personified everything for which Chortkov stood. His *zechus* and the *zechusim* of all the *tzaddikim* mentioned in the book should accompany us all until the coming of Moshiach speedily in our days. Amen.

Introduction

AMONG THE MANY GREAT *GEDOLIM* WHO ILLUMI-
nated the Torah world in the decades before the two World
Wars, a select few stand out as the major pathfinders of
Klal Yisroel. These personalities' every thought and deed
were devoted to helping *Klal Yisroel* as a whole. They made the important decisions and carried the heavy burden on their shoulders.

One of the largest and most famous chassidic dynasties in pre-
war Europe was the dynasty of Chortkov. No matter, large or small,
was decided on before the Rebbes of Chortkov were consulted.
Chortkov became the uncrowned capital of Orthodox Jewry in
Galicia, as the hundreds of letters that arrived daily could testify.

For over a century the Rebbes of Chortkov guided, taught, encouraged and protected the masses. The Rebbes of Chortkov were
considered to be among the greatest *tzaddikim* of their time. They

exercised immense influence on all aspects of Jewish life through-out Galicia, Poland, Romania and Russia. Their ways left an indelible imprint on the tens of thousands of *Yidden* who flocked to Chortkov from all corners of Eastern Europe and beyond. Their *divrei Torah* and every comment were eagerly awaited by the masses, who looked to the Rebbes for inspiration and direction in the difficult and turbulent times.

In the non-Jewish world, the ways and opinions of previous generations are often regarded as outdated and obsolete, no longer relevant in our constantly changing world. How can the views and morals of a person from a different era possibly dictate to a modern age? Even the greatest minds and thinkers of previous times are regularly regarded as old fashioned and out of touch with an ever evolving society.

Different, however, is the Torah outlook. The Torah exhorts us to take advice from the way in which previous generations acted. *"Zechor yemos olam binu shenos dor vador, she'al avicha v'yagedcha zekeinecha v'yomru lach* — Remember days gone by, understand the years of generation after generation. Ask your father and he will relate it to you, your elders and they will tell it you" (*Devarim* 32:7-8).

The outlook and perspective of those who view the world through the Torah are immune to the march of time. Their opinions and advice are always and will always remain essential for us and serve as our guide in ever-changing times. It was in this vein that the Chortkover Rebbe, Reb Yisroel, once said:

> It is my opinion that there is a higher form of *chochmah* that is hidden from sight. It is from this higher *chochmah* that true *tzaddikim* draw their wisdom. This is what Reb Meir meant when he said (*Avos* 6:1): "Anyone who learns Torah *lishmah* … from him people enjoy counsel and wisdom." For the Torah contains in it a blueprint of all aspects of life, according to their true values. Someone who learns Torah *lishmah* understands and sees the world as it should really be, according to higher levels and according to its true purpose. From such a person you can ask advice, and his answers will be correct and faithful.

Yet, even so, *tzaddikim* also have to be attuned to the specific requirements of their times and understand the unique needs of each generation in turn. At a conference of Agudas Yisroel in Warsaw in 1936, Reb Yisroel's son, Reb Dov Ber of Chortkov, stressed this point very clearly:

> The program of Agudas Yisroel is the handling and solving of all problems according to the dictates and ways of the Torah. This program is fixed and not given to change, but the ways to achieve this aim are many and varied and subject to change according to the place and time.
>
> Unfortunately, until today the Agudah has failed to understand this. It continues to employ only one method of action. It is true that from time to time people do put forward new ideas, but still the basic strategy has remained the same. We are living in difficult times, both physically and spiritually, and we must find new ways of dealing with the ever-changing challenges that face us.

The Rebbes of Chortkov were highly attuned to the ever-changing needs of the generations. This was especially true of the second Chortkover Rebbe, Reb Yisroel, whose life and ideals hold the center stage of this book. A founding and leading member of Agudas Yisroel, he did not hesitate to challenge old hallowed ways if he felt that they were no longer suitable or applicable. He was considered by many to be a pioneer in various fields, especially in social issues. He innovated drastic changes in the field of *chinuch* and also reshaped the way *Yidden* viewed work and the workplace.

In many ways the Rebbe was ahead of his times. His views and opinions may appear nowadays to be the standard opinion, but then it was not so. It took many decades for the validity of his words to become clear to all. Thus the Rebbes of Chortkov can be credited as being from those select few who laid the groundwork for ushering the Orthodox community into the modern era.

In this book, the lives of the Rebbes of Chortkov are revealed in all their extraordinary greatness. Containing a treasure of inspiring and moving stories, the reader will enjoy the profound lessons that the Rebbes have bequeathed to us, a heritage for all times.

PART ONE

MEZERITCH TO RIZHIN

CHAPTER ONE
The Maggid of Mezeritch

WHEN REB DOV BER, THE MEZERITCHER Maggid, was 5 years old, a fire broke out in his parents' home, destroying the whole house with all its contents. Reb Dov Ber's mother was heartbroken — for the fire had consumed all their possessions — and she refused to be comforted. Seeing her tears, her young son asked her in surprise, "Mamma, why are you so upset? All that was lost was a few broken cups and saucers. We didn't own more than that. Did they really mean so much to you?"

REB DOV BER'S MOTHER LISTENED TO HER SON'S WORDS and answered him, "No, my son, I am not crying about the loss of
The Family Tree our old and shabby belongings. It's the loss of our family tree that upsets me so much. Our family is descended from generations of famous *rabbanim* and *tzaddikim*. The tree listed their names all the way back to Dovid

HaMelech. It meant a lot to me and now that we have lost it how can I not weep?"

Reb Dov Ber comforted his mother and told her, "Mamma, don't be upset about the loss of our ancestry. I will start a new family tree that will replace the one destroyed. Until the coming of Moshiach our family will light up the world with its Torah and *kedushah!*"

The young boy kept his word and grew up to become the famous Maggid of Mezeritch, the *talmid* and successor of the Baal Shem Tov. After the Maggid's *petirah* he was succeeded by his son Reb Avrohom HaMalach (who was so called because of his great holiness) who was in turn succeeded by his son, Reb Sholom Shachna of Prohibisht. Reb Sholom Shachna's son was the famed Rebbe of Rizhin who founded the Rizhiner dynasty, which continues to light up the world to this very day.

⁂

Very little is known about the Maggid's early years. Not even the year of his birth is known for certain. Tradition has it that he was born just before the beginning of the 18th century (5460), a few years before the birth of the Baal Shem Tov.

As a young boy, Reb Dov Ber advanced rapidly in his learning and eventually his diligence earned him a place among the elite *talmidim* of the famed *gaon*, Reb Yaakov Yehoshua Falk, author of the renowned *sefer*, "*Pnei Yehoshua*."

The Pnei Yehoshua respected Reb Dov Ber highly and regarded him as his *chavrusa* and not just as a *talmid*. After some time, the Pnei Yehoshua left Lemberg to assume the *Rabbanus* in Frankfurt, and his son filled his position in Lemberg. Before leaving Lemberg, the Pnei Yehoshua instructed his son to bring difficult *sha'alos* to Reb Dov Ber and to follow his ruling.

When Reb Dov Ber reached marriageable age, he became engaged to the daughter of Reb Sholom Shachna of Torchin. After his *chasunah* he moved to Torchin where he continued his learning, while his wife supported them from a small shop that she owned. The townspeople soon realized the great potential that Reb Dov Ber possessed, and he was appointed to head the local yeshivah in Torchin.

During his years in Torchin, Reb Dov Ber delved into the hidden parts of the Torah — the *Zohar* and the writings of the Arizal. Hand in hand with his ascent in the secrets of the Torah, Reb Dov Ber's *mesiras nefesh* for every mitzvah and *minhag* grew as well. His intensity in *avodas Hashem* can be seen from the following story that was related by the Chortkover Rebbe, Reb Dovid Moshe, who was a descendant of the Mezeritcher Maggid:

> When my *zeide* Reb Dov Ber lived in Torchin, he would immerse himself daily before *Shacharis*. Since there was no *mikveh* in the area, Reb Dov Ber would *toivel* in a local river. Even when winter arrived and the river was covered with snow and ice, he would not desist from this practice. Due to his poverty Reb Dov Ber was unable to afford proper shoes. Therefore, every time he went to *toivel*, the soles of his feet would crack, and wherever he walked, he left a trail of blood behind him.
>
> Despite the severe cold, when Reb Dov Ber started to *daven* he would perspire profusely from great concentration. Hardly had he reached *Baruch She'amar* than he would have to remove the *tallis* from over his head in order to cool himself down.

Traveling Maggid

EVENTUALLY REB DOV BER GAVE UP HIS POST IN THE yeshivah to become a traveling *maggid*, going from town to town giving *mussar* and exhorting people to change their ways and do *teshuvah*. Like many *tzaddikim* of his time, Reb Dov Ber used to engage in extended periods of fasting. Often he would fast for days on end, only eating a few morsels of bread once it was night. Over the years this regime of fasting began to take its toll on his already weak body. Eventually the time came when he became so frail that he was no longer able to carry on learning properly. He also suffered from an extremely painful ailment in his foot, which prevented him from walking and from going to the *mikveh*. For a *maggid* who was constantly on the go, this was a major calamity.

At the time, the name of the Baal Shem Tov was beginning to be heard more and more. Some twenty years had passed since 1734, when the Baal Shem Tov had first revealed his miraculous powers. Now many *Yidden* flocked to him for help, when everything else had failed. Reb Dov Ber's family and friends urged him to also make the trip to the Baal Shem Tov and ask him to cure his ailments.

Reb Dov Ber, however, refused to hear of the idea. Like many other *gedolim* of the time he was very suspicious of the Baal Shem Tov. Less than 100 years had passed since the tragic episode of Shabsai Tzvi, who had misled the thousands of *Yidden* who had joined his movement, which he based on his perverted explanations of the *Zohar* and other *sifrei* Kabbalah. That episode climaxed with Shabtai Tzvi converting to Islam in the year 1666.

Although the Baal Shem Tov did not *chas vesholom* change the slightest iota from what was written in the *gemara* and *Shulchan Aruch*, he did put great emphasis on many Kabbalistic concepts which until then had been the domain of only the select elite. The Baal Shem Tov also rejected the time-honored practice of fasting as a way of *teshuvah*. He held that performing the mitzvos with true joy was a better way of coming close to Hashem than afflicting the body and thereby weakening oneself.

Meanwhile Reb Dov Ber's condition continued to deteriorate until he became totally lame in his left foot. His family's pleas to visit the Baal Shem Tov and to find a way out of his misery fell on deaf ears. The matter would have ended there had Reb Dov Ber not happened to meet one of the close *talmidim* of the Baal Shem Tov. Reb Dov Ber was very impressed by the *talmid* and finally he agreed to visit the Baal Shem Tov. The historic encounter between these two *tzaddikim* was recorded in the *sefer "Keser Shem Tov"* that was printed some forty years later in 1795.

WHEN REB DOV BER HEARD ABOUT THE GREATNESS OF
the holy Baal Shem Tov, and of the amazing results of his *tefillos*, he

Meeting the Baal Shem Tov
decided to visit him in order to see for himself
if the reports were true. Besides his great
geonus in all sections of the Torah, both *nigleh*
and *nistar*, Reb Dov Ber was also a great *masmid* who never wasted
a minute from his learning. Reb Dov Ber expected to hear some
deep and profound insights from the Baal Shem Tov. Much to his
dismay, when Reb Dov Ber finally arrived in Mezibuzh, the Baal
Shem Tov only related some stories about how he had gone on a
journey, and had run out of food for his horses. The following day
the Baal Shem Tov told Reb Dov Ber some more stories, all of which
appeared to be very meaningless.

Reb Dov Ber decided to return home immediately and didn't even
bother to ask for a cure for his illness. As he was preparing to leave,
the Baal Shem Tov sent someone to summon him. When he arrived
the Baal Shem Tov asked him, "Are you fluent in the whole Torah?"
Reb Dov Ber answered that he was, to which the Baal Shem Tov
asked him, "Are you also fluent in the whole of *Zohar* and *kisvei
haArizal*? Once again, Reb Dov Ber answered in the affirmative.

The Baal Shem Tov then took out the *sefer "Eitz Chaim"* (by the
Arizal) and asked him to explain a certain passage. That particular
passage is extremely difficult to understand. The Arizal explains the
names of various angels, and shows how the name of each angel
corresponds to its task and to its composition and being. Reb Dov
Ber looked at the passage and immediately explained it. The Baal
Shem Tov listened carefully and after Reb Dov Ber had finished he
told him, "You did not explain it properly."

Reb Dov Ber looked at the passage again and said, "My explanation is the correct one, but if his honor has a better *pshat* I will gladly
accept it." The Baal Shem Tov instructed Reb Dov Ber to stand up on
his feet. When they were both standing, the Baal Shem Tov started to
recite the paragraph in the *"Eitz Chaim."* As the Baal Shem Tov recited the names of the angels the room became filled with an
amazingly bright light and the angels became visible to Reb Dov Ber.
After the Baal Shem Tov finished reading, he turned to Reb Dov Ber

and said, "The meaning of the passage is indeed as you had said. But your learning was dry like an empty vessel without any *neshamah*."

After this revelation Reb Dov Ber decided to stay on in Mezibuzh and to absorb the teachings and ways of the Baal Shem Tov. From the beginning the Baal Shem Tov viewed Reb Dov Ber as his eventual successor, and prepared him for this task. To his *talmid* Reb Chaim Krasna, the Baal Shem Tov said, "Even before Reb Dov Ber came to me he was already a pure golden *menorah*. All I had to do was to light the candles."

The Rebbe of Rizhin once said, "People think that the Maggid was a *talmid* of the Baal Shem Tov, but it is not so. They taught each other. The Maggid was weak and therefore he wasn't able to absorb as much as the Baal Shem Tov, who was strong and healthy."

An amazing account of what Reb Dov Ber learned with the Baal Shem Tov can be found in the preface to the *sefer "Maggid Devarav LeYaakov."* The *sefer* was first printed in 1808 (5568), thirty-eight years after the Maggid's passing, by Reb Shlomo Lutsker, who was one of the Maggid's close *talmidim*. In his wondrous preface, Reb Shlomo writes:

> Who can possibly describe the great *kedushah* of our master Reb Dov Ber? People will not believe me even if I tell them his wondrous deeds, and how his *tefillos* and his every word were fulfilled, as we saw ourselves. Despite his great *madreigos* he was always the epitome of humility and lowliness, and the fear of Hashem could be seen etched on his face constantly. Occasionally he would voice the praises of our master Reb Yisroel Baal Shem Tov, and he once said to me, "Why are you surprised that I tell you that he was *zocheh* that Eliyahu HaNavi would reveal himself to him?"
>
> On another occasion I heard from his holy mouth that the Baal Shem Tov even taught him to understand the language of birds and trees, and he also taught him the meanings and secrets of the Divine Names of Hashem, and how to understand the writing of angels. He also told me that it was through these Divine Names that the Baal Shem Tov knew

every year in *Chodesh Nissan* who would be the new leaders and rulers in the coming year and how they would act.

After the Maggid related to Reb Shlomo Lutsker what he had seen and learned from the Baal Shem Tov, Reb Shlomo writes that he asked the Maggid a question:

> "If our master told me that the Baal Shem Tov learned with him all these things, then surely our master must also have mastered all these *madreigos*?"
>
> In his humility, however, he refused to answer me. I asked him why he doesn't want to reveal to me his *madreigos*, just as the Baal Shem Tov revealed his *madreigos* to him, to which he replied, "The Baal Shem Tov did not reveal his greatness to me. Only before his *petirah* did he admit that Eliyahu HaNavi used to frequent him. I, however, realized by myself his greatness from the first time that I came to him."

⥤⥢

ONLY THREE YEARS ELAPSED FROM WHEN THE MAGGID first came to Mezibuzh until the passing of the Baal Shem Tov on

The Maggid Is Crowned Successor

Shavuos 5520 (1760). Although most of the *talmidim* had come to Mezibuzh long before the Maggid, he was recognized as the Baal Shem Tov's main and favorite *talmid*. Despite the Maggid's special status, the Baal Shem Tov never officially appointed him as his successor and therefore the Baal Shem Tov's son, Reb Tzvi, was crowned as the new leader of the chassidim.

Reb Tzvi's position as leader lasted for only one year. The following Shavuos, all the *talmidim* came to Mezibuzh to observe the first *yahrtzeit* of the Baal Shem Tov. Reb Tzvi sat in his father's place at the head of the table, while all the *talmidim* sat around him.

Suddenly Reb Tzvi told them that he had an important message to relate to them. "Last night, my father came to me in a dream and informed me that the *Shechinah* and the Heavenly Court that used to be with him have gone over to Reb Dov Ber. Therefore my father has instructed me to transfer the leadership to him in the presence of all the *talmidim*. Reb Dov Ber will sit in my place and I will sit in his place."

When Reb Tzvi finished speaking, he got up from his place and went over to Reb Dov Ber and led him to his new place at the head of the table, and Reb Tzvi took Reb Dov Ber's old place at the side.

⌒⌒

AS LONG AS THE BAAL SHEM TOV HAD BEEN ALIVE, THE chassidic movement had been confined to a small, localized group of

Gaining Support of the Masses

talmidim and followers. The Maggid, however, sought to disseminate the teachings of his Rebbe far and wide, to spread the movement to the masses across Europe. Reb Dov Ber realized that in order to achieve this goal, he would have to attract and win the support of the *rabbanim* and the *gedolim* of the period. Once he had their support, then the masses would follow automatically. Within one generation Reb Dov Ber managed to realize this aim and by the time he was *niftar*, some twelve years after the Baal Shem Tov, large sections of Poland, Russia and Lithuania had communities of followers.

In the space of a few years, the Maggid succeeded in gaining the support and the following of many of the great *rabbanim* and *tzaddikim* of his era. It is not known exactly how he managed such an amazing feat, but it seems that much of it was due to his overwhelming personality, his unbelievable *geonus* and his great *kedushah*. The greatest *talmidei chachamim* felt themselves as simpletons in his presence. The greatest *mekubalim* and *tzaddikim* felt humbled to stand next to him.

Thus, for example, did the esteemed *gaon*, Reb Meshullam Feivish of Kremnetz, agree to become the Maggid's *mechutan*. Reb Meshullam Feivish was one of the greatest *geonim* of his period. In a *haskamah* to his *sefer* "Mishnas Chachamim," the Noda BiYehudah extols his greatness in Torah and he adds: "While I was still in Poland I already heard of his good name and that he is literally a '*yachid*' in the generation."

Although Reb Meshullam Feivish lived not far from Mezeritch, he refrained from visiting the Maggid for reasons of *bitul Torah*. One day a difficulty cropped up in his learning and Reb Meshullam was unable to solve the problem. In desperation, he decided to travel to Mezeritch to ask the Maggid. When Reb Meshullam arrived, the Maggid just looked at the *gemara* in question and immediately clarified all the difficulties.

Although Reb Meshullam had been opposed to the Maggid until then, he was so impressed by his explanation that he ended up becoming the Maggid's *mechutan*; the Maggid's only son, Reb Avrohom, married Reb Meshullam's daughter.

The Maggid was known to have thirty-nine *talmidim* who possessed *ruach hakodesh*. These *talmidim* were referred to as the "*Tal Oros* — The Thirty Nine Lights.*" It is impossible to list them all here, but some of the more famous ones are: Reb Aharon of Karlin; Reb Elimelech of Lizhensk; the Chozeh of Lublin; the Kozhnitzer Maggid; the Chernobyler Maggid; the Berdichever Rav, Reb Levi Yitzchok; the Baal HaTanya, Reb Shneur Zalman of Liadi; Reb Shmelke of Nikolsburg; and his brother the Baal Haflaah, Reb Pinchos Horowitz. All these *talmidim* also disseminated the Maggid's teachings in their hometowns, and thus in a short span of time much of Eastern Europe came under the influence of the Maggid.

⮜⮞

THE MAGGID'S DESIRE TO SPREAD CHASSIDUS WAS NOT only in order to promote more Torah learning and greater intensity

The Derech of Chassidus in *avodas Hashem*. Rather, he viewed Chassidus as a salvation from the new influences that were beginning to penetrate Jewish homes all over Europe. For hundreds of years, from the times of the *Rishonim*, *Yidden* had little or no contact with the outside gentile world around them. Confined to the ghettos, they had been insulated and sheltered from non-Jewish influences.

One of the famous *geonim* of the period, Reb Yaakov Emden, bemoaned "the evil that has come from France to Germany. *Yidden* lust after the non-Jewish styles of clothing, the shaving of their beards and *payos,* and the wasting of money to teach their children the French language and culture." In Poland and Lithuania, the Vaad Arba HaAratzos, which had looked after and safeguarded *Yiddishkeit* for over 200 years, was finally dismantled in 1762. No longer did the *rabbanim* have the power to decree new laws as they saw fit.

It was in light of these events that the Maggid felt the need to re-unite *Yidden* all over and to breathe new life into them. Thus the chassidic movement took on a dual role — to teach and further elevate the *talmidei chachamim* and also to unite and harmonize the masses, the ignorant and the illiterate. This dual role has often confused those who wanted to analyze and examine the *derech hachassidus* and to understand its purpose.

In his *sefer "Nezer Yisroel"* the Chortkover Rebbe writes:

> The Baal Shem Tov and the Mezeritcher Maggid spread and implanted a deep *emunah* in the hearts of many *Yidden.* It is this *emunah* which has helped us to survive until this very day. Before their times there were also many *gedolim* who taught and instructed *Klal Yisroel.* Their influence, however, only extended to the *bnei Torah* who were able to learn. The result was that the simple and the ignorant were totally ignored, and thereby a large gap was created between the *talmidei chachamim* and the masses.
>
> The Baal Shem Tov and the Maggid worked hard to rectify the situation. They tried desperately to be *mekarev* the simple people and to breathe into them *emunah* and love for the Torah and its *talmidim.* To achieve this end, the founders of the chassidic movement created a new *derech* — that the *gedolim* should set aside part of their time to listen to the everyday problems of the masses, and *daven* for them and also show them miracles. Through such actions, even those who were on a very low level were also drawn close to the *tzaddikim.* The children of these people would then be educated to become *talmidei chachamim* and thereby *limud haTorah* was strengthened and spread even among the masses.

An example of how the Maggid impressed the simple people can be seen from the following passage, which was written by a philosopher by the name of Solomon Maimon. Having heard about the Maggid, he decided to spend a Shabbos in Mezeritch to see for himself what it was all about. He was so impressed that he recorded the impressions of his visit in his autobiography (*Lebens Geshichte*, Berlin 1798):

> On Shabbos I came to the *tzaddik's* house where I found a festive meal awaiting us. A distinguished group of people had come there from various regions. Eventually the *tzaddik* came to the meal. His noble appearance aroused great respect from all who saw him. He was dressed in shiny white clothes — even his shoes and his snuffbox were white. The *tzaddik* greeted everybody individually and then we all sat down to the meal. Throughout the meal a respectful silence reigned. Afterwards the *tzaddik* sang a beautiful melody, which we all found very uplifting. He then placed his hand on his head and became lost in his thoughts, and then he identified each guest by name and place of origin. As can be imagined, we were very amazed by this feat.
>
> The *tzaddik* instructed all the guests to quote a *pasuk* from *Tanach*. He then proceeded to skillfully weave all these *pesukim* into a *derashah*. Even more amazing was the fact that in the part of the *derashah* which related to our respective *pesukim*, we all found precise hints and allusions to our private life and thoughts.

Indeed, the Torah that the Maggid would deliver at his discourses was not prepared ideas and thoughts that he planned to convey to his *talmidim*. The Maggid himself did not know what he would speak about until he actually started speaking, and then the words would flow freely from his mouth. In his *sefer* "*Ohr HaMeir*," the Maggid's *talmid*, Reb Zev of Zhitomir writes:

> Many times I saw with my own eyes that when he opened his mouth to speak words of Torah, he appeared as if he were not in this world at all. It seemed as if the *Shechinah* were speaking through him.

Once, I heard from the Maggid explicitly as follows: "I will teach you the best way to give over the Torah to others: The speaker should not be conscious of himself and the words should just flow from his mouth without his having to think about what to say. As soon as the speaker becomes aware of himself he should stop speaking."

And Reb Zev ends off:

I remember that sometimes the Maggid would stop speaking in the middle of a subject and sometimes he would stop even in the middle of a word.

This *derech* of saying Torah was adopted by many of the Maggid's *talmidim*, as is illustrated by the following story:

Before his *petirah*, Reb Nuchem of Chernobyl asked that all the *derashos* he had said over the years, which were written down, be given to him, so that he could see if they were fit to be printed. Reb Nuchem went through the many papers and divided them into two piles, one big and one small. The small pile was to be printed and the large pile was to be buried.

When he was asked what flaw he had found to make him disregard so many of his *derashos*, he replied, "All the *derashos* that are stacked in the big pile I remember quite clearly. I recall when and where I said them, and what I wanted to achieve with my speech. The *derashos* which are in the small pile, however, seem totally foreign to me. I don't recall ever having said them nor do I remember where or why I delivered them. Therefore I would like just these *divrei Torah* to be printed, for they are not my own *chiddushim* which I thought up, but ideas that Hashem put into my mouth so that I would be His messenger to give them over to *Klal Yisroel*."

Although many of the Maggid's *divrei Torah* were recorded in a number of *sefarim*, due to their tremendous depth, they have by and large remained the domain of a select few. Even the Maggid's own *talmidim* were hesitant to try to record the Torah discourses of their Rebbe for fear that they would not be able to do the job properly.

In his introduction to the *sefer "Maggid Devarav LeYaakov,"* Reb Shlomo Lutsker wrote:

> The truth is that I was very apprehensive to get involved in printing the holy words of our master, Reb Dov Ber, because these subjects are so exalted that not every person will be able to comprehend them. His holy words allude to many of the Torahs of the Arizal and the *Zohar*. When he would speak, his words would enter the hearts of those who heard them like a flaming fire and enflame their souls to serve their Creator. Because of the depth of these subjects it did not even occur to me to try to print them; just to try and simply write them down was beyond me. But one day our master asked me why I don't write down what I hear from him. I answered him that I don't feel capable of doing so, and I had also noticed that those who did record his teachings had often not understood him correctly and wrote according to their own understanding. He answered me that I should still record them, for however they will be written, they will still be an aid for those wishing to ascend in their *avodas Hashem*.

The Maggid's greatness was not limited just to his excellence in learning and performance of the mitzvos. His every action and movement was carried out with intense *kavanos* which were understood only by the greatest of his *talmidim*. The Berdichever Rav, Reb Levi Yitzchok, used to have a notebook in which he recorded everything that he saw and heard from the Maggid, even things that appeared to be just ordinary simple conversation. Once, on a Friday afternoon, the Maggid lay down to rest but was unable to fall asleep. After a few moments he summoned a *talmid* and told him to find Reb Aharon Karliner and tell him to stop reciting *Shir HaShirim*. His recital was causing all the heavens to tremble and this was disturbing the Maggid's sleep. When Reb Hillel of Paritsh would relate this story, he would add, "Look how great the Maggid's every action was. Although he said himself that Reb Aharon Karliner's *davening* caused the very heavens to tremble, his sleep was still more important!"

It was in this vein that Reb Leib Sarah's once remarked, "My trip to the Maggid was not just to hear his Torah, but even to watch how he would take off his socks and put them back on again."

Indeed, one of the early chassidic classics, *"Sifrei Tzaddikim,"* quotes Reb Leib Sarah's as once having said, "It is not enough for a person to be able to say over a *dvar Torah*. Rather he should see that all his actions should be part of the Torah, and that he himself should be part of the Torah. All his activities and his movements should be in accordance and in harmony with the Torah, until people will be able to learn how to keep the Torah just from observing his daily actions."

These words also echo a similar statement of the Baal HaTanya: "Elsewhere you learn how to master the Torah. In Mezeritch you learn how to let the Torah master you."

Many of the *divrei Torah* and the sayings of the Maggid put great emphasis on the need for a person not to fool himself. Before one can expect to ascend the ladder of Torah and *yiras Shamayim*, he must first realize on what level he is already. Only then can he hope to move further.

On one occasion he said, "There are those who learn Torah, and the more they learn, the haughtier and prouder they become. When my *talmidim* learn Torah I want them to realize how poor their understanding is and how inferior they are to those of generations gone by."

When Reb Aharon Karliner returned home after his first visit to Mezeritch, he was asked what he had at learned there. "Absolutely nothing," he replied. "I learned that I am absolutely nothing."

> A wealthy *Yid*, attracted by Chassidus, became a *talmid* of the Maggid, and soon after he lost all his money. The *Yid* asked the Maggid why such a punishment should have befallen him, just at the time when he was finally trying to

improve himself. The Maggid answered him, "*Chazal* have said, 'Whoever seeks wisdom should go to the south, whoever seeks wealth should head north.' You are trying to be in two places at once — which is an impossibility."

"Can nothing be done?" the man asked. "There is only one *eitzah*," the Maggid explained. "Somebody who humbles himself and becomes like nothing takes up no space at all and can therefore go both north and south ..." The Maggid's words penetrated the mind of the *talmid* and led him to work on the *middah* of humility; ultimately he regained his wealth.

Although the Maggid constantly emphasized to his *talmidim* the need to realize one's lowliness and insignificance, he also stressed the need to realize that Hashem values and treasures the *avodah* of every person regardless of his *madreigah*. Nobody should exempt himself and each person has to realize the great potential that he has — that his *tefillos* and his *avodah* will be accepted by Hashem. This point is driven home by the following story:

A simple villager and his wife once came to the Maggid and asked him to *daven* for them that they should be *zocheh* to children. The Maggid requested that they give him 52 golden rubles, equal to the *gematria* of *ben*, and then he would *daven* for them. The villager was horrified to hear what a large sum was demanded of him and he explained that he could not afford more than 10 rubles. The Maggid, however, refused to lower his price and told him, "Either 52 rubles or nothing." Hearing the Maggid's words, the villager grew angry and, turning to his wife, he exclaimed, "Let's take our money back, Hashem will help us without the Maggid!"

At the villager's words, a smile spread across the Maggid's face and he said, "This is what I was waiting to hear. Before you came here, it had not even occurred to you that you are also able to *daven* to Hashem. Since you now uttered these words with pure faith in Hashem, your words have made an impression in *Shamayim*." Within a year the couple had a baby boy.

With this concept the Maggid would often explain the words of the *gemara,* "Although (in the *Beis HaMikdash*) fire descends from Heaven, it is a mitzvah to kindle one's own fire." Although a person can often become aroused by his surroundings, from what he sees and hears, this is not enough. Such a *his'orerus* is only a temporary elevation, which will subside with the passage of time. Rather a person should kindle his own light, by working on himself and elevating himself without relying on external fires, which are easily dampened.

Never blessed with good health, the Maggid became steadily weaker until he was suddenly *niftar* on the 19th of Kislev 5533 (1772). Although he reigned for only twelve years, he had succeeded in transforming the movement into a major force which would help protect and safeguard *Yiddishkeit* all over Europe and beyond, for generations to come.

⋙⋘

Reb Avrohom HaMalach

BEFORE HIS *PETIRAH*, THE MAGGID INSTRUCTED THAT HIS only son, Reb Avrohom HaMalach, be appointed as his successor. Reb Avrohom, however, refused to accept the leadership. He wanted to serve Hashem in solitude without having to lower himself to the level of others. He once said, "There are certain types of *tzaddikim* who cannot lead their generation. The masses are too far removed from the ways of such a *tzaddik* to be able to understand and appreciate them, and the *tzaddik* himself, due to his great *madreigah,* cannot descend low enough to uplift them."

When Reb Avrohom HaMalach once visited the town of Kremnetz, a large crowd turned out to see him. But Reb Avrohom ignored them all and stared into the distance toward a tall mountain. The people waited respectfully to hear some comment or greeting from him but he remained lost in thought. Among those present was a young man who wasn't used to being kept waiting. In a fit of anger and annoyance, he approached Reb Avrohom HaMalach, and in a brazen manner he demanded, "Why do you keep on staring at that mountain? All it is is a clump of earth."

"I am staring and wondering," replied Reb Avrohom, "how such a simple clump of earth could be haughty enough to become a tall mountain!"

Reb Yitzchok Radviller was one of the *tzaddikim* of his generation. He used to say that at first he did not understand why Reb Avrohom HaMalach had been singled out for such an exalted title, to be likened to an angel. However, after spending a Tishah B'Av in Reb Avrohom HaMalach's presence, he could testify that he was indeed not a normal mortal being but a heavenly angel. As the *chazzan* began to recite *Eichah*, Reb Avrohom uttered a bitter and painful cry — "*Eichah.*" With that, he slumped forward, until he sat almost doubled over, with his head between his knees. No sound could be heard from him except for his constant sobbing, which filled the whole room.

After the recital of *Eichah* had ended and the congregation had gone home, Reb Avrohom HaMalach remained in his bent and crumpled position. Reb Yitzchok stayed in the shul until after midnight but Reb Avrohom still did not raise his head from between his knees. When Reb Yitzchok returned to shul the next morning, to his astonishment he found Reb Avrohom still in the same position. This was truly not a normal human being, for only a *malach* could sit doubled over like that without pause for so long.

Reb Avrohom HaMalach personified a statement that he made in his renowned Kabbalistic *sefer* "*Chesed LeAvrohom.*" Quoting the words of *tefillah* that we say every Shabbos morning, "*Vechol komah sich'tachaveh lefanecha* — And all who stand erect shall bow before You," he explained: "Only after a person reaches his full stature can he completely nullify and subjugate himself and bow to Hashem."

Reb Avrohom outlived his father by only four years, for on the 12th of Tishrei 5537 (1776) he suddenly passed away. Although they were now left without any main leader, many of the *talmidim* were already leading large groups of chassidim in their own right. These groups eventually evolved into their own distinctive dynasties, as we know them today.

REB AVROHOM HAMALACH LEFT BEHIND A YOUNG SON BY
the name of Reb Sholom Shachna. He was no ordinary child. When

Reb Sholom Prohibishter

the *tzaddik,* the Shpoler Zeide, saw him, he said:
"When one has a father a *malach* and a mother a
malachte, a child like this is born." Being only 6
years old when his father was *niftar,* Reb Sholom Shachna was
raised by the famed *tzaddik* Reb Shlomo Karliner. When he reached
marriageable age, he married the Rebbetzin Chava, who was a
granddaughter of the Rebbe Reb Nuchem of Chernobyl, author of
the classic *sefer "Me'or Einayim."*

Reb Sholom embarked on a new path in Chassidus. In contrast to
his father and to all the other *tzaddikim* who afflicted themselves and
denied their bodies everything except the basic minimum, Reb
Sholom acted differently. Rather than wear the drab and threadbare
robes of his forefathers, he dressed in smart well-tailored clothes. He
insisted on living in a comfortable home and not in a dilapidated
shack. This *derech* was later broadened by his son, Reb Yisroel of
Rizhin, and became famous as the "Rizhiner *Derech.*"

When his grandfather, Reb Nuchem Chernobyler, who did not
agree to this new path, questioned Reb Sholom, he answered him
with a *mashal*:

> Some duck eggs were once put into a chicken coop so that
> the hen should sit on the eggs and hatch them. When the
> chicks were born they stayed with their foster mother who
> regarded them as her own. One day, as the mother hen was
> walking along followed by the chicks, they passed a river. At
> the sight of the water, the chicks instinctively ran forward
> and jumped into the river. In terror and panic the mother
> hen screamed at them to come out at once before they
> drown. "Don't worry," they called back contently. "This is
> where we belong, we are quite safe here."

Reb Nuchem understood his grandson's answer and from then
on left him in peace.

When the Rizhiner was asked for an explanation of his own *derech*
and that of his father, he replied:

The Baal Shem Tov gave our *zeide*, the Maggid, a precious jewel — the path of true Chassidus. Knowing that the Satan would be only too eager to get his hands on this precious jewel, the Maggid hid it in a fortress of Torah and *tefillah*, but the thieves from Above, the Satan and his agents, broke into the fortress to destroy the gem. My grandfather, Reb Avrohom HaMalach, repaired the breaches and added to the fortress by means of fasting and affliction. But the Satan persisted. So my father devised a new strategy — he hid the stone in a rubbish bin of pride, glory and honor. This place proved much safer, for the thieves never expected to find a precious jewel there.

Reb Sholom moved to the town of Prohibisht in Russia where he opened his *beis hamedrash*. Highly respected by all the *tzaddikim* of his time, Reb Sholom Prohibishter — as he came to be known — was looked up to in awe and deference even by *tzaddikim* many years his senior.

Like his father the Malach, Reb Sholom was also *niftar* at a very young age. The Rizhiner attributed their early demise to the fact that they constantly cleaved to Hashem, never diverting their minds from *avodas Hashem* for a second. Therefore they completed their life's mission quickly.

Although Reb Sholom completed his life's task quickly, the special gift that he left behind him has not been quickly forgotten. His legacy lives on through the ways and teachings of his son, Reb Yisroel of Rizhin.

The Butatcher Rav, who was one of the most famed *gedolim* of his time, and author of the classic *sefer* "*Aishel Avrohom*," once made a startling comment about this legacy. He said as follows: "So great and exalted was the *neshamah* of the Rizhiner, that it needed the combined efforts of the Mezeritcher Maggid and Reb Avrohom HaMalach with Reb Sholom, to be able to bring such a lofty soul down into this world."

CHAPTER TWO
The Rebbe of Rizhin

THE MERE MENTION OF THE WORD "RIZHIN" IS enough to conjure up stories of fabulous wealth and undreamed of treasures. Indeed, the Rebbe of Rizhin was already a legend in his own lifetime. All of his personal belongings, even his everyday cutlery, were made of the most expensive materials. The buttons on his *bekeshes* were made of solid gold, studded with diamonds, and his pillowcase was woven from pure gold thread. Even though most people did not understand the reasons for the Rebbe's conduct, he was regarded as one of the greatest *tzaddikim* of his time.

The Young Tzaddik

MANY WERE THE PRAISES HEAPED ON HIM BY THE *gedolim* of his era: the Szanzer Rav, the Divrei Chaim, said that he could testify that the Rebbe of Rizhin was constantly *moser nefesh* for Hashem, every second of the day. Reb Moshe Kobriner exclaimed that even in the times of the *Tannaim* and *Amoraim* the Rebbe would have been considered a special person; and even when he blinks his eyes it's only *l'shem Shamayim*. The Chidushei HaRim spent three weeks traveling to the Rebbe in order to speak to him, and he later declared that during the half-hour they spent together, the Rebbe had taken him through half the Torah! Similar sentiments were echoed by the Apter Rav, who used to say that he had never seen anybody as well versed in the Torah as the Rizhiner.

The Rebbe was born to Reb Sholom, the Rebbe of Prohibisht, and his wife Rebbetzin Chava, a day after Rosh Hashanah in the year 1797. Even before he was born they knew that their child was destined for greatness. When the Rebbetzin Chava was expecting she went to see the Apter Rav to ask for his *berachah*. He stood up for her as she came into the room, telling her that he was standing up for the *Sefer Torah* she was carrying inside her. As a young child, the Rizhiner's phenomenal level of *kedushah* was already noticeable. When he was only a few years old he would often cry bitter tears but would refuse to disclose the reason for his crying. When his father told him that as a father he has the right to decree that his son tell him the reason for his tears, the child answered, "I am thinking to myself how many times I have lifted up my hands today *shelo l'shem Shamayim*."

At the age of 6, Reb Yisroel met Reb Shneur Zalman, the Baal HaTanya. Reb Shneur Zalman later related how deeply impressed he had been with a question the 6-year-old child had asked him. The Rebbe had asked about an apparent contradiction in *Krias Shema*. When a person says the *pasuk Shema Yisroel*, he must totally annul himself until he comes to the realization that Hashem is One and that he and everything else cease to exist in comparison. If so, how is it possible to immediately fulfill the next *pasuk* of loving Hashem, having just totally annulled all personal feelings? In reply, the Baal HaTanya told him a very deep explanation which took a few hours to relate, and the Rebbe later revealed that he had understood every word.

IT WAS AT THIS TIME THAT REB YISROEL'S FATHER, REB Sholom, was *niftar*, and he was succeeded by his oldest son, Reb

The Drunkard and the Royal Crown Avrohom, who was just 16 at the time. Reb Sholom was *niftar* on Erev Succos 5563 (1803), and the same night Reb Avrohom sat at the head of the table in his father's place. Among Reb Sholom's chassidim were a few who were not so happy with the confident attitude of the new young Rebbe. They were not pleased that he had become Rebbe without first obtaining the *berachah* of elder *tzaddikim*. Sensing their displeasure, Reb Avrohom related the following story:

> There was once a king who spent a fortune building a new palace. When it was finished he invited his subjects to come and view the palace, promising a reward to anyone who could find a fault with any aspect of the new building and its furnishings. Among the many experts who came to inspect the building was a simple villager. The man looked at the beautiful rooms and saw hanging on the wall a picture of a drunken man walking in the street holding a cup of wine. The villager went straight to the king and told him that he had found a major fault with the drawing. In the picture the man was holding a full cup and that was an impossibility. A drunkard sways from side to side and the wine in the cup would certainly have spilled. In reality the cup could be no more than half full. The king agreed with him, rewarding him handsomely.
>
> Pleased with his success, the man looked for more mistakes and soon proclaimed that he had found another fault, this time on a picture of the royal crown. The diamond did not suit the crown at all. This time, however, the king commanded his servants to punish the man for his insolence. The villager could not understand his crime and when he asked for an explanation the king said, "When it comes to a drunkard then you can offer your opinion, but how dare you, an uneducated man, offer an opinion about the royal crown?!"

AT THE AGE OF 7, REB YISROEL BECAME ENGAGED TO THE
daughter of Reb Moshe, the *Rosh Yeshivah* of Berdichev. The

**Admiration of
the Gedolim**

Berdichever Rav, Reb Levi Yitzchok, was invited
to the engagement. As he came into the room
and saw the *chasan*, he lifted up his eyes and exclaimed, "Hashem, You haven't got many *chasanim* like him!"

When Reb Yisroel was 13 years old the *chasunah* took place; when
he turned 16 his older brother, Reb Avrohom, was *niftar*, leaving no
children. He was then succeeded by Reb Yisroel. Despite his tender
age, he immediately began to attract masses of followers. The famous Chozeh of Lublin said that even though *Chazal* say that a
person does not achieve true understanding before he is 40 years old,
Reb Yisroel was an exception. Similar sentiments were also heard
from Reb Uri of Strelisk. Before Reb Uri was *niftar* at the age of 70, he
instructed his chassidim that after his *petirah* they should adopt Reb
Yisroel as their Rebbe even though he was then still in his 20's.

Not long after Reb Yisroel became Rebbe, the famous "Ostilla *chasunah*" took place. To this *chasunah* of two major dynasties came
thousands of chassidim, including dozens of great *tzaddikim*. The eldest guest was the Apter Rav, the grandfather of the *chasan*. As such,
he sat at the head of the table and was the center of attention. When
the Rizhiner entered the hall, the Apter Rav called out, "Make way,
make way." The Apter Rav's children didn't find it fitting that their
father should belittle himself so much, and told him so. The Apter
Rav ignored their pleas, telling them, "Do you know who is coming? *The Melech Yisroel* is coming."

On another occasion, when Reb Yisroel's *gartel* fell to the floor, the
Apter Rav picked it up and rewound it around Reb Yisroel's body,
saying that Heaven had granted him the opportunity to fulfill the
mitzvah of *gelilas Sefer Torah*. Stories such as these left a deep impression on the chassidim and thousands began to flock to
Prohibisht. The building where Reb Yisroel lived became too small
and he moved to the town of Rizhin, not far from Kiev in Ukraine.
It is by the name of this town that he is known until today.

One of the Rizhiner's greatest admirers was the Szanzer Rav, Reb
Chaim Halberstam. When his followers expressed surprise that he

should feel it necessary to make the long and difficult journey to visit the Rizhiner, he told them. "Why was the *Beis HaMikdash* built on Har Moriah (where the *Akeidas Yitzchok* took place), and not on Har Sinai (where the Torah was given to *Klal Yisroel*)? Because the place where a Jew was willing to be *moser nefesh* for Hashem's Name is more important than the place where the Torah was given. The Rizhiner is ready at all times to be *moser nefesh* for Hashem's Name."

WHEREVER THE REBBE WENT, CROWDS CAME TO SEE HIM. The Rebbe traveled in a beautiful carriage drawn by four white horses. On one occasion, the Rebbe was asked how he

Glory and Humility keeps himself from having haughty thoughts when he sees the many people pushing to see him. The Rebbe answered the question with a *mashal*:

> There was once a king who ruled over a country which was too big for him to control by himself. He therefore appointed a governor over each province. One day the king decided to visit one of his faraway provinces that he had never seen before. When the king arrived he asked the governor to accompany him for a stroll through the main street of the area. As they walked down the street together, crowds began to push each other to get a better view of their governor. The king, however, was not recognized by anyone. In the commotion to see the governor, the king got pushed and shoved around along with everyone else. Can you imagine how embarrassed the governor must have been? His importance came only from the king, and he must have felt terrible to see that the king was getting pushed around. "Similarly," ended the Rizhiner, "when I see the way people try to honor me, I think to myself, if only they would honor Hashem like this as well, and it makes me so upset that the idea of becoming haughty doesn't even occur to me!"

The Rebbe laid great emphasis on sanctifying his thoughts. He regarded this as one of the most important factors in a person's *madreigah*. He constantly exhorted his chassidim to strive toward the goal of sanctifying their thoughts. At the very least, the first thoughts a person has when he wakes up in the morning should be about Hashem. These first pure thoughts then stand the person in good stead for the rest of the day, even while he is working or eating. The Rebbe himself testified that if he were left alone in a house for 100 years without any *sefarim* he would not forget about Hashem for even one second. Often, from his great *d'veikus* in Hashem, he would go into a deep trance and remain so for hours at a time. His constant awareness of Hashem's presence was noticed by all. The famed *tzaddik*, Reb Mordechai of Nadvorna, would say that if one wants to see true fear of Hashem, one should watch the conduct of the Rizhiner: his knees would knock together with fright at the thought that he was standing in Hashem's presence.

One year, on Rosh Hashanah, no signal was received from the Rebbe's private room that he had finished *davening Shemoneh Esrei*. The Rebbe's oldest son, Reb Sholom Yosef, went into the room and saw that his father was still on the first page of *Shemoneh Esrei*. Reb Sholom Yosef turned the pages of the *machzor* for his father until the end of *davening*. Later the Rizhiner explained what had happened. When he realized that he was standing in front of Hashem, he suddenly became so overcome with fear that he was unable to move even his arm — as if he had been paralyzed — and therefore was unable to turn the pages of the *machzor* to continue *davening*.

Although from the outside it appeared that the Rebbe enjoyed all the comforts of this world, nothing could be further from the truth. In reality, the Rebbe afflicted himself terribly, denying his body even the basic necessities. This point is illustrated by the famous story of the Rebbe's boots. The Rebbe used to wear a magnificent pair of boots. It was rumored that even the Czar of Russia was jealous of these boots. Made of solid gold and studded with diamonds and other precious stones, they were the envy of all who beheld them. Once, on a bitterly cold night, the Rebbe went out in his boots to sanctify the New Moon. The Rebbe stood *davening* for a long time in the snow. When he left, the chassidim noticed blood where he had been standing.

An investigation of the Rebbe's boots revealed that they had no soles. Every time the Rebbe wore them he was really walking barefoot, and when he stood on the snow his feet became stuck to the icy ground, causing them to bleed when he began walking. When this story became known, even those people who had until then been opposed to his extravagant lifestyle, bowed their heads in deference, acknowledging that the Rebbe's every action was only for the sake of Heaven and not for his own pleasure.

The Rebbe would go for days on end without eating. On one occasion he commented that when the time came for him to be born, his *neshamah* did not want to descend into this lowly world until the body promised the *neshamah* that it would only partake of this world what it needs for its basic survival.

When the Rebbe was asked why he had chosen to follow an extravagant lifestyle unlike the other *tzaddikim* of the time who lived in poverty, he answered as follows: We find that the two traits of humility and wisdom are entwined with one another. Only somebody who is truly wise can acquire the trait of humility, and similarly, only someone who is truly humble can become wise. Moshe Rabbeinu is called the most humble of men, and if so, he must have also been the wisest. Shlomo HaMelech is known as the wisest of all men and therefore must also have been the most humble. The reason Moshe is praised for his humility is because a Rav has the right to be *mochel* on his *kavod*. A king, however, even if he wants to, may not be *mochel* on his *kavod* (*Melech shemachal al kevodo, ein kevodo machul*). Therefore Shlomo could only be praised for his wisdom. "What can I do," said the Rebbe, "it has been thrust on me from Heaven to take the way of royalty. It wasn't my choice and I haven't the ability to exempt myself from this *derech*."

In keeping with this *derech*, the Rebbe would often comment that a Yid's biggest *aveirah* is when he forgets that he is a "*ben hamelech*," a son of Hashem. As long as a person remembers who he is, he is less likely to fall to lower standards.

THE REBBE'S FAME SPREAD FAR AND WIDE AND PEOPLE came from all over to see him. Once, when the Rizhiner was in

Eisav's Clothes

Germany, the distinguished *tzaddik*, Reb Shamshon Raphael Hirsch, came specially to see him. Afterwards, when he was asked what impression the Rebbe had made on him, Reb Shamshon Raphael answered: "It is quite unbelievable to see how all the money and *kavod* is brought to him, and he himself is totally uninterested in it. His one and only concern is how to increase *kevod Shamayim* and the *kavod* of *Klal Yisroel*."

Indeed, the Rebbe was constantly occupied with trying to lift the *Yidden* up from their poverty and problems. As a small child he used to go to the cattle market and tell the butchers which animals were *treif* and therefore shouldn't be bought. When the Rebbe's father heard of this he ordered his son to cease this practice. The young Rizhiner protested that he wanted to save the *Yiddishe* butchers from losing their money.

The Rebbe sought to lighten the heavy burden of the *Yidden* as much as possible. When it was decreed that all the *Yidden* had to change their way of dress to that of the *goyim*, most of the *poskim* of the time held that a person should give up his life rather than change his mode of dress. When the Rebbe was asked what he held, he answered, "Yaakov Avinu received the *berachos* from his father Yitzchok, dressed in Eisav's clothes."

Even people who had fallen from the correct path could also hear a warm word from the Rebbe. In the times of the Baal Shem Tov and his disciples, it was mainly the elite who found a place at the Rebbe's table. The Rizhiner, however, sought to include even the simple and unlearned. He would constantly remind his chassidim about the importance of being with a Rebbe. He would say that even if they did not learn anything new while in Rizhin, it was still worth the effort to come.

Although always occupied with lofty thoughts, the Rebbe was able to speak to every person on his own level. When a simple person told him that he didn't know how to do *teshuvah*, the Rebbe retorted, "And to sin you did know? You just did it without thinking twice and later you realized that you had done an *aveirah*. Now too if you start mending your ways the *teshuvah* will follow automatically."

To another person, the Rebbe advised that his *teshuvah* would be to *daven* only using a *siddur*. Even the smallest *berachah* should only be said from a *siddur*. In due course, this *baal teshuvah* became known as a well-respected *tzaddik*.

The Rebbe would do his utmost to help others. He would say that just like metal becomes hot when placed in fire and freezing cold when placed in the cold, similarly he himself feels the pain and suffering of every *Yid* from one end of the world to the other. Not for nothing did the aged Rebbe of Vorka, Reb Yitzchok, proclaim that *ahavas Yisroel* such as he had seen in Rizhin was not to be found anywhere else!

When news arrived in Rizhin of an evil decree against the *Yidden*, the Rebbe would lock himself up for weeks at a time in his private quarters to *daven* that Hashem annul the decree. At such times it was literally impossible to see or speak to him: not even his closest family or *gabbaim* were granted access.

In his *tefillos* the Rebbe would constantly be *melamed zechus* on the *Yidden*. He would often repeat that when the Berdichever Rav would see a person carrying his *tallis* and *tefillin* on the way to shul, he would remark about the *tzidkus* of such a person who leaves his warm bed every morning in order to please Hashem. If so, then what can one say nowadays about a person who leaves his home to go to shul and doesn't know if his children are going to be snatched away to the army while he is out. Such a person can be likened to the Baal Shem Tov himself!

THE REBBE CARED NOT ONLY FOR THE *YIDDEN* IN HIS vicinity but also for those from far and wide. He took a special in-

Helping Yidden in Eretz Yisroel
terest in helping those living in Eretz Yisroel. At that time it was extremely difficult to live in Eretz Yisroel. Only 4,000 *frum Yidden* inhabited the land, living in very primitive conditions. A large number of them subsisted on money sent by Kollel Volhin. This organization looked after most of the needs of those in the Holy Land.

The Rebbe, who headed the Kollel Volhin, was in charge of raising and distributing the money to the needy. As a direct descendant of Dovid HaMelech, the Rebbe felt that it was his duty to see to their welfare. Anyone who wanted to immigrate to Eretz Yisroel first had to obtain the Rebbe's permission; otherwise he would not receive money from the Kollel. The Rebbe insisted that every person going to live in Eretz Yisroel must be able to support himself for the first

The Rizhiner Shul in the Old City of Yerushalayim; it was destroyed by the Arabs in 1948

three years, only afterwards would he be paid by the Kollel. In this way the burden on those already there was eased.

When word reached the Rebbe that the Russian Czar intended to build a big church in the Old City of Yerushalayim, the Rebbe summoned Reb Nissan Bak, who lived in Yerushalayim and was one of the Rebbe's faithful chassidim. The Rebbe gave him a sum of money and told him to rush and buy the plot of land before the Russians do so. Reb Nissan arrived there a few days ahead of the Russians and succeeded in buying the plot of land. When the Czar heard that the land had been snatched out of his hands, he exploded in a fit of rage and vowed to take revenge against the Rebbe. The Czar was forced to buy a different plot of land, known today as the Russian Compound. With the money the Rebbe sent, a big shul was built. Although officially called the Tiferes Yisroel Shul, it was popularly referred to as the Reb Nissan Bak Shul. It served as the main shul and center for Rizhiner chassidim in Yerushalayim until 1948 when it was destroyed by the Arabs.

Although the Rebbe longed to go and settle in Eretz Yisroel, he was unable to forsake his chassidim. He used to say that if he came to Eretz Yisroel he would be asked why he had come without his *Yidden*. On one occasion the Rebbe spoke about the final *geulah* and said that it would begin with the gradual immigration of *Yidden* to Eretz Yisroel. Just as there was no miraculous redemption in the times of Ezra, as there had been in Egypt, similarly, in our times if the generation will not be worthy, the redemption will also take place in a natural way. The countries of the world will decide to give the *Yidden* Eretz Yisroel as a land of their own and the *Yidden* will come back and rebuild the land. There will be great miracles but they will be hidden in the circle of nature, and after this we will see the final redemption. As the Rebbe finished these words he sighed and said, "Of course it bothers us that the *geulah* should start in such a way, but we have no more strength to wait. However it will be, let it start already."

THE RUSSIAN CZAR AND THE VARIOUS *MASKILIM* OF THE time were greatly distressed by the power the Rebbe wielded.

Prison Through his royal conduct the Rebbe greatly uplifted the level of the downtrodden masses. The *maskilim* had long been plotting to bring about the Rebbe's downfall, but without any success. When the Rebbe was 40 years old, he was arrested on charges of having had a hand in a murder. An informer brought evidence that the Rebbe had ordered the execution of a second informer. As the Rebbe was taken into custody he said, "*Gam ki eileich b'gei tzalmaves lo ira ra* — Even as I am to be locked up I am not afraid. One thing, however, upsets me, *ki Atah imadi* — that You, Hashem, will be with me, that the *Shechinah* will also be in *galus* with me."

Following the orders of the Czar himself, the Rebbe was locked up in the notorious Kiev dungeons. The Rebbe spent twenty-two months locked away under terrible conditions in a small, dark and damp cellar. No charges were ever brought against him, nor was he ever put on trial. The Rebbe was transferred to a second prison in Kaminetz for six months until he was finally freed on Shushan Purim. A few days after the Rebbe was freed he was given a tip off that the Czar had decided to rearrest him on charges of rebellion and had already passed a sentence of life exile to Siberia. The Rebbe was left with no option but to flee Russia.

As soon as the authorities realized that the Rebbe had disappeared, soldiers were sent to find him and prevent his escape. The Rebbe crossed the border into Austria in the middle of the night, and the Russians, having narrowly missed capturing him, returned home empty-handed. The Russian Czar, however, did not give up and demanded that Austria send the Rebbe back to Russia.

Meanwhile, "witnesses" were produced who testified that the Rebbe was really an Austrian citizen who had disappeared many years ago and had finally returned home to Austria. The Russians, however, also had witnesses to contradict this story and insisted on his return. The Austrian government, however, refused to comply. They knew that the Rebbe would attract tens of thousands of chassidim who would be good for the economy and businesses of the area. The Rebbe was simply too valuable an asset to lose.

When Reb Yitzchok of Vorka came to visit the Rebbe soon after he arrived in Austria, the Rebbe told him that he had not been imprisoned for his own sins, for in his life he had never transgressed even the smallest *issur d'rabbanan*.

Not long after the Rebbe settled in Austria he was asked by one of his chassidim why he didn't take revenge against the Russian Czar. Everyone knew that the Rebbe was able to work miracles, so why didn't he do something to destroy the Czarist regime?

"Do you believe in all the miracles that took place when Hashem took the *Yidden* out of Egypt?" the Rebbe asked him.

"Of course I believe," answered the *Yid*.

"And do you believe that Hashem still has the same power to perform such miracles?" the Rebbe continued, and the *Yid* answered him again, "Of course, Rebbe, I believe!"

"If so," the Rebbe asked him, "can you explain to me why Hashem doesn't punish the Czar for all his wicked actions? If Hashem doesn't feel that it is time to punish him, what's the wonder if I also keep quiet?"

The time came, however, when the Rebbe felt he could not keep quiet any longer. A few days before Purim the Rebbe requested that on Purim one of his chassidim should dress up as the Russian Czar. The chassidim understood that the Rebbe had deep *kavanos* in his request, and it wasn't just going to be a show. On Purim, as the Rebbe was in the middle of his *seudah*, suddenly the door opened and in walked the dressed-up Czar. The Rebbe rose respectfully to his feet and addressed the Czar. "Your Majesty the Czar, you have decreed harsh decrees against my people. I ask you, please annul these harsh decrees."

The Czar, however, refused: it was impossible to retract. The Rebbe's face became more serious as he once again asked, "Please, I beg of His Majesty to have pity and rescind the decrees."

"No, it is impossible, it cannot be done," the Czar answered with impudence.

The Rebbe's face turned white and, getting up from his chair, he walked over to the Czar and in an emotional voice ordered him immediately to leave the room and never return. Afterwards the Rebbe sunk down into his chair and in a broken voice he said: "*Chazal* tell us, '*Ein lecha adam she'ein lo shaah*,' every person comes to the world to fulfill a specific task. If this chassid would have realized that he should have agreed to annul the decrees, automatically in Russia they would also have been annulled. A great pity that this opportunity has been lost."

THE REBBE SETTLED IN THE TOWN OF SADIGER. SOME years earlier Reb Chaim Kosover had promised the people of the

His Legacy town that one day a great *tzaddik* would come to live there, and he would make the name "Sadiger" famous for all generations. Once again the Rebbe set up a magnificent court with a big shul. Tens of thousands flocked to Sadiger, and indeed much of the local population became his chassidim. The Rebbe lived in Sadiger for ten years, until his *petirah*. A few months before he was *niftar*, he started to drop hints of his imminent departure. Just before Rosh Hashanah 1851 he told his sons that he had prepared extremely beautiful living

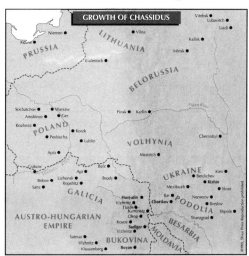

Map of the towns of Rizhiner Chassidus

The Rizhiner's kever in Sadiger

quarters for himself and he would be moving to them after the Yomim Tovim. As he walked into his *beis hamedrash* on Yom Kippur, he put his hands on the *mezuzah* and announced that he would be a *kapparah* for *Klal Yisroel*. Right after Succos the Rebbe became ill and was *niftar* on the 3rd of Cheshvan.

A few hours before he was *niftar* he asked one of his close chassidim if he knew what Esther *davened* before she went to Achashverosh. Without waiting for an answer the Rebbe himself answered, "She asked Hashem that He either help the *Yidden* or take her from this world."

Before his *petirah* the Rebbe said: "Reb Yehudah HaNasi testified about himself that he never had enjoyment from this world, not even the amount of a small finger. I testify about myself that I did not enjoy this world, not even the amount of a bit of thread (*kechut hasaarah*). The reason for my grand and royal conduct was totally *l'shem Shamayim*." With these words the Rebbe was *niftar*. He was only 54 years old. The doctor who examined him diagnosed that the Rebbe had been *niftar* because his heart had given way in its longing to be reunited with its Creator. The Rebbe's son, Reb Avrohom Yaakov, used to say that just as on Shabbos, Gehinnom is closed, the same is true on his father's *yahrtzeit*, the 3rd of Cheshvan —

The Rizhiner's third son,
Reb Dov Ber of Leova

Gehinnom is also closed. This statement can be reinforced with a story which occurred about eighty years ago:

> In Yerushalayim lived a Karliner chassid who used to make a *seudah* every year on the *yarhtzeit* of the Rebbe. Eventually this man was *niftar* on the Rebbe's *yarhtzeit*, the 3rd of Cheshvan. A few nights later, all his children had the same startling dream. In the dream their father suddenly appeared and told them that since he had died on the Rizhiner's *yahrtzeit* he was let straight into Gan Eden. The fact that all the children dreamt the identical dream on the same night showed that this was indeed not an empty dream that is to be dismissed out of hand!

The Rizhiner's *divrei Torah* preserved to this very day contain in them a message which is still as important as ever. But even more important than his Torahs was the physical inheritance that he left behind. "Everyone," he said, "leaves *sefarim* behind. I leave my sons. We will see who will achieve more."

The Rizhiner's sons continued in the footsteps of their holy father, each one setting up a large court with tens of thousands of followers. Famed for their great *ahavas Yisroel*, it was no wonder that the number of Rizhiner chassidim grew constantly, as did their influence throughout the whole of Eastern Europe and beyond.

Present-day descendants of Rizhin — from left to right: the Rebbes of Vasloi, Sadiger and Boyan

The Rebbe's *derech* was carried on through his six sons. Each of them moved to a different town where they set up their own court. The Rebbe thought very highly of all his sons. He used to say that just as people used to come to ask the *Urim VeTumim* in the times of the *Beis HaMikdash*, in the same way people will come to ask his sons for advice.

The Rebbe's oldest son, Reb Sholom Yosef, was *niftar* less than a year after his father and was succeeded by his son Reb Yitzchok, who became the first Bohusher Rebbe. The Rizhiner's second son, Reb Avrohom Yaakov, took his father's place in Sadiger. He had two sons; the eldest, Reb Yitzchok, was the first Boyaner Rebbe, and the younger son, Reb Yisroel, was Rebbe in Sadiger. The third son of the Rizhiner was Reb Dov Ber who was Rebbe in Leova, and the fourth son, Reb Menachem Nuchem, was Rebbe in Shtefanesht. Reb Dovid Moshe, the Chortkover Rebbe, was the fifth son, and Reb Mordechai Shraga, the Husyatiner Rebbe, was the sixth son.

PART TWO
R' DOVID MOSHE OF CHORTKOV

CHAPTER THREE

In the Shadow of the Rizhiner

FROM HIS YOUNGEST YEARS IT WAS APPARENT THAT the Chortkover Rebbe, Reb Dovid Moshe, was no ordinary child. At the time of Reb Dovid Moshe's birth, on the second day of Shavous 5587 (1827), the Rizhiner was conducting a *tisch* in honor of Yom Tov. The chassidim present asked the Rizhiner to serve a *l'chaim*, as is the *minhag* for a *baal simchah*. "Perhaps it's you who should provide the *l'chaim*," exclaimed the Rizhiner. "I have brought you today a great *neshamah* which will bring *Yiddishe* hearts closer to their Father in Heaven."

Reb Dovid Moshe Is Born

THE RIZHINER USED TO SAY THAT EACH ONE OF HIS SIX sons corresponded to one *seder* of the six volumes of the Mishnah. Reb Dovid Moshe, being the fifth son, corresponded to the fifth volume — *Kodshim*, and the Rizhiner would conclude, "And he is indeed *kodshei kodshim* (holy of holies)."

CHORTKOVER DYNASTY

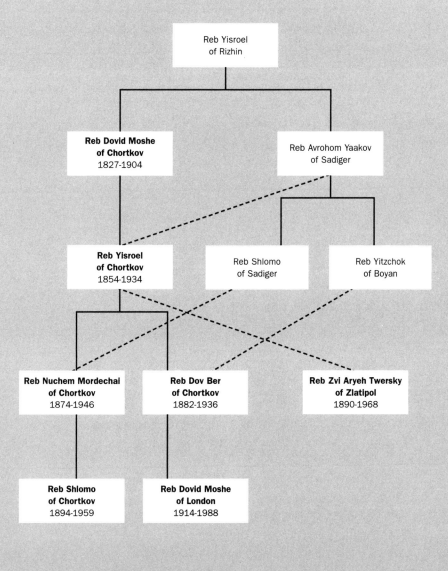

Reb Yisroel
of Rizhin

**Reb Dovid Moshe
of Chortkov**
1827-1904

Reb Avrohom Yaakov
of Sadiger

**Reb Yisroel
of Chortkov**
1854-1934

Reb Shlomo
of Sadiger

Reb Yitzchok
of Boyan

**Reb Nuchem Mordechai
of Chortkov**
1874-1946

**Reb Dov Ber
of Chortkov**
1882-1936

**Reb Zvi Aryeh Twersky
of Zlatipol**
1890-1968

**Reb Shlomo
of Chortkov**
1894-1959

**Reb Dovid Moshe
of London**
1914-1988

——— Father and son

- - - - Father-in-law and son-in-law

As a young child, Reb Dovid Moshe earned the nickname, "the *tzitzis Yidelle*." This name came about due to the following incident. The Rizhiner had the *minhag* that all his sons started to wear *tzitzis* from when they were 30 days old. When Reb Dovid Moshe was a few months old, it once happened that they forgot to put his *tzitzis* on him. No one noticed that he wasn't wearing his *tzitzis*, and so it would have remained, had Reb Dovid Moshe not alerted them.

He refused to eat or drink anything and he also did not stop crying. All his mother's efforts to calm him down and to soothe him met with failure. Fearing that the baby was ill, the Rebbetzin decided to call for a doctor. Before the doctor was summoned, she consulted her husband to hear his opinion. When the Rizhiner heard of the problem he laughed and said: "No doubt someone forgot to put the *tzitzis* on him." The Rebbetzin went to check and so it was. As soon as he was clothed in his *tzitzis* he stopped crying and agreed to eat.

When Reb Dovid Moshe was 10 years old, he was once learning with his *melamed* the words of Yirmiyah HaNavi who said to Hashem: "*Lo yadati daber ki naar anochi* — I do not know how to speak for I am still a child." "What!" exclaimed Reb Dovid Moshe in astonishment. "A *navi* was also once a child? I don't remember anymore when I was a child!"

And indeed, Reb Dovid Moshe never acted or behaved like a child. His only interest was the well-being of his *neshamah* and in striving to ascend the rungs of *kedushah* and *taharah*. When he was once confined to bed with a serious illness, he worried about the toll the illness was exacting on his spiritual well-being. Throughout the day the young boy lay in his bed moaning to himself: "How are you faring, my *neshamah*? What are you doing, my *neshamah*? Be healthy, my *neshamah*."

Thus it was hardly surprising that the Rizhiner would advise those who complained about their own lack of *yiras Shamayim* that they should watch Reb Dovid Moshe's conduct, and this would be a *segulah* for them to improve their ways.

WHEN REB DOVID MOSHE BECAME OF AGE, HE MARRIED Rebbetzin Feiga, the daughter of Reb Aharon of Chernobyl, who was

Marriage one of the great *tzaddikim* of the time. The Rizhiner was unable to physically participate in the wedding. Since the *chasunah* had to be held in Russia (the authorities had banned Reb Aharon Chernobyler from traveling abroad), and the Rizhiner was unable to enter Russia for fear of arrest, he accompanied the wedding entourage until the Russian border. On the way, they stopped in the forest between Husyatin and Kopitchinitz to rest and *daven Minchah*. After *davening* was over, the Rizhiner asked that all present should drink a *l'chaim* and bless him that he should have much *nachas* from Reb Dovid Moshe and all his future descendants for generations to come. He also asked that all present file past him and wish him the same *berachah*; he even requested that the simple and illiterate wagon drivers should bless him.

It is interesting to note the timing and location of this incident; it was just a few short miles from the town of Chortkov, where Reb Dovid Moshe was later to settle and by whose name he was to become famous.

At the border, the Rizhiner took leave of his son with the following words: "My father used to say, 'From my sons people will know who I am,' but I say differently, 'From my sons people will know who Hashem is.'" With these words Reb Dovid Moshe went to his *chupah*.

Reb Aharon Chernobyler held his son-in-law in great esteem and voiced his praises on many occasions. In a letter to his daughter Feiga, Reb Aharon exhorts her to be extremely careful to honor her husband properly, adding that the Rizhiner had told him that he had taken the choicest of his sons (*muvchar she'bebanai*). Although Reb Aharon was a Rebbe of thousands of chassidim, he would openly humble himself in front of his son-in-law. When Reb Aharon's sons remarked that it wasn't befitting for him to act in such a way, Reb Aharon answered them: "The truth is that I should really travel to Chortkov to learn and absorb his ways. Hashem, however, has decreed otherwise, that he should marry my daughter and therefore have to come to me. If so, how can I possibly not give him at least the honor due to him?"

❧

For twenty-four years Reb Dovid Moshe lived in the shadow of his great father, first in Rizhin and then in Sadiger. Before his *petirah*, the Rizhiner summoned his six sons and spoke to each of them individually. Although the children never divulged what their father's parting words were, many years later Reb Dovid Moshe hinted that the Rizhiner had spoken about the final *geulah* and their task in hastening its arrival. As Reb Dovid Moshe finished speaking, tears welled up in his eyes, and in a tear-choked voice he added: "I still remember what my father told me, I still remember what my father told me."

AFTER THE RIZHINER'S *PETIRAH*, HIS PROPERTY AND belongings were divided among his sons and daughters — each get-

Dividing the Inheritance

ting what they required — without argument or dissent. Only about one particular item, the *tefillin*, did a problem arise — to whom they should be given. This was no ordinary pair of *tefillin*; the Rizhiner had inherited them from his father, Reb Sholom, who, in turn, had been given them by his father, Reb Avrohom HaMalach, who had received them from his father, the Maggid of Mezeritch. The Rizhiner had treasured these *tefillin* more than all his other possessions, and therefore it wasn't surprising that all his sons wanted to inherit them. Finally, it was decided that each son would write on a slip of paper how much of the total inheritance he was ready to forego if the *tefillin* would be given to him.

The oldest of the brothers, Reb Sholom Yosef, didn't agree to this scheme. Why should they forfeit their rights to the inheritance in order to obtain the *tefillin*? The brothers then decided to draw lots for the ownership of the *tefillin*, and in that way they came into the possession of Reb Dovid Moshe.

After the division was completed, one of the older brothers, Reb Avrohom Yaakov of Sadiger said, "It would interest me to see what each of us had intended to give up for the *tefillin*." When he opened the slips of paper they saw that Reb Dovid Moshe had written that he was willing to forego his whole share in the estate in exchange for the *tefillin*.

About two years after the inheritance had been divided, Reb Avrohom Yaakov, the Sadigerer Rebbe, was sitting with a group of his chassidim and the topic of the *tefillin* came up in conversation. Reb Avrohom Yaakov remarked, "I envy my brother Reb Dovid Moshe, he has the *zechus* to wear the *tefillin* of our holy *zeide* the Mezeritcher Maggid." At these words, two young men in the crowd grew pale. Mustering up their courage, they announced that they had a confession to make. Knowing how much these *tefillin* meant to the Sadigerer Rebbe, they had taken upon themselves to get hold of the parchment scrolls inside the *tefillin* and bring them to their Rebbe. They had succeeded in removing the *parshiyos* from the *battim* of Reb Dovid Moshe's *tefillin*, putting in their place ordinary *parshiyos*, but as yet hadn't found an opportunity to hand them over to the Sadigerer Rebbe.

The Sadigerer Rebbe ordered his chassidim not to breathe a word of what had happened, and the next day he left Sadiger to go to see his brother. On his arrival he didn't mention a word about the reason for his visit. The next morning, Reb Avrohom Yaakov entered the room in which his younger brother used to *daven*. On the table he found two pairs of *tefillin* — the priceless pair inherited from the Maggid and another pair. When Reb Dovid Moshe entered the room, he approached the table, took up the Maggid's *tefillin*, sighed and returned them to their place, then picked up the other pair in order to put them on.

"Why don't you wear the Maggid's *tefillin* which you rightfully inherited?" Reb Avrohom Yaakov asked his brother. "I'll tell you the truth," replied Reb Dovid Moshe. "Not once in these two years have I donned these holy *tefillin*. You see, every time I pick them up, I don't feel any more their *kedushah*, and if I can't feel their *kedushah*, then I am not worthy of using them."

"No, my dear brother," Reb Avrohom Yaakov exclaimed. "You are indeed worthy of using those holy *tefillin*. It is not you who are at fault. The reason you didn't feel their *kedushah* is because the holy *parshiyos* have been removed from them! Now here they are. Return them to their place for you are truly worthy of using them!"

≈≈

AFTER THE RIZHINER'S *PETIRAH*, THE WHOLE FAMILY
gathered at the late *tzaddik's* estate in the town of Potik in Galicia, in

The Brothers Part Ways order to plan and to discuss their future. The Rizhiner had bought the estate when he had fled Russia in order to escape the clutches of the Czar, who demanded his return. According to Austrian law, a landowner in Austria could not be extradited to another country, and thus Potik provided the Rizhiner with a safe haven.

During the first few months after their father's *petirah*, all the brothers resided together in Potik while deciding on their next move. Many communities and delegations came to beg them to move to their towns but the brothers were in no hurry to go. Only after due deliberation did they finally leave to their new homes, each one setting up a large court with many chassidim.

Many Rizhiner chassidim journeyed during this time to Potik to decide for themselves to which of the six sons they felt attracted as their next Rebbe. In his *sefer "Tiferes Adam,"* HaGaon Reb Reuven Margulies relates the following story:

> Among those who came to Potik to select a new Rebbe was Reb Yossel Radviller, who was a *tzaddik* in his own right and a Rebbe in the town of Radvill in Russia. He had been intending to spend six weeks in Potik, one week by each son, and then to make his choice. In the end, however, things turned out differently and he was drawn to Reb Dovid Moshe.
>
> During the long and arduous journey from Radvill, Reb Yossel was constantly plagued with feelings of guilt about the many lost hours of learning that the journey was causing him. These thoughts refused to leave him, and almost caused him to regret undertaking the trip. When Reb Yossel finally arrived in Potik and introduced himself to Reb Dovid Moshe, the Rebbe told him the following story.
>
> "My *zeide* Reb Sholom spent the first few years after his *chasunah* in the town of Chernobyl, at the side of his wife's illustrious grandfather, Reb Nuchem of Chernobyl. One year, Erev Rosh Hashanah, everybody was in shul *davening* the last *Minchah* of the year with great devotion. Reb Sholom was also there, but for some reason felt unable to

concentrate properly. Throughout the *Shemoneh Esrei* he struggled and battled with himself, but to no avail. Reb Sholom was extremely upset over his failure, especially since this was the last *tefillah* of the year, but there was nothing he could do. He just wasn't able to concentrate on anything more than the most plain and simple *kavanos*.

"After *davening* was over, Reb Nuchem came over to Reb Sholom and congratulated him for his *tefillah*. 'My son,' Reb Nuchem exclaimed, 'Do you know what a storm your *tefillah* created in Heaven. Thousands of *Yidden* have been helped as a result.'"

Reb Dovid Moshe finished his story and turning to Reb Yossel he added: "You see that sometimes it happens that a person thinks that he has wasted his time and hasn't achieved anything, but in reality it is not so. Even if a person is on a journey and unable to learn and *daven* as he would like, his *avodah* can still achieve great heights."

Reb Yossel understood the message the story conveyed and his feelings of guilt evaporated. He decided to adopt Reb Dovid Moshe as his new Rebbe.

IN THE MONTHS AFTER THE RIZHINER'S *PETIRAH*, ALL THE brothers slowly but surely left Potik until only Reb Dovid Moshe re-

Remaining in Potik mained. His chassidim were sure that soon he would also leave Potik, but Reb Dovid Moshe refused all their pleas and requests. Potik was a small town far removed from the main Jewish centers. In addition, the family estate was in an outlying area of Potik, and when it rained, the road to the estate became almost inaccessible. This suited Reb Dovid Moshe just fine. Here he was free to serve Hashem without the disturbances that a large Chassidus would entail. His close chassidim protested to him that in Potik it would be impossible to set up even a small Chassidus, but their pleas fell on deaf ears.

One Friday night, heavy rain prevented most of the local chassidim from coming. When the Rebbe saw the small group that had braved the weather, he commented: "My *zeide* Reb Sholom used to say that he is happy when he has only a few people at the *tisch*. And if some of them fall asleep during the *tisch* then he is truly delighted. That way they won't disturb him from his *avodah*." And so, despite all his chassidim's complaints, Reb Dovid Moshe remained in Potik and became known as the Potiker Rebbe.

⊰⊱

In Service of Hashem ALREADY AS A YOUNG MAN THE REBBE BECAME FAMOUS for his extraordinary self-denial, abstaining from even the most basic minimum needed to keep his body and soul together. His nightly sleep was never more than two hours, and even then not always in bed, but sitting in the chair where he had been learning. As a rule he never went to sleep on Friday night; he would say that we have been commanded to guard the Shabbos (*sh'mor es yom haShabbos*) and who has ever heard of a guard sleeping on duty! Similarly, on other occasions, such as Seder night and Yom Kippur, he would also not go to sleep.

One year, in the Rebbe's later years, when Seder night fell on Motza'ei Shabbos and the Rebbe had already denied himself two nights' sleep, his son, Reb Yisroel, went to his father on Shabbos af-

Reb Dovid Moshe in his younger years

ternoon to try and convince him to rest a bit, and said to him, "Dear father, it is already two nights that you have gone without any sleep. Since tonight and tomorrow night are the Seder, this means that you will miss another two nights, and I am worried that it could ruin your health. If you are concerned that because of the many years you didn't sleep on Shabbos, this practice has the strength of a vow, I'll call in three *talmidei chachamim* and they will annul the vow."

The Rebbe answered his son and told him, "Listen, my son, to what you are saying. In order to annul a vow one must regret what one has undertaken. For many years I haven't slept on Shabbos, and now, because of a half hour's sleep, I should regret and uproot my *minhag* of so many years?"

On another occasion, when he had already gone for four nights without sleep, and with the arrival of the fifth night he didn't show any intention of going to sleep either, his Rebbetzin begged him with tears in her eyes to have pity on himself and to rest a bit. The Rebbe answered her, "If a person cleaves to Hashem with all his might, he can do without food and sleep for as long as forty days." Indeed, the Rebbe was once heard to comment that he had worked on himself until he achieved the state that whether he eats or not, or he sleeps or not, is immaterial.[1]

Once, after Tishah B'Av, the Rebbe received a visit from his nephew, Reb Levi Yitzchok of Ozeranah, who said, sighing deeply, "What more can we do? The *Yidden* dutifully mourned the destruction of Yerushalayim and have fasted as the *din* requires, yet the *geulah* has still not arrived."

"Do you think that fasting means merely abstaining from food and drink?" replied the Rebbe. "A person may eat and drink and at the same time he can be fasting. How is that possible? A person who refrains from transgressing when he has the opportunity to sin is also practicing a form of fasting. For example, if he has the chance to violate the Shabbos, slander someone or do anything the Torah has forbidden, and he stops himself from doing it because Hashem forbids it, in a way he is also fasting. If we would all fast that kind of fast, then we would be able to look forward to the coming of Moshiach."

True to his words, the Rebbe cut himself off from all this world's pleasures. He would tell his chassidim, "This world isn't worth anything. It's the next world that is important."

Once, before Pesach, the chassidim bought a beautiful golden dish for the Rebbe as a present. The dish had cost a fortune and

---

1. Although the *gemara* writes that it is impossible for a person to go for more than three days without sleep, Reb Moshe Cordovero writes in the *sefer* "*Tefillah LeMoshe*" that the *gemara* refers only to ordinary people. But a *tzaddik* who has elevated himself above the ways of nature can exist much longer without sleep.

the chassidim wanted very much to hear the Rebbe make a *birchas Shehecheyanu* (which one recites on receiving an expensive gift) in appreciation of their efforts. The Rebbe, however, refused to recite the *berachah* and said that the dish should be placed on the table at the Seder and when he recites the *Shehecheyanu* then, he will also have in mind the dish. At the Seder, before the Rebbe recited the *berachah*, he whispered a few words in his son's ear. The chassidim later found out that he had said, "Gold and silver have no value to me!"

Throughout the year Reb Dovid Moshe was gripped with an intense fear of Heaven. The Maggid of Kolomei, Reb Yitzchok Weber, wrote in his memoirs:

> One never saw even the slightest sign of lightness from the Rebbe. Even during a meal he would sit with trembling, and the fear of Heaven was etched all over him. This seriousness of mind never left him, ever. Even at the weddings of his grandchildren, when the whole town was caught up in the celebrations and the joyous occasion, the Rebbe would not change his earnest composure and would remain closed in his room totally immersed in his holy *avodah*. Only when the *chasan* and *kallah* were ready to walk under the *chupah* would the Rebbe finally remove his *tallis* and *tefillin* and join in the happy event. Once the *chupah* was over, the Rebbe would return to his *sefarim* and continue to learn, oblivious to the crowds circulating under his window.
>
> I was present at one such wedding. After the *chupah* I sat in the waiting room to the Rebbe's quarters. While I was there, a messenger of the Husyatiner Rebbe arrived, to ask if the Husyatiner Rebbe could have an audience with his uncle the Rebbe. The Rebbe's *gabbai* went into the room and returned a moment later. "Not now," the *gabbai* answered. "It's not possible." This occurred three times during the next hour; each time the *gabbai* went in and each time he came out with the same reply. The Husyatiner Rebbe's messenger was rather taken aback at the Rebbe's refusal. The Rebbe had the greatest respect for the Husyatiner Rebbe and normally

(1) (2)

Reb Yisroel of Husyatin (1) and Reb Moshenu Boyaner (2)

would never have kept him waiting. The messenger asked the *gabbai* for an explanation.

"Why are you so taken aback?" the *gabbai* explained. "The Rebbe is learning! Each time I entered the Rebbe's room, he immediately put his finger to his lips and signaled to me not to interrupt him, and that he cannot stop now. Thus I was unable to speak to him and tell him who is waiting."

This was the *madreigah* of the Rebbe. Even at his own grandchildren's weddings when everyone else was caught up in the joyous occasion, his mind did not deviate for a moment from his holy *avodah*. While the guests and the masses were singing and rejoicing, the Rebbe carried on his learning and *davening* as usual.

With the approach of the *Yomim Noraim*, the Rebbe's *avodah* intensified even more; his fear and dread could be felt by all around him. Once, on Erev Yom Kippur, the Rebbe was sitting in his room, hot tears running down his cheeks as he reviewed his actions of the past year. When the Rebbe's son, Reb Yisroel, entered the room, he was taken aback by his father's sobbing and his white and ghostly appearance. "You see, my son," Reb Dovid Moshe exclaimed, "this is how one must cry when one isn't *ehrlich!*"

CHAPTER FOUR

The Move to Chortkov

REB DOVID MOSHE LIVED IN POTIK FOR SIXTEEN years, and would probably have remained there for the rest of his life had he not felt forced to leave. The local council decided that the time had come to build a new church in the area. According to local tradition, all citizens of Potik had to contribute, even the *Yidden*. This put the Rebbe in a predicament; to evade payment could create hostility toward the local *Yidden* and even give rise to a pogrom. On the other hand, to contribute toward a church was also unacceptable. The only option was for the Rebbe to leave Potik.

ALMOST IMMEDIATELY THE REBBE'S *GABBAIM* STARTED TO search for an alternative site. This in itself was no easy feat. The new

Leaving Potik

mansion would not only have to be big enough to accommodate the Rebbe and his family plus *gabbaim*, but would also have to host the many chassidim who came to the Rebbe. In addition a large dining room, reception area and rest rooms

The palatial home of the Rebbe in Chortkov;
on the right-hand side is the hall where the Rebbe would hold his tischen

would be needed, to host visiting Rebbes and other dignitaries. Such large properties were extremely hard to find and were rarely for sale.

As if by a miracle a suitable place was found almost immediately. On the outskirts of the town of Chortkov in Galicia stood a beautiful building which impressed all who saw it. This was no regular mansion or stately house, it was a veritable palace. Set in its own gardens, the palace boasted fifty-four rooms including large conference halls and dining halls. It was no wonder that the Kaiser Franz Joseph had elected to stay there during a recent tour of Galicia. No sooner had the Kaiser left than the owners decided to move to Paris and to sell the palace. The owners were in such a hurry to go that they were not even willing to wait to find a buyer who would offer them a serious price. Thus the Rebbe was able to acquire the palace for a fraction of its real value. And so, in the year 5627 (1867), the Rebbe finally left Potik and moved to Chortkov.

Moving to Chortkov

SITUATED STRATEGICALLY ALONG THE MAIN ROUTE between the cities of Tarnopol and Chernovitz in Eastern Galicia, the town of Chortkov had a large and important *kehillah*, which dated back hundreds of years. The earliest record of *Yidden* living in the town is mentioned in a document dated 1427, which states that there was a place named after its owners "Chortkovichi," and that Jews settled there at that period of time. Over the years the *kehillah* grew until the *Yidden* comprised over half the town. Many great *rabbanim* had lived in Chortkov, perhaps the most famous being Reb Hershele

The magnificent shul of the Rebbe in Chortkov

Chortkover, who was the father of the Rebbe Reb Shmelke of Nikolsburg and Reb Pinchos, the Baal Haflaah. The town also had the honor of hosting the Baal Shem Tov, who spent some time in Chortkov, as did the Berdichever Rav.

Next to the beautiful palace was built the Rebbe's shul. This was also no ordinary building. Designed by the Rebbe's son Reb Yisroel and built to special specifications, its beauty stunned all who laid eyes on it. Measuring approximately 150 feet long by 120 feet wide and 40 feet high, and flanked by two outer towers, the shul was indeed impressive. Beautiful ornate decorations gave the finishing touches to this unique work of art.

Upon its completion the Rebbe praised the special beauty of his shul and said: "*Chazal* have told us that when Moshiach comes, all the shuls in *chutz laAretz* will relocate themselves to Eretz Yisroel. I will not be embarrassed to go with my shul to greet Moshiach."

It is interesting to note that although Chortkov was not spared the ravages of the two World Wars during which much of the town — including the Rebbe's beautiful palace — was destroyed, the Rebbe's shul was left intact. Miraculously the shul has survived both the Nazis and the Communists, and still stands to this day, awaiting the arrival of Moshiach!

A third large building called "The *Salash*" (hall) was also built. In the *salash* the Rebbe would conduct the *tisch*. These three buildings were not linked together although they were in close proximity, all being situated in the Rebbe's court.

ALTHOUGH THE REBBE LIVED IN A PALACE SURROUNDED by riches and luxury, not only did he not partake of them; he did not even notice them. When the famed *posek*, Reb Meir Arik, was in Chortkov for the first time, he was upset by the beautiful gardens surrounding the Rebbe's house. Most of the Rebbes of the time lived in dire poverty and Reb Dovid Moshe's luxurious surroundings were not what Reb Meir had expected. Noticing his concern the Rebbe asked him what was troubling him, to which Reb Meir answered him that he was not used to the idea of a Rebbe being surrounded with beautiful gardens and flowers.

The Rebbe's Palace

"What gardens? What flowers?" the Rebbe asked him. "I don't know what you mean!" Reb Meir later related that when he heard the Rebbe honestly say that he didn't know of the gardens' existence even though he walked through them a few times a day, that's what made him into a fervent and zealous Chortkover chassid.

The Rebbe was once learning the *pasuk* in the Torah where it is written that Moshe Rabbeinu was the most humble person alive, more than any other person on the face of the earth, when he suddenly burst into tears. "You see what's written," the Rebbe told those around him, "Moshe Rabbeinu was the most humble person on the earth. Now, how is it possible that Moshe Rabbeinu, who spoke to Hashem 'face to face' and wrought so many miracles, could possibly be so humble as to think that he was the lowest and the most insignificant of all the *Yidden*?

"The answer is that Moshe thought to himself: it is not surprising that I serve Hashem properly. I was on Har Sinai for forty days and nights where I saw things that no one else has seen, and heard things that no one else has heard, and therefore I am not tempted anymore by ordinary mundane matters. But a simple *Yid* who does not understand much and whose *yetzer hara* is constantly trying to win him over, and even so he doesn't give in and continues keeping the Torah and mitzvos, such an *avodah* is much more precious to Hashem than mine."

Similarly, the Rebbe was also convinced that he was just a simple ordinary *Yid*. The fact that he lived in a palatial villa surrounded by thousands of chassidim made absolutely no impact on him. He remained convinced of his insignificance, as if he were no different than anyone else, simply regarding himself as another downtrodden Jew.

When the Rebbe's brother, the Sadigerer Rebbe, came to Chortkov on a visit, he asked for a lit candle. The Sadigerer Rebbe took the light and proceeded to inspect the palace, room by room, corner by corner, as one does on the night before Pesach. When the Sadigerer Rebbe was asked what he was looking for, he answered: "People say[1] that you can't truly know someone until you have been in his house and seen how he lives. I have inspected my brother's home and have seen that every room and every corner is saturated with an aroma of *yiras Shamayim*!"

⸙

THE REBBE'S MOVE TO CHORTKOV PROVED TO BE A turning point not just in his own life but also in the lives of the thou-

Chortkov Becomes a Center

sands of *Yidden* living in Chortkov. In an article (*Sefer HaZikaron*, Chortkov) written after the Second World War, one of the old inhabitants described his memories of the area and the Rebbe's impact on the town:

---

1. See the commentary of the *Meiri* on the Mishnah: "Don't judge your fellow man until you have reached his place" (*Avos* 2:5).

Welcome to Chortkov,
the sign that greets you nowadays

Thanks to the Rebbes of Chortkov, the place changed from being a quiet provincial town to become a center for many thousands who came from across Russia, Poland, Volhin, Ukraine and Hungary. The town became a magnet for the hearts and souls of thousands of chassidim, until people would say: "Why is the town called Chortkov? Because the Rebbe of Chortkov lives there."

Who among us could fail to be moved or influenced by the sights and scenes of a Shabbos or Yom Yov? From faraway towns and distant villages many thousands would arrive, united together with great *simchah* and *d'veikus*. During such times it almost seemed that the Rebbe's very court had become alive and was rejoicing also. Such a *simchah* could only have taken place in Yerushalayim, when the *Beis HaMikdash* was still standing.

A second local *Yid* wrote as follows:

Due to the Rebbe's court, life in Chortkov was totally different from that in other towns. It was never dull or boring in Chortkov. Every day brought more traffic and more new faces who came to see the Rebbe. Whoever saw how they danced outside the Rebbe's house on Yom Tov, or the dancing in the town squares as they made their way to the Rebbe's *beis hamedrash,* will never forget it. Their joy was the result of their total and unswerving faith in their Rebbe.

Even those *Yidden* in Chortkov who had strayed from the path of the Torah also benefited from the Rebbe's presence and from his court. One such *Yid* recalled:

It is our duty to remember the happy memories that we had thanks to the Rebbe's court. The court was a bustling and thriving center and it played an important role even in our lives. There one could meet all types of people who had come from far and wide.

The vast gardens around the court provided us the only safe area in which to stroll and relax. Chortkov had no park, and the forests outside the town were too dangerous. The *goyim* often attacked lone *Yidden* outside the town. The Rebbe's garden was open to all *Yidden* and as long as we behaved there in keeping with the wishes of the *gabbaim*, we were never disturbed. In contrast to other chassidic groups who made us feel like outcasts, in the Rebbe's gardens we were always made to feel at home.

THIS IS HOW ANOTHER OLD CITIZEN OF THE SECULAR community in Chortkov recorded his impressions of the impact the

A Changed Environment

Rebbe made on the town:

Chortkov was always bubbling and full of life. As long as religion was in supremacy, the town was renowned with its great Rabbis, learned and erudite men. Of the personalities active at various times in some fields of life in Chortkov, I want to mention here Rabbi Dovid Moshe Friedman, the founder of the Rizhin dynasty of rabbis in Chortkov, active in the second half of the 19th century. His influence reached far beyond the boundaries of the town.

He was a modest, G-d-fearing man who kept away from world affairs, and was mostly engaged in the study of the Torah and in religious subjects: the whole of his being said spirituality. In an atmosphere of luxury and abundance — as was customary in the courts of this dynasty — he lived a life of suffering and torment. As if forbidden by vow, the pleasures of life he denied to himself. His influence lay in the strong belief that thousands of his disciples had in their Rabbi, whom they admired, listened to for advice, and whose commands they obeyed.

Thanks to him the town became famous all over the world. The great stream of people from without, who used to come into the town throughout the year, especially on the eves of festivals and the High Holy Days, was of great importance, both from the social aspect and from the economic one. The people who used to come from far and near relieved the town of dreariness and breathed life into it. The influence of the chassidic Rabbi's "court" turned Chortkov into an important cultural and Torah center for the surrounding villages in Eastern Galicia. Chortkov's name became well known and its reputation spread over the borders of Galicia and Poland into the bordering countries.

Even the local non–Jewish residents of the area recognized the Rebbe's importance and his valuable contribution to the town and its life. One year before Rosh Hashanah, a serious epidemic broke out in the area around Chortkov. The local government decided to ban the weekly market in the towns of the area in order to halt the spread of the disease. Not only was the market closed but all large gatherings were also forbidden. The Rebbe's court, however, was not included in the ban. One day a government official turned up in the Rebbe's home and informed them that the chassidim would be permittted to gather there as usual. The government recognized the importance the Rebbe placed on being in contact with his chassidim, and they were sure he would pray that no harm befall them.

ANOTHER ASPECT OF THE REBBE'S COURT THAT ATTRACTED much publicity was the famous *chazzan* and choir that used to perform in the Rebbe's shul. In Chortkover Chassidus strong emphasis was placed on the importance of music in the service of Hashem. The Rebbe, however, did not permit just any *baal tefillah* or *chazzan* to *daven* in his shul. Only someone with the highest caliber of *yiras Shamayim* was allowed to hold such a post. In addition the *chazzan* had to possess a powerful and beautiful voice that would move and elevate the listeners to even greater concentration and devotion in their *davening*. Finding such a *chazzan* was not an easy job and only select individuals qualified for the post. Over the years a number of *chazzanim* served in Chortkov and earned that coveted title of "Court *Chazzan*." The most famous of these was Reb Chaim Munish, who was popularly known

Munish Chazzan

as "Munish *Chazzan*." Under his directive the Chortkover *nusach* and *niggunim* reached new heights. Not only was he a superb *chazzan* but he was also a composer of music. For every Yom Tov and occasion he composed new *niggunim* which later became the staple for many families at their own Shabbos tables.

It is interesting to quote the words of one of Munish *Chazzan's* pupils who sang in his choir and later recorded his memories (*Sefer HaZikaron*, Chortkov) for posterity:

> When I was 9 years old, I visited the home of Reb Munish for the first time, and I was warmly welcomed. Reb Munish listened to my voice and tested it. After I repeated a few sounds he decided that my voice was worth training. He invited me to come and visit him twice a week. There were two reasons for those visits: to develop my voice and to teach me how to read musical notes. There was a lot of improvement in my voice from the training; Reb Munish was able to develop my "alto" voice so well that it sounded like a silver bell.
>
> In the breaks during rehearsals, Reb Munish's wife gave us tea with milk. While we were drinking our tea Reb Munish practiced the parts where we had to accompany him with a soft humming. I remember that one of the parts was in the Rosh Hashanah *davening* in the section *BeRosh Hashanah Yikaseivun*. After the choir finished singing all the parts of *U'nesaneh Tokef*, Reb Munish started with *BeRosh Hashanah Yikaseivun* while we were humming. I remember that once, during Rosh Hashanah, when we reached that part we suddenly realized that the program had unexpectedly changed. After we had finished singing *U'nesaneh Tokef* we started to hum the way we had practiced. Suddenly one of the choir members, Chaim Shorr, frantically started to wave his hands, as a sign that we should stop humming.
>
> I looked around and realized that all the choir members seemed like they had frozen in their places. Reb Munish had suddenly started to *daven* from his heart with great *d'veikus*. I felt that I was witnessing an original musical improvisation that was created on the spot by an experienced and spiritual

composer who had a natural musical talent — a *chazzan* who expressed his inner *hislahavus*, who poured out the sorrows of his heart and created on the spot a *niggun* that pierced my heart. A shiver passed from my head to my feet. I turned my head slowly as a show of respect and I noticed our teacher, Reb Zalman Shechter. Tears were running down his cheeks from emotion. I am sure that he also felt the originality of the *niggun* that was created in front of us at that moment.

The many compositions that Reb Munish wrote were well written and well organized. If his work were ever published it would have created a large and complete library of original chassidic music. It is very sad that his compositions were never printed and published. With the destruction of the Jewish world in Europe by the Nazis, the voice of this most famous *chazzan* was silenced forever. All his compositions, which were stored in his cabinet, were also destroyed and lost forever. Only a few crumbs of his *niggunim* survived, and I am sure that they have become distorted through their many journeys. We have to be thankful for the few remnants of his *niggunim* that have survived, because they recall to us the memory of one of the most important Jewish musicians in the history of Chassidus.

CHAPTER FIVE

A Shabbos in Chortkov

OVER THE YEARS THE REBBE'S FAME GREW UNTIL he became universally recognized as the *"tzaddik hador."* Thousands would converge on Chortkov to spend a Shabbos or Yom Tov with the Rebbe and to taste for themselves the *kedushah* which permeated the air there. In Rizhiner Chassidus great stress was laid on going regularly to see the Rebbe. The Rizhiner himself once said, "If people would only know how I clean and rinse their *neshamos,* fathers would tie up their sons and drag them to me."

ALREADY LONG BEFORE A CHASSID LEFT HOME TO GO TO HIS Rebbe, he would start to prepare himself for the moment when he would meet his Rebbe face to face. The Rebbe himself once gave his chassidim guidance as to how to prepare themselves before setting out to Chortkov. These were his words as recorded in his *sefer "Divrei Dovid"*:

Preparation

*The haskamah of Reb Yisroel of Chortkov
to the sefer "Divrei Dovid"*

The most important part of the journey is the *hachanah*, the preparation. Traveling to a *tzaddik* is no different than any other mitzvah. Just as all other mitzvos need preparation beforehand, so does the mitzvah of traveling to a *tzaddik* require prior contemplation and reflection. This preparation consists of two parts. The first part is the general *hachanah* that one needs to have in mind before the performance of every mitzvah — to realize that you are doing the will of Hashem and thereby subjugating yourself and your actions to Him. The second half of the preparation is to delve into the deeper meaning of the particular mitzvah being performed. This second half is dependent on the person's own level of *yiras Shamayim*. The greater his fear of Heaven, the more he will realize and appreciate the depth of the mitzvah.

A person who travels to a *tzaddik* after he has prepared himself properly is like a vessel waiting to be filled. Such a person will be able to absorb the *kedushah* of the *tzaddik* who feels his preparation and is waiting to help him. If, however, a person comes without preparation, he is comparable to a blind man standing next to a bright light. He won't see anything and the trip will not help him. It could even cause a *chillul Hashem,* and strengthen those who think that one goes to a *tzaddik* in order to enjoy himself and to drink and dance.

These words of the Rebbe left no room for misinterpretation. Anybody who wanted to go had to first prepare himself. In the town of Munkatch lived a *dayan* by the name of Reb Menachem Weiss. He once came to Chortkov to *daven* at the *kever* of an ancestor who was buried there. While he was there, he decided to take the opportunity to visit the Rebbe as well. When he entered the Rebbe's room, the Rebbe did not greet him with the customary "*Shalom Aleichem.*" Instead the Rebbe said to him: "You did not come to me, you came to your *zeide* who is buried here." Reb Menachem was amazed that although the Rebbe had never seen him before, he still knew and felt why he had come to town. After Reb Menachem had regained his composure, he quickly replied that he had come to the Rebbe as well. Only then did the Rebbe stretch out his hand and wish him "*Shalom Aleichem.*"

It is interesting to read the words of Reb Alter Meir of Sonik. He describes his preparation as follows:

> On Shavous 5662 (1902), when I was still a young *bochur,* my father called me aside and told me that in a few weeks he would be going to Chortkov. He was willing to take me along, but only if I would double the hours I learn until then. He also demanded that I review all that I had learned that summer plus the previous winter. That way, he said, he wouldn't be embarrassed of me in Chortkov. For the next few weeks I did not stop or rest.

Although very few chassidim recorded their impressions and memories of the Rebbe and his holy *avodah,* one or two did, thereby giving us a glimpse into a vanished world. One such chassid who recorded his impressions was Reb Yitzchok Stein. He was in Chortkov sometime during the 1880's. After the Rebbe's *petirah* in 1904, he described his visits in a series of newspaper articles:

THE FIRST THING CHASSIDIM DO WHEN THEY
reach their Rebbe's town is to immerse themselves in a

Meeting the Rebbe *mikveh*, purifying themselves before meeting the Rebbe. Just as a magnet attracts metal, so I felt pulled to the Rebbe. Therefore I didn't spend long in the *mikveh*; I immersed myself three times, had a few thoughts of *teshuvah* and with that jumped out.

When I approached the Rebbe's door, I could feel my heart thumping inside me like a thief caught in the act. Any minute the door would open and the holy Rebbe would appear. I started to make a *cheshbon hanefesh* before I showed my face to the Rebbe. As my mazel would have it, I suddenly remembered a string of long forgotten *aveirahs* that I had not yet done *teshuvah* on. It's true that they were not serious *aveirahs*, but nevertheless an *aveirah* is an *aveirah*. How could I possibly greet the *tzaddik* in such a state? While these thoughts were rushing through my confused mind the door suddenly opened and the Rebbe appeared.

Already from the first glance the Rebbe made a tremendous impression on me. I felt a new breath of life sweep through me. My tired and weary *neshamah* felt uplifted. The Rebbe's totally white face — without any hint of color — together with his aura of *kedushah* and purity made you feel that you were in the presence of greatness. He was the true *tzaddik*, whose every action was to do only the wish of Hashem without any personal interest or gain.

The Rebbe left his room to go to *daven*. Although his hand was outstretched to shake the hands of the newcomers, the Rebbe's eyes remained almost closed. Even when I went forward to touch the ends of his fingers he didn't lift his eyes for a second.

Another chassid who recorded his memories was the Banila Rav, HaGaon Reb Aryeh Mordechai Horowitz:

The first time I was *zocheh* to see the holy Rebbe was when I was 11 years of age. When the Rebbe started to recite *Kiddush* I became so overwhelmed that tears streamed down

The Banila Rav,
Reb Aryeh Mordechai Horowitz

my face. From then until the Rebbe's *petirah* I was *zocheh* to spend many Shabbosim in Chortkov, for my father took me along every time he went.

The Rebbe's *minhag* was to greet those who came for Shabbos after *lecht bentching* (candlelighting). The Rebbe would stand with his eyes closed and his hand outstretched. The visitors filed past to shake his hand, and the Rebbe wished everyone "*Shalom Aleichem.*" It made no difference who the guest was — even if he was a famous Rebbe or Rav — all were greeted the same way.

It seemed that the Rebbe did not know whom he had greeted, but in reality this was not so. One of my father's *talmidim* once told me that he arrived in Chortkov on Sunday, just as all the Shabbos guests were filing past to receive a *berachah* before leaving. The young man joined the queue, but instead of receiving a farewell *berachah*, the Rebbe greeted him with the words "*Shalom Aleichem.*" It was quite clear that the Rebbe knew exactly who was there for Shabbos and who wasn't!

IF JUST GREETING THE REBBE LEFT SUCH AN IMPRESSION, all the more so did the Rebbe's *Kiddush* leave a permanent and searing mark on all who witnessed it. As the Rebbe started **Kiddush** the first words of *Kiddush*, a terrible dread and fear fell on all those assembled. The Rebbe's *Kiddush* made such an impact on those who heard it that even many years later the chassidim who had witnessed it would shed hot tears as they reminded themselves of the event. In order to explain what was so special about the Rebbe's *Kiddush*, a few words of introduction are needed.

Unlike most Rebbes who used to act as the *chazzan* on Shabbos or Yom Tov, in the Rizhiner dynasty such a thing was unheard of. In addition the Rebbes of Rizhin did not even *daven* in the same room as their chassidim, but would *daven* in an adjoining room, unseen and unheard.

In his memoirs, the Banila Rav writes:

Reb Meir Arik was famed as one of the foremost poskim of his era

> A Belzer chassid who was once in Chortkov and was inspired by the Rebbe's *Kiddush* commented that it was a pity the Rebbe didn't *daven* in front of the *amud* and thereby lift *Yidden* to even greater heights. But he didn't understand that the Rebbe was like the Kohen Gadol on Yom Kippur about whom is written: "*Vechol adam lo yihiye b'Ohel Moed bevo'o lechaper bakodesh* — No one may be in the *Ohel Moed* when he comes to provide atonement in the *kodesh*."

Thus there was never a chance to see the Rebbe's *avodah* except during *Kiddush* or a *tisch*. Although a number of descriptions of the Rebbe's *Kiddush* have been written down, the common thread running through them is that it is impossible to convey on paper how it really felt. Even famous *gedolim* felt inadequate to fully explain the true depth of the feelings that were aroused by the Rebbe's *Kiddush*.

The *gaon* Reb Meir Arik was a frequent guest in Chortkov; every few months he made a point of spending a Shabbos by the Rebbe. One winter his family tried to dissuade him from his customary trip. There was a deep snow outside and in addition, Reb Meir had been suffering recently from ill health. Reb Meir, however, refused to give in to their demands that he cancel the trip.

When someone asked him why it was so imperative that he go, Reb Meir answered: "The climax of every *Yid's avodah* is the *tefillah* of *Neilah* on Yom Kippur. Which *Yid* would not want to experience such an intense *his'orerus* during the year as well? Believe me! When I hear the Rebbe make *Kiddush*, I experience the same intense sensation that grips me on Yom Kippur at *Neilah!*"

Among the many *gedolim* and *tzaddikim* who flocked en masse to Chortkov was the Shiniva Rav, Reb Yechezkel Halberstam. When the Shiniva Rav was asked to describe the atmosphere in Chortkov he replied: "How is it possible to describe the *ruchniyus* that one feels in Chortkov? All I can say is that I looked around me while the Rebbe was holding a *tisch*, and I noticed that when he called out suddenly in deep *d'veikus*: 'Heiliger Tatte! Heiliger Rachamim of the whole world,' there wasn't a dry eye in sight, as each and every person there was gripped with intense feelings of *teshuvah*."

One of those who recorded his impressions of the Rebbe's *Kiddush* was Reb Yitzchok Stein; he writes as follows:

> After *davening* was finished, the Rebbe stayed in his private room, alone, for about an hour. What he did there, no one knew for sure. Often one could hear his voice as he called out, "*Heiliger Tatte! Heiliger Rachamim!* Help! Help!" At 10 o'clock the large *tisch* hall is packed to capacity. Everyone is waiting for the Rebbe's entry. Suddenly silence falls, the door from the Rebbe's room has opened. A moment later the Rebbe makes his entry. A shudder goes through all present. His face an almost deathly white, the *tzaddik* starts to recite "*Shalom Aleichem*." An unearthly silence descends on the vast hall, only the Rebbe's soft voice can be heard. As the Rebbe proceeds and starts to recite *Kiddush*, everyone's eyes are glued to his face. His normal deathly white complexion has changed to fiery red. If I hadn't seen it myself I would not have believed it. The Rebbe's normal white complexion was the result of years of fasting. He was extremely thin, just skin and bones, not a drop of color was ever visible on his face. Only when he was engaged in a mitzvah did his complexion change.

Not a hint of color was
ever visible on the Rebbe's face

Then his face would shine a bright red. One could see clearly how his *neshamah* was in control of his body, how the spiritual ruled over the physical.

Although the Rebbe stands still without swaying, his whole being is trembling, a byproduct of his great fear of Heaven. The Rebbe's fear of *Shamayim* isn't lost on those present. As the Rebbe continues to recite the words of *Kiddush*, a terrible fear and awe overcomes the chassidim, a true *pachad Hashem*, unlike anything one has ever felt before.

During the *Kiddush*, the wine in the Rebbe's cup appeared as if it were boiling, like a pot of water on a fire. The wine froths and jumps up above the cup and then falls down again back into the cup. I once heard a natural explanation for this wonder from a doctor. After studying the Rebbe's movements, he reported what he had seen to his colleagues in Lemberg. They came to the following conclusion: If a cup of water were placed in the hand of a dying man, the convulsions of the throes of death would also make the water in the cup froth and jump!

After the Rebbe finishes reciting *Kiddush* one doesn't hear from him anything else, but one feels. One feels a new level of *kedushah* which fills the whole body. One feels like a new person, clean and pure. One appreciates the meaning of the words *"oneg Shabbos,"* and one understands what *"Yismechu b'malchuscha shomrei Shabbos v'kor'ei oneg"* means. We have experienced the words of *Chazal* — that Shabbos is a taste of *Olam Haba*.

In his memoirs, the Maggid of Kolomei, Reb Yitzchok Weber, also relates his impression of the Rebbe's *Kiddush*:

Who can possibly describe the intensity of the Rebbe's *avodah*? Those who saw how he wept, and those who heard his heavenly voice felt as if a fiery flame was enveloping them, cleansing them from all their impurities. The words emanating from his holy mouth pierced the very heart, causing tears to well up in the eyes. Anyone who had just the slightest knowledge in our holy Torah could see with his naked eye how the Rebbe's every move and act was performed with intense *kavanah* far beyond our understanding.

The Banila Rav adds:

Who can possibly describe the *his'orerus* that gripped us when the Rebbe recited *Kiddush*. Happy are those who merited hearing the *Shechinah* emanate from his mouth. Just to see how the Rebbe entered the hall where he made *Kiddush* was a lesson in itself. His *d'veikus* and humility were such that he never noticed whether the hall was full of people or empty. A number of times my father told me that he was convinced that if everyone would file out of the hall the Rebbe would not even notice. Such were his *d'veikus* and his humility.

AFTER *KIDDUSH* WAS OVER, THE *TISCH* BEGAN. THIS WAS AN opportunity to watch the Rebbe's *avodah* while he was eating.

The Rebbe's Tisch

Once again we shall rely on the testimony of Reb Yitzchok Stein:

Hardly had the *tzaddik* eaten a piece of challah than he started *tzu arbeten maasim*, to work wonders. With his thin and slender fingers he banged on the table and gave an ear-piercing cry: "*Heiliger Tatte! Heiliger Rachamim* of the whole world!" An awesome shudder gripped all the chassidim; almost everyone had tears in their eyes.

This testimony can be backed up by the words of the Shotzer Rebbe, Reb Sholom Moskovitz of London. Although he was a Belzer chassid, he also used to frequent Chortkov. In his later years Reb Sholom was once asked what had made the most profound impact on him from all that he had seen by the various *tzaddikim* he had encountered. Reb

Sholom thought for a moment and answered that the scene of the Chortkover Rebbe banging on the table and crying out to Hashem had affected him in a way unparalleled by anything else he had seen.

Indeed it was no wonder that the effect the Rebbe had on his chassidim was not quickly forgotten. In an article compiled in 1964, the chassid Reb Dovid Moshe Spiegel writes:

> I knew many great chassidim who were close to the Rebbe, and when they used to tell me about him, tears would stream down their faces. This was always a source of amazement to me. I once visited HaGaon Reb Nuchem Leiberzohn and we spoke about the Rebbe. Hardly had we begun when he started to cry. I wanted to comfort him and I said, "But the Rebbe left behind him a son like himself who is the glory of all *Klal Yisroel*. He possesses all the qualities enumerated by *Chazal* that a leader must have." "You are right," Rav Leiberzohn answered me. "It's true what you said, but if you would have known the Rebbe, you would cry as well."
>
> Recently I visited HaGaon Reb Yoel Fink, who is the only person still alive who was present at the Rebbe's *petirah*. I had a few points that I wanted to clarify, and I spoke to him for a long time, and again I witnessed this same wonder. During our conversation Reb Yoel had to dry his eyes from his tears a number of times.

Thus, the time and effort invested into going to the Rebbe left an indelible and everlasting mark that time could not erase. It is worth noting that the Rachmistrivka Rebbe, Reb Yisroel Mordechai Twersky, often says that he knew many old Chortkover chassidim who were *zocheh* to bask in the Rebbe's presence. All these chassidim, observed the Rachmistrivka Rebbe, had about them a special aura of *yiras Shamayim* that others do not have.

Similarly, the Potiker Rav, Reb Shlomo Zalman Horowitz, related that his *zeide* Reb Moshe Schechter was *zocheh* to travel to the Rebbe fifty times. When Reb Moshe once mentioned this fact to the Rebbe's son and successor Reb Yisroel, he jumped up from his seat and exclaimed: "If so you must be one of the select and special people of the generation (*yechidei segulah shebador*). You don't need me or my *berachos!*"

≈⌒

ALTHOUGH THE REBBE'S *KIDDUSH* AND *TISCH* WERE undoubtedly the highlight of any chassid's trip, the night's *avodah* was not over yet. In his article Reb Yitzchok Stein continues:

A Chassidishe "Sitz"

It was already after 1 o'clock in the morning by the time the Rebbe's *tisch* finished. Many of the chassidim, exhausted from the day's activities, headed for bed. The senior chassidim, however, those who were regarded for their lofty and exalted ways, and their sharp heads, had more important things to take care of than a few hours sleep. They looked down on sleeping as of secondary importance, a partial death from which one must flee as much as possible. Instead, they made their way to the inn where they spent most of the night engrossed in stories of *tzaddikim* and their wondrous ways.

There were three chassidishe inns in Chortkov. There, chassidim would sit in informal gatherings, and over a "*glaizel bronfen*" discuss what new insights they had absorbed from the day's events. The greatest minds used to assemble in "Dovid's Shenk" or in "Peretz's Shenk." There one could often find men of stature like Reb Itzikel Titover, Reb Shaul Bulkamener, Yosele Dobromiler, Itzikel Tarnopoler and many others like them. The third inn was called "Miriam's Weinshenk," and those who were known for their sharp minds, such as Reb Chaim Ber Brasskover or Reb Moshe Cohen from Phelenstein, assembled there.

Many of the young chassidim would also push themselves into the inns in order to hear and observe the insights of the senior chassidim. I also entered one of the inns. My sleep could wait until I was back home. I needed to have some fresh stories and new insights to relate to the chassidim back home. Those who hadn't been fortunate enough to go to the Rebbe always expected that at least they would hear something new from those who had.

The chassidim arranged themselves around a long table, while the *yungerleit* stood behind them. Glasses and wine were placed on the table but before anyone could even contemplate drinking, the discussion had started. One of the senior chassidim opened the discussion: "Tonight's *tisch* was something really special," he declared. "It is a long time since I last saw the Rebbe in such a state. His *d'veikus* when he sang the *niggunim* and his fiery *avodah* was like that of a *malach*. One could feel the *kedushah* throughout one's body."

I wasn't surprised to hear the elderly *Yid's* words. True chassidim find a new sensation and feeling at every *tisch*. This is the *madreigah* referred to by our sages — to feel every day's *avodah* as if it is new (*bechol yom yihiyu b'einecha kechadashim*).

A second *Yid* echoed the words of the first speaker. "We have to thank Hashem," he added, "that we were *zocheh* to spend a Shabbos with the Rebbe. Any *Yid* who has even the smallest spark of Chassidus in him knows that a person can only be a true chassid if he is in the Rebbe's presence at every opportunity."

"It's not exactly as you say," someone interrupted. "A true chassid is someone who feels attached to the Rebbe even when not in his presence. If he truly believes in the Rebbe, then he will be attached to the *tzaddik* regardless of where he is. I have a story just about this point involving our holy Rebbe."

Everybody present picked up his head to hear this new story. Turning in the direction of the speaker, all the chassidim listened attentively.

"I HEARD THIS STORY FROM REB ASHER ZELIG from Ostilla," the speaker continued. "I presume that everyone knows who he is and the close relationship that he enjoys with the Rebbe. Reb Asher Zelig and his brother Reb Velvel Sofer have never missed a Shavous with the Rebbe, even

Old Chassidim Remember

when he lived in Potik. One year, however, Reb Velvel was unable to go; something had occurred that simply made his trip impossible. Reb Velvel wrote a letter to his brother telling him what had happened, and asked him to at least mention to the Rebbe how upset he was not to be there.

"After Yom Tov was over, Reb Asher Zelig was granted an audience with the Rebbe. At that time he presented a *kvittel* on behalf of his brother and added how upset his brother was not to have spent Yom Tov with the Rebbe. 'Your brother was here for Shavous,' the Rebbe told him. 'We even drank *l'chaim* together.' Reb Asher Zelig wondered greatly at the Rebbe's words but didn't dare ask for an explanation. After he left the Rebbe's room he asked the elder chassidim for an explanation but they were just as puzzled.

"When Reb Asher Zelig met his brother and told him the Rebbe's words, Reb Velvel wasn't surprised. 'It's true,' Reb Velvel exclaimed. 'We did drink *l'chaim* together. Come, let me explain what I mean.

"'The first day of Yom Tov at the hour when the Rebbe normally starts the *tisch* I was sitting at home with a heavy heart. To miss being at the Rebbe's *tisch* was a bitter pill to swallow. While I was engrossed in my thoughts, I dozed off in my chair for a few moments and I started to dream. In my dream I found myself in Chortkov standing at the Rebbe's *tisch*. Everything was crystal clear just like in real life. I did not receive any wine with which to drink *l'chaim*, but the Rebbe noticed and commanded the *gabbai* to pour a cup for me. I drank *l'chaim* and reached out to touch the Rebbe's hand. As I touched his holy fingers a slight smile lit up his face. My joy was indescribable, not just in the dream, but also when I woke up a few seconds later. I was positive that through his heavenly influence, the Rebbe had felt my sorrow and had wished me *l'chaim*!'"

⌒⌒

It is worth noting that this idea of the Rebbe being in touch with his chassidim even when far away was mentioned by the Rebbe himself on a number of occasions. In his *sefer "Divrei Dovid,"* the Rebbe is quoted as follows:

> A *tzaddik* can be compared to a rope, as it is written: *"Yaakov chevel nachalaso* — Yaakov is the rope of His inheritance." When a person shakes one end of a rope it can be felt the whole way through, to the other end. Similarly, when a person attaches himself to a *tzaddik* and he feels constantly connected to him, then the *tzaddik* will feel all that is happening to that person and assist him even from afar.

Indeed there are many stories which can back up this claim of how the Rebbe felt and assisted his chassidim from afar. Although it is not the aim and purpose of this book to relate *mofsim* (miracles), the following story can be understood in the previous context.

One of the great Torah disseminators in pre-war Romania was the *gaon* Reb Dovid Zimering, who was *Rosh Yeshivah* of the famous Keshinov yeshivah. He was a close *chassid* of the Chortkover Rebbe and the words and sayings of his Rebbe were constantly on his lips. In the preface to his monumental *sefer* on *Shas,* the following story is recorded:

> Reb Dovid was once traveling on a train when he began to feel sick. In order to clear his head, he opened the window and leaned out of the stuffy cabin. Suddenly he heard the voice of the Rebbe calling his name: "Dovid! Dovid!" Reb Dovid immediately moved his head back inside the cabin in surprise. The cabin, however, was empty save for a few sleeping *goyim.* Just at that moment a train passed by in the opposite direction. In horror Reb Dovid realized that in his quest for fresh air he had totally forgotten about the danger from trains passing in the opposite direction. If not for the voice that had beckoned him back in the cabin, the other train, which passed only inches away from his carriage, would probably have killed him.
>
> When Reb Dovid was next in Chortkov, the Rebbe's opening words to him were: "Tell me, Dovid! Are we not commanded to guard our lives and to act in a responsible manner?"

CHAPTER SIX

A Life of Kedushah

JUST AS THE REBBE'S *KEDUSHAH* WAS CONSIDERED TO be beyond ordinary human grasp, so was his physical strength also above everyone's comprehension. Even in his later years when he appeared weak and frail, he continued his almost daily fasts. He also denied his body even the basic minimum amount of sleep. On the days when he did sleep, it was never more than two hours, normally between 5:30 and 7:30 a.m.

AROUND 9 O'CLOCK EVERY MORNING THE *GABBAIM* would bring the morning's post to the Rebbe. So much post would **Daily** arrive that it had to be delivered twice daily, once in the morning and once in the evening. Each session **Schedule** lasted approximately one hour; the *gabbaim* would read the letters to the Rebbe, and he would answer them on the spot. The *gabbaim* would then proceed to write the exact language and answer the Rebbe had given. Almost always, the Rebbe's answers were given straightaway without any hesitation. It was very rare for the Rebbe to say that he needed time to think over his answer.

At 10 o' clock the Rebbe would receive the many chassidim who needed to speak to him. Again this lasted about an hour. The Rebbe's replies were quick and concise, thus enabling him to see a large numbers of people in a short time. The Maggid of Kolomei, Reb Yitzchok Weber, writes:

> The speed of the Rebbe's mind was beyond human understanding. In less than a second after being asked he would already give his answer on the most serious issues and on a course of action. I once needed to speak to him about a problem, and I thought that I would need at least 2 minutes to explain the case. No more than 12 seconds after I started, the Rebbe already interrupted me with the answer.

IT WAS DURING THIS HOUR THAT THE CHASSIDIM witnessed almost daily occurrences of the Rebbe's *ruach hakodesh.* Often two people in the same predicament would ask the Rebbe the same question and each one received a different answer. This was especially prevalent in regard to young men who asked for advice as to how to be freed from army service.

Reading a Kvittel

As is well known, one of the terrible decrees that faced Russian Jewry was that of forced conscription into the Czar's army. Young men who were 18 years and over were sent far away from home, for years at a stretch, and forced to violate the Torah. Many men would flock to Chortkov hoping to receive the Rebbe's *berachah* that they be spared this fate. So many people would come for this problem alone, that there was a special queue just for them. Unlike everyone else, they were not required to give a *kvittel* and they would file by in turn. The Rebbe would give his *berachah* to each person and accordingly the person often knew what his fate would be.

When Reb Yisroel Shusterman of Zinkov received his call-up papers, he made his way to Chortkov to receive the Rebbe's *berachah* that he be freed. As his turn came, the Rebbe looked at him and said: "We find in the Torah that there were three categories of people exempt from the army. 'Someone who has built a new house and not yet inaugurated it. Someone who has planted a vineyard and not yet redeemed it. Someone who has betrothed a woman and not yet married her.' There was, however, a fourth category who also did not go to the army. They were not exempt, rather they were unfit. 'Somebody who was scared and faint-hearted should not go, lest he influence others.'

"Those people who were faint hearted," the Rebbe explained to Reb Yisroel, "had not received an exemption like the other three groups. Therefore those *neshamos* now have to make it up! You must make sure to complete your army service, do not attempt to evade it." Reb Yisroel listened to the Rebbe and did his tour of duty. Not only did he complete his regular army duty but he even served for an extra year. Due to some unknown reason they refused to free him after the allotted time and insisted on keeping him for another year!

WHEN THE REBBE READ A *KVITTEL*, HE ALWAYS KEPT HIS eyes glued to the paper. The chassidim understood that the Rebbe

Between the Lines was not merely glancing at the written request. He was looking beyond the paper, into higher realms where other people could not see, in order to help the person before him. The chassidim had countless stories to back up their claim.

When the well-known philosopher, Reb Aharon Marcus, was in Chortkov for the first time, he hoped to analyze the Rebbe's conduct. He soon came to the conclusion that through such a method he would never understand who the Rebbe really was. The Rebbe could not be explained through natural means. It didn't take long for Reb Aharon to find this out firsthand.

When Reb Aharon was granted an audience with the Rebbe, he presented him with a *kvittel* in which he had listed all the names of his family. The Rebbe stared intently at the names and then he asked: "How is your Shlomo doing?" Reb Aharon didn't understand the Rebbe's question. Why had he singled out only this one child? In order to answer the *tzaddik* who was waiting for a reply, he said: "*Baruch Hashem* he is fine, and he is a well-behaved boy." Again the Rebbe took the *kvittel*, looked at it intently, and then he asked: "Was Shlomo ill when you left home?" By now Reb Aharon had become nervous. "No," he answered. His son had been fine when he had left home. "Hashem should help that he be totally healthy," the Rebbe assured him.

After Reb Aharon left the Rebbe's room he asked the main *gabbai*, Reb Yisroel Rapporport, for an explanation, but he was also mystified. It didn't take too long before Reb Aharon heard that he was being searched for. A telegram had arrived for him. With trembling hands Reb Aharon opened the telegram. It was from his wife. Their son Shlomo was seriously ill with a lung infection. He should ask the Rebbe for a *berachah* immediately ... Reb Aharon remained a Chortkover chassid for the rest of his life. His son, Reb Yisroel Marcus, became one of the Rebbe's close confidants.

Reb Yitzchok Stein writes the following story, which he says he heard from a reliable source:

> A young man from the town of Bendin in Poland once came to the Rebbe for Yom Tov. Although the *minhag* in Chortkov was that only upon leaving one gave the Rebbe a *kvittel*, if a person needed a *berachah* for something that did not bear delaying, he would be granted entry to the Rebbe upon his arrival. This young man asked to be let in on his arrival. His wife had recently started to suffer from frequent migraine headaches, and there was no reason to prolong her agony.
>
> No sooner had the Rebbe looked at the *kvittel*, than he stuck out his hand to the young man and bid him farewell. Thinking that perhaps the Rebbe thought that he was about to leave, the young man explained to the Rebbe that he had just arrived, and was intending to stay for Yom Tov. The reason why he had come in now and not on his departure was only to secure a *berachah* for his wife.
>
> Again the Rebbe examined the *kvittel* and looked at the request. Putting the *kvittel* face down with the writing against the table, he bid the young man farewell. Although the young man did not understand the Rebbe's actions, the *gabbaim* knew what had happened. Only after the Rebbe's *petirah* did they reveal their secret. Whenever the Rebbe received a *kvittel*

about someone who had already died or whose fate had already been sealed and was beyond help, the Rebbe would place the *kvittel* face down with the writing toward the table.

The Bendiner young man arrived home to find that his wife had suddenly passed away while he was on the way to Chortkov.

⁂

A Faithful Servant AT 11 O'CLOCK THE REBBE WOULD START TO *DAVEN Shacharis*. (The Rebbe was once asked why he *davened* after the time prescribed by the *Shulchan Aruch* but he refused to answer.) The *davening* took him most of the day — until late afternoon or early evening. The Rebbe of Slonim, Reb Shmuel Weinberg, was once present when the Rebbe's *gabbai* came into the room to inform him that it was time to *daven Minchah*. Reb Shmuel later related that when the Rebbe heard that it was time to stand up in prayer in front of Hashem, his hair stood up on end in fright, such was his fear of Heaven.

No chassidim were ever present in the Rebbe's room to see how or what he *davened*. The Rebbe's brother, Reb Menachem Nuchem, who was Rebbe in Shtefanesht, once watched the Rebbe at prayer in his private room. The comment that he later made to describe the Rebbe's *tefillah* became famous among the chassidim.

"I am sure," the Shtefaneshter Rebbe said, "that when my holy brother takes his *Tehillim* in his hand, Hashem says to him: 'Dovid Moshe, My son, the whole world is yours. Do with it what you please.' Now, if I were in his position I would already know what to do with it. He, however, is such a faithful and trustworthy servant that he returns it to Hashem just as he received it."[1]

An example of the Rebbe's faithfulness can be seen after the *petirah* of his eldest son, Reb Nuchem Mordechai. Not long after Reb Nuchem Mordechai's *petirah* at the tender age of 21, the Rebbe's

---

1. Reb Yossel Halpern of Manchester pointed out that this concept has its source in *Midrash Tanchuma* [*Parshas Behar*]: "Hashem said: I sold the entire world to Avrohom; he, however, presented it back to Me, as it is written (*Bereishis* 14:22): *Konei shamayim vaaretz*."

second and last child, Reb Yisroel, also fell ill with the same illness that had claimed his brother. Reb Yisroel's condition was critical and the doctors had already given up hope on him. The Rebbe went to visit his sick son and to see how he was doing. As Reb Dovid Moshe left the room, he was overheard muttering to himself, "If this is Your wish, Hashem, that he should join his brother — I won't say anything ..."

Reb Yisroel of Chortkov as a young man

THE REBBE ALSO GUIDED HIS CHASSIDIM IN THIS WAY, TO come to the realization that everything that happens to a person,

All Is for the Best even things that seem bad, are ultimately for his good. In his *sefer* the Rebbe is quoted as follows:

There are those who wonder — often we see people who ask a *tzaddik* to *daven* to Hashem to help them in difficult times and the prayers of the *tzaddikim* go unanswered. Surely our sages have told us that even when Hashem has decreed something, a *tzaddik* can annul the decree through prayer.

The truth, however, is that when something bad befalls a person, it is really a blessing in disguise, a hidden benefit, as the *pasuk* informs us: "*Mipi Elyon lo seitzei haraos* — From Above will not descend evil." Unfortunately we often do not realize that ultimately everything is for our good and even the sorrows have in them a spark of goodness. When such a person comes to a *tzaddik* and asks him to remove his suffering the *tzaddik* is faced with a predicament. He can and wants to relieve the *Yid* from his sorrow, yet he knows that to do so would not be in the *Yid's* long-term interest.

Not every *tzaddik*, however, is capable of seeing the ultimate goodness in every sorrow. Only the *tzaddik hador* who can see the person's whole being, from his roots to his end, is in the position to have the full picture. Therefore it can happen that a person might beseech a great *tzaddik* to help him and his cries and tears go unanswered. Yet when this *Yid* turns to a lesser *tzaddik* for help, his problem is solved right away. The reason for this is that the lesser *tzaddik* is unable to see the ultimate good which the present sorrow heralds and therefore does not hesitate to remove it.

Once, during a *tisch*, the Rebbe turned to a wealthy chassid, Reb Yitzchok Kapeler from Zalishtik, and said to him: "Sometimes a *tzaddik* sees that a person is going to suffer, yet he doesn't want to take away the sorrow, for he knows that it is for the person's good. Still the *tzaddik* is distressed at the problem. In such cases the *tzaddik* davens that the damage should be as light as possible under the circumstances."

Realizing that the Rebbe had meant to give him a personal message, Reb Yitzchok hurried home, fearful that something had happened to his family. Before he arrived home he already knew to what the Rebbe's words alluded. A large fire had broken out in his business and had reduced the building to rubble. Reb Yitzchok, realizing that if not for the Rebbe's intervention, worse could have been awaiting him, thanked Hashem that the punishment was wrought only on wood and stones and not on his family.

A story of how the Rebbe was once coerced into giving a *berachah*, which in the end turned out to be a living curse, became famous across Galicia:

> One of the greatest chassidim in Chortkov was Reb Itzikel Titover. He was regarded by all as a true chassid, a person who had purified himself over decades. He was also one of the Rebbe's closest confidants, and could gain access to the Rebbe without delay. Reb Itzikel was also the only person who was able to bring a smile to the Rebbe's lips. On Purim he would dress up and act as a *badchan* in order to gladden the *tzaddik*'s heart.
>
> Despite his cheerful appearance, Reb Itzikel carried inside him a deep sorrow. Although he was married for many years, he had not yet been *zocheh* to children. Being a true

and faithful chassid, he never bothered the Rebbe about this. In his *kvitlach* he would always ask for a *berachah* for children but that was it. He never pressured the Rebbe into promising him a child; the Rebbe knew his sorrow and if he had not promised him on his own accord, that meant it was not to be. (An explanation of this concept is to be found in the *sefer* "*Shevet Mussar*," Chapter 24.)

There came, however, a time when Reb Itzikel could bear it no longer and he decided to approach the Rebbe at all costs. He chose to wait for Purim when the Rebbe would be in a joyous mood and perhaps more willing to promise him a child. That Purim, when Reb Itzikel was performing his antics and causing a smile to spread across the Rebbe's face, he begged the *tzaddik* to promise him a child. No sooner had he uttered the words than the smile vanished from the *tzaddik's* face.

"Itzikel!" the Rebbe answered in a stern voice. "Don't you know that if you haven't been granted a child it shows that the time has not yet arrived." "Have pity on me," Reb Itzikel wailed. "I can't take it any longer." The Rebbe took Reb Itzikel's hand and wished him a son, a *berachah* that was fulfilled that very year.

Reb Itzikel's joy, however, didn't last long. His only son, into whom he put great effort to teach him all he knew, did not go in his father's ways. As the boy grew older it became more and more obvious that he would not give his parents much *nachas*. Slowly but surely he forsook the path of the Torah until he no longer even kept Shabbos. Eventually he became a *maskil* who tried everything in his power to cause other *Yidden* to sin and belittle the Torah. Reb Itzikel was left with no option but to banish his son from his house. Afterwards he sat *shivah* after him and never mentioned his name again.

Another chassid, who pressured the Rebbe and later regretted it, was HaGaon Reb Yisroel Berger, the Rav of Bucharest. In his well-known *sefer* "*Eser Oros*" he writes as follows:

In the winter of 5647 (1887), I needed the Rebbe to write for me a very important letter which concerned my future. The Rebbe dictated the letter to his *gabbai*, who then handed it to me. I wasn't happy with the Rebbe's choice of words and I asked him to alter it. I had to plead with him the whole day until he finally agreed to change the text.

That evening when I finally received the new draft the Rebbe said to me: "Don't think that your begging has changed my mind, I am still of the opinion that the original letter was correctly written and would be better for you. It's just that when I saw what anguish it caused you, I gave in to your demands so as not to cause you anymore pain, but not because I agree with you."

Reb Yisroel Berger finishes off as follows:

Since that incident nineteen years have passed, and now I see that the Rebbe was correct. If only I would have listened to him then, I would not have had to endure all that I did, and I would have been far better off both spiritually and physically. I can't explain all the details, but what I can say is that my whole future would have been different had I only listened then.

⋙⋘

BY THE TIME THE REBBE HAD FINISHED *DAVENING*, MOST of the day had passed and evening was already well on its way.

Eating L'Shem Shamayim
Until the Rebbe had *davened* he would never eat or drink anything, thus spending the majority of the day fasting. Often he would refuse to eat then also, saying that since it wasn't long anymore until nightfall, he wanted to complete the day as a *taanis*.

When the Sadigerer Rebbe was once in Chortkov for a visit, he noticed how thin and pale his brother looked. He begged his sister-in-law, the Chortkover Rebbetzin, to carefully watch her husband and to make sure that he did not fast too much. The Rebbetzin replied that she tried her best, but she was often unable

The Rebbe's nephews:
Reb Avrohom Yaakov
of Sadiger (r.)
and
Reb Mordechai
Shlomo of Boyan (l.)

to ascertain when he was fasting. The Rebbe was particular to eat in total privacy, thereby preventing anyone from knowing if he had actually eaten his food or not. His plate was always empty when it was collected, but no one knew if the Rebbe had actually eaten the food. Sometimes he would hide the food in a drawer and later give it to a *gabbai* to remove.

The Rebbetzin herself once related the following incident about how she got her husband to break his fast. One day, a coffee was brought into the Rebbe's room. A few minutes later the Rebbetzin entered and found the cup already empty. In the sink could be seen signs that he had poured his coffee down the drain.[2] The Rebbetzin approached her husband and said: "Think carefully, what is more precious to Hashem, your fasting or your eating?" Without further ado the Rebbe asked for another coffee to be brought in and he promptly drank it.

Indeed it was clear to all that the Rebbe's eating was not a mere physical activity but rather a continuation of his *avodas Hashem.* The Rebbe himself once said: "A person can live 70 years, learning and *davening,* but if he hasn't learned how to eat properly, it's all worth nothing." In his *sefer "Avir Yaakov,"* the Rebbe's nephew, Reb Avrohom Yaakov of Sadiger, writes:

---

2. See *Piskei Teshuvos Siman* 171 section 2, that the prohibition of wasting food (*bal tashchis*) does not apply if food is wasted in order to conceal one's spiritual level, i.e. that one is fasting.

There are some *tzaddikim* who know how to serve Hashem only through spiritual acts, such as learning Torah and *davening*. There are other *tzaddikim,* however, who know how to serve Hashem with all their actions, even through mundane and physical acts. I was still *zocheh* to see my holy uncle from Chortkov during a meal in his house. I saw that even while he was eating on a regular weekday he was trembling with such fright of Heaven, far more than others do during *davening* on Yom Kippur.

The Rebbe once received a gift, a new *bekeshe,* which a chassid had tailored for him using the best and most expensive materials. The Rebbe wore the new garment for *davening* and then sat down to eat something. Fearing that the new *bekeshe* might get slightly stained, one of the *gabbaim* suggested that the Rebbe use the new garment only for *davening* and not for eating. "I don't understand you," the Rebbe replied in wonder. "Is eating not also a form of *davening*?"

This comment can be understood with the words of Reb Yaakov Emden, who writes in his commentary on the *siddur* as follows: "You already know and have heard from me that *tefillah* and eating are almost the identical activity. Just that *tefillah* is food for the soul and eating is food for the body." Similarly the famous Rebbe, Reb Hershele Zhidichover used to often say: "In my younger years I used to *daven* that I achieve with my eating what I achieve with my *tefillah. Baruch Hashem,* I now *daven* that I achieve with my *tefillah* what I achieve with my eating."

☙☜

AFTER THE REBBE HAD FINISHED HIS SOLITARY MEAL OF the day, the night program began. Reb Alter Meir from Sonik writes

Night Program

as follows:

It is close to fifty years since I was in Chorkov for the first time. The Alter Rebbe, Reb Dovid Moshe, was still alive then. Just as our sages tell us that during the *Simchas Beis Hasho'eivah* in the *Beis HaMikdash,* there was no time to

Reb Alter Meir of Sonik

sleep, so it was in Chortkov. The nights that we spent in the Rebbe's presence left us with no time to even contemplate sleeping. We went from one *avodah* to the next *avodah*: *Minchah* followed by learning and then *Maariv* followed again by learning until midnight. Then the Rebbe would receive those chassidim waiting to speak with him. One could hear someone ask for a *berachah* for his wife for an easy childbirth and the Rebbe would bless him and also tell him what name to give. From this the man knew whether it would be a boy or a girl. The next person would ask the Rebbe to prescribe for him a way of atoning for his many sins. Often the Rebbe would answer such a request by advising the person to stop delving into the past and rather concentrate on perfecting the future.

And so the night passed until the clock read 3 a.m. Now it was time for the next *avodah*, to hear the Rebbe's *Krias Shema* with *Vidui*, before going to bed. This took over two hours and by then it was almost 6 o'clock.

Just as the Rebbe's *Kiddush* left a deep impression on all who witnessed it, so did the Rebbe's *Krias Shema*. In the introduction to the *sefer "Imrei Naftoli"* by HaGaon Reb Hershel Schmerler, it is written as follows:

> Reb Hershel used to relate that his grandfather, the Rav of Monistritch, took him to Chortkov when he was still a young boy. The amazing sight of the Rebbe saying *Kiddush* never left him, and remained firmly imbedded in his mind all his days. Reb Hershel would say that he was so moved that a stream of tears poured down his face, and he would add that he was not exaggerating. He also related that he merited being present when the Rebbe said *Krias Shema* and *Vidui* before going to sleep at night. The Rebbe paced up and

down in his room with great *d'veikus*, totally oblivious to all around him. Reb Hershel added that it was apparent that the Rebbe never noticed them at all. These scenes made an everlasting impression on him.

ॐ

More often than not, the Rebbe did without any sleep, going for days without rest. This wonder, which sounds hard to believe but is known to be true, gives us an insight into his greatness. Even his close family sometimes feared for his health, but each time the Rebbe would reassure them that they need not worry. He would often say: "If a person is truly attached to Hashem, he can go without food or drink." On one occasion he said that he was capable of going forty days without eating or sleeping. Thus it seems that the reason why he did eat and sleep was not a physical exercise but a spiritual one. Indeed the Arizal once told his *talmidim* that there were certain secrets of the Torah that could only be revealed to him while he was asleep.

The heavy burden of *Klal Yisroel*, however, did not allow the Rebbe to indulge in the luxury of sleeping, spiritual or otherwise. Once, the Rebbe was in a terrible state; for days he had been pacing up and down in his room deep in worry. Seeing the Rebbe's nervous state, his *gabbai* asked him to rest a little bit. The Rebbe answered him, "It is easy for you to ask me to rest! But how can I rest when my whole being is in a torment of indecision over the future of a *Yid* who needs my help, but I am unable to help him. How can I possibly rest?!"

To what lengths the Rebbe went to help his fellow *Yidden* can be seen from the following incident, which occurred in the Rebbe's last years. Every night, after the Rebbe had finished seeing his chassidim, he would remain closed in his room for a long period of time. Curious to know what the Rebbe did during this time, one of the Rebbe's close chassidim, HaGaon Reb Dovid Zeideman, climbed up a tree from where he was able to peek into the Rebbe's room. The Rebbe was busy reviewing all the *kvitlach* that he had received that day. Hundreds of pieces of paper were piled up in front of him and

Reb Dovid Zeideman (standing in left corner) watches the actions of Reb Nuchem Mordechai of Chortkov. Reb Dovid was one of the foremost Chortkover chassidim.

the Rebbe was meticulously going through all of them. While Reb Dovid was watching, the Rebbe came across a *kvittel* that he was unable to read. The Rebbe held the piece of paper this way and that way as he tried to read the messy writing, but without much success. The Rebbe got up from his place and, walking over to the center of the room, he held the *kvittel* up to the lamp, in an attempt to decipher the *kvittel*, but to no avail, the writing remained as illegible as beforehand. Finally, in desperation, the Rebbe climbed up on a chair and, holding the *kvittel* right next to the lamp, he succeeded in reading the messy writing.

CHAPTER SEVEN

Showing the Way

ALTHOUGH THE REBBE WAS VERY EXACTING WITH himself, when it came to others his kindness was legendary. He never refused any request made to him, and it was unheard of that he should lose his temper or even show the slightest sign of anger. Each person was warmly greeted and granted the Rebbe's gentle heartfelt *berachos*. "I decided as a child of 7 not to annoy any creature," he used to say. When he was asked, "What would you do if a *goy* were to molest a *Yid* and you were asked for help?" he replied: "I would pray to Hashem for the *Yid* to be saved and not for the punishment of the *goy*."

OVER THE YEARS, THERE WERE MANY INSTANCES WHEN the Rebbe would have been justified in becoming angry.

Ignoring Provocation Occasionally it happened that one of the *gabbaim* overstepped his authority and issued a wrong directive, or a close confidant neglected to do what the Rebbe had requested of him. Still, the Rebbe never grew angry and never showed any feelings of being upset in any way.

The Rebbe's *gabbaim* were not happy that the Rebbe never reacted to any situation or provocation. They viewed it as a failure on the Rebbe's part not to uphold his dignity and honor, which in the long run would not be good for the running of the Chassidus. When the *gabbaim* made their concern known to the Rebbe, he answered them with a story:

> My father once told me the following incident and he added that he is telling it to me because there will come a time when I will need to know it. My *zeide* Reb Sholom was once granted access to the interior of Gan Eden. He went from one chamber to the next, going higher and higher. Eventually he arrived in a very exalted chamber, which was decorated in a most fabulous fashion. In the middle of the room was a table and chair, which were also made from the most beautiful materials. On the table stood a crown adorned with diamonds and jewels.
>
> Seated on the chair was a very great *tzaddik*. ("I know who this *tzaddik* was," the Rebbe added, "but I do not intend to tell you.") Reb Sholom was informed that this wondrous crown was created as a result of the Torah and mitzvos that this *tzaddik* had performed. But since this *tzaddik* used to act in a strict and stern way he was not allowed to wear the crown that was created by his deeds.

The *gabbaim* understood the message the Rebbe had given them and from then on they did not attempt to influence the Rebbe to act in a stern or strict fashion.

It once happened that a certain Rav came to Chortkov and the Rebbe honored him according to his status. Among the chassidim were a few people from this Rav's town and they were not so pleased with all the *kavod* that their Rav was receiving. They had many grievances against him, and felt that he was not really worthy of being Rav of the town. Thus the honor bestowed on him was like a stab in their backs. The chassidim decided the time had come to let the Rebbe know of their feelings.

Reb Yaakov Husyatin (center)

A delegation went to the Rebbe and informed him that they felt their Rav should be removed from his post. "What is wrong with him?" the Rebbe demanded. "To me he makes a fine impression." "Our Rav is not what he appears to be at first glance," they explained. "If the Rebbe would just examine the inner recesses of the Rav's mind and heart, he would see that he is not as pure as he pretends." Turning toward the delegation the Rebbe exclaimed: "Perhaps you would also like me to examine the insides of your minds and hearts."

An interesting story illustrating to what lengths the Rebbe's goodness went was related by the Husyatiner Rebbe, Reb Yaakov:

> A new kitchen helper was hired to work in the Rebbe's home. It soon turned out that he was more trouble than he was worth. He would shout and verbally abuse anyone with whom he came into contact. Even the Rebbetzin wasn't immune to his taunts, but she concealed the matter, hoping that he would soon change. The situation, however, did not improve; if anything it got worse. One day the man picked up a pot and flung it at the Rebbetzin, wounding her head in the process.
>
> That evening, when the Rebbetzin entered her husband's room, a large bandage adorned her forehead. She told the

Rebbe that one of the newly hired employees had taken to constantly cursing her. Today he had gone a step further and thrown a pot at her. Whereas most people would have become angry and demanded to know who the perpetrator was, the Rebbe had other priorities. "And how did you react to his cursing?" he asked her gently. "I never reacted at all," she answered. "I simply ignored him." "And what did you say today after he wounded you?" the Rebbe persisted. Again the Rebbetzin answered that she had not uttered a word to the man. "*Oi*," the Rebbe sighed. "I am so envious of what you have done."

It was in this vein that the Rebbe used to say: "The Mishnah in *Avos* tells us that '*Siyag lechochmah shesikah* — Keeping silent is an aid to wisdom.' Our sages inform us that when a *Yid* ignores provocation and insults and doesn't answer back, he is on his way to acquiring wisdom. If keeping quiet is only an aid, a *siyag* to attaining wisdom, what is the actual wisdom? When will one know that one has actually achieved the stage of acquiring and become a *chacham*?"

The Rebbe answered, "A *chacham* is someone who not only does not answer back, but does not even take to heart what has been said. A person who has learned to become immune to taunts and insults has reached and attained the level of a true *chacham*!"

❦

THE REBBE'S INTENSE FEAR OF HEAVEN GOVERNED ALL HIS actions and thoughts. A *Yid* once came to the Rebbe and told him
A Bad Deal about a brilliant deal which he had just been offered. A *poritz* wanted to sell him a vast forest for a fraction of its real value. The *Yid* had carefully thought through the offer and decided to purchase the forest. Before completing the deal he came to the Rebbe to receive his *berachah*. He explained to the Rebbe that such a good opportunity could not be wasted. The wood could be chopped down and sold as timber for many times the price for which he had bought it. From the profit he would be rich until the end of his days and all his financial worries would be

at an end. He had already tested the wood for worms and decay, and found it to be of the highest quality. The Rebbe listened carefully to the man's story and when he had finished, the Rebbe told him not to buy the forest.

The *Yid* left the Rebbe's room in shock; he could hardly believe his ears. He hadn't come to seek the Rebbe's advice, he had come just to receive his *berachah*, and now he would have to let this marvelous opportunity slip through his fingers. In the end the *Yid* decided not to listen to the Rebbe and he bought the forest from the *poritz*. After the trees were chopped down and ready to be made into timber, disaster struck. It became obvious that almost all the trees were wormy and rotten, and were totally useless. Obviously the test hadn't been done properly. The *Yid* who had invested all his money in the deal became a pauper overnight. Feelings of shame and guilt overcame him for having disobeyed the Rebbe's words, and for a long time he didn't show his face in Chortkov.

When he finally plucked up the courage to see the Rebbe, he begged his forgiveness, and at the same time he asked the Rebbe how he had known that the trees were wormy; surely it must have been either *ruach hakodesh* or a *mofes*! "It was neither," the Rebbe told him, "I didn't know that the trees were wormy. It was just that when I heard how you were speaking about this deal — with such an air of confidence as if it were impossible for you to lose money on it —I thought to myself, 'Such a deal, which has already made you forget totally about Hashem, that He is the One Who decides who will be rich or poor, such a deal can't be a good thing,' and therefore I told you not to go ahead with it." Now that the *Yid* had learned his lesson, the Rebbe blessed him that he should regain his money, and indeed not long afterwards he regained his lost wealth.

ONE OF THE TOPICS THAT THE REBBE SPOKE ABOUT the most was *emunah* and *bitachon* in Hashem. Constantly he
Emunah and Bitachon stressed the need for total faith and acceptance of all that Hashem does to us. The Rebbe's son and successor, Reb Yisroel, writes in his *sefer* "*Nezer*

Yisroel" that the *derech* of *emunah* was the main theme that his father constantly preached and that was the *derech* he bequeathed to his family and chassidim after his *petirah*.

The Rebbe once inquired about the welfare of a certain chassid who was undergoing hard times. The *gabbaim* told the Rebbe that the *Yid's* situation had not improved and according to the laws of nature the outlook for him was bleak.

"I am sure that he does not have proper *emunah*," the Rebbe responded. "Otherwise he would have been helped by now. To Hashem it makes absolutely no difference if something can be achieved by natural means or by special means that supersede the laws of nature. We find many instances in the *gemara* where *tzaddikim davened* for a miracle to help them and they were answered. Someone who has total faith in Hashem and doesn't give up hope even when the normal pattern of events indicate otherwise, such a person has elevated himself to have *emunah* beyond the call of nature. Therefore, in return, he will be helped even when it entails superseding the laws of nature. If, however, a person's *emunah* is limited by the boundaries of nature, then similarly his salvation will also be limited by the boundaries of nature."

A chassid once gave the Rebbe a *kvittel* regarding a certain matter and he added that he had already approached the Rebbe about this matter but without any results. He told the Rebbe that he was concerned that the continued failure to produce a solution would have a detrimental effect on his faith.

Hearing his words, the Rebbe's face turned a fiery red and he exclaimed: "If one wants to question the ways of Hashem there are many questions that could be asked. The truth is, however, that we must contain ourselves and have total faith in the same way the *Yidden* did in their hour of crisis at the shores of the *Yam Suf*, as it is written, 'And they believed in Hashem and in Moshe His servant.'"

Sometime later this chassid came back to the Rebbe with joyous news. The problem that had been bothering him for so long had finally been solved. "You see," the Rebbe replied, "Hashem does help."

≈≈

NOT ONLY DID THE REBBE EXPECT OF HIS CHASSIDIM TO have complete *bitachon*, he also demanded of them to continue being

Serving Hashem With Joy *b'simchah* regardless of the severity of their situation. Every Motza'ei Yom Tov the chassidim would dance in the courtyard underneath the Rebbe's room. The sounds of the dancing would become louder and louder and ever livelier. Just as the dancing reached its peak, the Rebbe would go outside onto his balcony to watch the joyous chassidim below.

One year as the Rebbe got himself ready to go, he noticed one of the chassidim standing on the side. When the Rebbe inquired as to why he wasn't taking part in the dancing, the *Yid* poured out his heart to the Rebbe. He had been incriminated in a serious crime. His court case would soon be taking place, and if he was found guilty he could spend the rest of his life in prison, or even worse. Thus he was in no state of mind to join in the dancing.

"Let me tell you a story," the Rebbe comforted him:

> One year on Motza'ei Yom Kippur, in the town of Mezibuzh where the Baal Shem Tov lived, clouds obscured the moon, thus preventing the *Yidden* from fulfilling the mitzvah of *Kiddush Levanah*. The Baal Shem Tov foresaw that their failure to perform this important mitzvah immediately after Yom Kippur did not bode well for the coming year. It was a sign that the year would be a sad and difficult one. He started to *daven* with great *kavanah* to get the moon to appear, thereby signaling that the decree had been annulled. However, his efforts produced no results and the moon remained hidden.
>
> Meanwhile, the Baal Shem Tov's *talmidim*, oblivious to the situation, had started to dance joyously, as they did every year. When their dancing reached its climax, they dared to push themselves into their Rebbe's room and form a circle around him. The *talmidim* then asked him to join in the dance, and he agreed. Hardly had the Baal Shem Tov started to dance than the clouds parted, leaving the moon shining brightly for all to see.
>
> Afterwards the Baal Shem Tov informed his *talmidim* about what had happened and he told them that they had

accomplished with their *simchah* what he had not managed to do through his *avodah* and *tefillah*.

The Rebbe finished the story and he added to the chassid: "You see how great is the power of mitzvos performed through *simchah*. Even when a person is faced with despair, if he strengthens himself to believe in Hashem with joy, despite his circumstances, he will merit salvation." With that the Rebbe instructed the *Yid* to join in the dancing and promised him that thereby his court case would have a favorable outcome.

We can see from the following incident to what extent the Rebbe had strengthened himself to accept every sorrow with joy. The Rebbe's oldest son, Reb Nuchem Mordechai, was *niftar* on the 26th of Tammuz 5630 (1880), at the young age of 21. When news of his *petirah* reached his father, he started to pace up and down in his room. As he paced up and down he repeated to himself over and over again the words of the *pasuk*: "*Hod vehadar lefanav oz v'chedvah bimkomo* — Glory and majesty are before Hashem, might and joy are in His place." Turning toward his family he explained, "Glorifying Hashem is only possible when a *Yid* is joyful. When a *Yid* tries to overcome his personal tragedy and to remain happy, knowing that he is in Hashem's presence, such behavior glorifies the *Shechinah*."

❧

On the topic of serving Hashem with joy, the Rebbe is quoted in his *sefer* "*Divrei Dovid*" as follows:

> During the *Simchas Beis Hasho'eivah* celebrations on Succos the Rebbe once asked. "We need to understand what all the joy is about. We no longer have a *Beis HaMikdash* so what are we celebrating?"
>
> We find that Shlomo HaMelech writes in *Koheles*: "Do not say that the olden days were better than now." Surely, asked the Rebbe, the olden days were far better than nowadays. We had the *Shechinah*; we had the *Beis HaMikdash*, the

Kohen Gadol and the constant revelations of the Divine presence. Nowadays we have no *Beis HaMikdash* and wherever we go there is only darkness, the *Shechinah* being hidden from our eyes.

The reality is, however, that although we are lacking all these benefits, as far as *avodas Hashem* and *yiras Shamayim* are concerned, there is no difference between now and then. At *Krias Yam Suf* even the lowest maidservant merited greater Divine revelation than Yechezkel HaNavi did, yet they carried an idol with them through the *Yam Suf*. At Har Sinai the *Yidden* were on such a level that they were able to hear Hashem Himself speak to them and give them the first two commandments. Even so, look what happened to them afterwards, how they fell from their *madreigah*. Oi! Oi! Nebech! Nebech!

Similarly, throughout their journey in the wilderness they witnessed constant miracles — the Manna, the Well of water, and the *Ananei HaKavod*. Yet each time they fell from their *madreigah*.

The reason this happened was because they had a tremendously strong *yetzer hara*. Since they had such open revelations and daily miracles, the temptations of the *yetzer hara* also had to be greatly magnified, in order to preserve the balance of *bechirah*. Therefore the *Yidden* were unable to withstand the pull of the *yetzer hara*. Thus on the one hand they had tremendous revelations but on the other hand they had a very enticing *yetzer hara* to deal with.

And so, although nowadays we are surrounded by darkness and we don't know which way to turn, the power of the *yetzer hara* has also been reduced. This is what Shlomo HaMelech meant when he said that the olden days were no better than now. A person's ability to choose the correct path and defeat his *yetzer hara* has not changed and will not change, regardless of the time and period in which he lives.

IT WAS THIS THEME OF KEEPING THE BALANCE OF
bechirah which once led the Rebbe to make a very unusual and un-

False Tzaddikim

characteristic comment. In his *sefer Tiferes Adam,"* HaGaon Reb Reuven Margulies writes:

> A letter was once sent to the Rebbe from a group of chassidim from Russia. A *machlokes* had broken out between two different groups of chassidim in a certain town, as a result of the death of a person who was known to be of dubious character. In order to provoke and anger the other group of chassidim, the dead man had purposely been laid to rest next to the grave of this group's Rebbe.
>
> While the Rebbe's *gabbai* was reading this letter, he was unable to contain himself and he cried out. "Is this the *derech* of Chassidus that the Baal Shem Tov left us! Is this how chassidim behave?"
>
> The Rebbe sat in his chair listening to his *gabbai's* words. His whole face radiated *kedushah* while he became lost in his thoughts. Finally he aroused himself and said. "I once heard in the name of Reb Yitzchok Radviller that the Satan came with a complaint to Hashem. His job is to cause people to sin. The *tzaddikim*, however, have managed to influence so many people to follow their ways that the Satan is no longer able to overcome them. The balance of *bechirah* has been tipped against him. The Satan was asked what he demanded in order to balance the scale again, to which he replied that he wanted his own *tzaddikim*.
>
> "Therefore there are people nowadays who go around masquerading as Rebbes or *rabbanim* and really they are just agents of the *yetzer hara*. Since one can no longer assume that everyone who is dressed in the robes of the rabbinate is fit for the post, the balance of *bechirah* has been saved. A person can run to a false *tzaddik* and delude himself that he is on the correct path." The *gabbai* understood the Rebbe's answer. This Rebbe, next to whom the man of dubious character had been buried, was also no great *tzaddik* and was of the same nature as his new neighbor!

The Rebbe was also not in favor of those who liked to copy the actions and movements of *tzaddikim*. About such people he once made the following comparison. "When a cup is filled to the top it overflows down the sides onto the saucer. Similarly *tzaddikim* have absorbed inside themselves a full measure of Torah and *yiras Shamayim*. The part that is noticeable to outsiders is the excess that bubbles over from the *tzaddik,* who is likened to an overflowing well. Those, however, who copy and mimic just the external movements and ways of a *tzaddik,* can be likened to pouring water down the sides of a cup, while the inside of the cup remains empty."

≈⌒

THE REBBE ONCE SAID ABOUT HIMSELF THAT HE HAD achieved the *madreigah* of never moving a limb in his body unnec-

Every Action for a Higher Cause

essarily. HaGaon Reb Moshe Kliers, the Rav of Tzefas, was in Chortkov a number of times. On one occasion, after he had just left the Rebbe's room, he realized that he had forgotten to give the Rebbe a second *kvittel* that he had brought with him from Eretz Yisroel. Reb Moshe debated going into the Rebbe's room a second time in order to give him the other *kvittel*. When the Slonimer Rebbe, the Divrei Shmuel, who was also then in Chortkov, heard of his dilemma, he advised him not to bother the Rebbe again. "What's so terrible if I go in again?" Reb Moshe asked. "After all, I have just come the whole way from Eretz Yisroel."

"You should know," the Slonimer Rebbe told him, "the Chortkover Rebbe puts more effort and more concentration into his every move than you have put into the entire journey from Tzefas to here!"

The Maggid of Kolomei, Reb Yitzchok Weber, wrote in his memoirs:

> Anyone who had just the slightest knowledge in our holy Torah could see with his naked eye how the Rebbe's every move and act were performed with intense *kavanah* far beyond our understanding.

Reb Yitzchok wasn't just referring to the Rebbe's actions when performing a mitzvah but even to actions pertaining to mundane matters. The concentration and *kavanah* that the Rebbe invested in his every move once came to light through the following incident:

Every chassid knew that the Rebbe was the epitome of humility and goodness. He never grew angry with anyone and he was never *makpid* about his *kavod*. Every *Yid* was addressed in the polite form *"Ihr"* rather than the more common and familiar form, *"Du."* Similarly, he always refused the services of his *gabbaim*, and when he needed something he would get it himself rather than bother one of his attendants.

Yet it once happened that the Rebbe became upset with his *gabbai* Reb Hershel Sternberg, for something which seemed to be almost of no consequence. Or so it seemed to most people. When the Rebbe would speak to the various chassidim Reb Hershel would stand behind the Rebbe's chair in order to ensure that everything ran

The Rebbe's every move and action were done for higher purposes. This fact is discussed in the classic halachah sefer "Minchas Shabbos," concerning moving objects for no reason on Shabbos.

smoothly. From time to time he would also remove from the Rebbe's table money or written petitions that people had given to the Rebbe.

Once, as Reb Hershel was clearing the table, he picked up the Rebbe's beautiful silver snuffbox (*tabak pushka*), and put it down a few inches from its original resting place. Immediately the Rebbe stopped what he was doing and placed the *pushka* back in its original place. Reb Hershel, however, didn't grasp the severity of his actions and a few minutes later he again moved the *pushka* slightly. This time the Rebbe put down the *kvittel* he was reading, and in a strict tone he addressed the *gabbai*:

"Why do you play around with the *pushka*? Can't you understand that if it has been placed in this spot, then that is where it is supposed to be? Are you not aware that the Rebbe Reb Mechel Zlotchover said that someone who plays with a *tzaddik*'s possessions might transgress the *issur* of rubbing out Hashem's Name? A *tzaddik*'s every move is done in conjunction with various thoughts and ideas, which allude to or are symbolic of the attributes of different Names of Hashem. Therefore, interrupting this cycle is likened to erasing the Name of Hashem!"

⤙⤚

There is a well-known saying of the Baal Shem Tov based on the words of *Chazal* (*Tosefta Shevous* 3:3), that "if a person sees a flaw or blemish in another *Yid*, it is proof that he has the identical flaw, for it is like a person looking into a mirror." The Rebbe took this saying very seriously. On the rare occasion that he witnessed a wrongdoing, no matter how slight it was, he immediately understood that he had been given a message that he possessed the same flaw.

One Friday night as the Rebbe was about to make *Kiddush* in front of his chassidim, he noticed one of the chassidim move a *muktzeh* object. The Rebbe felt that the fact that he had witnessed this wrongdoing indicated a fault in his own person. A look of worry appeared on him and his face grew ashen. Deeply anguished, he told his chassidim that he would not be able to recite *Kiddush*, for he first had to seclude himself and make a *cheshbon hanefesh*.

For a long time the Rebbe sat in his room, until the chassidim had almost given up hope that he would re-emerge. Suddenly the door to his room opened and the Rebbe appeared, ready to make *Kiddush*. He explained that he had not yet finished his *cheshbon hanefesh*, but it would no longer deter him from making *Kiddush*.

"When we recite *Vayechulu* in *Kiddush*," the Rebbe explained, "we are acting as witnesses to the fact that Hashem created the world in the six days of creation and that He rested on the seventh. The *gemara* (*Kiddushin* 65b) says that a witness is only needed when there is some reason to doubt the truth. If no one doubts the truth and all are in agreement, the statements of the witnesses lose their importance. Precisely now, when we have seen someone violating the holiness of Shabbos, contradicting the truth as it were, is our testimony needed."

CHAPTER EIGHT

Leader of His People

I N ADDITION TO ACTING AS A GUIDE FOR THE MASSES, the Rebbe was also venerated by many *gedolim* who turned to him with their own problems and regarded him as their ultimate authority. Dozens of famous *rabbanim* and Rebbes considered themselves Chortkover chassidim and traveled to the Rebbe like regular chassidim. Not for nothing was the Rebbe hailed as the Rebbe of Rebbes and the *tzaddik* of *tzaddikim*. His opinion was decisive and was normally accepted as the final word on every matter.

THUS, FOR EXAMPLE, WHEN THE REBBE APPROVED THE selection of one of his chassidim, Reb Avrohom Shorr (later he was a Rav in Yerushalayim) to become Rav of the town of

Leader of Leaders Monistritch, the Vishnitzer Rebbe, the Ahavas Yisroel, wrote to his chassidim to accept the Rebbe's decision

and he added: "Since the holy and esteemed *tzaddik* of Chortkov has decided that this Rav is the suitable candidate, it is obvious that every *Yid* who is concerned about the word of Hashem will not ignore the wishes of the holy *tzaddik,* which is the word of the Torah."

The Ahavas Yisroel was wont to sing the Rebbe's praises on many occasions and once he even proclaimed, "If it were not for the fact that I have to sit on my father's chair in Vishnitz, I would also travel regularly to Chortkov as a chassid!"

Indeed, there were many *gedolim* who traveled regularly to Chortkov. From Poland came the Rebbes of Ostrovza, Amshinov, Radzamin and Radomsk; and from Lithuania came the Rebbes of Slonim and Karlin. From Hungary came the Shiniva Rav; the Krasna Rav, Reb

The famed posek, the Maharsham

Boruch Lichtenstein; the Minchas Elozor of Munkatch; and the Atzei Chaim of Sighet. Galicia was also well represented with the famed Rebbes: the Spinka Rebbe, the Chakal Yitzchok; Reb Shlomke of Zhevil; and Reb Yisroel of Modzitz to name but a few.

Side by side with the Rebbes sat the greatest *poskim* of the era — the Maharsham, Reb Meir Arik, Reb Shlomo of Felestein (author of *Ginzei Chaim*), Reb Shmuel Bornstein (author of the classic *Minchas Shabbos*), Reb Meshullam Rot of Chernovitz, Reb Meshullam Katz of Tarnov, and Reb Yaakov Weidenfeld and his son Reb Dov Berish, the Tchebiner Rav. These are only a few names from the lengthy list of *gedolei Yisroel* who were faithful Chortkover chassidim.

Once in Chortkov many of these famous *tzaddikim* used to mix freely among the crowds, behaving as just one of the regular chassidim.

One of these elite chassidim was the Amshinover Rebbe, Reb Menachem Kalish. Whenever he was in Chortkov, Reb Menachem was particular to remove the special velvet robes that he normally wore as a sign of his status. Instead he wore just a plain simple *bekeshe* like a regular chassid.

The Slonimer Rebbe, the Divrei Shmuel, was also an avid chassid of the Rebbe. When someone once asked the Slonimer Rebbe during one of his trips to Chortkov how many *gabbaim* he had brought with him, he exclaimed: "Can't you see that not only have I left the *gabbaim* behind but the 'Rebbe' I also left at home."

The famed *gaon* and *posek*, Reb Avrohom Yaakov Horowitz (author of the classic *sefer "Tzur Yaakov"*), was also a regular visitor in Chortkov. Whenever he would arrive in Chortkov, he would get off his carriage at the town gates, and from there until the Rebbe's house he would continue on foot as a sign of respect to the Rebbe. Such was the *kavod* and the esteem in which the Rebbe was held by the *gedolim* of his time.

IN ADDITION TO THOSE *TZADDIKIM* WHO TRAVELED TO Chortkov, there were many more who were unable to make the long

Responsible for the Nation

trip. Nevertheless many of them still considered the Rebbe their ultimate authority and sent him their questions by post. From all corners of Europe and beyond, questions flooded in, awaiting the Rebbe's response and direction. One of the *gedolim* who never made it to Chortkov but still consulted him was the famed *gaon* Reb Eliyahu Chaim Meisel. Originally from Lithuania and a product of the Volozhin Yeshivah, he was Rav of the city of Lodz in Poland, which boasted a *kehillah* of over 200,000 *Yidden*. Only Warsaw had a larger *kehillah,* but they had no Rav. Thus, in effect, Rav Meisel reigned supreme as the most senior Rav and *posek* in the world, his name uttered in reverence and respect in all circles. In the newspaper *Machazikei Hadass* (Lemberg, May 17, 1912) is printed a letter that Rav Meisel sent in his later years to the Rebbe.

In his letter Rav Meisel states that he cannot divulge his problem in writing and instead is sending a messenger to explain his worry to the Rebbe in full. Nevertheless his letter is still interesting to us by virtue of the tremendous respect that this Lithuanian *gadol* displayed for the Rebbe and his total awe of him. Here are some excerpts of the letter:

> To the holy and awesome man, like a Heavenly *malach* in our midst in his pure fear of Hashem, the great one in Torah who lights up Yisroel, his holiness Reb Dovid Moshe:

After prostrating myself in front of his holiness with my blessings, may his holiness permit me to reveal the anquish of my heart in front of him. Woe is to me if I say and woe is to me if I don't. I worry that perhaps I will stumble with my words when I speak about our holy nation.

A father who seeks the good of his child will not hesitate to reveal to a doctor his child's blemishes so that the doctor can help him. Our Chosen Nation has fallen ill with a spiritual disease. I have decided not to hide their condition lest the illness take root and cannot be removed. Therefore I will reveal their illness to his holiness who is a spiritual doctor and healer. It is impossible to write here the extent of the problem, therefore I am sending a messenger to discuss the matter with his holiness and to bring us back the advice of his holiness for which we are waiting. These are the words of the youngest of the *rabbanim* who yearns for the Rebbe's response.

17th Av 5660 (1900)
Eliyahu Chaim Meisel
Av Beis Din, Lodz

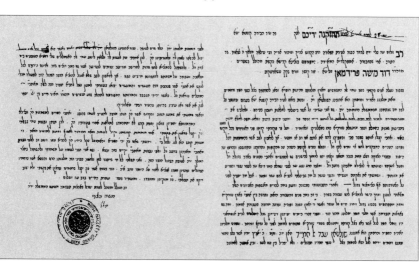

Letters flooded into Chortkov from around the globe.
This letter is from Reb Moshe Halevi, the Chief Rabbi of Istanbul.

IF THROUGHOUT THE YEAR THE REBBE'S LIFESTYLE WAS saturated with *kedushah*, all the more so were the weeks of Elul and

Which Shul to Daven in

the *Yomim Noraim*. "It is very difficult to be a leader of *Klal Yisroel*," the Rebbe once revealed to his family. "Whereas every person only has

to give an accounting for his own actions, a *manhig* bears resposibility for the actions of his followers as well."

During the weeks of Elul and the *Yomim Noraim*, the Rebbe's every word and thought centered on the topic of *teshuvah*. Anyone who saw him then — even somone who had a heart of stone — could not help being influenced to repent his wrongdoings and become a better person. During *davening* the unusually loud sighs that were heard from the Rebbe's room filled the hearts of his followers with dread.

The fear that a *tzaddik* inspires in the hearts of those near him once caused the Rebbe to give an interesting answer to the following

A proclamation by the Rebbe and his brother, the Rebbe of Sadiger, on behalf of the Machazikei Hadass organization

question. A *Yid* asked the Rebbe's advice concerning which shul he should *daven* in. There were a number of shuls in his town, but he was unable to decide which one he should make his home. The Rebbe asked him if any of these shuls had in them a *Yid* whose heart trembled from fear of Hashem. When the man replied in the affirmative, the Rebbe told him to *daven* there even if the other shuls had more members.

The Rebbe explained that the Torah tells us that before *Klal Yisroel* would wage war against its enemies the commanding officer would proclaim, "Who is the man who is afraid and fainthearted? Let him return home and not cause his fellow soldiers to also become afraid." From here we see how one man's fear causes those around him to also become afraid. Similarly, when a person *daven*s near someone who is a true *yirei Shamayim*, the person will become influenced by his ways and some of the fear of Heaven will rub off on him as well.

Although the Rebbe would never *daven* in front of the *amud* as a *chazzan*, on a few select occasions he would lead the *tefillos* and act as the *sheliach tzibbur*. On these occasions thousands of chassidim would converge on Chortkov to hear for themselves the Rebbe's *davening*. One of these rare occasions was during *Selichos*, when the Rebbe would recite aloud the paragraph *Aneinu* at the end of the *Selichos*. The Rebbe's *avodah* was then like that of a *malach*. Although he stood still without swaying, his whole body would shake and tremble as he *davened* in front of Hashem. It was plainly clear to all that when the Rebbe *davened* to Hashem everything else in the world ceased to exist. If there were any who doubted this, an incident happened which removed this doubt.

ONE YEAR WHEN THE REBBE CAME OUT TO SAY THE *Selichos*, the large crowd surged forward toward the front. Due to the masses of people the front of the shul near the Rebbe's place became very hot and humid. As a result of the crowded and stuffy conditions, the Rebbe's son, Reb Yisroel, suddenly fainted. The chassidim tried to revive him but were unable to do so. A panic overtook the crowd, people shouted to bring a doctor, while others brought water and splashed it on Reb Yisroel in an attempt to revive him.

Oblivious to Worldly Matters

While all this was going on, the Rebbe continued *davening*, totally oblivious to the commotion around him. It was quite apparent that he hadn't noticed or heard anything. When the chassidim saw that they could not revive Reb Yisroel, one of the *gabbaim* dared to interrupt the Rebbe and tell him what had happened to his beloved son. Even then the Rebbe refused to interrupt his *avodas hakodesh*. He made a sign with his hand to carry his son outside and then he continued with his *tefillos* as if nothing had occurred.

One year, among the large crowd who had assembled to hear the Rebbe were two of his nephews, Reb Shlomo and Reb Nuchem Ber of Sadiger. Surprised by their sudden arrival, the Rebbe asked them why they had come, to which they told him that they had come to hear him say the *Aneinu's*.

"I *daven* only to Hashem, and not for people to listen to," the Rebbe told them, and that year he refused to *daven* in front of the *amud*. Until he had been told explicitly that people had journeyed to listen to his *davening*, it hadn't even occurred to him that all the thousands assembled had also come specially to hear his *tefillos*!

The Potiker Rav, Reb Shlomo Zalman Horowitz, used to relate what his father, Reb Aharon, had told him from his memories of *Yomim Noraim* in Chortkov. Reb Aharon was once present as the Rebbe left his home escorted by two *gabbaim* to say *Kol Nidrei*. As they were walking along, the Rebbe, who was then in his last years, suddenly gave a loud sigh, and he called out in alarm: "Where are you taking me? To give an account of my actions in front of Hashem! But I haven't yet managed to do *teshuvah*." And with these words the Rebbe broke down crying. Whenever Reb Aharon would repeat this story tears would well up in his eyes and he would add that he was sure that he would never again experience such intense feelings of *teshuvah* as he did on that occasion.

Indeed, as far as the Rebbe was concerned no *teshuvah* could adequately make up for the damage wrought through an *aveirah*. The Rebbe once said as much to one of the great *tzaddikim* of the generation, the Ostrovza Rebbe. Among the many *gedolim* who traveled to

The Chortkover Rebbe in his later years;
in Rizhin the custom is for
the Rebbes to wear a streimel
with the center elevated

The Rebbe of Pishkan, Romania,
Reb Moshe Yehudah Leib;
he was the son-in-law of
Reb Nuchem Dov of Sadiger

Chortkov was the famed *gaon* and *tzaddik*, Reb Yechiel Meir, the Rebbe of Ostrovza. Reb Yechiel Meir would tell the following story, which he had experienced himself:

> Normally every time Reb Yechiel Meir arrived in Chortkov he was immediately ushered into the Rebbe's room. On one occasion Reb Yechiel Meir arrived in Chortkov and the *gabbai* informed the Rebbe of his presence. This time, however, the Rebbe sent back a message to Reb Yechiel Meir that he should wait. While waiting, Reb Yechiel Meir thought to himself. "No doubt I have sinned in some way, and therefore the Rebbe doesn't want to see me before I have done *teshuvah*." With that he started to ponder to himself what it must have felt like to receive *malkus* — thirty-nine lashes that were dealt out in the times of the *Beis HaMikdash* to those who had committed serious *aveirah*s.
>
> While he was in the middle of his thoughts the door suddenly opened and Reb Yechiel Meir was ushered into the Rebbe's room. After an introductory "*Shalom Aleichem*," the

Rebbe said to him, "It is written in the Torah that a person who commits certain serious *aveirah*s is to be given forty lashes, yet in practice *Chazal* instruct us to give only thirty-nine lashes. Why did *Chazal* deduct one of the lashes which had to be given? The reason is that a person must always realize that he can never do enough to fulfill his obligation to his Creator. If a person who committed an *aveirah* would be given forty lashes he might think that he is now totally innocent of any crime, for he has already received his due punishment. *Chazal* had pity on such a person — who had transgressed an *aveirah* and was still capable of thinking that he is a *tzaddik*. Therefore they commanded to give only thirty-nine lashes, so that a person should realize that he still has to carry on doing *teshuvah*; he can never do enough *teshuvah* to atone for his sins."

❦

With the approach of the *Yomim Noraim*, the Rebbe did not allow chassidim to write individual requests. Instead everyone received the same *berachah* for a good year, a *kesivah vachasimah tovah*. Woe to the person who did not receive such a *berachah*; he could rest assured that the future did not bode well for him. This point is illustrated by the following incident, which was related by the Rebbe's nephew, the Mezibuzher Rebbe, Reb Yisroel Sholom Yosef Heschel.

Only the Pure Truth

REB YISROEL SHOLOM YOSEF HESCHEL WOULD travel every year before Rosh Hashanah to his *shver*, the Sadigerer Rebbe. On the way he would stop off in Chortkov to visit the Rebbe and wish him a good year. The Rebbe would use Reb Yisroel Sholom Yosef as his messenger to send his wishes for a good year to his brother, the Sadigerer Rebbe. This practice continued for many years, until the Sadigerer Rebbe's *petirah* in 1883. That year Reb Yisroel Sholom Yosef went as usual to Chortkov but this time, however, the Rebbe made no mention of his brother and did not wish him a good year.

The Rebbe's nephew,
Reb Yisroel Sholom Yosef,
the Mezibuzher Rebbe

Reb Yisroel Sholom Yosef knew very well that his uncle's every action and word were not by chance. He realized that if the Rebbe had not inquired about his brother's welfare there must be a good reason for it. His heart trembled at the thought that perhaps his *shver* had just passed away and the news had not yet reached him. Upon leaving the Rebbe's room he rushed to catch a coach to Sadiger, but when he arrived, he found the town peaceful.

A new predicament now faced Reb Yisroel Sholom Yosef. What was he to say when his *shver* would ask him what his brother had said? How could he possibly reveal that the Rebbe had not even inquired after him or sent him his wishes for the new year? Fearing for his *shver*'s health, Reb Yisroel Sholom Yosef decided that under the circumstances it was permissible for him to deviate from the truth and tell his *shver* that his brother had indeed wished him a good year.

When he arrived in the Sadigerer's house, he received a warm welcome from the Rebbe, who rejoiced to see and hear from his beloved son-in-law. Hardly had Reb Yisroel Sholom Yosef begun to tell his *shver* about his visit to Chortkov and that his brother wished him a good year, than the Sadigerer Rebbe interrupted his son-in-law and exclaimed: "Is that what my brother really said...?" With that, the Sadigerer Rebbe picked himself up and walked out of the room, leaving a shame-faced son-in-law behind.

Reb Yisroel Sholom Yosef later related that he learned then to appreciate the words of the *pasuk: "Doveir shekarim lo yikom l'neged einai* — A speaker of untruths will not stand before me."

When the Sadigerer Rebbe was *niftar* during the course of

the new year, Reb Yisroel Sholom Yosef finally understood why the Rebbe had not wished him a good year and how his *shver* had realized that he had not spoken the truth. Through his *ruach hakodesh* the Rebbe had known that his brother's life was coming to its end. Therefore greetings for a full and prosperous year would have been out of place. In the same vein the Sadigerer Rebbe also knew that it was his last year and therefore impossible that his brother could have sent him such greetings. The only explanation to the greetings was that his son-in-law had been economical with the truth!

⇌

THIS ABILITY OF THE REBBE TO SEE THINGS THAT ARE hidden from others manifested itself in many different ways. Not **Eiffel** only did he know events of the future, he was also able to see things or events taking place in faraway places. The **Tower** following story was told by the Rebbe of Slonim, Reb Avrohom Weinberg.

An assimilated Jewish journalist who was always on the lookout for bits of news to relate to his readers wanted to see the *tzaddik* of Chortkov and went to visit him at his court. Upon his arrival he requested permission to have an audience with the Rebbe and permission was granted.

The Rebbe discussed various wordly topics with the journalist and soon the topic centered on the recently built Eiffel Tower in Paris. The Rebbe said: "This tower was built with amazing architectural insight. Did you ever notice the unique window built into the tower on such and such a floor? This small window is a most innovative engineering feat. It is made to perfectly regulate the circulation of air and the penetration of light throughout the entire tower."

The journalist was filled with wonder and curiosity. He had been to the famous Eiffel Tower numerous times and had recorded all the interesting features of the tower but he had never noticed the amazing skylight of which the Rebbe had spoken. Was there any credence to the *tzaddik's* words? Out of politeness, he did not express his doubts nor ask any questions, but took leave of the Rebbe with his blessing and went his way.

Back in his hometown of Vienna, the journalist searched the souvenir shops and book stores until he found a brochure made for travelers who wished to visit the Eiffel Tower. It contained every minute detail about the tower. Quickly he looked up the facts about the special skylight and discovered to his amazement that everything the Rebbe had told him was true.

The journalist could not contain himself. From where had the Rebbe — who secluded himself — gotten his information? The question gave him no peace.

At the first opportunity the journalist boarded a train back to Chortkov, where he would be able to ask the Rebbe himself. When he entered the Rebbe's room he voiced his amazement. "How did the Rebbe know all those facts about the skylight? Has the Rebbe ever been to the Eiffel Tower?" he asked.

The Rebbe answered him patiently. "I have never visited the Eiffel Tower. But every morning, when I say the morning blessings with *Shem* and *Malchus*, before I pronounce the words *Melech HaOlam*, I contemplate and view the universe over which I am about to crown Hashem as King. I look around and once while I was looking I happened to see this wonderful skylight in the Eiffel Tower."

The Rebbe had spoken simply, as if it were only natural that before pronouncing the words *Melech HaOlam* he should perceive with his holy penetrating eyes the vast universe over which he was crowning Hashem in his prayer. But his words pierced the journalist's heart like an arrow and the man's knees buckled beneath him and he fainted.

The Rebbe's *gabbaim* ran to the man's aid and revived him. In a few minutes he regained his composure, but he did not return to his career. He underwent a complete transformation. The journalist became totally distressed over his former lifestyle and became a *baal teshuvah*, for the amazing encounter with the Rebbe did not allow him to go on with his life as before.

INDEED IT WAS CLEAR TO ALL THAT THE REBBE POSSESSED a higher level of *ruach hakodesh* that enabled him to see and to know

Ruach things that other *tzaddikim* were unable to see:

HaKodesh A *Yid* once came crying to the Rebbe, for every one of his children had died in infancy, and he begged the Rebbe to promise him healthy children. The Rebbe told him that when his next child would be born he should give the baby a name that is mentioned in the *haftorah* of the week in which the child is born.

Sometime later the man's wife gave birth to a baby girl. The man looked in the *haftorah* of that particular week — *Parshas Nasso* — but could not find any mention of a woman's name. The *haftorah*, which speaks about Shimshon, does, however, mention Shimshon's mother, even though it does not refer to her by name. The *gemara* in *Bava Basra* informs us that her name was Sallfonis. At first the man couldn't understand why the Rebbe had chosen this name for his daughter, but he soon found out the reason. One of the classic commentators on the *gemara*, the *Maharshal*, writes in his notes on that piece of the *gemara* that the name Sallfonis prevents the evil eye from harming a person who has that name. Needless to say the girl lived to a ripe old age.

Another extraordinary example of the Rebbe's *ruach hakodesh* is the following story, which was related by Reb Shlomo Zalman Horowitz, the Rav of Potik:

A young man returned home one day to find that his wife had disappeared. They had been unhappily married for some time, so he realized that she must have run away. All his efforts to locate her were in vain, and after a time he decided to obtain a *heter me'ah rabbanim* so that he could remarry.

When he had already obtained ninety-six signatures he decided to go and ask the Rebbe for a *berachah* that he should soon find a suitable *shidduch*. When he told the Rebbe his story, the Rebbe said to him, "I advise you to go to Reb Leib, the *Dayan* of Toyest, to obtain his signature." The man was surprised at the Rebbe's words, for although the *Dayan* of Toyest was a respected *talmid chacham*, the Rebbe had absolutely no connection with him. When the young man arrived in Toyest and told the *Dayan* that the Rebbe had sent him, he was equally surprised. After the young man told the *Dayan* his name, he exclaimed, "When were you in Chortkov?"

"Yesterday afternoon at 12 o'clock I spoke to the Rebbe and that's when he told me to come here," the young man replied. The *Dayan* could hardly believe his ears. Just yesterday at 12 o'clock midday the postman had delivered a letter from a friend of his who was a Rav in America. In the letter he wrote that he had been summoned to a hospital to attend to a very sick woman. She told him that she had run away from her husband to America and she now regretted the anguish she had caused him and would therefore like the Rav to seek out her husband and let him know that she is ready to accept a *get*. The woman mentioned in the letter was none other than this man's wife!

מכתב תעודת אדמו"ר הרה"ק מטשארטקוב שליט"א

ב"ה יום ב' י"ב תמח תרס"ז לפ"ק טשארטקוב

ברכות ישע וכט"ס לכבוד קדושת הרה"צ בר אהבן קדישא פאר מקדושים גוע אלים ותרשישים
כקשית מו"ה......שליט"א
מאד יראב לבי על כ"ק כי אחר אשר תקוה טובה נשקפה לו כי יבא בקרב לידי פירוד
בדרך הטוב והנאות נסתתה ונתהרסה על ידי מיאון זגתו תחי' אחרי אשר יגע ועמל על
ידי כמה השתדלות להגיע לזה אל ידי פשר ולא עלתה בידו וברצונו ליקח לעצמו היתר
מרבנים עפ"י דעת תה"ק ומאד נכמרו רחומי על מצבו הנכחי, כי יושב גלמוד זה שנים
רבות. לכן לא אוכל עוד לעכביהו ולעצריהו שימתני עד, אחרי שניסה כל הדברים
והדרכים להביא הדבר לידי גמר טוב ונעים. לזאת הנני מוכרח כעת לתת
הסכמתי שיפנה כרצונו כנ"ל אל הרבנים להוות לו הדרך אשר ילך על פי דעת תה"ק.
ה' הטוב יניחהו במעגלי צדק ובקרב יוציאהו מכבלי העיגן כחפץ לבבו וחפץ לבבי דו"ש
מברכו בכל טוב.

ישראל במוהר"ר דוד משה זצ"ל

A letter from Reb Yisroel of Chortkov allowing someone to seek a heter me'ah rabbanim

CHAPTER NINE

Giving Tzedakah

AMONG THE MANY PEOPLE WHO FLOCKED TO THE Rebbe for his advice and help would also come the poor and destitute, who knew that they would receive money from the Rebbe, and some warm food from the court kitchens. The kitchens provided food on a daily basis for the dozens of chassidim who lived in the Rebbe's court. These chassidim were known as *yoshvim* (dwellers). They were people who cut themselves off totally from the outside world and devoted themselves to Hashem's service. They lived in the Rebbe's court and many of them stayed for months or even years, during which time the Rebbe provided for their food and lodgings.

THUS THE CONSTANT AVAILABILITY OF READY HOT FOOD was like a magnet for the poor and hungry. The Rebbe saw to it that **Helping the Poor** the meals were given on schedule, and from time to time would inquire if everything was running smoothly. It happened once at the end of a fast day that the meals were not ready right away. This occurred because the person whose job it was to have the food ready, went to *daven Maariv* before seeing to the food. When the Rebbe heard about the incident he demanded that this *Yid* be relieved of his job. "A *Yid* who cannot feel the weakness of another *Yid*," the Rebbe exclaimed, "is not fit to be in charge of distributing food and drink."

Besides the hot meals, many of the poor also received donations from the Rebbe. The Rebbe himself never personally distributed the money; it is very doubtful if he ever handled money or was even familiar with the different notes and coins. Rather he would instruct the *gabbai* to give a sum of money. One *Yid* once received a double donation from the Rebbe. When this *Yid* had approached the Rebbe for a donation, the Rebbe had instructed the *gabbai* to give him something, but for some reason the *gabbai* did not do so and the Rebbe had to tell the *gabbai* a second time. Therefore, since the Rebbe had requested twice that this *Yid* be given money, it was decided to give him a double amount, one for each time the Rebbe had asked.

SOMETIMES IT HAPPENED THAT THE DISBURSEMENT OF *tzedakah* was so great that the Rebbe's funds almost dried up. Reb

Hated Money
Reuven Margulies reports on such an occasion in his *sefer "Tiferes Adam"*:

> One year before Pesach the Rebbe commanded the *gabbai*, Reb Hershel Rapporport, to send money for the upcoming Yom Tov to a large number of *talmidei chachamim* and *ehrlicher Yidden* who were in financial difficulty. While Reb Hershel was preparing the *tzedakah*, placing the money into the various envelopes, the money ran out before the list had been completed.
>
> "If only the Rebbe had as much money as Baron Rothchild," Reb Hershel sighed, "then the Rebbe would be able to give *tzedakah* to his heart's content."
>
> Hearing the *gabbai's* words the Rebbe's face changed colors and in a tone of wonder he exclaimed, "What did you say? That I should wish myself money? What a stupidity!

Where can one rather acquire a bit of *yiras Shamayim*? *Oi!* Where can one truly find a bit of *yiras Shamayim*?"

ON ANOTHER OCCASION WHEN THE REBBE RAN OUT OF money to distribute to the poor, he summoned his son Reb Yisroel

An Accusation in the Heavenly Court

and commanded him to go around town and solicit money from the various people. When the *gabbaim* heard the Rebbe's instructions they were aghast. Reb Yisroel was considered by all to be a prince of his people. To reduce him to the level of a collector would be an insult to his status and dignity. In addition, Reb Yisroel's every minute was spent immersed in Torah. How could the Rebbe possibly contemplate forcing his son to act like a common beggar and spend his time collecting money? The *gabbaim* approached the Rebbe and told him of their concerns and they offered to go instead of the Rebbe's son.

A letter from Reb Yisroel of Chortkov in support of a poor man

מכתבי 6

האדמורי״ם הצדיקים הקדושים הגאונים הגדולים המפורסמים בעולם כאו״א לפי״ע נדלו נאונו וקדושתו ד׳ עליהם שליט״א.

המכרתבים הרפסתי כפי הזמן שקבלתי אותם מידם הקדושה.

ב״ה

שפעת חיים ושלום וברכת ישע ברכה והצלחה לכבוד אניש היקרים הרבנים הגדולים הגבירים הנכבדים הנגידים הישרים רודפי צדקה וחסד בכל מקומות מושבותיהם ד׳ עליהם יחיו:

אחרי דרישתי ועתירתי על שלומם טובתם והצלחתם כל הימים הן כאשר המוכיח הרב המופלג בתורה וחכמה יקר ערך הוו״ח היר מענדל ראוויצקי ני׳ אשר נסע עוד לאאמו״ר צי״ע וצוקלל״ה זי״ע והי׳ חביבותי׳ נבי׳ כי הוא נפש סגולה ולפנים הי׳ על נפי כיומי העושר והללוהו צדיקים ורבים רבים במעשיו הטובים ולאסונו ירד עשר מעלות אהורנית מאינגרא רמא לבירא עמיקתא ר״ל ועתה עפ״י גלגולי׳ סבות קשות נאלץ לעקור דירתו לארץ גאליציא ומה מאד נבכמו נחוכי על האי נברא יקירא אשר מעת הכרתיו ראיתי כי הוא איש איש נעלה מאד ועתירתי ובקשתי מאנ״ש היקרים שיקבלוהו בספי׳ ויתאמצו לתמכו במסחרו על נרם הכבוד בכל האפשרות ומאד יחשב הדבר בעיני וזכות המצוה הרבה הלוז ינן על העושים והמעשים להתברך בכל הטוב הנועד להמחזיקים בתורת ד׳ ויושעו בכל משאלותיהם לטובה. דברי המעתיר בעדם ובעד כלל ישראל כל הימים לטובה.

ישראל במוה״ר **דוד משה** זצ״ל
מטשארטקאוו.

"I'll tell you a story about my *zeide*, the Rema (Reb Moshe Isserles)," the Rebbe replied. "He too never used to go collecting until he was summoned to a court case in Heaven by the drunkard Moshe Shiker of Cracow." The Rebbe proceeded to relate:

> It was a sight the people of Cracow were familiar with. Every Friday at about midmorning, Moshe the Shiker, as he was known, would emerge bleary-eyed from his lodgings. His pockets jingling with the coins that he managed to collect that week, he would make his way to the local tavern and spend all his money on wine and alcohol.
>
> One Friday as he made his way as usual, a destitute woman sighed and called out bitterly, "There goes Moshe Shiker to buy his drinks and I don't even have money to buy candles for Shabbos!"
>
> Moshe Shiker stopped in his tracks and thought to himself for a moment. Then, before he could change his mind, he ran over to the woman and gave her the entire sum that he had collected that week. Since he no longer had any money with which to buy drinks, Moshe Shiker retraced his steps and headed back home. A few hours later he suddenly passed away.
>
> That Motza'ei Shabbos the Rema was engrossed as usual in his learning when he was suddenly disturbed by the entry of Moshe Shiker, who informed the Rav that he was summoning him to a *din Torah*.
>
> The Rema had never had any personal contact with the town's drunkard and told Moshe Shiker that he had no time for jokes. The Rema gently reprimanded him, and asked him to leave the room so that he could continue his learning.
>
> "I am not joking," Moshe Shiker replied. "I was *niftar* this past Friday and have been sent by the Heavenly Court to warn you that in Heaven they are not pleased with you." No sooner had Moshe Shiker finished his words than he disappeared.
>
> The Rema was disturbed by the drunkard's words and he summoned his *gabbai* to bring Moshe Shiker back again.

When the *gabbai* heard the Rema's request he told him that Moshe Shiker was no longer alive — he had died that Friday.

Realizing that this was no simple matter, the Rema sat in his room and waited for Moshe Shiker to return and repeat his demand. Sure enough the drunkard soon returned to repeat his accusation against the Rav of Cracow. The Rema used to go collecting *tzedakah* only at the houses of the rich where he was honored and welcomed, but he never frequented the houses of the poor, and so he prevented them from fulfilling the mitzvah of *tzedakah*. Since Moshe Shiker's last act in this world had been an act of *tzedakah*, he had been chosen to tell the Rema of the accusation against him.

"I have accepted your rebuke," the Rema answered solemnly. "Go and tell the Heavenly Court that from now on I will go to all the inhabitants of the city and knock even on the doors of those houses which are not according to my honor."

"So you see," the Rebbe concluded, "if in Heaven it was felt that fundraising was not too menial a task for my illustrious *zeide* the Rema, surely it is not below the dignity of my son either!"

To Have an Honest Job

AMONG THOSE WHO CAME TO THE REBBE TO SOLICIT funds were also a number of people who were descended from illustrious Rabbinical families. They were hoping to receive from the Rebbe a letter of recommendation that would boost their status and thereby increase their ability to raise money.

The Rebbe, however, rarely agreed to give such letters of recommendation. He did not approve of those who sought to make money through their *yichus*. He regarded the idea of using the names and *zechusim* of *tzaddikim* in order to raise funds as belittling the memory of the particular *tzaddikim* involved. He assured one young man that if he would not reveal his *yichus* when he goes collecting, in that merit he would be helped.

Instead of giving a letter, the Rebbe would help the person as much as possible. If this wasn't possible the Rebbe would write a letter to one of his chassidim and ask him to employ the person in his business. Thus the person would be able to earn a wage in an honorable fashion rather than having to embarrass himself and his great ancestors by going collecting.

∽〰

One of the mitzvos that we are commanded to keep is, *"Lo saashok es rei'echa* — You shall not cheat your fellow" (*Vayikra* 19:13). On this *pasuk* the famous commentator, the *Ohr HaChaim,* offers a very interesting interpretation:

> I have heard in the name of the Arizal that the reason why *tzaddikim* often are poor is because the world cannot absorb the full measure of goodness that the *tzaddikim* deserve. Therefore Hashem only bestows wealth upon average people, and through them the *tzaddikim* will also be supported. Thus the riches that the average person have amassed are supposed to serve the *tzaddikim* as they feel fit. Therefore, someone who withholds money from a *tzaddik* has trangressed this prohibition of cheating his fellow man.

IT IS WITH THESE WORDS IN MIND THAT ONE CAN understand the following incident that the Maggid of Kolomei,

Owned All the Money Reb Yitzchok Weber, wrote in his memoirs. It is a story that his father, Reb Elozor, who was one of the Rebbe's closest chassidim, had witnessed firsthand:

> The Rebbe once sent a letter to the town of Kaminetz asking the *Yidden* there to contribute to a certain *tzedakah.* One of the local *rabbanim* in Kaminetz wasn't so happy about the Rebbe's request and voiced his opposition to the appeal in a derogatory manner. Before long this Rav suffered a number of personal tragedies. He realized that it was probably a punishment for the belittling tone he had used to attack the letter that the Rebbe had sent. The Rav therefore decided to go to the Rebbe and ask for his forgiveness.

After the Rav had approached the Rebbe and asked him for *mechilah*, the Rebbe told him that he would like to tell him a story:

The Apta Rav, Reb Avrohom Yehoshua Heschel, was once conducting a *tisch* when a man with tears in his eyes came into the room and shamefacedly made his way to the Apta Rav. Noticing this person's arrival, the Apta Rav told the *rabbanim* seated there that he had the following case to present and he wanted to hear their opinion.

"Before I came down to this world," the Apta Rav told the assembled *rabbanim*, "I was alloted a very large sum of money for all my needs. But because I had to become what I am, how could I achieve that if I had to take care of so much money? Therefore the Heavenly Court distributed the money to various people who would take care of it for me.

"This man here was entrusted with 20,000 rubles of mine. Recently I needed 300 rubles to help a poor man marry off his daughter. Since I knew that this man had 20,000 rubles of mine, I sent him a letter asking for 300 rubles.

"When this man received my letter he refused my request. Since then he has slowly but surely lost all his money, and he is now penniless. He has come to me now to ask me for forgiveness and for a *berachah* to regain his wealth. The question is — can he be trusted with my money? Can I rely on him and deposit my money with him again?"

The assembled *rabbanim* ruled that since the man had demonstrated that he was truly sorry, the Apta Rav can trust him and deposit his money with him. With that the Apta Rav blessed the man that he regain his lost wealth.

The Rebbe finished his story and turning toward the Rav from Kaminetz he added: "Hashem knows the truth — that all the money in the world belongs to us, and according to the laws of the Torah we have the right to demand our money, whether for our needs or for the needs of others!"

CHAPTER TEN

The Last Days

ALL HIS DAYS, THE REBBE LONGED TO GO AND settle in Eretz Yisroel; a number of times he even prepared himself to go but each time something else cropped up and he had to drop his plans. The Rebbe was once seen walking up and down in his room in great *d'veikus*. Suddenly, he exclaimed: "Master of the Universe, what does it bother You if I will go to Eretz Yisroel? I promise You that I will not speak badly about the land, I won't get upset at anything I will see. I beg of You, please, let me go and live there."

ALTHOUGH THE REBBE NEVER MOVED TO ERETZ YISROEL nevertheless he left his imprint on the Holy Land. Through the Rebbe's efforts, groups of his chassidim moved to **Moving to Eretz Yisroel** Eretz Yisroel and founded a number of shuls. Two of the shuls — in Yerushalayim and in Tzefas — function to this day.

The stamp of the Chortkover shul in Tzefas

A document from the Beis Din of Tzefas in the year 1883 concerning the ner tamid that the Rebbe had instituted

The Rebbe felt very attached to the *kever* of Rebbi Shimon bar Yochai in Meron. On a number of occasions he even mentioned that there was a connection between his *neshamah* and that of Rebbi Shimon bar Yochai. Although a large and grand building was built over Rebbi Shimon's grave, surprisingly it had never occurred to anybody to install a *ner tamid* next to the *kever*, until the Rebbe inquired about its existence. When he heard that there was no permanent *ner tamid*, he sent money to construct one. One night the Rebbe came in a dream to the *gabbai* of the *kever* in Meron and told him that the *ner tamid* had blown out and he should rekindle it. In haste, the *gabbai* run to the *kever*, and — lo and behold — the light had indeed gone out!

Throughout his life, the Rebbe regularly sent money to Meron to pay for the oil needed to kindle the light. After his *petirah*, the Rebbe's son Reb Yisroel continued his father's tradition of financing the *ner tamid*. This practice is still kept today by his descendants.

Half a year before his *petirah*, the Rebbe told his chassidim, "In another six months I am ascending to Eretz Yisroel; I shall close myself into a small room and I will not allow anybody to disturb me."

By way of explanation for this comment, the Rebbe told his chassidim that when a *tzaddik* is *niftar*, the *neshamos* of the *tzaddikim* buried in Eretz Yisroel go out to *chutz laAretz* to welcome the *neshamah* of the *niftar*. They then pass back through Eretz Yisroel as they escort the *niftar* through the Holy Land on the way to his place in *Olam Haba*.

IF THE REBBE'S LIFESTYLE WAS SATURATED WITH *KEDUSHAH*, all the more so were the final months before his *petirah*. It was

The Final Months clearly evident that he was preparing himself to leave this world. His every conversation centered on stories about the *petirah* of various *tzaddikim*.

In his younger years the Rebbe was *makpid* to visit his father's *kever* each year during the month of Elul. There he would ask his father to beseech Hashem to grant the *Yidden* a good year. In his last years, the Rebbe's advanced age did not permit him to make the trip. Instead he appointed Reb Meir Trachtenberg, the Prilikover Rav, to go in his place.

When the month of Elul (1903) came around, the Rebbe summoned Reb Meir as usual. This time, however, he instructed Reb Meir to tell the Rizhiner an extra message. "Prilikover Rav, you should tell my father that I no longer have any strength to carry on. As far as I am concerned it's enough already."

Although the Rebbe was then 77 years old, he was still in the best of health. Nevertheless, when the Rebbe's family and chassidim heard of the Rebbe's words, they were sure that very soon he would be departing from their midst. Within a month, the bitter decree had become a reality.

The Rebbe (r.) walks across his garden from his home (in the background) to his shul. He is accompanied by the gabbai, Reb Aharon Dehol.

In his last weeks the Rebbe gave many signs about his imminent departure. A few days after Rosh Hashanah he stopped seeing his chassidim. Normally this was one of the peak seasons of the year, when thousands waited anxiously to receive the Rebbe's *berachah* for a good year. "It is the duty of a *tzaddik* to worry about the welfare of *Klal Yisroel*," the Rebbe explained. "Nevertheless there comes a time when even the greatest *tzaddik* has to turn away from others and have himself in mind."

ON HIS LAST EREV YOM KIPPUR HE CALLED IN HIS ONLY son Reb Yisroel and told him, "On Yom Kippur the Kohen Gadol

Reunited With the Shechinah

would enter the holiest place on earth, the *Kodesh HaKodashim*. Can you imagine what it must have felt like to be inside there, together with the *Shechinah*? *Oi!* My heart is longing to also enter into the Holy of Holies, to be reunited with the *Shechinah*."

Right after Yom Kippur the Rebbe fell ill with a lung infection. The chassidim, who realized that their crown was about to be removed from their heads, implored the very heavens to have mercy on their holy Rebbe, the last one of the Rizhiner's children. The Rebbe's condition deteriorated from day to day. Normally the Rebbe would have an *aliyah* to the Torah on the first day of Succos. When the *gabbai* asked the Rebbe if he wanted an *aliyah* this year as well, the Rebbe thought for a moment and said, "An *aliyah*! Yes, yes, I want an *aliyah* but not today. On the last day of Succos I'll have an *aliyah* ..."

The Rebbe spent his last Shabbos in bed; the doctors had already given up hope, and said they could do no more. Despite the Rebbe's precarious condition, it was clear that his mind was occupied with matters other than just his health. At midnight, the time when the Rebbe would normally start his *tisch*, the Rebbe's facial features changed. Suddenly he called out loud, over and over again, "*Heiliger Tatte! Heiliger Rachamim* of the whole world," just as he would during a *tisch*. And just as during a *tisch* his ghostly white complexion would change to a fiery red, so now it also changed. It appeared that in his mind the Rebbe was conducting a *tisch*.

When the end of Shabbos came, the Rebbe refused to recite *Havdalah*, and insisted that his son Reb Yisroel say it instead. It seemed that he felt he no longer had any connection with the coming week.

SUNDAY AFTERNOON, EREV HOSHANA RABBAH, THE REBBE called his *gabbai* Reb Hershel Rapporport and asked him, "Hershel, perhaps you can tell me why it has become so dark?"

The Last Day

"I haven't noticed that it has become dark," the *gabbai* replied. "You haven't noticed? How can that be? A real darkness has descended on us," the Rebbe said a second time.

When the night of Hoshana Rabbah arrived, the night of the Rebbe's *petirah*, the Rebbe asked for a *siddur* and for over an hour he *daven*ed with intense *kavanah*. "It's never too late to pray for the salvation of *Yidden*," he told those around him. Afterwards he commented to his son Reb Yisroel, "You see, my son, what has happened! When I was healthy I helped all of *Klal Yisroel* with my *tefillos*. Now that I am ill, all of *Klal Yisroel* are unable to help me."[1]

ONE HOUR BEFORE THE REBBE'S *PETIRAH*, HE ASKED THAT his chair (on which he would sit during a *tisch*) be brought into the room. When it was brought in, the Rebbe turned to

Crowning a New Rebbe

his son and instructed him, "Sit on my chair, my son, and take over my position." Reb Yisroel answered his father in a choked voice, "*Oi, Tatte*, what are you saying?" and refused to sit until his father commanded him a second time. Even then, he got up right away. Only when the Rebbe asked him a third time to stay seated did he finally remain in his father's chair. His father then told him, "You shall be Rebbe and all the *berachos* with which you shall bless *Klal Yisroel* will be as if I had blessed them, and you should be worthy to ascend to Eretz Yisroel together with all the *Yidden*." Reb Dovid Moshe then asked his son to reply, "Amen," to which Reb Yisroel answered, "Amen, together with you."[2]

---

1. These words mirror those of Moshe Rabbeinu as quoted in *Medrash Rabbah* (*Ki Savo* 7:10): "When Moshe was about to die and they didn't *daven* for him, he told them, 'One person saved 600,000 after the sin of the Calf, and 600,000 are incapable of saving one person?'"

2. In his last years Reb Yisroel explained that the reason why his father's dying *berachah* to him was not fulfilled was because he did not answer "Amen" as instructed, but said, "Amen, together with you"!

The original matzeivah of the Rebbe was destroyed during the war.
The present matzeivah was erected some ten years ago.

After the Rebbe had crowned his son Rebbe, he closed his eyes and started to recite the *tefillah* "*Nishmas kol chai*" with great *d'veikus*. It took the Rebbe almost an hour to recite the *tefillah*; some of the words he repeated countless times, again and again. As he finished the last words of the *tefillah*, "*LeDovid, borchi nafshi es Hashem*," his holy *neshamah* ascended upwards.

The Rebbe's *levayah* took place early in the morning, before *Shacharis*. Since it was Hoshana Rabbah, there was no *shivah*, and Reb Yisroel took over the mantle immediately. Hardly had he finished *davening*, than a long queue of *rabbanim* and senior chassidim had formed, eager to be among the first to present the new Rebbe with a *kvittel* and to show that they accept his leadership.

That night Reb Yisroel danced the traditional *hakafos* with great joy; it was impossible to notice on him that he had just lost his father. Only once did his pain and anquish come to the surface. Before the dancing commenced, the Rebbe recited aloud the prayer "*Atah hareisa*" and the *pesukim* which follow. When he came to the *pasuk*, "*Baavur Dovid avdecha al tasheiv pnei meshichecha* — For the sake of Dovid Your servant do not turn away the face of Moshiach," the

Rebbe repeated the *pasuk* twice, an innovation which from then on became the standard *minhag* in Chortkov. As the Rebbe repeated the *pasuk* for the second time, his voice suddenly cracked and it was evident that he was close to tears. He later explained that he had said the *pasuk* twice, once in the merit of Dovid HaMelech and once in the merit of his own father.

After the *hakafos* had ended, the Rebbe recited *Kiddush* for the first time in front of his chassidim and delivered his first Torah as Rebbe. The Rebbe's opening words were from a *pasuk* in *Kesuvim* — "And Shlomo HaMelech sat on the throne of Hashem as King instead of Dovid his father."

In his address the Rebbe acknowledged that it was a difficult task for him to sit on the chair of such a great and holy person like his father, which can be compared to the throne of Hashem. He hoped and *davened* that he prove himself worthy of the tremendous position that he had assumed.

In a subsequent discourse, he commented that during a father's lifetime, the mitzvah of *kibbud av* is that one may not sit in his father's place. Now, however, the mitzvah is the opposite: to sit in his father's place and take over his position and through doing so, to bring honor to his father.

As long as it was Yom Tov, the Rebbe showed absolutely no sign of mourning for his father, but right after reciting *Havdalah* at the end of Yom Tov, he burst into tears. Reb Yisroel never stopped crying for his father, and even many years later would burst into tears at the mere mention of his father's name.

The tens of thousands of Chortkover chassidim accepted Reb Yisroel immediately as the heir to his father's position, for even before Reb Dovid Moshe's *petirah*, Reb Yisroel had played a major role in the daily lives of the chassidim.

NEWS OF THE REBBE'S SUDDEN *PETIRAH* BROUGHT A terrible wave of sadness and mourning across Europe and beyond.

Hespedim Rarely in history did the *petirah* of one person bring such grief to whole towns and communities. Across

Galicia, Poland, Russia and Hungary the Rebbe was eulogized by the greatest and most famous *rabbanim* of the period. Some of these *hespedim* were later printed and they serve to give us an insight into the depth of grief that gripped Eastern Europe with the Rebbe's *petirah*. The popular mass circulation newspaper, "*Machazikei Hadass*," reported the *petirah* as follows:

> Like the branches of a tree on a stormy day, so our hands are shaking as they undertake their task, to grasp the pen which will inform *Klal Yisroel* of the calamity that has befallen them. Woe is to the hand that has to write these lines, our bodies are trembling and our knees are knocking in fright as we record that the blazing sun has set at noon. The great light that illuminated our lives has been extinguished. The Prince of *Klal Yisroel*, the light of the world, who was *kodesh hakodashim*, similar to a heavenly angel, our master and teacher, Reb Dovid Moshe, the Chortkover Rebbe, left our midst on Hoshana Rabbah and has gone to his eternal rest.
>
> Although no man can dare to say that he is able to eulogize the "*Ish Elokim*," we cannot restrain ourselves from

אבל כבוד

כיום. א. שבוע. זו. היכף. אחר. תפלת. ערבית. דרש. הרב הגאון
הגדול מרא דאתרא שליט"א הספד מר בבכיה גדולה על אדמו"ר
ההצ הקדוש בוצינא קדישא חסידא ופרישא מטשארטקוב זי"ע
זצב"י, וכמעט כל העיר אנשים ונשים וטף גם רבים מעיירות
הסמיכות שהי' בביהמ"ד בכו בכיה גדולה בעת אשר הה"ג שליט"א צעק
בבכיה גדולה' אבי אבי רכב ישראל ופרשיו, ואח"כ ישב הרה"ג
שליט"א. כרבע. שעה על הארץ ואחרי' ישבו כל העם על. הארץ
צעקו צעקה גדולה ומרה.
והמנחם אבלי ציון וירושלים, הוא ינחם אותנו במהרה.
יום ב' פרשת נח תרס"ד ברעזאן.

Notice of the hesped that the Maharsham delivered in the town of Barzhan.
"Almost the whole city — men, women and children, who were in the beis hamedrash — cried bitterly ... afterwards the Rav shlita sat on the ground for about a quarter of an hour, and after him all the people sat on the ground and cried out with bitter wailing.

ס.פ.ר

מקור דמעה

והוא מספד מר על מאורן של ישראל. ראש גולת אריאל. אדומו״ר קודש
הקדשים. הרב הדומה לאראלי תרשישים. פאר הדור והדרו. אלפים ורבבות
מישראל הלכו לאורו. צדיק יסוד עולם. אור טמיר ונעלם. רשכבה״ג. לו
דומי׳ תהלה. אור ישראל וקדושו. ממזרח שמש עד מבואו נודע שם קדשו

רבינו הגדול **דוד משה** זצוקללה״ה **ממשארמקוב**

נצחו אראלים את המצוקים ונשבה ארון הקודש בליל הו״ר תרם״ד לפ״ק

אשר קרא לנבכי ולמקפד כבוד הרב הגאון המובהק כ״י ע״ה פה״ח שלשלת
היוחסין כש״ת מו״ה זאב וואלף האומים שליט״א אבדפ״ק זאלישטשיק והגליל
אור ליום ועש״ק פ׳ בראשית שנת חיה כבוד אדוננו ורבינו הסתהור לפ״ק

ונסתפח לזה קונ׳ פרי תאר פלפולים נחמדים אשר כבוד הרב השיב
לשואליו הנכבדים

הבאתיו לביה״ד אנכי זעירא דמן חבריא מאיר ווארמבראנד מאלישטשיק.

זאלישטשיקי
בדפום של היה מו״ה שמואל גלאסם
שנת תרס״ד לפ״ק

M E K O R   D I M O H
Druck v. S. Glass Zaleszczyki, 1903.

*Over sixty hespedim about the
Rebbe were printed;
this particular hesped
was delivered in the town
of Zalishteshik, Galicia*

offering a few words concerning this *tzaddik*, about whom
Klal Yisroel is shedding and weeping rivers of tears. Who
didn't know of the Rebbe's extreme *kedushah* and *taharah*?
From his youngest years he had cut himself off from the
world's pleasures. Who didn't know of the Rebbe's holy *avodah* in Torah and *tefillah*? The Rebbe, who served Hashem
with his every breath, acted as a messenger for us. We have
been deprived of our connection between our lowly world
and the higher world. Who can describe the pain that has
overtaken the world with his passing.

We can only hope and *daven* that the *zechus* of the Rebbe
will protect us. He who comforts the mourners of Zion will
dry our tears. We accept upon ourselves the decision of
Heaven and we state that the ways of the Creator are just
and without wrongdoing. *Baruch Dayan HaEmes.*

CHAPTER ELEVEN

The New Rebbe

WITH THE ASCENT OF REB YISROEL TO THE position of Rebbe, a new chapter was opened in the annals of Chortkover Chassidus. In truth, a new era was starting not just for the chassidim, but also for many other *Yidden* across Poland and Galicia and beyond.

UNLIKE HIS FATHER BEFORE HIM, WHO USED TO SECLUDE himself behind locked doors and rarely left the confines of his home, **A Changing World** Reb Yisroel soon became known as one of the most active and foremost leaders of *Klal Yisroel* who did not shy away from standing up and directing the people as a whole.

He became extemely involved in all aspects of communal life and his mark was felt in all quarters. During his reign, the world started to enter the age of modernization, bringing with it many changes and dangers, from which no house was immune. No

The holy Rebbe,
Reb Yisroel of Chortkov

longer could one afford to ignore the winds that were blowing from outside. In the years before and after the First World War, a storm was blowing across Eastern Europe. Many *bochurim* left the *beis hamedrash* in pursuit of more "modern" pastimes. Those who had already forsaken the Torah and mitzvos did their utmost to persuade their former companions to join them. The Jewish Socialist party, known as "The Bund," actively targeted the *chareidim*, as did the Zionist Party and many other groups. Each one offered different promises of happiness and equality, but their aims were all the same — to do away with Torah and *Yiddishkeit*.

Chortkov offered a *bochur* or a young man shelter from these strong winds which sought to uproot him. Here he was once again reminded that only through Torah and mitzvos could he hope to survive. Although the Rebbe counted his every word, for the young *bochurim* he always had plenty to say.

The Rebbe would often stress that one must remember that the young generation is the future of *Klal Yisroel* and they must be taken care of properly. Many a *Yid* could truthfully say that it was only the loving care and attention the Rebbe had shown him that gave him the strength to carry on and not give in.

⇒)⇐

REB YISROEL WAS BORN ON THE 10TH OF IYAR 5614 (1854), and it was immediately apparent that he was destined for great-

The First Years

ness. On the day of his birth, the chassidim were sitting together in Chortkov as usual, when the esteemed chassid, Reb Alter Rimonover, proclaimed that he had some good news to reveal to them. Reb Alter was no ordinary chassid. He was considered a *tzaddik* in his own right, a person about whom the Rizhiner had already said decades earlier that he possessed *ruach hakodesh*. Therefore his words were always taken note of and treated with the utmost seriousness and respect.

"Last night," Reb Alter related, "I had a dream. In the dream I saw our master the Rizhiner holding a newborn baby. He said that he was presenting us with a *berachah*, with someone who would fill

חגיגת אבן הפנה קלויז טשאָרטקוב מאנשסתר
י' אייר תשס"ג לפ"ק

*The Rebbe's birthday, the 10th of Iyar, used to be observed as a day of celebration
and thanksgiving among Chortkover chassidim. In 1993, the 10th of Iyar
marked the Even HaPinah celebration for a new Chortkover Kloiz in Manchester.*

his place. This was in keeping with what the Rizhiner had said before his *petirah*, that his *neshamah* would return again to this world
and be known by the name Yisroel." A few hours after Reb Alter had
made his dream public, the town of Chortkov was aglow with the
happy news. The Chortkover Rebbetzin had given birth to a boy!
Although this was not the Rebbe's first child (an older brother, Reb
Nuchem Mordechai, had been born some years earlier), still Reb
Alter's words about the greatness of the new arrival drove the town
to even greater *simchah*. When Reb Nuchem Mordechai was *niftar* as
a young man leaving just Reb Yisroel to succeed his father, the ac-
curacy of the dream became evident to all.

When Reb Yisroel was 3 years old, his mother took him to her father, Reb Aharon, the Rebbe of Chernobyl. Reb Aharon Chernobyler
was not able to take his eyes off the small child, exclaiming that if he
had not known that this was his daughter's son, he would hardly believe that the child is a *yelud ishah* (regular mortal). Reb Yisroel's
uncle, the Rebbe of Sadiger, also once commented that even though

The Rebbe in his younger years

all the grandchildren of the Rizhiner were something special, Reb Yisroel was unusual even among them (*chiddush she'be'chiddushim*).

As a young child Reb Yisroel delved deeply into the sea of Talmud and would often speak in learning with the various *rabbanim* who came to see his father in Chortkov. Reb Yisroel became especially close to Reb Shlomo Dreimar of Skola (author of *"Yashreish Yaakov"*) and every time the Skola Rav came to Chortkov they learned together. Reb Yisroel, who was only 14 years old at the time, wrote two lengthy responsa on the topic of *"bitul berov,"* which the Skola Rov published in his classic work *"Beis Shlomo."* Another complicated *pilpul* on the topic of monetary interest, which the Rebbe wrote at the age of 14, was printed in the *sefer "Ateres Yaakov VeYisroel."*

מאמרי אגרא דכלה

משא וזמן של הלכה אשר היה בן המחבר הרב המאוה"ג האבד"ק
פרינבווא שלימ"א ובין מחו' הרב הקדוש מו"ה ישראל פרידמאן שלימ"א •
בנו של מרן קודש הקדשים מטשארטקוב שרימ"א • בימי טל ילדותם
בהיותם שניהם מבני תלימד וארביסר •

ב"ה

יום גימל זך ניסן וזהו כבוד שמו רפ"ק
משארטקוב •

רב שמום וברכה לכבודו מעלת ידידי
הדרין ובקי השנון זית רען' יפה
פרי תואר, ההדור הועדה כש"ת מוה'
ישראל כי' שלומו ישא ובואיתו יצליח :

הן סונד לי אשר מתא של שלומי עם תשותה
מניחי שלטו מי יד' זרים • ולאי לכבודי
וה'

ישראל במ"ה דוד משה שלימ"א.

On another occasion, the famed *posek,* the Maharsham, who also frequently came to Chortkov, asked Reb Yisroel if he owned a certain rare *sefer* that spoke about a difficult *she'elah* in *hilchos gittin.* It was well known that Reb Yisroel had a vast library, which took up several rooms. He

A pilpul on the topic of ribbis that the Rebbe wrote when he was 14 years old

bought every new *sefer* available; in addition he also owned many manuscripts of *sefarim* which had never been printed. Thus he was an address for anyone seeking a rare or ancient *sefer*. Reb Yisroel wanted to know what the *she'elah* was and when the Maharsham told him, Reb Yisroel proceeded to tell him all the different opinions and how one should act *halachah lemaaseh*. The Maharsham, who had been quite unaware of Reb Yisroel's vast knowledge until then, asked his permission to ask him about all the difficulties that he encountered during his learning. Reb Yisroel answered him that he never does anything without first obtaining his father's consent. The Alter Rebbe, however, did not give his consent.

The Rimolover Rav, Reb Yaakov Weidenfeld, once told the Alter Chortkover Rebbe, Reb Dovid Moshe, how impressed he was with his son. Reb Dovid Moshe immediately called his son and sternly rebuked him, saying, "Why does the Rav of Rimolov have to know that you are a *lamdan*; is that what I have worked so hard to achieve?" From then on Reb Yisroel was careful not to display his learning in public, and only on select occasions did he offer his opinion after being pressed to answer.

REB YISROEL UNDERSTOOD THAT HIS TASK IN LIFE WOULD not be to *pasken sha'alos* and issue halachic rulings. Rather than focusing just on the external confines of the *halachah*, he

My Job Is to Daven

was to concentrate on the service of the heart and soul of the Torah. His job would be to elevate the *neshamos* of *Yidden* and bring them ever closer to their Father in Heaven. This role is well illustrated by the following story which was recorded by the *gaon* Reb Tzvi Hirshorn: (He was Rav of the town of Yebrozna in Galicia, and one of the distinguished chassidim of Chortkov. He was killed during the Second World War.)

> It was *Shabbos Bereishis* in the vast shul of the holy Rebbe, Reb Yisroel of Chortkov. Reb Meir Shapiro, who was then a young man and Rav in the town of Sonik, had come to spend a Shabbos in the company of his Rebbe.
>
> After *krias haTorah* had ended, the door of the Chortkover Rebbe's private room suddenly opened and

there on the threshold stood his radiant form. "I honor Reb Meir Shapiro with Rosh Chodesh *bentching* and *Mussaf*," the Rebbe declared.

In Chortkov it was a very rare event for the Rebbe himself to honor anyone with *davening* before the congregation. Normally this was left totally to the *gabbai's* discretion. Reb Meir, however, was known not only to be a brillant *talmid chacham*, but also a genius of the emotion and the heart. His fiery *tefillos* captivated the hearts of all who heard them and his *davening* softened even someone who had a heart of stone.

And so with his beautiful and melodious voice Reb Meir led the congregation. He *davened Mussaf* with such emotion that all the thousands of listeners were completely caught up with his devotion.

After *davening* the Rebbe invited Reb Meir into his room, where he remained for some time. When he emerged, Reb Meir's face was radiant with joy. Later on, while eating the Shabbos meal together with the other chassidim, Reb Meir related a small snippet from his conversation with the Rebbe. The Rebbe had revealed to him what his mission in this world was to be.

Since the Rebbe had mentioned Reb Meir's gift for *davening*, and his ability to inspire others, Reb Meir had asked him, "If my power of *tefillah* is so great, perhaps I should become a regular *chazzan*?" The Rebbe pondered his chassid's question and after a few moments of silence, he answered. "I would like to tell you a story about the Rebbe, Reb Zishe of Annipoli.

"Reb Zishe was once on his travels, going from town to town. Eventually he reached the town of Zalkova where he made his way to the local shul. The Rav of the town, who was known as Reb Yuzpah, was delivering a complicated *shiur* at the time, and thus no one took any notice of Reb Zishe as he took a place at the back of the shul.

"When the *shiur* was over, Reb Zishe made his way over to Reb Yuzpah, who was one of the *gedolim* of the period, and thanked him for the *shiur*. Although Reb Zishe was dressed in worn-out clothes and had the appearance of a beggar, Reb Yuzpah sensed that there was more to him than met the eye. 'What is it about you that so attracts me?' Reb Yuzpah asked him. 'I have no special traits,' Reb Zishe answered. 'I hardly know how to learn. The only thing I know is to *daven* a little bit.'

"Reb Yuzpah wasn't satisfied with the answer. Which *Yid* does not know how to *daven*? Perhaps Reb Zishe could show him what he meant that he knows how to *daven* a little bit. The two of them entered a side room and Reb Zishe started to instruct his host in the secrets of *tefillah* and the Kabbalistic ideas contained in every word, until Reb Yuzpah could not contain his amazement.

"'I can see that I do not yet know how to *daven* properly,' Reb Yuzpah exclaimed. 'Perhaps I should leave my post and follow you, so that I should at least know how to *daven* properly?'

"Reb Zishe, however, refused to allow Reb Yuzpah to leave his post. He told him, '*Chazal* have told us that just like no two people look the same, similarly no two people have the same inner mind and attitude. Accordingly every person has been given a different task to perform in this world, one to which only he is suited according to the way he has been created. Your job is to sit and learn and give *shiurim* and my job is to *daven*.'"

The Chortkover Rebbe finished his story and, turning to Reb Meir Shapiro, he said, "You have the gifts and the potential to become a great Torah disseminator. You have the ability to establish yeshivos and produce fine *talmidim*. This must be your goal! As for *davening* and inspiring *Yidden* to greater *kavanos*, that you can leave to me, that is my job."

"With these words," Reb Meir concluded, "the Rebbe directed me on my life's mission. He showed me that I had been appointed to educate the younger generation and to spread the Torah far and wide."

᠅

"Ateres Yisroel," a booklet of the first divrei Torah that Reb Yisroel delivered upon becoming Rebbe

At His Father's Side

FIFTEEN YEARS BEFORE the Alter Chortkover Rebbe was *niftar*, he suddenly stopped saying *divrei Torah* at his *tisch* or at public occasions. The chassidim were very upset by this sudden change and begged the Rebbe to resume.

The Rebbe refused, saying, "More than the calf wants to drink, its mother wants to feed it." When the chassidim persisted in their request, he told them to go to his son, Reb Yisroel, and he would say Torah for them.

Thus it became the norm in Chortkov that at the end of every *tisch* Reb Yisroel would say Torah to the chassidim. On the occasion when the Alter Rebbe did not give a *tisch*, Reb Yisroel would sit with the chassidim and inspire them with his penetrating and stimulating *divrei Torah*. In an article, one of the chassidim described his impressions as follows:

> Already when he was a young man, all the chassidim regarded Reb Yisroel as a full-fledged Rebbe in his own right. Even the great *rabbanim* and the saintly chassidim looked up to him with the greatest respect and awe imaginable. This was clearly evident from their behavior toward him, and especially when in his presence.
>
> Reb Yisroel's way of sitting with the chassidim was unique. In all rabbinical circles, regardless of their background, it is the time-honored practice for a son to continue his father's *minhagim*. Reb Yisroel, however, broke with this

תעודת הרב הצדיק הקדוש והטהור עטרת
ראשנו עמודא דנהורא נזר ועטרת
תפארת ישראל סיני ועוקר הרים דבריו חיים
וקיימים גאון ישראל המפורסם בכל קצוי ארץ
אור הבהיר שמן תורק שמו כ"ק שם תפארתו
מו"ה **ישראל** שליט"א ממשארטקאב.

גם למראה עיני כ"ק עטרת ראשנו קדוש **ישראל**
שליט"א היה הספר „ברכות חיים" שחיבר
ידידנו החסיד המופלא מו"ה חיים ברוך כהנא נ"י
והוטב בעיניו. והבטיח לו כאשר יזכה המחבר הנ"ל
ויוצא מחברתו מאור הדפוס יקח גם הוא ספר אחד
במחיר אשר יושת עליו . וע"ז באתי עה"ח יום ב'
דר"ח כסליו שנת תרח"נ מ ש א ר ט ק א ב .

דברי הכותב בפקורת כ"ק אהרן דאהל :

tradition. He did not
sing the same tunes as
his father did; even the
Kiddush and the pre-
ceding *Shalom Aleichem*
were not recited in the
same way as his father. He also did not *daven* at a late hour
like his father did; rather he was particular to *daven* punctu-
ally as stated in *Shulchan Aruch*. This creation of a new and
individual style signaled to the chassidim that Reb Yisroel
would create his own trail-blazing path in years to come.

After Reb Yisroel would make *Kiddush*, he would give a
lengthy *dvar Torah*, which could easily take up to three-
quarters of an hour. All the chassidim would "lick their
fingers" at his words, because Reb Yisroel was not only a
very interesting speaker, but also a true *gadol* in Torah.
Every word that he said contained in it an echo of his brilliance and his genius.

The discourses that Reb Yisroel delivered became famous in their
own right and were later printed under the title *"Tiferes Yisroel."*
When a copy of the *sefer* came into the hands of the great *gaon* and
posek, Reb Yitzchok Shmelkis of Lemberg, who was often vocal in
his criticism, he said admiringly, "If even the Rebbes who are busy
all day with their chassidim can produce such *geonus*, what are we
rabbanim to answer?" The *gaon* Reb Shlomo Zalman Auerbach once
learned a *dvar Torah* from the *sefer "Tiferes Yisroel."* He later commented to his son Reb Mordechai, "This *sefer* is a masterpiece, it is
a beautiful blend of chassidishe *geonus*."

The Rebbe's first sefer
was called
"Tiferes Yisroel."
Further volumes were
printed in later years.

Indeed Reb Yisroel's greatness in Torah earned him the undiluted praise of even the most senior *gedolim* of his time. Surviving letters and correspondence serve to demonstrate to us the awe in which Reb Yisroel was held by even the most senior *gedolim*. This, for example, is how the esteemed *posek*, Reb Meir Arik, describes and prefaces Reb Yisroel's name in a letter printed in the *sefer "Shaarei Taharah"*:

> To the great Rav, the holy light, who is like a river stream-ing with wisdom. Who has ten measures (*eser yados*) of *nigleh* and *nistar*, who shines with a brilliant light like the morning star: our master and teacher, the holy Reb Yisroel son of the Rebbe the *kodesh hakodashim*, the head of the Diaspora, from Chortkov.

So, although Reb Yisroel was already 50 years old when he be-came Rebbe, he was no newcomer to public life. For years he had occupied a standing which was perhaps unique in the chassidishe world. Whereas in other courts no son would play an active role during his father's lifetime, with Reb Yisroel things were different.

This unique role is perhaps best described by Reb Dovid Moshe Spiegel in the booklet "*Pe'er Yisroel*":

> I once heard from the elder chassidim that after the *petirah* of the Alter Rebbe, the heads of the chassidim came together to bemoan their loss and to strengthen and comfort each other. The tears flowed freely as they recounted what was no more, until one of the *Yidden* stood up and exclaimed, "Why are you all sobbing like lost sheep? We have a new Rebbe who is fully capable of filling his father's place. He is great in all spheres of the Torah and is able to lead us in the same way his father did."
>
> "It is true that the new Rebbe is a great and wonderous *tzaddik*," another *Yid* answered. "We also don't underestimate him for a moment, we are all well aware how fortunate we are to have him. However, until now we had two Rebbes, and now we are left with only one. Until now when a *Yid* didn't know how to approach the Alter Rebbe or how to phrase his question, Reb Yisroel would guide him and prepare him. Similarly, not always were the Alter Rebbe's short and concise answers understood by all. Again the present Rebbe would explain his father's words. At the same time he would show us where this answer could be found in the words of *Chazal* or in another source, thereby demonstrating the *geonus* of the Alter Rebbe which lay hidden beneath a veil of simplicity. In practical matters he would also explain how to put his father's advice into practice. Thus until now we were blessed with two Rebbes, and now we are crying that we are left with only one Rebbe."

An example of the Rebbe's role during his father's lifetime was related by the *gaon* Reb Shmuel Halpern, the first Rav of Zichron Meir in Bnei Brak:

> When Reb Shmuel received his call-up papers to enlist in the Russian army he went to ask the Alter Rebbe for a *berachah*

that he be spared. Before being freed from the army a young man could not hope to get married. No girl wanted to marry someone who might be forcibly conscripted for years, or might never come back again. The Alter Rebbe told him that he need not worry, everything would work out fine and he would be spared. When Reb Shmuel related to Reb Yisroel his father's words, Reb Yisroel told him. "The truth is that there is cause for worry, but since my father has said that everything will be fine, you can rest assured that you will not be conscripted."

Reb Shmuel got married and settled in the town of Brizov. One day, soldiers descended on the town; they had come to arrest Reb Shmuel on charges of desertion. In a panic Reb Shmuel made up a story that he had served in the army and had already been discharged. The soldiers demanded to see his discharge papers, to which Reb Shmuel replied that he had left them in his hometown. The soldiers ordered him to get hold of the papers and promised to return to see the papers. As if by a miracle, they never came back!

In an article, one of the elder chassidim, Reb Alter Meir from Sonik, relates his memories from the period when Reb Yisroel acted as a junior Rebbe at his father's side. At the time Reb Alter Meir was a young *bochur*, and he describes the impression Reb Yisroel made on him and on his friends:

> It is almost fifty years since the first time I was in Chortkov. The Alter Rebbe was still alive then ... The Rebbe's son, Reb Yisroel, with his sharp eyes, recognized us instantly as *bnei Torah*. Although he had never seen us before, he came over to us and inquired as to where we were from. During our stay in Chortkov he was *mekarev* us and urged us to learn even better. He asked us what we were learning and delved into the *gemara* with us. He listened carefully to what we had to say and took part in the discussions.
>
> We were very impressed with his Torahs and with all the attention he gave us, and we drank thirstly his every word,

and that of the elder chassidim too. Soon we began to feel part of it all, as we sat to eat and drink with the others in the Rebbe's court. When we left to go home, we were different people than when we had arrived. Suddenly all the wordly desires had lost their sparkle and appeared to us remote and worthless. No longer did they attract us. Instead we joined the chassidim, becoming part of their circle. From every gathering of the chassidim, whether on Shabbos or during the week, we drew inspiration and *chizuk*. Our learning and understanding of the *gemara* also increased. We could not return to Chortkov empty-handed.

In communal matters Reb Yisroel took an active role as well. Often the Alter Rebbe would rely on the decisions of his son before deciding or issuing a ruling on a problem. The many letters which have survived until today bare witness to Reb Yisroel's involvement in all aspects of the *kehillah* and Chassidus, from a very young age.

Even when it came to giving a *haskamah* on a new *sefer*, the custom was for father and son to give a joint letter, a practice that was unheard of elsewhere.

ALTHOUGH REB YISROEL acted as his father's right-**I Am Not My Father** hand man, this did not in any way remove the great awe that he had for his father. He would not enter his father's room without permission. Often he would ask his mother to see if it was convenient for the Alter Rebbe to see him.

A joint haskamah from both Rebbes to the sefer "Divrei Yisroel" by the Rebbe of Modzitz

Even when he had entered the room, he would not speak until his father addressed him first.

Even decades after the Alter Rebbe's passing, Reb Yisroel would speak with awe and longing about his father. To one chassid who remarked that he needed an immediate salvation the Rebbe groaned and said, "I hope you won't be so foolish as to compare me to my father. When my father promised a person his *berachah*, he was helped instantly. I, however, am not my father, I cannot do what he did."

Even in his last years the Rebbe would break down in tears when speaking about his father. To one surprised onlooker he explained, "I long for my father so much, in every matter I am missing his advice and his guidance."

Nevertheless, when the time came for Reb Yisroel to assume his father's position, he did so with authority and leadership. To a close chassid he commented that he had always hoped to remain a child at his father's table, and although Hashem had decreed otherwise, he was grateful that he had at least managed to complete the whole of *Shas* over forty times before he had to take the first *kvittel*!

CHAPTER TWELVE

His Marriage and Family

WHEN REB YISROEL BECAME OF AGE HE married his first cousin, the Rebbetzin Ruchoma Bas-Sheva, the daughter of his uncle the Alter Sadigerer Rebbe, Reb Avrohom Yaakov Friedman. The great *simchah* that enveloped the chassidim at this majestic wedding reverberated throughout Galicia for a long time. The unusual wording of the invitation that the *chasan's* father sent to all his chassidim explicitly conveyed the message that this was not an occasion to be missed. In his invitation to the chassidim, the Alter Chortkover Rebbe wrote:

> AFTER INQUIRING AFTER THEIR WELL-BEING and success all the days: with praise to Hashem, I bless this
> **Marriage** day, the day that I have waited for and chosen, to bring my dear and only son, who is the glory of Israel, under the marriage canopy. The *chupah* shall take place

The Rebbe's invitation to the wedding of his son, Reb Yisroel of Chortkov

b'shaah tovah u'mutzlachas on the 18th of Sivan. It should be a mazel tov for us and for all of Israel. My heart is sure and confident that on the occasion of my simchah, the heavens and earth will also rejoice. The heavens will bestow upon us their berachos and from the earth will rise up salvation. Therefore I hope that my letter shall bring rejoicing like a lost treasure that has been discovered.

The Rebbetzin Ruchoma Bas-Sheva was known as a tzadekes in her own right. Occasionally Reb Yisroel would tell his chassidim to mention their problems to the Rebbetzin so that she should daven for them as well. He once commented, "She helps me in my avodah with her tefillos!"

The Rebbetzin stood faithfully at her husband's side throughout his life. Her great devotion to him came to light after the Rebbe's petirah in 1933. Throughout the year of mourning, the Rebbetzin attended davening every day in order to answer the Kaddish prayer of her sons. As they said the Kaddish, the Rebbetzin's sobbing could be heard throughout the shul.

Eleven months after the Rebbe's petirah, the Rebbetzin participated in the hakamas matzeivah. While she was standing next to the Rebbe's kever she suddenly broke down in tears and exclaimed: "You promised me that you wouldn't leave me here a long time by myself in this world. It is almost a whole year and I see no sign of your promise."

The Rebbe's mechutan,
Reb Avrohom Yehoshua of Adjud,
father of Reb Menachem Nuchem

The next day the Rebbetzin fell ill and ten days later, on the 24th of Cheshvan 5694 (1934), she was *niftar*.

The Rebbetzin bore five children to her husband. The oldest child, Reb Chaim Aharon, was born soon after their marriage, in 1873. Although he was groomed as his father's eventual successor, in Heaven things were planned differently. Reb Chaim Aharon was *niftar* during his father's lifetime, on the 26th of Elul 1926. For his father, his loss was an irreplaceable blow, as he himself said: "Only with *techiyas hameisim* will I be comforted!" Reb Chaim Aharon's descendants were all killed during the war.

Reb Yisroel of Chortkov (center). The Rebbe's oldest son, Reb Chaim Aharon, is on the extreme right, and the second son, Reb Nuchem Mordechai, is on the extreme left. Reb Nuchem Mordechai's son, Reb Shlomo, is next to him, and Reb Yisroel of Husyatin is on the other side.

In 1874 the Rebbetzin gave birth to a second son, Reb Nuchem Mordechai, and in 1882 to a third son, Reb Dov Ber (see more about them in Chapters 23-24). In addition she also gave birth to two daughters, the Rebbetzin Miriam and the Rebbetzin Chava. The older daughter married her cousin Reb Menachem Nuchem Friedman of Shtefanesht. He was acclaimed as a major *talmid chacham* and served as Rav of the town Itzikan in Romania. He too was *niftar* as a young man in his *shver*'s lifetime, on the 20th of Sivan 1933. His children and grandchildren were all killed in the war. The second daughter, Rebbetzin Chava, married Reb Tzvi Aryeh Twersky of Zlatipol (see more about him in Chapter 24).

AFTER HIS *CHASUNAH* REB YISROEL STAYED FOR A TIME under the shadow of his great uncle and *shver*, the Sadigerer Rebbe.

The Sadigerer Rebbe

It is worthwhile devoting a few pages to the stature of the Sadigerer Rebbe, who was considered to be one of the greatest *tzaddikim* of his time. He exercised immense influence on all aspects of Jewish life throughtout Russia, Galicia and Poland. His ways left an indelible imprint on Reb Yisroel, whose awe for his *shver* knew no bounds and whose sayings and *divrei Torah* were constantly on his lips.

☙❧

Reb Avrohom Yaakov was born on the 20th of Cheshvan 5580 (1820). During that particular time, Russian Jewry was undergoing a painful and difficult period. The accursed Czar Nikolai had embarked on his plan to destroy the Jewish nation; each day brought terrible new decrees, in an attempt to bring the *Yidden* to their knees. When one of the chassidim asked the Rizhiner in desperation, "Is there nothing that can be done to topple this terrible man?" the Rizhiner answered him, "My son Avrohom Yaakov, he will topple the Czar ... Concerning him it is written, '*Hakol kol Yaakov.*'" And, indeed, not long after Reb Avrohom Yaakov became Rebbe, the Czar committed suicide — on Purim 1854.

At Reb Avrohom Yaakov's *bris*, the *mohel*, Reb Aharon of Klivan, dropped the *milah* knife after reciting the *berachah* "*al hamilah.*" The Rizhiner, who acted as *sandek,* later asked the *mohel* what had caused him to drop the knife. Obviously shaken, Reb Aharon, who had been a *talmid* of the Baal Shem Tov, explained that he had seen a vision of his Rebbe.

Hearing his words, the Rizhiner told him that he was not surprised. "The Baal Shem Tov said before his *petirah* that if Moshiach does not come in the next sixty years, he (the Baal Shem Tov) would have to come back to this world again. It is now sixty years since his *petirah.*

"I would even have named the baby Yisroel after the Baal Shem Tov, if my name weren't Yisroel," the Rizhiner continued. "Instead I named him Yaakov which is a corresponding name to Yisroel. The name Avrohom is after Reb Avrohom Broide, for the baby possesses the *neshamah* of the Baal Shem Tov, but the head of Reb Avrohom Broide."

When Reb Avrohom Yaakov turned 13, his father asked him, "You know that the *yetzer hatov* joins a person when he becomes bar mitzvah. Yet his *yetzer hara* is with him right from birth. Tell me, how were you able to stand up to the *yetzer hara* all these years without the help of the *yetzer hatov*?" Reb Avrohom Yaakov answered his father, "Whenever my *yetzer hara* tried to tempt me to sin, I put him off with a convincing argument. I told him that the *halachah* forbids a judge to hear the arguments of one of the parties in a case if the other one is not present. So he would have to wait until I turn 13 and then my *yetzer hatov* will be able to refute his persuasive arguments."

When Reb Avrohom Yaakov became of age he married Rebbetzin Miriam, the daughter of Reb Aharon Karliner. Before the *chupah* the Rizhiner told his son, "My father used to say, 'From my sons people will know who I am,' but I say differently: from my sons people will know who Hashem is. My dear son, you should know that you possess a very holy *neshamah.*" And with these words, Reb Avrohom Yaakov went to his *chupah.*

NOT LONG AFTER REB AVROHOM YAAKOV BECAME REBBE he was imprisoned by the Austrian authorities in the notorious dun-

Prison geons of Chernovitz. When the Rizhiner was *niftar* the Russians confidently believed they had seen the end of "Beis Rizhin." Thus when they realized that the Rizhiner's successor was proving himself both competent and beloved, they were furious. They were ready to do anything to get rid of him, and when the opportunity presented itself they grabbed it with both hands.

The police apprehended a *Yid* who was a forger of Russian banknotes. In his possession they found a letter from the Rebbe blessing him in all his endeavors. The local *maskilim*, who long regarded the Rebbe as a thorn in their side, grasped this golden opportunity. They went to the police and testified that the Rebbe was also mixed up in forging banknotes and was in partnership with the forger.

On the strength of the false evidence provided by the *maskilim*, the Russian government demanded the arrest and imprisonment of the Rebbe on charges of being involved in circulating forged Russian banknotes. A few days after Pesach 1856 the Rebbe was arrested and imprisoned in the dungeons of Chernovitz.

The Rebbe was thrown into a tiny, dark cell in which there was hardly room to turn and nowhere to sit or lie down. To add to his discomfort, his jailers put another man with him in the cell. This man, a hardened criminal, who was known to be a violent anti-Semite, delighted in annoying the Rebbe with his remarks and coarse talk. He disturbed him during his *davening* and purposely got in his way whenever the Rebbe wanted to lean against the wall after the many long hours of being forced to stand on his feet.

After several days of this cruel torture, the warden of the prison was bribed to permit an armchair to be placed in the cell, so that the Rebbe could sit down during the daytime. No sooner was the armchair brought in than the criminal carved crosses all over it, knowing only too well that the Rebbe would not sit on a chair with such decorations and thus he would be able to use it himself.

And so the days and nights passed, until one Monday morning when the Rebbe was *davening Shacharis*. As he recited the words: "Look from Heaven and see how we have become a scorn and a derision among the nations," he burst into sobs of anguish and misery.

Quickly the Rebbe controlled himself and cried out, "Nevertheless, we have not forsaken Your Name, Hashem, please do not forsake us." He repeated these words several times.

Suddenly a surprising thing happened. The criminal collapsed on the floor writhing in agony, his whole body gripped in excruciating pain. He began screaming at the top of his voice, "Help! I'm dying! Help! Help!" The guards came rushing toward the cell and threw open the door. Inside, the Rebbe stood immersed in *tefillah* with his face to the wall. On the floor, writhing in pain, was the criminal, screaming, "Take me out of here! I'm dying! The Rabbi is tearing me to pieces!"

Not knowing what to do, the guards rushed into the warden's office to ask for instruction. But the warden too was writhing on the floor unable to speak. In terror the guards returned to the Rebbe's cell and dragged the criminal out of the room. Only then did he and the warden recover. The Rebbe was transferred to a larger cell where he spent fifteen months until he was finally released.

A Human Korban

THE REBBE EMERGED FROM PRISON A DESPERATELY ILL man. The many hours spent standing on his feet, and the damp and cold conditions, plus the lack of basic food had seriously damaged his health. A few days later the Rebbe's condition worsened and his life hung by a thread. The Rebbe's brothers converged on Sadiger to visit him and to *daven* to Hashem to revoke the decree. With tears in their eyes, thousands of chassidim stood in the great *beis hamedrash* pouring out their hearts in *tefillah* to Hashem. Suddenly the Chortkover Rebbe, Reb Dovid Moshe, walked up to the *bimah* and called out, "We have done all that we can, but the Gates of Heaven remain closed. Call in all the townspeople, the simple and the ignorant, let them join us in our *tefillah*. Perhaps the pure *tefillos* of the simple will succeed where the *tefillos* of the *tzaddikim* failed."

Within a few minutes the *beis hamedrash* was packed with the local laborers and workers, their voices joining the crying and wailing of those already present. After a few more minutes the Chortkover Rebbe mounted the *bimah* for the second time and called out: "The crown is falling! Only a short while remains until our crown will be removed! Who is willing to offer himself as a *korban*, to accept the Rebbe's illness on himself? I guarantee *Olam Haba* to whoever will take on himself the Rebbe's illness."

A deathly silence descended on all those assembled. Suddenly a *Yid* called Reb Mordechai Mishel of Linsk jumped up and said, "I am willing to be a *kapparah* for our holy Rebbe, I accept on myself to be his *pidyon nefesh*." No sooner had he finished speaking than scores of chassidim also jumped up saying they were willing to be the Rebbe's *kapparah*. "Mordechai Mishel was first," the Chortkover Rebbe announced, "only he has been *zocheh* to become the *kapparah*."

That evening Reb Mordechai Mishel fell ill. As his condition deteriorated, so the Rebbe's condition improved. With jolly spirits Reb Mordechai Mishel told his visitors how happy he was that he had been found fit to be the Rebbe's *korban*. As he lay on his deathbed, he asked that a *l'chaim* should be brought in. With his last breath he whispered, "The Rebbe should have a *refuah sheleimah*, and myself — a place *tachas kanfei haShechinah*."

Years later, on Reb Mordechai Mishel's *yahrtzeit*, the chassidim wanted to drink a *l'chaim*. The Rebbe told them, "*Nu*, you have finally remembered him! I haven't forgotten him, not for one second. When he arrived in the next world he was looked upon as something of a wonder. No, no, he doesn't need your *l'chaim* at all. He is supported by my holy father on one side and my grandfather on the other." From then on, whenever the chassidim spoke about Reb Mordechai Mishel, they would add the words "*zechuso yagein aleinu*," as one does when speaking about great *tzaddikim*.

AFTER THE REBBE'S RECOVERY THE DOCTORS WARNED the Rebbetzin to watch the Rebbe's health carefully and prevent him

The Worst Person

from straining his weak heart. The Rebbe's *minhag* was to stay in shul wrapped up in his *tallis* and *tefillin* from the morning until 1 or 2 in the afternoon. During this time he would often stand transfixed at the window, gazing at the heavens in holy *d'veikus* with his Creator. Anyone who saw him then felt such a terrifying awe that no one could approach him. As a result of this practice, the Rebbe would eat his first meal very late in the day.

The Rebbetzin made it her duty to make sure that the Rebbe ate regular meals and under her supervision his health slowly improved. Getting the Rebbe to eat, however, was not always such an easy task.

One day the Rebbe stood transfixed at a spot, totally ignoring the food that had been prepared for him. The Rebbetzin waited for an opportunity to catch his attention but his holy demeanor was so awesome that she dared not disturb him. She made a noise by moving the table and chairs, coughed, and finally called out to him, "It's late and you must not strain your heart." But the Rebbe heard nothing.

Finally, in desperation, the Rebbetzin tugged at his clothes and said, "How long will you stand like this?" Only then did she succeed in getting his attention. He sighed a long heartbroken sigh and said, "*Oi!* What can I do? I am the worst person in the world!"

The Rebbetzin was shocked to hear her husband's words and replied, "How can you say such a thing. I myself heard from your father that the *pasuk*, '*Titein emes leYaakov* — Give truth to Yaakov,' could be applied to you! So how can you say that you are the worst person in the world?"

The Rebbe thought for a moment and then asked in wonder, "Did you really hear that yourself from my father?"

"Yes, yes!" she cried. "I heard it myself from your father!"

The Rebbe remained quiet for a moment and then he said, "*Nu*, if so then you can surely believe me that I am telling the truth when I say that I am the worst person imaginable."

AFTER THE REBBE HAD FULLY RECOVERED, THE SADIGERER Chassidus started to increase and expand even more. *Tzaddikim*

Captivated His Chassidim would say that the Sadigerer Rebbe's very holiness was "contagious." As his name and fame spread ever wider so did the numbers of his chassidim grow. Every week new faces appeared, eager to experience for themselves a Shabbos in Sadiger. Already hours before a *tisch*, the vast hall was jam-packed with chassidim who hurried to grab a place.

The magnificent shul of the Sadigerer Rebbe

Often the crowd was so great that it was impossible for them all to fit into the hall, but still they came. They knew that even if they could not see the Rebbe, he could still see them and feel their presence.

Once, while the Rebbe was wishing a *l'chaim* to those at the *tisch*, he suddenly called out: "*L'chaim* to the *Yidden* in the town of Nesiveilitz." At the time no one understood the Rebbe's words, but after Shabbos had terminated, his words were understood by all. A large group of chassidim who had been hoping to spend Shabbos with the Rebbe arrived in Sadiger on Motza'ei Shabbos. Their journey had taken longer than anticipated and they had been forced to spend Shabbos in the town of Nesiveilitz. Although they hadn't been able to see the Rebbe, he had seen them.

Besides his tremendous influence on all matters concerning European Jewry, the Rebbe also had such an overwhelmingly powerful personality that those who had met him could not forget him. A Sadigerer chassid had a son who took to modern ways until he finally became a *mechallel Shabbos*. Grief-stricken, the father turned his back on his son.

The next time the chassid journeyed to Sadiger the Rebbe asked him about his son. "I no longer want to know of him," answered the chassid. "He has forsaken the Torah and mitzvos."

"A chassid who was once at my *tisch* cannot forsake the Torah," the Rebbe told him. "If he has sinned, he will not die without doing *teshuvah*." When the *Yid* returned home he found that his son had indeed repented his former ways and returned to *Yiddishkeit*.

The Rebbe's brother, Reb Menachem Nuchem of Shtefanesht, once said, "If my brother wanted to, he could make all his chassidim so wealthy that they could travel in wagons with golden wheels. He, however, concentrates on a totally different undertaking; he has managed to achieve that whoever visited him once will not have to return to this world!"

NOT FOR NOTHING WAS THE SADIGERER REBBE HAILED as the greatest Rebbe of his era. It was commonplace to hear from

A Living Mussar Sefer

him about events which were about to happen in faraway countries and cities. One of the Rebbe's closest chassidim was the *gaon* Reb Meir Leibish, the Rav of Turka. In his memoirs he writes:

> It is impossible to describe what our eyes have seen and what we have heard from the Rebbe; every different aspect of the coming year was known to him: if food prices would rise or fall, if there would be rain for the crops or not, and also the running of the monarchy — if there would be peace or war. In short, all the future events of the coming year we heard from him long before they happened, and it was so commonplace that it didn't surprise anybody.

When the famed *maggid* and preacher, Reb Hillel of Kolomei, was in Sadiger the Rebbe called him in and told him: "Your job is to travel through the towns giving people *mussar* and encouraging them to change their ways. I want you to also tell me some *mussar*, tell me how I can improve my ways." Reb Hillel didn't feel up to giving the Rebbe *mussar*, but after the Rebbe insisted for a second time he told him: "I have only one observation to make, and that is, why doesn't the Rebbe give *mussar* to his chassidim?" The Rebbe listened to Reb Hillel's words of rebuke and told him, "Our holy father taught us that it is not enough just to say *mussar*, our actions and behavior must also be a living *mussar sefer*."

On another occasion the Rebbe met Reb Isaac'l of Zhidichov who asked the Rebbe to tell him a story, a *maaseh* from one of the Rebbe's zeides. The Rebbe told him: "We know of only one *maaseh*, the words of *Chazal* who say: A person is obligated to say: 'When will my *maasim* (actions) reach the *maasim* (actions) of my fathers?'"

True to his words, the Rebbe's every action was a living *mussar sefer*. In his memoirs, the Rebbe's trusted confidant, Reb Meir Leibish, writes:

> The Rebbe is careful not to waste even a split second, not a moment passes which isn't totally utilized to serve Hashem. Even when he speaks mundane matters with those who have come to see him, the *kedushah* doesn't leave his face for a second, and even while he is busy with those around him it is clearly noticeable that his thoughts are far away in the highest Heavens.
>
> During mealtimes his whole face glows with *kedushah*, and indeed, a simple person as myself cannot possibly grasp or understand his great *kedushah*, but from what I see it is clear that his eating is an *avodah* just like *davening* or putting on *tefillin*.
>
> Where is the pen that can attempt to describe the sweetness of his voice when he makes a *berachah*? It is clearly visible that as he recites the words his physical being ceases to exist, becoming totally subservient to his *neshamah*. The sight of him making a *berachah* is so captivating that afterwards the onlooker doesn't know whether he will be able to resume his daily mundane life, having just felt that this world is really an empty shell.

Once during a *tisch*, the Rebbe's son-in-law, Reb Yisroel Sholom Yosef of Mezibuzh, knocked over a glass of wine, spilling it on the tablecloth. After a few days, Reb Yisroel Sholom Yosef noticed that his *shver* seemed to be upset with him and he realized that it must be due to the incident at the *tisch*. He went up to the Rebbe and apologized, adding that it had been a pure accident, he hadn't spilled the wine on purpose. "That's why I'm upset," the Rebbe answered him. "How can a person move one of his limbs without any *kavanah*?!"

Descendants of the first Sadigerer Rebbe:
the Rebbes Reb Mordechai Sholom Yosef of Sadiger (l.) and Reb Mordechai Shlomo of Boyan (r.)
They were also both sons-in-law of Reb Yisroel Sholom Yosef of Mezibuzh.

THE REBBE WAS VENERATED NOT ONLY AMONG *YIDDEN*, but also by prominent *goyim* (*lehavdil*). Articles about him appeared in

Venerated by the Goyim

the press of Vienna, Berlin, Frankfurt, Prague and elsewhere. It was not unusual for princes, counts and famous writers to journey to Sadiger to see the "Wonder Rabbi" and to speak with him. For such audiences the Rebbe relied on a translator, since he himself spoke no German.

One prominent figure who came to see the Rebbe was Sir Laurence Oliphant, a wealthy and eminent landowner. He was said to have an enormous influence on the English government. For political reasons, he took an interest in the settlement of Palestine. At the time (during the 1870's) there was talk of eventual partition of Turkey. Oliphant tried to convince his government that the Jews should, in that event, have Palestine, the land of their fathers, where they could once again make their home.

Although exactly what he spoke about to the Rebbe was a secret, the Rebbe's translator years later told the chassidim in hints

A grandson of the Sadigerer Rebbe, Reb Menachem Nuchem of Boyan-Chernovitz

and allusions about the contents of their conversation. Oliphant, believing that the Sadigerer Rebbe was the leader of World Jewry, wanted his help to establish a national fund to buy Palestine from Turkey. The Rebbe was supposed to have refused on the grounds that he was a Turkish subject living on a Turkish passport. Moreover, he believed Jews must await redemption by a miracle, not by purchasing land.

After the Rebbe's *petirah* in 1883, Oliphant described his visit in a Viennese journal:

When I was in Vienna, people l trusted told me so much about the Sadigerer Rebbe. I very much wanted to meet him. I thought, come what may, a person who by spirit alone rules thousands of people cannot be an ordinary commonplace human. Since I was then situated near Sadiger, I advised the Rebbe that I would like to meet him. Arriving in the Rebbe's house, I was led into a room much like a princely court, furnished with precious gold and silver antiques. There I met the Rebbe accompanied by two servants. Regal authority was in his face; he spoke intelligently about the situation of the Russian Jews. Though I did not quite understand his conduct, I was nevertheless convinced that he could lead and command his people with just the barest gesture.

IN THE REBBE'S LAST YEAR HE STARTED TO PREPARE himself to leave this world. More and more he secluded himself, sitting for hours on end in deep *d'veikus*. He refused to see people, cutting himself off totally from his surroundings. Although he had never eaten much — just a few spoonfuls a day — he now refused even the bare minimum.

The Bright Star

The home (hoif) of the Rebbe of Sadiger

With the onset of the Yom Tov of Shavuos, thousands of chassidim journeyed to Sadiger to spend Yom Tov in the company of their Rebbe. The chassidim, who drew conclusions from every word the Rebbe did or did not say, could not help but notice the change in his behavior. During *davening* the unusually loud sighs emanating from the Rebbe's room filled the hearts of his followers with dread.

Every year the highlight of the Yom Tov was when the thousands of chassidim would gather in the massive courtyard underneath the Rebbe's room. When the singing and dancing reached their peak, the Rebbe would go outside onto his balcony overlooking the courtyard. With a slight smile on his face the Rebbe would watch his chassidim dance below.

This year, however, even though the chassidim's singing pierced the very heavens, the Rebbe did not appear in front of his chassidim. Instead he stayed in his room surrounded by his sons and *gabbaim*. The Rebbe was deep in thought, quite oblivious to the sounds going on outside. Suddenly the Rebbe aroused himself from his deep *d'veikus* and said, "Each *tzaddik* is given a certain period of time during which he may procure a *yeshuah* for *Yidden*. When this time comes to an end, the *tzaddik* loses his power to do anything, and he is called to the Next World, from where he continues to worry for his people. At this time the *tzaddik* feels as if a voice from Heaven is calling him saying, '*Lech shuvu lachem leoholeichem,*' tell the people who are close to you that the time has arrived for them to return home, '*ve'atah amod poh imadi,*' because you have to leave them and be with Me."

When the Rebbe finished speaking he signaled to his sons to leave the room; he instructed his *gabbai* to tell the chassidim to stop their singing, and instead to go and sit with his sons.

In his last months a very bright star was seen over the skies of Sadiger. When the Rebbe was informed of its presence his expression became very serious and he exclaimed, "Is that so? There has appeared a star." It seemed as if he had been expecting its appearance, as if it foretold news of what was about to happen. The star appeared every night until the night of the Rebbe's *petirah*, after which it was never seen again.[1]

On the night of the 11th of Elul 5643 (1883) the Rebbe's holy *neshamah* ascended upwards. His *petirah* was described by his faithful chassid, Reb Meir Leibish:

> Until the second of his *petirah*, the Rebbe did not rest from his holy *avodah*; even when it appeared that his *neshamah* had already departed, his lips were still moving in constant *tefillah*. Those who saw him in his last minutes understood and realized what *madreigah* he had reached. It is not possible to write at length, for my hands still tremble when I remember what I saw, wonder of wonders …

Zechuso yagein aleinu.

---

1. Before the *petirah* of the Chozeh of Lublin, a bright star was also seen in the skies of Lublin every night until the night of his *petirah*. In the *sefer* "*Tov HaAretz*" (Yerushalayim, 1891) the author writes that every *neshamah* has its own star which is its representative. A *tzaddik* has a brighter star than others, and as his life draws to a close, so the star grows in brightness, sometimes even becoming visible to the human eye.

CHAPTER THIRTEEN
Founding Yeshivos

THROUGHOUT HIS LIFE, REB YISROEL CONCERNED himself with caring and worrying for the youth of the generation. Constantly he urged and exhorted his chassidim about the importance of educating the young. Times had changed and one could no longer afford to presume that the youth would grow up to be the *ehrlich*er *Yidden* their predecessors had been, unless they were provided with a solid foundation.

AT EVERY OPPORTUNITY HE STRESSED AGAIN AND AGAIN the importance of the youth, how they were the future of *Klal Yisroel*. In an article (*Dos Yiddishe Togblatt*), Reb

Concern for the Youth
Alter Yechiel from Reisha recalls the great love that the Rebbe showed to the youth:

> On one Yom Tov, as the chassidim were singing and dancing their lively dances outside the Rebbe's room, the Rebbe appeared on his balcony to watch the dancing. Suddenly

the Rebbe signaled to make a pause in the dancing. In a voice filled with emotion the Rebbe looked at the many *bochurim* present and exclaimed: *"Ashrei yaldoseinu shelo biyeshah ziknoseinu* — Happy is our youth that has not put to shame our elders" (*Succah* 53a).

During a visit to Germany in 1923, the Rebbe addressed a delegation of communal leaders. He explained to them the importance of educating the young and said as follows:

> We find in *Tehillim* (8:3) an interesting statement, *"Mipi o'lelim veyonkim yisadeta oz* — From the mouths of infants and babies You established the Torah." Our Sages (*Medrash Tehillim* Ch. 8) revealed to us a deep insight into the meaning of this *pasuk.*
>
> When Hashem came to give the Torah to *Klal Yisroel,* He demanded that the *Yidden* provide a guarantor that they would indeed keep the Torah properly. They answered Hashem that their fathers and grandfathers could serve as guarantors. Hashem said to them that they were also obligated and could not serve as guarantors. "Who then can we bring?" the *Yidden* asked. "Your children!" Hashem answered. "They can serve as your guarantors."

Sitting, from left to right: the Rebbe, Reb Avrohom Yaakov of Boyan-Lemberg, Reb Nuchem Mordechai of Chortkov

Why was it that Hashem refused to accept the fathers and *zeide*s as guarantors, yet he accepted their children? The reason is because even if we have such great *zeide*s as Avrohom, Yitzchok and Yaakov, this does not yet guarantee the future of the Torah. But when there are generations of children who keep the Torah, this guarantees the survival of the Torah and of the Jewish people.

≍

HARDLY HAD REB YISROEL BECOME REBBE THAN HE embarked on his first major innovation — the founding of yeshivos in Galicia and Poland. In order to understand why **The First Yeshivah** this was such a major innovation, and why it had not been implemented until then, a full historical picture is needed.

Even before *Klal Yisroel* became a people, the yeshivah had already assumed its task of transmitting the Torah from one generation to the next, as *Chazal* inform us (*Yoma* 28b):

> From the earliest days of our Fathers the yeshivah did not cease from them. Avrohom Avinu learned in yeshivah, Yitzchok Avinu learned in yeshivah, Yaakov Avinu learned in yeshivah. In Mitzrayim they had a yeshivah, in the *Midbar* they had a yeshivah.

Already then there existed two types of yeshivos. Yeshivas Shem V'Eiver catered to and taught only those who came to learn in their *beis hamedrash* (see *Migdal Oz, Hilchos Acum* p.1 hal. 3), while the *Avos* were *moser nefesh* to travel around and spread the word of Hashem to whomever they met. The Rambam describes to us quite clearly how the *Avos* spread the teachings of Hashem to their generation and for all future generations:

> Avrohom would travel from one city to the next and he would gather together the townspeople and call out, as it is written, "And he called out in the Name of Hashem, G-d of the Universe." When the people would gather around him

and ask him questions, he would explain to each person according to his understanding until he changed his ways to the *derech ha'emes*. Thousands flocked to him, and they became the *"anshei beis Avrohom."* He implanted in them his teachings and he wrote *sefarim*, which he passed on to Yitzchok who also taught them. And Yitzchok passed this on to Yaakov and appointed him to teach. Yaakov taught his sons, from whom he separated Levi and appointed him the head, and placed him in yeshivah to teach the *derech Hashem* and to keep the mitzvos of Avrohom. And he commanded his sons that there should never cease to be a leader from the sons of Levi so that the Talmud would never be forgotten. And through this process came about a nation that knows Hashem.

And so throughout the ages the yeshivah did not cease from *Klal Yisroel*. At the time of darkness and destruction before the *Churban Beis HaMikdash,* the one and only request of Rabban Yochanan ben Zakkai was, "Give me Yavneh and its scholars." Later on, after the great yeshivos of the *Tannaim* and *Amoraim* in Bavel came the yeshivos of the *Rishonim* and the *Baalei Tosafos* in Europe and then of the *Acharonim* in Poland.

A DESCRIPTION OF THE YESHIVOS IN POLAND IN THE YEAR 5408 (1648) just before the outbreak of the infamous massacres of the

History of Yeshivos in Poland
Geziros Tach VeTat is given to us by the *gaon* Reb Nosson Hanover who writes as follows:

There is no need to bring proof to what is well known, that there was never so much Torah learning throughout *Klal Yisroel* as there was in Poland. Every single *kehillah* had its own yeshivah. They would pay the *Rosh Yeshivah* a handsome wage, so that he could delve into the Torah without worry, and would not need to leave his house except to go to the *beis hamedrash*.

Every *kehillah* would support the *bochurim* with a weekly payment and if the *kehillah* had fifty *baalei battim* they would support at least thirty *bochurim*. There was hardly a house in

Poland in which Torah wasn't learned. Either the head of the house was a *lamdan,* or one of his sons or sons-in-law, and often they were all *lamdanim.* All the *bochurim* and all the *chachamim* and anyone who had just the slightest bit of *yiras Shamayim* would go to the yeshivah to be with the *Rosh Yeshivah.* When the *Rosh Yeshivah* arrived people would ask him their difficulties and he would answer. Afterwards silence fell and the *Rosh Yeshivah* would say the *chiddushim* that had occurred to him.

Great honor was given to the *Rosh Yeshivah* in every *kehillah,* and his words were listened to by all: the poor and the rich alike. He had the power to decree as he felt fit and to punish those who disobeyed him. But even so, he was respected and admired by all, and on Shabbos and Yom Tov the whole *kehillah* would accompany him home.

⤳⤶

THE TERRIBLE MASSACRES AND DISTURBANCES OF *TACH VeTat* (1648) bought an end to this golden period in Poland. The

Learning in the Shteibel great *kehillos* and yeshivos were destroyed and hundreds of thousands found themselves impoverished and homeless overnight. The *Yidden* in Poland never managed to regain their former glory and from then on for the next 300 years a new system of learning cropped up. No longer were the great yeshivos the domain of Torah study. Instead anyone who desired to learn Torah would go to his local shul or *shteibel* where he joined those already there. It was from these informal little *shteiblach* that many famous *geonim* emerged, and indeed the lack of yeshivos did not seem to have much of a detrimental effect on the level of Torah learning.

In a description of his local *shteibel* written over 100 years ago, a *Yid* from Bialystok in Russia wrote:

> How nice and how pleasant it is to enter the *beis hamedrash.* Sitting around the tables are the young and the old, the wise and the simple, the rich and the poor, and they all sit and

learn together. How pleasant it is to walk along the road and to hear the sweet sound of their learning which rises to the very heavens. Here many of the workmen, the tailors, the butchers, and the water-drawers are all great *yirei Hashem* and fluent in all of *Shas*. Even during the night, organized *mishmaros* learn until the morning; many of these *mishmaros* comprise over twenty people and they are increasing steadily.

Although the system of learning in the shuls produced many great *geonim*, it also had a number of major drawbacks. While it worked fine for the clever and for those who enjoyed their learning, there was no extra help or stimulation to encourage those who needed extra attention. Apart from the *shiur*im of the Rav or *Rosh Yeshivah* there was little formal structure or supervision of their progress and growth. Over the years a few major yeshivos were set up in various cities but these did not differ greatly from the *derech* of the *shteiblach*. Although referred to as a yeshivah, they had little in common with the modern-day image of a yeshivah. The curriculum tended to be much more haphazard than what we are accustomed to today. There were neither dormitories nor eating facilities, and as a result the *bochurim* often suffered terribly from deprivation. This in turn lowered the honor of the Torah in the eyes of the masses and caused many to forsake the ways of their elders.

IT WAS DUE TO THESE REASONS THAT IN 1803 THE *GAON* Reb Chaim of Volozhin opened a yeshivah, which was established

Volozhin Yeshivah within a framework that would provide all the needs of the *bochurim*. Volozhin has become recognized as the first modern-day yeshivah. Volozhin was a completely independent institution; it had its own *beis hamedrash* and a staff that continually watched and guided the *bochurim* who were under their command. The *bochurim* were released from all their previous burdens and were able to devote themselves totally to their learning. The yeshivah paid the local *Yidden* in Volozhin to house and feed the boys, and as the yeshivah grew, there was hardly a home in the town that did not house a *bochur*. Not only were the yeshivah *bochurim* not viewed as an imposition by their hosts, they were even a welcome source of income. Indeed Reb Chaim was careful not to ask the local population to contribute to the yeshivah in any way. He did not want them to regard the yeshivah as a burden. Instead *meshulachim* were sent to all corners of the land to raise funds.

Although the Volozhiner Yeshivah was extremely successful and proved to be the first of many such yeshivos in Lithuania, in Poland and Galicia the idea was frowned upon and did not gain any support. The first yeshivah with dormitories and eating facilities was opened in Galicia over 100 years later, in 1905. The exact reason why the chassidim refused to copy the Volozhin style of yeshivah is not known, but in his *sefer "Divrei Chaim,"* the Szanzer Rav makes known his disapproval and he writes:

> There are no yeshivos here in our country for a number of good reasons, which I heard from my *shver* (the Baruch Taam) from Leipnik. Instead groups gather together in the shuls and *batei medrash*, and there they learn the Torah and the *gemara*.

Although the Szanzer Rav does not divulge his reasons for opposing the founding of yeshivos, it is possible to guess what worried him. Until then it had been the norm for everyone to learn together in the local *shteibel*. There, fathers would learn with their sons and grandsons, and the tradition and ways of one generation were passed down to the next generation. These benefits might be lost in the yeshivah, where the *bochurim* learned together and were severed from their family and *kehillah*. This reason and others is given in a letter written by one of the chassidishe *gedolim* of the time, Reb Tzvi Hirsh of Liska:

> The *minhag* of not introducing yeshivos here in Poland is in my opinion justified for a number of reasons. In the *batei medrashim* whole *kehillos* sit and learn together in purity. Here *bochurim* are able to learn side by side with their elders and can be influenced from their ways, a benefit which is not always possible when youngsters sit by themselves in yeshivos.

Thus, while in Lithuania the yeshivos became the accepted way of education, in Poland and Galicia things continued in the time-honored fashion and the *bochurim* continued to learn in their local *shteiblach*.

However, at the beginning of the 20th century, the *gedolim* in Poland decided that the time had come to abandon the old *derech* and to open modern yeshivos as had been done in Lithuania.

The reason for the change was not due to the failure of the old system but because of the new dangers against which the local *shteibel* offered little protection. The *maskilim* and other secular groups were slowly but surely making their influence felt in Poland. Many *bochurim* became ensnared in their trap and left the *beis hamedrash* in pursuit of other studies. Those who had already forsaken Torah and mitzvos did their utmost to persuade their former companions to join them. The yeshivos offered a *bochur* shelter from those influences that sought to uproot him from the Torah. Here he was protected from the schemes of the rebellious youths who roamed the streets. Under the watchful gaze of the *Roshei Yeshivah*, the *bochurim* were insulated from the foreign influences that had engulfed many *kehillos*.

≈)⸚

Bradoshin Yeshivah

IT IS WORTH MENTIONING THAT THE PERSON WHO HAD the *zechus* to open the first modern yeshivah in Poland was not one of the famous *rabbanim* or *gedolim*, but a *Yid* by the name of Reb Doniel Shternfeld. He was one of the respected *talmidei chachamim* of the town of Bradoshin in East Galicia. The yeshivah, known as Yeshivas Toras Chaim of Bradoshin, opened its doors for the first time on the 1st of Iyar 5665 (1905), and already for its first *z'man* it attracted over 100 *bochurim*.

The yeshivah owed much of its initial success to the Chortkover Rebbe, who was one of the main forces behind its opening and its continued existence. Since Reb Doniel Shternfeld was only a private individual he could not hope to succeed without the support and backing from the *gedolim* of the time. This backing he found in Chortkov.

In a letter published at the time, in the newspaper "*Machazikei Hadass*," the Rebbe stressed the importance of the new yeshivah. He urged everyone to do their utmost to ensure "that this house will indeed produce *talmidim* who are true *talmidei chachamim*." He also

expressed his hope that "everyone in *Klal Yisroel* will realize and
understand the tremendous importance of supporting yeshivos
like these, and will willingly contribute to promote the growth of
Torah, which acts as a pillar of
fire to light up the way for *Klal
Yisroel.*" The Rebbe ends off the
letter with an assurance that
"such yeshivos will protect us
from the evil waters that seek to
flood every house and dwelling."

The influence the Rebbe's letter had on the general populace can
be gauged by the great importance the yeshivah attached to his
words. The Rebbe's letter was followed by an appeal from the *hanhalah* of the yeshivah in which they wrote:

> We have no words to thank the *Nesi Elokim*, the Glory of
> Israel, the *manhig* of thousands and myriads of *Yidden*, our
> teacher Reb Yisroel of Chortkov, for his backing and his help
> to found and support our yeshivah. In addition to his advice
> and *berachos*, he has also given us sizable amounts of money.
>
> No doubt his pure words will leave a deep imprint not
> only in the Heavenly spheres but also here in this world.
> Who of all our brothers, who listen to the Rebbe's every word
> and action, will not heed his words? The Rebbe himself has
> already twice donated large sums of money for which we
> cannot do enough to thank him.
>
> We cannot adequately express our gratitude for all that
> the Rebbe has done for our yeshivah. May his reign be
> long and prosperous and in good health.
>
> From all the *hanhalah* and members of the holy yeshivah
> Toras Chaim in Bradoshin who bow toward his honor and

*Title page of the rules of Yeshivas Bradoshin
(printed 1905)*

consider themselves like dust under the Rebbe's feet.

Reb Doniel Shternfeld distributed a booklet across Galicia in which he outlined the conditions of acceptance:

This yeshivah is open both to the rich and the poor, both from this town and from other towns. Whoever desires to learn in the yeshivah must first send a letter inquiring if there is a place for him. Together with the letter must also be sent a letter of recommendation from his Rav about his standard of learning and his *middos*. I implore the *rabbanim* not to give certificates to those who do not learn with *hasmadah* nor to those who have bad *middos*, for such *bochurim* could *chas vesholom* destroy the whole yeshivah. "*Chachamim hizaharu b'divreichem!*" The *bochurim* will be carefully looked after and we shall worry for them as a father cares for his only son.

The yeshivah was probably the most modern of its time. Hygiene was given top priority, as Rav Shternfeld wrote, "The rooms of the dormitory are large and airy and conform to the highest standards of cleanliness set by the government." In the list of *takanos* of the yeshivah the boys were instructed, "The *talmidim* must take care to keep their clothes extremely clean, and the *mashgichim* will be very strict about this."

Next to the *beis hamedrash,* which could seat up to 200 boys, was a kitchen (an innovation which did not even exist in Volozhin where the *bochurim* dined at the homes of locals). The Rav of Bradoshin, Reb Pinchos HaLevi Horowitz, was appointed *Rosh Yeshivah*. Rav Horowitz was acclaimed as one of the great *poskim* of Galicia and authored a number of important *sefarim*. Rav Horowitz would deliver a daily *shiur* and would also spend much of the day in the yeshivah learning with the *bochurim* and supervising their progress. Two additional *maggidei shiur* were appointed, plus a *mashgiach*.

In hindsight one can say that although the yeshivah did not emerge as one of the great yeshivos of its time, it nonetheless achieved a major goal. It was the catalyst for many other yeshivos, which soon sprang up across Poland and Galicia, saving many families and *kehillos* from total destruction.

WITHIN HALF A YEAR OF THE OPENING OF THE YESHIVAH in Bradoshin, so many *bochurim* besieged it, clamoring to be ac-

Stanislov Yeshivah cepted, that it became necessary to open a second yeshivah in the neighboring town of Stanislov. Like its predecessor, this yeshivah was also supported by the Chortkover Rebbe, who made an emotional plea to his chassidim to help sustain the yeshivah.

The Rebbe publicized a letter telling of his immense pleasure that the yeshivah had opened, and he added:

> This is truly a *davar be'ito*. Indeed for a long time it has upset me to see the terrible lack of yeshivos which can be felt across Galicia. Due to this, many of those who originally dedicated themselves to learning Torah have become weakened; and without the right center where they can ascend properly in Torah, they gradually slip away, one by one. They forsake the Torah and instead bury themselves in the pits of the *haskalah* and slowly the Torah is *chas vesholom* becoming forgotten day by day.
>
> Therefore my heart rejoices that Hashem has given us the *hatzlachah* to open a general yeshivah which is to be led by a Rav who is great in Torah who will lead the yeshivah and teach the *bochurim* until they will be on the level to receive *semichah*. I have no doubt that the name of this yeshivah will be praiseworthy and will increase the *kavod haTorah*.
>
> I am therefore sending my contribution of 72 rubles to support this holy institution and with the help of Hashem, I shall

bli neder every year send the sum of 26 rubles. I also hereby ask all our chassidim to give generously to the yeshivah, both from their own private funds and also from the communal funds in every *kehillah* and city. Thereby the yeshivah will be able to support the poor who learn in its ranks, and from whom the Torah is destined to shine forth. Through this, the honor and glory of the Torah will be uplifted and will illuminate the surroundings like the blazing sun. In this merit we should be worthy of the *geulah*, as *Chazal* have told us that we will be redeemed in the *zechus* of the Torah.

The yeshivah in Stanislov was headed by the world-famed *gaon* Reb Aryeh Leib Horowitz, who was Rav of the town and author of the classic responsa *sefer "Harei Besamim."* The *Rosh Yeshivah* was Reb Eliezer Kuterdosky, who had the distinction of being a well-known chassid of the Rebbes of Rizhin and also a product of the Volozhiner Yeshivah. A second acclaimed *gaon*, by the name of Reb Yekusiel Kamelhar, was appointed as deputy *Rosh Yeshivah*. Under their guidance the yeshivah prospered and soon became venerated throughout Galicia. The change that the yeshivah wrought on its surroundings is evident from an article written at the time by a *Yid* from Stanislov:

> The *kol Yaakov* which had fallen silent in our city and the *kol haTorah* which had almost ceased to be heard in the *batei medrashim* has aroused itself and is once again to be heard in the streets. Every time we pass by the holy yeshivah our hearts become full of joy to hear the *kol Yaakov* ring out from the voices of the *bnei yeshivah* who sit and learn with diligence and desire. The new wind that emanates from the yeshivah's windows warms the heart of every *Yid* to the Torah.
>
> The holy yeshivah blooms and blossoms, and we are all hopeful that the *berachah* of the *gaon* and *tzaddik*, the Rebbe of Chortkov, that the yeshivah will light up the surroundings like the blazing sun, will speedily be fulfilled. And the whole land will soon be full of Torah and *yiras Shamayim*.

IN ADDITION TO OPENING YESHIVOS, THE REBBE REALIZED
that other methods were also necessary in order to protect the youth

**Catering to
the Youth**

from outside influences. The Stanislover *Rosh
Yeshivah*, Reb Yekusiel Kamelhar, recorded an interesting conversation that he had with the Rebbe, in
connection with catering to the youth of the time.

Reb Yekusiel had written a book detailing various episodes of
Jewish history from previous ages. When he brought the book to
the Rebbe as a present, the Rebbe told him that he was grateful
that someone had finally taken upon himself to record the history
of *Klal Yisroel*.

"No doubt you are surprised that I advocate spending time writing history," the Rebbe said. "Twenty years ago, I would not have
encouraged you like I do now. Then the shuls and *batei medrash* were
full of boys and young men who learned Torah day and night. They
had no need for such books. Now, however, times have changed.
Today's *bochurim* want and expect to know about worldly matters.
If they can't find their information from *frum* sources then they will
turn to other sources of information."

Reb Yekusiel told the Rebbe that he had received a fair amount of
criticism from various *rabbanim*. They found it demeaning that an
acclaimed *Rosh Yeshivah* should waste his time writing stories when
he could rather be composing and writing brilliant *divrei Torah*. Reb
Yekusiel writes that when the Rebbe heard these words, he gave a
deep sigh and in a pain-filled voice he exclaimed: "These *rabbanim*
do not understand the true situation of the youth of nowadays, they
fail to comprehend the real needs of the moment!"

Another well-known Rav, Reb Moshe Leiter, writes that the
Rebbe actually approached him and asked him to write a series of
books about Jewish history according to traditional rabbinical
sources. Reb Moshe told the Rebbe that a certain Reb Zev Yaavetz
had already compiled such a work. The Rebbe requested that he be
sent the books so that he could see if they fulfilled the necessary
requirements.

Despite the Rebbe's efforts in opening and promoting yeshivos,
many parents still did not understand the urgency of sending their
sons to a yeshivah. The parents themselves had never learned in a

yeshivah and they did not see the terrible crime if their sons also did not.

When the Rebbe asked one man whose son was in danger of falling by the wayside, why he refused to allow his son to go to yeshivah, the man answered: "The Rebbe must understand that he is from the olden times. My son is from the modern generation. Going to a yeshivah is simply not in keeping with the times."

"I am the one who is from the modern generation," the Rebbe retorted. "You are the one who is old fashioned. In the Haggadah we say: '*Mitechilah ovdei avodah zarah hayu avoiseinu* — At first our forefathers were idol worshipers and now Hashem has drawn us near to His service.'"

The *gemara* tells us that the *Beis HaMikdash* was destroyed due to the fact that "They did not first recite a blessing on the Torah." This difficult statement has been explained by the various commentaries in many different ways. In his *sefer* "*Ginzei Yisroel*," the Rebbe added his own thoughts, based on the trials the youth of the day were facing:

> One must understand why nowadays when a young man studies secular topics he immediately forsakes the Torah and becomes *hefker* and loses his *Yiddishkeit*. In generations gone by, this was not the case. *Gedolei Yisroel* studied other sciences and were even renowned among the *goyim* for their knowledge and understanding. The extra subjects did not harm or influence them in any manner. We must understand what has brought about this change.
>
> It appears to me that in former times *Yidden* realized that Torah and *yirah* was their real goal and it formed the basis and foundation of their life. The Torah was their staple diet and the extra subjects were viewed only as of secondary importance and were regarded as a side interest. A child was first educated in Torah and only after he had filled himself with a proper dose of Torah did he venture out to learn additional topics. Nowadays, however, secular subjects are injected into the pupils from a very young age, before they have had a chance to fill themselves with Torah. The result is

that the Torah gets relegated to a back seat while the secular studies occupy the first place. *Chazal* alluded to this woeful system in their statement that "they did not first recite a blessing on the Torah." At that time also they did not give priority to their Torah studies over their secular studies.

∾)∾

WITHIN THREE OR FOUR YEARS OF THE OPENING OF Yeshivas Bradoshin, more than ten other yeshivos were opened across Poland and Galicia. In the town of Barzhan the Maharsham opened Yeshivah Daas Torah, and in Ger the Gerrer Rebbe opened Yeshivas Darchei Noam, to name just two examples. The First World War, however, brought a sudden end to all these new yeshivos, and most of them did not reopen after the war. Nevertheless the impact and the importance of the yeshivos wasn't quickly forgotten by the *Yidden* of Poland.

Keren HaTorah

After the war, Agudas Yisroel set up a special organization called Keren HaTorah whose job it was to support existing yeshivos across Poland and Lithuania and to further encourage and finance the building of new yeshivos. These efforts culminated with the opening of the world-famous Yeshivas Chachmei Lublin, which was the foremost Torah establishment in Poland. This yeshivah owed much of its success to the unstinting efforts of the Rebbe in promoting the yeshivah and convincing the general populace about the importance of such an institution (see at length in Chapter 21).

In addition to the help that the Rebbe offered yeshivos and *mosdos*, he also gave freely of his time and strength to speak and be *mechazeik* boys on a personal level. In the Lubliner yeshivah over a quarter of the *talmidim* were Chortkover chassidim. After the Rebbe's *petirah* in 1934 these *talmidim* issued a public proclamation to *bochurim* across Poland in which they voiced the part that the Rebbe had played in their lives:

> Dear Brothers! For many years we have shared the same aims and goals. We have become united with one destiny. Your joy was our joy and your problems our problems.

Fundraising coupons, signed by the Rebbes of Chortkov (1) and Ger (2)

Together we journeyed every year to Chortkov to see the holy Rebbe and there we joined together like brothers.

Therefore we trust that you will give thought to our words. We are witnesses today to the spiritual decline that has drowned many precious *neshamos*. Many young Jews are falling into the trap of the powers of evil while we stand by, helpless to stop it.

*A letter from
the Rebbe in support
of Yeshivas Chachmei Lublin*

We must realize that if we have been so fortunate as to be spared the same fate, it was only in the *zechus* of the holy Rebbe who shielded us with his *kedushah*. Through his influence we remained united and he purified all who were attached to him.

After the Rebbe's *petirah*, a Chortkover yeshivah was opened in his memory in Yerushalayim (see at length in Chapter 25). This was considered a fitting and appropriate tribute to the Rebbe, a project that perpetuated his life's mission.

With the destruction of *Yiddishkeit* in Europe in the Second World War by the accursed Nazis, it seemed to many as if the glory of the great yeshivos of Poland had come to an end. But today much of the glory has been restored and the *kol haTorah* is to be heard once again. New yeshivos have been built and are continuing to be built and opened at an unbelievably fast pace. The yeshivah world is alive and as vibrant as ever!

CHAPTER FOURTEEN

In Support of Work

ANOTHER INNOVATION WHICH THE REBBE PIO-
neered was the opening of the "General *Cheder*," a
network of schools and training centers where boys who
were not capable of learning Torah were taught a pro-
fession, so they would be able to fend for themselves and not have
to rely on charity.

ALTHOUGH THE REBBE PUT HIS UTMOST INTO THE OPEN-
ing of new yeshivos and centers of learning, he realized that they

**Pioneering
New Ideas**

formed only part of the defense against the ever-
growing threat from the non-Jewish world. The
Rebbe knew that if the *chareidim* were to win the
fight against the *maskilim* and the other foreign influences that
sought to penetrate into every *frum* home in Galicia, it was vital that
the *chareidim* broaden their horizons. Yeshivos provided protection
for those inside their walls, but what would happen to those who

were not gifted enough to continue learning? What would happen to those who had learning difficulties and never succeeded in their learning? Therefore the Chortkover Rebbe proposed that every community set up its own workshops (*batei melachah*) where such *bochurim* would be taught a trade. The workshops would be staffed only by *frum Yidden,* thereby sheltering the *bochurim* from having to turn to *goyim* or secular *Yidden* for help.

Nowadays it has become the accepted fact that not all boys are able to cope in a regular yeshivah system. Allowances must be made for those who are incapable of progressing in their learning. A hundred years ago, however, such an idea was considered to be something of a revolution. Every boy was expected to learn all day regardless of his capabilities, and there was no alternative arrangement for those who could not keep up. The Rebbe knew that it would not be easy to educate a whole generation but he was willing to try. He would have to face much opposition, but nevertheless he felt that he could not keep quiet.

⸙

Recognizing a Person's Mission in This World

THERE ARE MANY INTERESTING STORIES TOLD OF HOW the Rebbe would often decide the future of his chassidim. He instructed some of them to stay in learning and make the Torah their life's occupation. He advised others to leave the yeshivah and head into the world of business and commerce.

The Potiker Rav, Reb Shlomo Zalman Horowitz, would often recount how he had ended up in the *Rabbanus*. These are his words as recorded in the foreword to his *sefer "Beis Aharon"*:

> It is only due to the Rebbe that I became a Rav. As a *bochur* I never dreamt about such an idea. Then it was the standard practice for a *bochur* to learn for many years *Shas* and *Shulchan Aruch*, regardless of his future plans. We all knew that as *bochurim* we were expected to sit and learn and become *talmidei chachamim*; this is how it was among

Old chassidim reminiscing about days gone by. Reb Yossel Halpern of Manchester (r.) visiting the Potiker Rav in his home on the East Side of New York.

Chortkover chassidim. Although I had received *semichah* from various *gedolim*, I had never intended to actually use it.

A number of years after my *chasunah*, my father and my *shver* decided that the time had come for me to start to earn a living. The three of us went to the Rebbe to discuss with him the different options available to me. Suddenly the Rebbe said, "Why not *Rabbanus*?" I answered the Rebbe that although I would do whatever he told me, I begged him to leave me out of the *Rabbanus*. "Why don't you want to be a Rav?" the Rebbe persisted. I explained that I was afraid to assume the responsibility to *pasken sha'alos*. In addition I was concerned that my standard of learning might not be good enough as befits a Rav. The Rebbe did not answer me directly. Instead he turned to my father and exclaimed: "In this orphaned generation that we live in, who else should become a Rav, if not someone who is afraid? Is it better to take someone who is not afraid?" And thus I ended up in the *Rabbanus*.

Another young man whom the Rebbe forced into the *Rabbanus* was the Rav of Yebrozna, Reb Tzvi Hirshorn, who became known in prewar Galicia as a prominent and active leader on behalf of the *Yidden*. He was also a gifted writer and his deep and penetrating essays were printed in a number of newspapers (a few of his articles are quoted in this book). His great future was cut short during the war, when he met a martyr's death. In a letter, Reb Tzvi recounts the Rebbe's involvement in getting him to enter the *Rabbanus*:

> During my stay in Chortkov, I consulted my teacher and mentor, the Rebbe of Chortkov, about my future in life, which way I should go and what path I should take. The holy Rebbe advised me that after my *chasunah* I should not go into the business world. Rather, he said, I should perfect my knowledge of *Shas* and *Shulchan Aruch*. He added that it would be a big loss for *Klal Yisroel* if a person with my capabilities went into business. He assured me that I would have a great future in the *Rabbanus* and would be able to bring much *berachah* to Orthodoxy as a whole.
>
> I protested that I wasn't suited for such a life. I had no desire to be in the limelight and was too shy to stand up and guide others. In addition, the idea of having to be dependent on the *kehillah* for my wages was against my nature. I was not descended from a rabbinical family and regarded myself as just a regular person. I also lacked the necesssary qualifications to act as a Rav, being unfamiliar with many of the *halachos*.
>
> The Rebbe, however, pushed aside all my protests. He told me that as a Rebbe he is commanding me to accept his ruling. He said that I did possess the talent to become a Rav and leader. After my *chasunah* I was to dedicate myself to learning. Once I had completed my learning and was ready to assume a position, I would not find it difficult to get a post. The Agudah would also lend me their support and backing.

Reb Tzvi moved to Kobrin where he became one of the prized *talmidim* of the *gaon* Reb Pesach Pruskin. Later on Reb Pesach gave him *semichah*, after which he embarked on the path that the Rebbe had outlined for him.

The Rebbe once asked him to speak in the great shul in Chortkov in front of hundreds of *Yidden* who had assembled at the Rebbe's request. The Rebbe honored the gathering with his presence. Throughout Reb Tzvi's speech the Rebbe sat there listening to his words. This was a rare and almost unique gesture from the Rebbe to his chassid.

≈≈

There were others, however, who came to the Rebbe hoping to receive his *berachah* to enter the *Rabbanus*, but left disappointed. To one such *talmid chacham* who asked the Rebbe why he hadn't allowed him to become a Rav, the Rebbe replied. "There are no shortage of people of your caliber who serve as *rabbanim*. However, if you remain a *baal habayis*, you will serve as an example to others. People will look up to you as someone who has succeeded in combining being a *talmid chacham* and also being a successful businessman. Therefore you will achieve more as a role model by remaining a businessman than by becoming a Rav."

A very unusual incident happened to Reb Menachem Distenfeld from Lemberg, when he approached the Rebbe for advice about his future. Reb Menachem had decided to become a Rav and he wanted the Rebbe to guide him about where to start his studies. The Rebbe listened to his question and then he answered that Reb Menachem should attend medical school in Vienna. After a few moments of awkward silence, Reb Menachem's father, who was also present, tried to clarify the issue, thinking that perhaps the Rebbe had not understood the question. His son wanted to know whether he should go to yeshivah in Warsaw or Lemberg — and not to attend medical school in Vienna.

A haskamah from the Rebbe in which he tells of his pleasure that a businessman who is busy making a living is still able to delve into the Torah and write chiddushim on the Rambam

מכתב תעודת קודש

מכבוד קדושת אדמו״ר צדיק יסוד עולם, אספקלריא המאירה, רבן של ישראל, מופת הדור והדור, המפורסם בכל קצוי תבל, כקש״ת מרנא ורבנא תפארת **ישראל מטשארטקוב** שליט״א החונה כעת בוויו

ב״ה ד׳ לך תרפ״ט וויעו.

שלו׳ רב לכבוד ידידינו היקר הוו״ח המופלא ומופלג מו״ה אהרן רייטער נ״י,

אחדשה״ט, מכתבו הגיעני כן הקונטרס ממחברתו הגיע, והי׳ למראה עיני טוהר כ״ק אדמו״ר שליט״א והוטב בעיני קדשו שאיש סוחר שטרוד להביא טרף לביתו קובע עתים לתורה ויגע ועמל לעשות פרחים וצמחים בשדי הרמב״ם ונושאי כליו, אך ידע כבודו אשר כ״ק אדמו״ר שליט״א אינו נותן הסכמה על ספרים, אך האצל ברכתו הטהורה עליו שהשרית יעזור לו שיומל לישב באהלה של תורה בהרחבה ונחת לאיוש״ט וספרו ימצא חן בעיני כל רואי.

והנני בזה ידידו דורש המזכירו לטוב בקורש הכותב בפקודת קדשו

יוסף שטערנבערג

They soon found out that the Rebbe had understood their question quite clearly. The Rebbe looked at Reb Menachem and said: "Your name is Menachem and you will be an *ehrlicher* doctor who consoles and helps people. Not only that, but by being a doctor you will save your own life as well as the lives of others."

The Rebbe instructed Reb Menachem to move to Vienna. As for the concern that it was a city of loose morality, the Rebbe reassured him. He told him that even at the most secular place in Vienna it would be to him as though he was at his Rebbe's *tisch*.

Reb Menachem did indeed attend medical school in Vienna. There was, however, one very anti-Semitic professor who always went out of his way to fail Jewish students. He did so by especially giving the hardest lectures on Shabbos, those that dealt with the composition of the head and the mind. Many Jewish students struggled to keep up and were confronted by the prospect of failure, because even if they attended the lectures they were unable to take notes. Reb Menachem informed the Rebbe of the problem. The Rebbe had told him to become a doctor but he would not pass the exams without remembering the lectures on the head.

One day, not long before the exams, the Rebbe summoned Reb Menachem to him. They stayed in a closed room for several hours. Reb Menachem emerged ready to take the exams. The Rebbe had spent several hours explaining to him in great detail how the brain functions. No note-taking was necessary because no chassid ever forgot any word spoken to him by the Rebbe. Reb Menachem passed the exams without a problem.

With the outbreak of the Second World War, Reb Menachem was sent to a concentration camp. One day the Nazis *ym"s* came looking for Jewish medical personnel to fight a typhus epidemic among their staff. Reb Menachem was permitted to leave the camp and was able to escape to the forest through the back door of a patient's house. He was picked up by Ukrainian partisans who would have killed him on the spot, but for their own need for a doctor. Many other *nissim* which he experienced were related directly to his having become a doctor, and for the rest of his life, even when he came to America, he viewed himself as a *sheliach* of the Rebbe.

Thus the Rebbe had a fixed philosophy that not everyone had come into this world to become a Rav or hold a rabbinical position. Every person was governed by the personal capabilities or limitations with which he was created. It was this same view that the Rebbe sought to impose on the wider public, when he announced the formation of the General *Cheder*. Not every person was destined to climb to great heights. Still, that was not a reason to abandon these people and leave them to their own fate.

⁊⁊

REB YEHOSHUA BAUMOL WAS ONE OF THE DISTINGUISHED *rabbanim* in Poland. (He was killed during the Second World War.)

Combating the Despair In a biography about his Rebbe, the Lubliner Rav, Reb Meir Shapiro, who was instumental in opening one of the first General *Chadarim*, Reb Baumol discusses the issue of the General *Cheder* at length:

> In Galicia at the time a new trend had emerged that became too obvious to be ignored. A dire shortage of jobs and increased competition meant that there was an ever diminishing prospect of earning a decent living. In order to combat the problem, more and more *bochurim* were turning to the secular world for help. Slowly but surely, the steady trickle of boys leaving the confines of the shuls and yeshivos increased, until it became a virtual flood.
>
> The effects of this mass walkout could be felt throughout the community. Long before a *bochur* reached the stage of worrying about his future, he had already been poisoned by the air of despair around him. As they began to learn about the world of reality in which they lived, the young *bochurim* soon lost all interest in their *sefarim*. A cloud of worry and foreboding hung over their heads. If they continued with their yeshivah studies in the time-honored fashion, they would later be unable to find themselves a job or a roof over their heads.

Thus the *chadarim* and yeshivos began to lose their precious students to the local colleges and universities. This changeover often caused the boys to change their lifestyles as well. No longer did the Torah dictate their priorities in life.

It was at this point, in the year 1912, that the famous chassidic Rebbe of Chortkov, who was renowned as one of the greatest *tzaddikim* in Galicia, devised a way out of the dilemma. As he understood it, there was a vital need for a basic change in the *cheder* and yeshivah system. Alongside the traditional *cheder*, a new type of *cheder* would be opened, the *"Cheder Klali —* General *Cheder."*

All children would be tested to assess their abilities and then divided into two groups. Those children who showed promise in their learning would go to the traditional *cheder*, and the others would go to the General *Cheder*.

In such places, along with the traditional studies, a craft or trade would also be taught, that would enable the person to earn a living when he left the *Talmud Torah*. In addition, the program of schooling would also be different than that of a normal *cheder*. Since most of these boys would not be going on to a long and comprehensive stay in yeshivah, their program must be designed with this in mind. To this end, the hours of *gemara* study would be kept to a minimum and more time spent instead on *halachah* and practical *Yiddishkeit*, which was vital if the boys were to lead an observant life.

The Rebbe of Chortkov was under no illusion as to the difficulty of the task that lay ahead of him. As simple and obvious as his plan might seem, for many his idea was totally revolutionary. Once he tried to put his plan into effect he would meet with powerful opposition from many quarters who wanted to resist any new modern adjustments to the time-honored system of the *cheder*.

The Rebbe understood the concerns and worries of those who disagreed with him. Still, he could not sit by idly and watch whole communities crumble and disappear. The

Rebbe could not just ignore the massive cracks in the old education system of the *cheder*. He would have to take action.

≈≈

THE REBBE'S FIRST COURSE OF ACTION WAS TO CALL A conference of *gedolim* to discuss the problem and to let them know

Agudas HaChareidim

firsthand the full extent of the calamity. The Rebbe knew full well that in order for his plan to succeed, he needed the consent and the backing from all circles of *Klal Yisroel*. To this end the Rebbe formed a new group called "*Agudas HaChareidim*," comprised of the Rebbes of Boyan, Sadiger, Husyatin, Vishnitz, Antonia and other *gedolim*. Afterwards the Rebbe called for an inaugural meeting of the new group in the town of Chernovitz.

Already before the conference took place rumors were rife about the upcoming event. The newspaper "*HaMitspeh*" wrote as follows:

> This coming Monday, Erev Rosh Chodesh Nissan (1912), a secret meeting of the Rebbes of Galicia and Bukovina will take place in Chernovitz. The purpose of the meeting is to combat the downward slide in *Yiddishkeit* and in living standards that has gripped Galicia, and to reverse this trend. The reason why the meeting has not been widely publicized is apparently due to the wish of the organizers. They say that it is not a secret meeting but rather a private meeting. The reason given, they explain, is because any plan that has not been fully developed is not yet ready to be presented to the broader public. What is known is that the conference is the brainchild of the Chortkover Rebbe who has been campaigning for change for some time. We have also heard that right after the meeting they will issue a public letter in which they will explain their plans and decisions.

In an open letter written half a year later, at the founding of Agudas Yisroel, the Rebbe explained the meeting in Chernovitz as follows:

The holy idea to found an organization to help Klal Yisroel also occurred to me and to the other leaders of Klal Yisroel in our district. We saw that the major principles of our faith are being eroded, and that the younger generation is no longer able to prevail in the difficult battles from inside and out. We therefore decided, myself and the *rabbanim* and *tzaddikim*, that it is not the time to keep still. To this end we came together during the previous Nissan to work out how to defeat the evil and to stop the storm enveloping the four corners of our religion.

And now my fellow brothers, you can see which way we are heading and what our goal is. If you share the same worries and also the same ideas and solutions as we do, we will be prepared to join with you. Let us hope that our combined efforts will create a strong bond and we will indeed succeed in healing the wounds of the nation and uplifting the honor of Yisroel and the Torah.

After the conference had adjourned, a public proclamation was issued which the Rebbe signed, together with the other *gedolim* who had attended. In the proclamation they pledged to undertake a series of measures to curb the need to seek help from secular sources. Firstly, a branch of *Agudas HaChareidim* would be set up in every town and city across Eastern Europe and beyond. These branches would then bear responsibility to establish a "General *Cheder*" where all would be accepted regardless of their ability to pay. To this end the Rebbe had amassed the astronomic sum of over a million Austrian crowns to fund the project.

A radical change in the General *Cheder* was the departure from learning only Torah the entire day. Two hours a day of secular studies would be introduced, namely the language of the country and arithmetic. The teachers of the secular studies were to be only *frum* people who would not harm the children with their views.

The second paragraph pledged to open a number of regular yeshivos where *bochurim* with a bright and promising future would be able to advance their learning in a comfortable environment. They would also receive hot meals daily.

בהתאספנו יחד לטכס עצה על דבר צרכת הדור הזה, בראותנו לדאבון נפשנו איך התורה הקדושה הולכת ומשתכחת חלו מנערי ב"י כל בתי כנסיות ומדרשות ריקנים. אסור וחנבשר מסכ"י בתי שרוס. כי הערים ידעו לבתי ספר העמים ולבתי המדרשות הדורים. ובהם שלא כרצון הדיים. וכולם תחת מסה הסצורים, שמכרחים רגם לכנס להם איזה בסם צרכת שינצילדו. וסוף הדבר אשר כל בתי לאם. ידאכו נהרהרים ומשטחדת הדת מסני חילול שבת בכתי הספר לעמ'ס. בחלי סריק על' תורה ומצות בכלל. ואף המשרדים בתיים חסר אשר ארכת התורה כנגד כלבם. ונלדם לטמט תורה ללמוד בהשיטות שנחימכו בכסת סירה בכאלידיצא וכנאמונא מסני הראשכת. הלא ובנלתי מכובדת בעיני הברירים כאמנגד אלה כי הערים הם הערער בכל בכר עבר ונגה רבה חנעונה בקרב הרוד הצעיר לכן לטמן שום טצצוור לדאם השוטם והולך בכל ערי ישראל. הם לא נדר לכנס איזה עצה חרומם יחומו חד כל נערי ב"י כבאםם כלים משפחות דרת. היוצאות הנצאות חד תחם יהלוך טרוזוי חחרום. הועד יה אם רוזבן חיל התאחדנו באיש אחר כלנ אחד בדדה אחד. אשר בנצבד העת הנוראה האה, לטמן הסיק חין ארבת הדוהצ הקרושה בכל צעירי עמנו ב"י. וגם להחזיק דרת בין סדרות העם בכלל בדוך בדדי שתמשרת לו מן הצכון ברוך הוא. והנאמרת כו מן האדם.

(א) שחומדינה אנודות חרידים בכל עיר ועיר אשר ראשית מטרתם יהיו ליסר חלמוד תורה כללית בכל עיר אשר ילטו שמה. יחד עשי וענ' כלי סום סרות. ובכל בדרכות ועתר. מסי מלמרים מוטחים וידא'ה. ולטמ נרצם לנו את בנידם. להחהר הכללי של אנודות חדידים ללטדות תחהק וירטנו כראם שלא יאמרו בשום אומן לחנך את בנידם. הם בלישון תוה'ק מכל' שדרצו עכ'ם שם המדינה. הצרצגה כהים בכל מסר. וגם מצט הנטשכלם ירה רוכן גנשטה ללטוד הד' מדריונה. ובלכן ישלחו עילטה לבתי ספר העמים. אשר הם רוא אך השע' הראשון. ושמם ילכו ילבי הלאה. הלאה. לבתי הנטשנהם. רסירו מכל דדך התוהה כאתו. לכן כדי לחציל את טאריית עמנו טטרתה הד'. בעת הנוראה הואת מצאו לננתל לחסכ'ם סירמנו כהתטמד חובה ובלכ'ה עם בער ב"י כסאני טעת שם המדינה. חטמנו רק שיהי' הכל עם'ת' השבתת מנחלקים ידאו הד' שישטרות לכבות נצהד שם הטריות איש כזה שלא יסוהם חיד אם הרעהים. ושירי עוני המטרות. צוטרות בצד הכללי בשטרה ליטדר' וחל שטא יסטיע חיד הטראה בד' חרצרה על הנעדים שום הטשקצו. הפוצוחה. רק ללטד עכ'ם ליטוד ספר המרות. וחטק ובהכל ברוה תורד' והאתונה טוטרת אבות – ויהיו הליטוד'ם וחל רק כתור אצאינים כדי לבהי את הנעדים למחהק לטטטד עי'ת אם כבוד העם שטחנו את בנידם להדעדים הכללים מאנודה הורידים וטמלא החאות שרטארתנו יטטירים שירד אנשים כשדים תאטצים לד' ולתורתו.

(ב) ליסר איזה ישיבות גדולות בכאליציא ובאקווינא אשר הערים הצעונים שהונט כבשרף נעלה להשתלב בתחק ולטרו שטה לטטם אצל ראשי ישיבות גדולים בחורה ויראי הד' רורו מכללכלים וטסחקים בכבוד וארדחתם יתנו להם טטוסם הבוטר אשר תחוטר אריה כמטרה ה.

(ג) לאחת כטה כטה שנטצאו הבדל ליטר נאטבה שערי תחטים תה'ק והוא תורה וטלאכה. אשר תכול הוקדי בכל כטט הטביאו הסטיאו לדנריל כבוד בעלי' טלאכה'. הצדבים סיני'ע כסירם. ולהצליה חד נחון ליסר בכאלידיצא וכאקווינא איזה בת'. מלאכה עצחוי ולחבב את המלאכה בעיני' העם אשר הנערים שאינם מנכשרים להתטחח בלישון תחהק ידטרו וירבטאר באיצו אוטנות. שטה. תחת מבטלים ירחו זה וגם יבטעו שטה איזו שעת לליטוד התחק ובשי'ע יהיו סגרים כל הוט ליטטוד תורה וטטרי טוסר.

(ד) גם נדבר בהאסיסה הלזו. שנורע להשטדיל הרוטטה ירה בענן נורה שביתת יום הראשון. שהטטשף חטרה הגדול על כל אלה שטרי' שבת שלא ידרם כיחס חד טשהרחה שני יום בשבוע וגם רעשות צעדים לסעול אצל הטטשלה הדוטטטת הטוטה ירה בענן הכבר טאכלם טס' ותהחק לאורב'ר הטוברים בחיל צבא המלך.

כל **התהבנוה** דבר מצאנו כלנו בדצף אחה. לחצצה חותר נכונה. לתוג כתרים כמני דטרטניות הגרול השרד כעת כטאבה עדבנו עלבנו בנונט לסיום תוחק ולשבחדה. הרה. אך לאשר אננתני אינגו באי כח חד הטם. וגם יש בכל דבר כטה סרטים ואוטצים להחיצע איך מציאם יציאתם לטצעל ובכל מעיף וטעיף נחון לבדאר אנשים המצטצכם חד על כן חלטטגו לכנס בהאטרה בעיני העם בשטצים אצטראי בראשטם הטטה לסני הצ' עטנו מבאליצגא לעשות בוסטבא רובכב לעטות בוטבטטא רזאו ראשטי העם צדיק'ו. ורבנו גדולים כהורה. לכן כאשר טהטתיום כ'הצות הרדירים בעיים כניל אטי תטלהנה את ציריהצ להאטסה טכל ראשי רבחורה כלל העדים מטרה חרמם הגרול. ואם כאשר יתאטסה אריה הצדים וציריהם ורגולה יסר רטור אשר נטר אריה טדר הכחורה. לכן באטר תסארנוה אהות הרדירם בעיים כג'ל אוי תוטלחנה את צדירהם והטרלה יסר רשדר אשר נטטד אריה טד טבחורה הגרולה. ואם כאטר יתאטטה אריה הצדים דבינו הרוטני'. רטטי הטם צדיקם ונכבדירם החינף אננתני יחד אריה על כל סרט ומם. הטעיר על טצא אבטם. הטרכזות המצוטטה. וטר הרוטה הכללית. וגם על אוטצי חקת חטטה. טוזת שידיו לחברי אנטדה הדירים בניל וטחה אריה טטר סרנטה שתדאנץ אריה הטנרה הכללית להכל ליה הטטה טטרתם כ'י שאטצא אריה האטסה ובכללית הג'ל. כטה שידי' כאטטטר.

בערים דבטאנוה שאיץ בכחם להחזיק חד כללי כנטס לבד. אוי תוזאל אריה הטרצה הכללית להחטר טטט'ם וכוטמם. טרטבטסד בכללי אשר יתחזנו אריה בעת הטכטה הטרולה. כי ירוטו הטה בכל סרטי התקנות הג'ל שם בהאטמטה הגרולה מני אריה תטר'ע דבט רוב דטות מטר'י אנטדה הרדירים הצ'ל אשר ידהו כוה רטת הטטלוחדם בכל סרט' תקנות הג'ל. אבל יה אריה חד הטלם. האחהדום בענן הג'ל הטטצמת מדאטטט.

כל **שאלה** או ספק אשר יה' לאיט אנודה כביאר ענן התיטרתה. או בכל ענן החטבה ונכבדה הלו. ובענן האטסה הגדולה. תטל לטגות יטר לכל אחד מאתגו ועד הטטעטו דדעם להודיע להם מאטטדה שיטדה וטבכל מטבה בטדה כהוק.

חברים להאנודה מתקבלים כל אוד תטרלטן סכך שני כתרים לטטלה יה נטרא יטר האטורה להתטם מזבית בגיל. ועל האטסה הגרולה יחטלם את אריה בכל ענני תטרלטן חברי האטורדת על איון אוטם שיהי ובטף דטי החקבלה האצטרום יהי טבה לעצ' אצל איש כטה בעיר האטורה בכל כטט התנטרחזה.

כל **אנודה** שטמטרה יטלה לטני טאות חברים תהי' לה. הכוזה לטלח ציר אחד להאטטה. ותדולה ויתר מטני צדירם אין זכות לטם אנודה לטלח אם לאנודה הוותר נחדה בכטם מטטרה. ה'ו יכון טטדון יריון ונוכה לראות טטרה קרן התורה. וכרן היהדות הנאטבה. ולחזצאות סעולות טוריות לטובת עטגו בכלל ובטרם. באנו עה'ח אחר יום ב' ר'ח ניטן חערב לסיק טה טשערנווים'ד

יצחק במוהדרר אברהם יעקב זצ'ל (בארון)

ישראל במוהדרר דוד משה זצ'ל (משוארטטקנ)

ישראל במוהדרר מרדכי פיבוש (חסיאטיף)

הק ישרא' בההדצ מודר'ב צללההדה (וויזניא)

הק משה בהדב הצדיק מכאסיב לערץ (מאטו)

הכ חיים בהדב הצ מהר' ברוך זצללהדה (סנמינאן)

יצחק מאיר במודר אברהם יהושע העט'ל זללה'ה (קאטסטינ'ץ)

אברהם יעקב במודר ישראל (סאראוורא)

אברוי צרוטה לזכרי הדדיקים הקדוטים הג'ר שלי'מא

בנימין אריה הכהן חיים הבד'צ הג'ל וטגליל

Proclamation issued by the Agudas HaChareidim after their conference

Reb Meir Shapiro was among the first to heed the Rebbe's call to open a General Cheder

The third paragraph addressed the problem of workshops and jobs. Here they pledged to instill in the masses a resolve and a duty to have a job, as is evident from many statements of *Chazal*. Special workshops and training centers would be set up to help those in need of a job. In addition, a number of large factories would be opened where those who hadn't found themselves another career, could be employed.

⁀‿

ONE OF THE FIRST TO HEED THE ADVICE OF THE *AGUDAS HaChareidim* to open a General *Cheder* was Reb Meir Shapiro (who

The General Cheder

later became reknowned as the Lubliner Rav). At the time he was living in Tarnopol, and he embraced the idea wholeheartedly. In his position as a Rav he could see for himself how many *bochurim* had fallen by the wayside, working at jobs where they were forced to compromise on their *Yiddishkeit*, even forced to work on Shabbos. If *Yiddishkeit* was to be saved, effort would have to be made to help all sections of the community.

In a *derashah* given in 1922 at the national convention of Agudas Yisroel in Poland, Reb Meir explained the reasons for the General *Cheder* as follows:

The problem of finding a suitable job is of grave concern to the young generation. They worry about their future, about establishing for themselves a stable economic position. Unfortunately, the atmosphere in the workplace, where *Yidden* have to work, is not a *Yiddishe* atmosphere. This is the result of many years of neglect by the *rabbanim* in this sphere.

It is not my wish to turn yeshivah students into workers and laborers, for if there are no *talmidim* in the yeshivos, *Klal Yisroel* has no future. It is my wish, however, to assist those who anyway will not remain by the *gemara* and are destined to work. Why should they be punished and denied the right to be educated and to work in a *Yiddishe* enviroment?

Therefore, when a boy turns 13 or 14 and he is unable to continue learning Torah the whole day, he should be given lessons in learning a trade. In addition, the Torah lessons that he does receive must be compatible to his level and not as was the norm — that all boys learned the same way, regardless of their understanding. In short, we must ensure that these boys receive, in the short time available to them, the maximum possible.

⤎⤏

ALTHOUGH THE REBBE'S IDEA RECEIVED WIDESPREAD approval and in many homes grateful parents heaved a sigh of re-

In Face of Opposition

lief, not everybody was so happy with the news. As the Rebbe had expected, there were some *gedolim* who frowned at the idea and accused him of embarking on a new system of *chinuch* which was at odds with the time-honored *derech*. They felt that by encouraging such *chadarim*, the Rebbe was playing into the hands of the *maskilim* and other secular groups, who sought to undermine the importance of Torah study.

Although the Rebbe held the opinions of these *gedolim* in the highest esteem and respect, he did not agree with their charge that he was pioneering a new and controversial *derech*. He said that he had based his scheme on a similiar one which had been instituted a few hundred years earlier. In the year 1638, Rabbeinu Yoel Sirkis, who is famed for his monumental *sefer,* the *"Bach,"* and by which name he is known, made new rules for the *chadarim* in Cracow, where he was Rav. Among the rules that he instituted was the following:

> When a boy reaches 14 and is not suitable to learn *gemara,* he should be given a job or be employed as a helper by a local *baal habayis*. It is the duty of the *Talmud Torah* to see that these boys are properly taken care of. Those boys who have no teacher to learn with them, should also be taught a trade. If no one wants to take them as apprentices one may take from the funds of the *Talmud Torah* to train them.

The Rebbe hoped that after the initial outcry, those who opposed the General *Cheder* would relent and withdraw their resistance. This, however, was not to be. Thus, instead of people coming forward to champion the cause of the General *Cheder* and to take up the challenge, they felt intimidated by those hostile to the innovation. People everywhere paid great lip service to the Rebbe's idea and they left it at that.

One of the *gedolim* who had originally disagreed with the Rebbe's plans did acknowledge some years later that he had not been fully aware of the true situation. If he would have known the full extent of the problem he might not have opposed the Rebbe. By then, however, it was too late.

Thus instead of the General *Cheder* becoming a universally recognized concept, it took hold only in parts of Poland and Galicia, where the Rebbe's influence was strongest. When the Rebbe was asked why he didn't fight his opponents if he knew he was right, he answered, "The damage caused by large scale arguments and rifts in the community outweighs the benefit of the General *Cheder*."

The Rebbe realized that any heated debate between himself and other *gedolim* would not remain an argument between a few individuals. It could easily spill over onto the thousands of *Yidden* on each side, and before long, the fire of *machlokes* would have left a trail of destruction in its path. This the Rebbe wanted to avoid at all costs.

The outbreak of the First World War in 1914 brought the progress of the previous two years to a swift end. Those branches that did open were nipped in the bud before they had a proper chance to prove themselves. After the war, Agudas Yisroel accepted on itself the job of carrying out the Rebbe's project — to open special *chadarim* coupled with workshops. In Warsaw the famous *Talmud Torah* known as the "Mesivta," which was under the direction of the Gerrer Rebbe, also introduced secular studies and training in its curriculum.

In an interview in 1929 with the daily newspaper "*Dos Yiddishe Tagblatt*," the Chortkover Rebbe was asked what were the most pressing points on the Agudah's agenda. The Rebbe gave his reply:

> *Chinuch* is our first priority. Our whole future is dependent on *chinuch*. This includes *Talmud Torahs*, yeshivos, Bais Yaakovs and also *batei melachah* — workshops. We have to work with all our strength for these institutions and especially for the *batei melachah*.
>
> For many years I have been stressing the need for *batei melachah*. Not all the children in the *Talmud Torahs* are going to become *rabbanim*. We have to worry for their future as well. Otherwise the Torah has no future, *chalilah*. How many thousands of *neshamos* has it cost us until everyone finally understood this? The terrible poverty that afflicts *Yidden* in Poland must urge us to give the *batei melachah* our full attention.

This issue of opening *batei melachah* remained high on the Rebbe's agenda for the rest of his life. After his *petirah*, his son and successor, Reb Nuchem Mordechai, also continued to constantly press for more to be done in this field. At the Knessia Gedolah in Marienbad in 1937, Reb Nuchem Mordechai told the assembled:

> We also have to open more workshops for those who want to work, and to create jobs for those who are not suited to pursue further studies in yeshivah. Once, people were embarrassed to admit that they were working and not learning, but such an approach is totally incorrect. A businessman works hard for his *parnassah* and adheres to the *pasuk*, "You

should eat the labor of your hands and it shall be good for you." The workshops must be run under *frum* supervision so that those who want to learn a trade should not need to compromise on their *Yiddishkeit*. All these issues have to be discussed and resolved during this Knessia.

Although, at the time, many did not agree with the Rebbe's words, his efforts have not been in vain. Nowadays, it is accepted that there are many boys who cannot cope with a regular yeshivah system, and they have to be catered to in an enviroment designed for their needs. It has also become a widely accepted fact by all parts of the community that the *rabbanim* must concern themselves not just with the yeshivos but also with workshops and professional courses for those who are no longer in yeshivah, which will lead them to a proper job and steady income.

CHAPTER FIFTEEN

The Royal City of Vienna

FOR TEN YEARS THE REBBE LED HIS CHASSIDIM IN Chortkov, during which time his name and fame became a by-word in households across Europe. The advent of the First World War in 1914 brought this period to a close. The fighting between the Russians and the Germans uprooted whole *kehillos*, causing hundreds of thousands of *Yidden* to flee from the front lines of the battles that raged around them.

CHORTKOV WAS ALSO NOT SPARED THE RAVAGES OF THE war. Fierce fighting took place in the city, during which much of

The First World War

the town, including the Rebbe's beautiful palace, was destroyed. The Rebbe's shul, however, was left intact.

Although the Rebbe lost his home and most of his belongings during the war, he accepted their loss with love and complete faith. When he learned of his palace's destruction, he commented: "Our Sages have told us that *'setiras zekeinim binyan* — the demolition of elders is not a negative act of destruction but is in its essence a positive act of building.' All the more so the destruction that is an act of G-d is definitely only for our ultimate good and is no doubt part of the preparation needed to herald a truly splendid building, that of the *Beis HaMikdash* — speedily in our times. It is this belief that gives us the strength to overcome our suffering, for we are sure that this is all for the ultimate good."

NOT LONG AFTER SHAVUOS 1914, the Rebbe traveled from Chortkov to

Crowds greet the Rebbe on his travels

Vienna a spa in Germany on the advice of his doctors. When the Rebbe came to the border where Austria, Germany and Russia all met, the Rebbe stopped and looked to the sky and said, "Austria says the earth is mine and so say Germany and Russia. I, however, say that the earth and the whole world belong to Hashem. My holy father told me not long before his *petirah* that he saw in a dream a black cup: the day will just start to brighten and will then become totally dark … My holy *shver* (the Rebbe's uncle, the Rebbe of Sadiger) also said that Vienna is a royal city, and Vienna is a good place to make *Kiddush*."

At the time, no one could understand the Rebbe's words. When, however, the First World War broke out just over a month later and the Rebbe escaped to Vienna, the meaning of his words became apparent to all.

The First World War caused thousands to flee in panic to Vienna, which was a safe haven, far away from the battlefront. Many of the Rebbes of the Rizhiner Dynasty took refuge in Vienna, as did some of the foremost *rabbanim* of the time. The great *geonim*, Reb Meir Arik, Reb Yosef Engel, Reb Avrohom Steinberg and Reb Yeruchem Altshteter also took up residence there.

CONCERNING THE REBBE'S ARRIVAL IN VIENNA, REB DOVID
Moshe Spiegel writes in his memoirs as follows:

A Broad Ahavas Yisroel   The Sadigerer Rebbe, Reb Avrohom Yaakov, told me that he was one of the first Rebbes to arrive in Vienna at the beginning of the war. Soon afterwards, many other Rebbes and *rabbanim* followed in his footsteps. Hardly had they arrived when they were visited by a delegation from the local *frum kehillah*. They had come on behalf of the Shiff Shul, which was the main *heimishe shul* and *kehillah* in Vienna. The *kehillah* was headed by the *gaon* Reb Yeshaya Furst, and he took it for granted that the Rebbes of Rizhin would want to be affiliated with his *kehillah*. The Sadigerer Rebbe answered that he was unable to answer on behalf of all the other Rebbes and they would be best off waiting for the Chortkover Rebbe to arrive, for he would decide on their behalf.

When the Rebbe arrived in Vienna, the heads of the *heimishe kehillah* came to invite him to be a member of their *kehillah*. They told the Rebbe at length about the services that they provide, the *Talmud Torahs*, the *mikvaos*, their own *shechitah*, and all the other amenities that they offered. At the end of the conversation, the delegation told the Rebbe that they hoped he would become a member in their *kehillah*, which was the only fully *frum kehillah* in Vienna.

The Rebbe asked the delegation how many *Yidden* lived in Vienna. "There are 200,000 *Yidden* living in Vienna," was the answer. "And how many of them are actually in your *kehillah*?" asked the Rebbe. "Ten thousand," they answered.

"So you want me to constrict my *ahavas Yisroel* from 200,000 *Yidden* to 10,000 *Yidden*?" the Rebbe retorted. "This is against what I received from my holy fathers! They took care and worried about those who had fallen by the wayside! Chassidus was founded to help *Yidden* from all walks of life, and to bring closer those who have become distanced. Therefore I cannot accept the invitation to join your *kehillah*. Instead, I accept upon myself the task of rectifying the broken fences and rebuilding *Yiddishkeit* in Vienna. I will do everything in my power to rescue the wider community and I hope that you will assist me in every way possible."

The Rebbe did not waste any time and soon formed a committee of *rabbanim* and influential people who held a series of meetings with the heads of the main *kehillah*. They came to an agreement to form a new Orthodox committee that would be responsible for spreading *Yiddishkeit*. In the committee were such *gedolim* as the Alter Boyaner Rebbe, the Husyatiner Rebbe, Reb Meir Arik, Reb Avrohom Steinberg, Reb Yosef Engel, and Reb Benzion Katz — to name just a few. One of the Rebbe's close chassidim — Reb Mechel Shechter, who was a *shochet* — was appointed to oversee the kashrus of the *shechitah*. Under his careful scrutiny, the *shechitah*, which had been on a very low standard, was brought up to scratch. Through the committee, the *kehillah* was transformed, new *Talmud Torahs* were opened and hundreds of children who until then had received almost no Torah education were taught to keep Torah and mitzvos.

THE REBBE'S INVOLVEMENT IN BUILDING *YIDDISHKEIT* IN Vienna is evident from one of his surviving letters. In the letter ad-

Helping Refugees

dressed to Reb Meir Tzvi Jung who was a well-known and respected Rav in Germany, the Rebbe asks for his assistance in setting up new *Talmud Torahs*:

> I still remember his honor from when he visited me in my hometown, therefore I am approaching you about a great and important matter. Due to the terrible war and the sword that hangs over Galicia, I am unable to return home. Not only did the Russians rob me of all my property and belongings, but they also destroyed my house. I remain here until Hashem has mercy on us.
>
> While I am here, I have noticed that a *cheder* and *Talmud Torah* is sorely lacking for our fellow brothers who have taken refuge here. They are overexposed to the secular world, yet when it comes to *limudei kodesh* they are rationed with meager doses. These children are growing up without

any guidance, and when they mature and reach adulthood they will be powerless to stand up against the spirit of lawlessness that can be felt in every corner.

My heart is extremely distressed at this dreadful situation and I have already urged others in this matter. Hashem has helped me to gather a respectable sum of money for a *Talmud Torah*. Praise is to Hashem that I have succeeded in acquiring a beautiful and pleasant building in the center of the city, in the district where the *Yidden* live.

But a large sum of money is still needed to equip the building for the purpose for which it has been bought. Also it is important to send the children on holiday during the summer. Many of them are extremely weak and thin. Why should they be treated any differently than the other children whom the American committee paid for, to rest and heal their bodies?

Since I know that his honor understands the importance of this matter, I hope that he will exercise his influence on those good-hearted people in his midst, and they will contribute for this cause. I am confident that a wise man will seize the mitzvah that has come his way.

In addition to the *Talmud Torahs* that the Rebbe set up for the general public, he also established his own private *Talmud Torah* and yeshivah. Known as the "Chortkover Talmud Torah" (it was situated at 36 Bauerle Gasse in the 20th District), it catered to boys right through from *aleph-beis* until *Shas* and *poskim*. The Rebbe took a direct and personal interest in the daily running of the *Talmud Torah*. When there was a public prize-giving to the *talmidim*, the Rebbe would even make an appearance and hand out the prizes.

In the Rebbe's residence in the Heinestrasse, a Chortkov in miniature was established. Although the new shul was only a fraction of the size of the great shul back home in Chortkov, nevertheless a pulsating chassidic life developed there. It was one of the few places in Vienna which had constant *minyanim* on a daily basis. Similarly a constant *kol Torah* rang out from the shul throughout the day.

ഔ

The Rebbe's fame spread among the Jews of Vienna and many of them came to receive his *berachah*. The Rebbe used the opportunity to coax them into keeping the Torah.

HaGaon Reb Shmelka Pinter of London related a typical story:

> A wealthy businessman planned to open three new branches of his bank, and wanted a *berachah*. Reb Shmelka's father advised the man to go to the Rebbe for a *berachah* and sent his son to accompany him. When they entered the Rebbe's room, the businessman told the Rebbe what he wanted. The Rebbe displayed a great knowledge of banking affairs and at the end he stood up, grasped the business-man's hands in his and asked him to promise to keep the banks closed on Shabbos. The man immediately refused, saying that it was impossible. The Rebbe asked the man again, and again he refused. Suddenly hot tears began to flow down the Rebbe's cheeks as he pleaded with the man not to desecrate the holy Shabbos. The businessman became very distressed that he had caused the Rebbe to become so upset and finally promised that the banks would stay closed on Shabbos, a promise that was indeed kept. By the end of

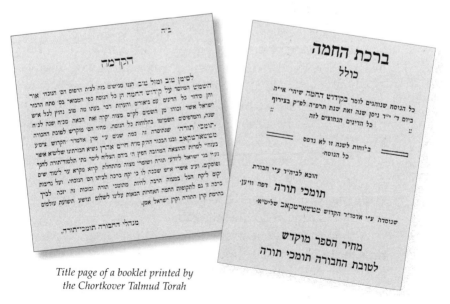

Title page of a booklet printed by the Chortkover Talmud Torah

the war, over sixty people had personally promised the Rebbe to keep their shops closed during Shabbos.

MANY VIENNESE *YIDDEN* WOULD QUEUE UP AT THE Rebbe's residence at 35 Heinestrasse, to ask for an audience with the "Wunder Rabbiner." Non-*frum* people would also ask for help, confident that Heaven would not allow the Rebbe to err. Although they were not *frum* themselves, they still looked up to the Rebbe in awe and reverence. The impression that the Rebbe left on them and on their lifestyle was not quickly forgotten. One Viennese *Yid*, by the name of Reb Mordechai Gotfried, printed a booklet of his memories of the Rebbe. Here are a few excerpts:

True Wisdom

> I had a close relationship with the Rebbe, an inner spiritual connection, and thus I feel the need to write about him. He was my teacher and mentor as he was for myriads of other *Yidden*. What did I learn from him? Not regular *shiurim* or the normal standard lessons. But what? The secrets of *kedushah* and knowledge of the *Shechinah*!
>
> Many of the Rebbe's sayings, his comments and ways are engraved in my heart, and wherever I go these spiritual messages accompany me.
>
> Great care is needed not to profane or tarnish the beauty and the essence of his holy words which came from a pure heart. Therefore I treasure them greatly and guard them as much as is possible for a commoner like myself.
>
> I once confessed to him that I find it difficult to keep all the mitzvos properly, although I am aware of their importance. The Rebbe answered me, "The body must become subservient to the *neshamah*, then you will manage to keep all the mitzvos properly. If a person has an inner spirit, he must push aside his bodily desires to make way for this inner need that cries out to him to do the mitzvah."
>
> Although everyone praised him as a true *chacham* and genius, his wisdom was different than that of others. Whereas wise men derive their knowledge from reading and learning, or hearing from others, his wisdom was different. For sure,

the Rebbe learned a lot and had received much *chochmah* from others, but there was more to it than that. His wisdom descended from upper spheres and emerged from a heart overflowing with feeling and emotion. This type of wisdom is only revealed to great *tzaddikim* who have elevated themselves, it is the product of a lifetime of *kedushah*, and not a mere physical understanding that comes from the intellect.

It was in this vein that the Rebbe once said to me, "It is my opinion that there is a higher form of *chochmah* that is hidden from sight. It is from this higher *chochmah* that true *tzaddikim* draw their wisdom. This is what Reb Meir meant when he said (*Avos* 6:1): 'Anyone who learns *Torah lishmah* … from him people enjoy counsel and wisdom.' For the Torah contains in it a blueprint of all aspects of life, according to their true values. Someone who learns *Torah lishmah* understands and sees the world as it should really be, according to higher levels and according to its true purpose. From such a person you can ask advice, and his answers will be correct and faithful."

YOUNG PEOPLE WOULD ALSO COME TO THE REBBE TO TALK over their problems with him and to consult him on major decisions

Rescuing Those by the Wayside

that had to be made. Vienna was famed for its universities and colleges, and people came from all over to study in their halls. The Rebbe would do his utmost to convince the students and their families not to study in university, The student's stay in university never did much to enhance his level of *Yiddishkeit* and often resulted in the student leaving the path of *Yiddishkeit* altogether. Because of this the Rebbe was opposed to anyone studying in university, and often attempted to talk students out of the idea.

Once, one such person challenged the Rebbe and said, "Did the Torah not obligate a person to learn a trade that he be able to fend for himself? Without studying in university I cannot find myself a job!" The Rebbe answered the man and replied: "The *halachah* is also quite clear that every boy is obligated to have *bris milah*. Nevertheless, a boy whose two older brothers have died due to *bris milah* is exempt from the mitzvah. Similarly, if attempting to fulfill the mitzvah of learning a trade turns people into secular Jews, one is exempt from the mitzvah."

A young man once came to the Rebbe to discuss with him what subject he should study in university. He couldn't make up his mind whether he should study law or medicine. The Rebbe was rather taken aback by the question and exclaimed: "Do you think that I encourage *Yidden* to go to university?" The young man assured the Rebbe that he was going to university regardless of whether the Rebbe approves or not, therefore the Rebbe doesn't have to feel guilty to advise him.

"If so," the Rebbe answered him, "I advise you to study medicine. That way, after you are *niftar*, you will at least be able to defend yourself in front of the *Beis Din Shel Maalah* that you learned medicine in order to save peoples lives (*pikuach nefesh*). But what answer can you give if you become a lawyer?"

The Rebbe wasn't content to be *mekarev* just those *Yidden* who came to see him. He would send messages to various people that he would like to speak to them. If the person ignored the message, the Rebbe sent him a second and a third message, until he finally turned up. He especially concentrated on the many Jewish students who came from all parts of the land to study in Vienna. To one such student who told the Rebbe that he is embarrassed to wear a yarmulka in public, the Rebbe explained, "A soldier who receives a medal is not embarrassed to wear it. On the contrary, he is proud of his award. A yarmulka is like a medal that should be worn with pride. It shows that you are a member of the Chosen Nation!"

In a similar vein the Rebbe explained to him the importance of keeping Shabbos. Observing Shabbos is not a liability, rather it is a privilege which Hashem has granted only to a select few. This student, who had been on a very low level of *Yiddishkeit* until then and only came to the Rebbe after numerous summons, repented his ways. Today he has descendants who number among the finest *frum* families in London.

⇒⇐

DURING THE WAR MANY *YIDDEN* WERE CONSCRIPTED INTO the army, where they met their deaths or were badly wounded. The

False Tears Rebbe tried to help *Yidden* avoid conscription. It soon became well known that the Rebbe aided and abetted *Yidden* to get out of army service, and scores of young men found refuge under the Rebbe's protection. Eventually rumor of the Rebbe's activities reached the army headquarters. The authorities decided to investigate the allegations and sent a spy to the Rebbe's home to find out the truth. They dressed up one of their officers as a *Yid* and sent him to the Rebbe to spy on the Rebbe's activities.

The man went into the Rebbe's room and started to cry, telling the Rebbe that he has only one son who had been called to perform his army service. He begged the Rebbe to have pity on him and help his son evade the army. The Rebbe listened to the man's story and when he had finished, asked the man to repeat the story. The man again told over the whole story, crying bitter tears for his son. When he had finished the Rebbe asked him to tell over the whole story again.

When the man finished his story for the third time, the Rebbe said sternly, "Don't you know that you have to obey the laws of the country? It is strictly forbidden to evade army service." A few days later, a high-ranking officer came personally to thank the Rebbe for sending people to do army service. They had heard rumors that the Rebbe helped people to avoid the army and they were pleased that the reports were not true.

The chassidim were convinced that it was only through a miracle that the Rebbe had known that the crying man was a disguised officer. The Rebbe sought to dispel this miracle and explained to them how he had suspected the truth. "Normally, when a *Yid* tells me his personal sorrows," he explained to them, "I feel inside me part of his pain and suffering. Yet when this man told me his story, his tears did not touch me at all. At first, I thought that it was my fault that perhaps I am not on the *madreigah* to feel another's suffering. I decided, therefore, to ask him to tell over his problem again. Perhaps I would then feel part of his pain. I still, however, did not feel touched by his story and I also felt that this man himself was not truly upset by his own problem. I asked him then to repeat it a third time and then I noticed that it was indeed as I had thought. The man was not

Reb Nuchem Leiberzohn was Rav of the town of Yas in Romania and one of the great Chortkover chassidim. He was known to have finished Shulchan Aruch over 101 times.

really upset and that was the reason that I had not been able to feel his pain. I therefore knew that his story was not true and he was lying."

It is worth noting that this quality of feeling another's pain was considered by the Rebbe to be a vital ingredient that a *tzaddik* must possess in order to be a Rebbe. One of the foremost Chortkover chassidim was the *gaon* Reb Nuchem Leiberzohn. He would often recount that the Rebbe had said to him: "Only someone who truly feels the pain and suffering of his fellow Jews is capable and worthy of being a Rebbe and accepting *kvitlach!*"

One of the Rebbe's chassidim who had connections in the army wanted to be the one to inform the Rebbe that the First World War had ended. On the day the cease-fire was signed, he ran to tell the Rebbe the happy news that at long last peace had arrived and the fighting was over. The Rebbe, however, showed no joy, and when the chassid showed signs of astonishment, the Rebbe told him "The war has not ended. It will only end with the coming of Moshiach!"

Unfortunately, the Rebbe's words have proven to be only too true. Just over twenty years later, the world erupted again in the Second World War. Since then peace has not come upon us. Hardly a day goes by in which one doesn't hear of war and bloodshed.

WITH THE WAR'S END IN 1918 THE TENS OF THOUSANDS of refugees who had fled to Vienna began to return to their home-

Refusal to Forsake Viennese Jewry towns. The chassidim took it for granted that the Rebbe would also go back to Chortkov, especially since Vienna was far away and totally out of the chassidishe camp. It came as quite a shock to them when the Rebbe announced that he intended to stay in Vienna. Over 300 people had promised him that they would keep Torah and mitzvos and if he moved back to faraway Chortkov, many of these people might go back to their old ways.

The chassidim would not take "no" for an answer and sent many delegations to plead with the Rebbe to change his mind. When they saw that it was impossible to move the Rebbe, they begged that at least he should leave Vienna and come to live in a town that was nearer to Galicia. The Rebbe again refused. Vienna was nearer to Eretz Yisroel than Galicia, and now that he had started the journey in fulfillment of his father's *berachah*, he did not want to turn back.

On a different occasion, the Lubliner Rav, Reb Meir Shapiro, begged the Rebbe to change his mind and return to Galicia. The Rebbe told him that it would cost a lot of money to build a new house for him and therefore it was preferable that he stay in Vienna. Reb Meir Shapiro offered to travel around Europe to raise the required sum, adding that he was sure the chassidim would donate the money with great joy. "True," the Rebbe answered him. "They would indeed give the money with great joy, but how is it possible to ask them in such difficult times?"

Indeed, the Rebbe's absence in Galicia was felt far and wide, and not only by his chassidim. The Belzer Rav, Reb Aharon Rokach, was known as a great admirer of the Rebbe, and during a visit to Vienna even gave him a *kvittel* and asked the Rebbe to *daven* for him. On a number of occasions he commented how Galicia was not the same without the Rebbe. To this end, he sent his personal messenger to ask the Rebbe to return to Chortkov. The Rebbe explained his reasons for being unable to do so, to which the Belzer Rav insisted that at least the Rebbe should visit regularly.

In Vienna the Rebbe was extremely careful not to change even the smallest iota from his ways and lifestyle in Chortkov. The Rebbe himself stressed a few times, "In Vienna one must be extra careful and extra vigilance is needed. The old *minhagim* must be kept with even more care." To a chassid from Galicia who changed his traditional chassidic garb to a regular suit, as was the norm in Vienna, the Rebbe said: "Your conduct is in breach of tradition. Although

Viennese *Yidden* do not dress in chassidic garb, you, however, used to wear chassidic clothes and now you have changed. That is a breach of your *minhag*."

The Rebbe's nephew, Reb Shlomo Chaim of Sadiger

VIENNA WAS FAMOUS THROUGHOUT EUROPE FOR ITS modern hospitals and expert doctors. Patients would come to **In the Field of Medicine** Vienna from all over for medical treatment. While in Vienna, many patients would take the opportunity to visit the Rebbe and receive his *berachah* and advice. It didn't take long for the doctors to hear about the great miracle worker in their midst. Sometimes, on their own accord they would send patients to the Rebbe saying, "This is a case for the 'Grosse Rabbiner Friedman,' only he can help you."

The following amazing incident is an example of the Rebbe's great powers. It was related by the children of the Rebbe's nephew, Reb Shlomo Chaim of Sadiger, who were present and witnessed it themselves:

> Reb Shlomenu (as he was fondly known) lived in Vienna after the First World War. It was there that he became dangerously ill with a lung infection. His condition worsened until he eventually lost consciousness and slipped into a coma.
>
> The doctors gave up hope and said that there was nothing they could do. It was at this point that the Rebbe announced

that he wanted to go to the hosptial to visit his nephew. Reb Shlomenu's family were standing around his bed when the door suddenly opened and the Rebbe strode in. He did not greet or acknowledge those in the room. Instead he briskly walked straight to the patient's bed. The Rebbe put his hands on Reb Shlomenu's shoulders and started to shake him, at the same time calling out, "Shlomenu get up! Shlomenu get up!" After a few moments Reb Shlomenu opened his eyes and regained consciousness, much to the surprise of all present. Without further ado, the Rebbe quickly left the room. Once outside, he took out a small *Tehillim* and said a few chapters for Reb Shlomenu's complete recovery, and with that he left the hospital. Reb Shlomenu made a full recovery and lived for many decades afterwards.

The Rebbe opposed dangerous or drastic operations. Often he said to ignore those doctors who tried to frighten their patients into obeying their rash decisions and undergoing potentially hazardous treatment.

In his *sefer "Tekufos VeIshim,"* Reb Shabsi Sheinfeld brings the following story:

A *Yid* in distress came to the Rebbe. The doctor had told him that unless his wife undergoes a dangerous operation on her head, she would live for only three months. Should she have the operation or not?

"No one has yet promised me that I will be alive in three days time," the Rebbe remarked in wonder. "And this doctor can promise life for three months?" The Rebbe concluded, "The Torah has given a doctor authority only to heal and that is all. He has no right to give up on someone else's life and hand down predictions of doom. The Torah has not given him a license to forecast when a person will die! Therefore you are not obliged to listen to him."

To another man who had been told that he must have his leg amputated or expect to die, the Rebbe exclaimed. "Your doctor has no regard for a Jewish body, he thinks that the flesh of a *Yid* is *hefker*, to be cut away at will. I, however, have more respect for a Jewish body. One doesn't cut off the limbs of a *Yid* so quickly." The *Yid* listened to the Rebbe and didn't have the amputation. He lived for many years afterward.

The Rebbe himself once related at a *tisch* an incident about a man who had come to him crying for help. This man's 7-year-old daughter had suddenly became paralyzed from head to foot. The man had taken his daughter to the top doctors and specialists in Vienna, but they were all perplexed as to the cause of her condition and how to treat it. In desperation the man came to the Rebbe, who gave him a certain *segulah*. Within a short time the girl had made a complete recovery. When the girl was completely better the Rebbe instructed her father, "Take your daughter and go back to all the doctors that you consulted, and show them that there is a *Ribbono Shel Olam* in the world!"

Occasionally the Rebbe used to hand out his own remedies or potions, which always worked wonders. Reb Avrohom Ochs (later of Queens, New York), was a close chassid of the Rebbe. He would relate an interesting story, which he himself witnessed, concerning these private remedies:

> One day Reb Avrohom's mother developed a swelling on her nose. The swelling was accompanied by very high temperature which refused to subside. Despite all the doctors' efforts, the temperature could not be lowered and she steadily became weaker and weaker. Eventually she stopped eating and it became apparent that if a cure wasn't found soon, her life would be in danger.
>
> In a panic, Reb Avrohom made his way to the Rebbe and told him about his mother's condition. The Rebbe left the room and came back a few minutes later holding a large book which he opened. Reb Avrohom saw that the whole book was in the Rebbe's handwriting. He could also see that it contained all sorts of remedies for a wide range of illnesses. The Rebbe asked a number of questions about the exact location of the swelling, its size and coloring and the symptoms of her illness. The Rebbe leafed through his book,

looking at the various remedies he had written. After a few moments the Rebbe told him, "Go to the butcher's and ask for the eye of a freshly slaughtered calf. The eye must be placed on the swelling and with the help of Hashem she will soon get better." Reb Avrohom did as instructed and procured the calf's eye as quickly as possible. Within a few hours the swelling had gone down and the temperature returned to normal!

CHAPTER SIXTEEN
On the Go

ALTHOUGH THE REBBE LIVED IN VIENNA AFTER the war and refused to move back to Chortkov, he did not forget about his many chassidim scattered throughout Poland, Romania and Galicia. To another Rebbe who complained to him that since he took up refuge in Vienna he has lost all contact with his chassidim, the Rebbe retorted, "If you don't forget about them, they won't forget about you!" The Rebbe maintained contact with his chassidim through letters, hundreds of which arrived daily. So great was the flow of the post to the court, that it took the Rebbe several hours every day to deal with all the correspondence. Similarly, the Rebbe's *divrei Torah* were printed regularly and distributed to his chassidim far and wide.

IN ADDITION, THE REBBE VISITED HIS CHASSIDIM IN CHORTkov once or twice a year, notably during the months of Tishrei and

Keeping in Contact Sivan. Every year the town of Chortkov came alive again for the few weeks that he was there. Tens of thousands poured into the town to be with the Rebbe.

The Rebbe's divrei Torah were printed and distributed far and wide. This particular discourse is from Parshas Bo 1912.

Even the buildings in Chortkov, which had been specially built to accommodate large numbers, were packed. The Rebbe's *beis hamedrash* could comfortably hold a few thousand people. On Yom Tov after the *tefillos* were over, the Rebbe would go out onto a balcony overlooking a large courtyard where the chassidim would dance while the Rebbe watched them.

THE YEARLY JOURNEY OF THE REBBE FROM VIENNA TO Chortkov became a major event in the lives of his chassidim. The

On the Go

Rebbe traveled by train and at each town on the way thousands came to greet him. This is how Rav Yosef Mordechai Baumel remembers the event:

> The Rebbe's train was due to pass through the town late at night. Already a few days earlier the unusual flurry of activ-

ity was noticeable. The railway station was specially cleaned for the occasion until it shone like new. It was almost as if there was a family *simchah*. Everyone was excited at the chance to see the radiant face of our holy Rebbe.

Finally, at the appointed time, the whole town made their way toward the station: men, women and children, all dressed in their Shabbos best. Chairs were prepared on the platform for the *rabbanim* of the town and the elderly. As the train came into view, the whole crowd respectfully rose to their feet. Suddenly, their hearts missed a beat. Standing at the window was their Rebbe, the Rebbe who cared for all their needs and problems. During the 10 minutes that the train was in the station, the assembled filed past to receive the Rebbe's *berachah*. After the train left, the crowd dispersed, each one going home with a full and contented heart and treasuring the few words the Rebbe had exchanged with them.

In an article, Reb Elisha Roter recounts those precious few moments in the Rebbe's presence:

The Rebbe blesses his chassidim during a stop in a town

After the war, the Rebbe came every year to Chortkov. Those who were unable to make the trip spared no effort to meet up with the Rebbe on the way. Throughout the day and the night they traveled to the railway station in order to catch a glimpse of their beloved Rebbe. To look into his great and merciful eyes dispelled the surrounding darkness and instilled us with new hope. I remember well how my father spoke a few words to the Rebbe and came back with tears in his eyes, because the Rebbe had said to him, "*Nu*, Avremele, how are you doing?" It is hard to describe the deep feelings that his chassidim had for him.

REB ZEV FISHER IN HIS BOOK ABOUT LEMBERG GIVES US a description of the Rebbe's visit to the city in the year 1921:

Lemberg The Chortkover Rebbe excelled as an unbelievable *chacham*. His approach to his chassidim, or for that matter to anybody who came to him, was an example for all to copy. The Rebbe had outstanding love for every single *Yid*, even more so for the youth and especially for the *bnei Torah*. The Rebbe imparted this *middah* to his many chassidim. Similarly, his active role in communal affairs and Agudas Yisroel also served to impress on his chassidim the importance of helping a fellow *Yid* in need.

In 1921 the Rebbe came to Lemberg on his way from Vienna to Chortkov. Thousands of his chassidim came from all parts to bask in his presence. This was a massive show of *kavod haTorah* for the *gadol hador* which left a strong impact in its wake. The elderly *tzaddik* made an unforgettable impression on all who saw him. His royal manner and his penetrating eyes made you feel that you were in the presence of greatness.

The Rebbe received people in the glass factory on Liganov Street that belonged to one of his chassidim, Reb Moshe Griffel. Hundreds of people queued in line with their *kvitlach*, each one getting a few seconds to pour out his heart to the Rebbe. The Rebbe listened to each person with great patience and with love, he was interested in each point, he asked and answered, and blessed each person with a heart full of warmth and fatherly love

Behind the Rebbe's chair stood his close chassidim, Reb Hirsh Leizer Zeif, a great *talmid chacham*, and also the *baal Mussaf* in the Chortkover *Kloiz* in Lemberg. Next to him stood Reb Herzl Horowitz, a pious *Yid* with pure thoughts. All the different organizations in the city came to receive the

ועד חסידי טשאָרטקוב

KOMITET „CHASIDEJ CZORTKOW"
pod adresem: J. B. HORN
— LWÓW, SZPITALNA 7. —

Chortkov had branches throughout Eastern Europe. This is the letterhead of the Chortkover chassidim in Lvov, Galicia.

Rebbe's *berachah*. They all left overawed by their meeting with him; from their faces it was evident that they were more than satisfied with what they had heard.

A SECOND DESCRIPTION, THIS TIME FROM THE REBBE'S visit to Lublin in 1930, comes to us from the columns of the secular newspaper, *"Der Moment."* In his article under the large **Lublin** heading *"Beim Chortkover Rebben in Lublin,"* the journalist, a certain Aharon Pearlman, writes as follows:

> The Rebbe of Chortkov is considered to be one of the most important figures in the chassidic world. Therefore I decided to obtain an interview with him for our newspaper. I must confess that this is the last time I am going to undertake such a meeting. To arrange an interview with the Rebbe is even more difficult than to meet a government minister.
>
> I went yesterday at 5 o'clock, which was supposed to be a time of rest. I soon realized that I had made a big mistake. A Rebbe doesn't rest, especially not the Rebbe of Chortkov, who doesn't know what the word rest means. The building where he was staying was crowded with people, while all the time more people were trying to force their way in.
>
> The crowd stood for hours in the queue; although the heat was unbearable, no one left the line. These people are used to standing many long hours at their Rebbe's *tisch*. The longer it took the more desperate everyone became to see the Rebbe.
>
> The entrance to the four-story building was locked and bolted. To my mazel I knew a family that lived in that building. I went outside, phoned them, and asked them to open the door for me. Now that I was inside, I thought my problems would be over.
>
> Once in the building, a further wait of two hours greeted me until I finally received access to the flat where the Rebbe was staying. It was only with the help of the police that I was eventually admitted.
>
> Because I am a journalist and the Rebbe's interview had to appear in the paper the next morning, I was allowed to skip

a few places in the queue. Suddenly, however, the *gabbai* announced that the Rebbe was about to *daven Maariv* and all interviews would be suspended.

A hot sweat covered my face; six hours I had been pushing and waiting to see the Rebbe, my strength was waning and I knew that I would not manage to hold out until the Rebbe had finished *davening*. With my last strength I pushed my way forward to the Rebbe's room and shouted aloud, "Let me through to the Rebbe!" The door of the Rebbe's room suddenly opened, and the Rebbe's son appeared. When he heard that I am writing for today's paper he let me in for a few moments.

The Wet Pillow

THESE YEARLY TRIPS TOOK A SEVERE TOLL ON THE REBBE'S health but still he refused to give them up, even in his later years. *Yidden* were waiting to see him and he couldn't let them down. One year, as the Rebbe was preparing himself to leave Vienna, a number of anti-Semitic attacks broke out across Galicia. This, coupled with general unrest, meant that the Rebbe's personal security would be at risk. His high profile trip would be bound to elicit a reaction from those looking to make trouble. The Rebbe, however, ignored all the requests for him to cancel his trip; *Yidden* needed him and that's all there was to it.

In desperation, the *gabbaim* summoned the Lubliner Rav, Reb Meir Shapiro, and asked him to speak to the Rebbe. Perhaps he would succeed in changing the Rebbe's mind. Reb Meir entered the Rebbe's room and explained to him in great detail the dangerous period the country was going through. He mentioned the hardships facing Galician Jewry, the constant backlash from the neighboring *goyim*, and the general feeling of unrest that could be felt throughout the country.

After Reb Meir had finished his argument, the Rebbe uncharacteristically raised his voice and exclaimed, "Why am I a Rebbe of chassidim if not that I should be with them in their time of sorrow? Am I not here to listen to their cries when things are difficult and to comfort them and be *mechazeik* them? If things are really so terrible in Galicia, it is even more vital that I go there as soon as possible!"

In the Rebbe's last year he didn't make his traditional journey to Poland and Galicia. When the influential chassid Reb Melech Backenrot from Drohibisht asked the Rebbetzin why the Rebbe wasn't coming, she replied: "Every time the Rebbe comes back from a trip, I find that his pillow is wet from the many tears that he cried during the night, over the plight of his fellow *Yidden*. Until now I never said anything, knowing how desperately the chassidim need him. Now, however, that he has become so weak, I cannot allow him to go, he can no longer carry the terrible strain from so much suffering."

⌒⌒

THE REBBE'S FREQUENT TRIPS ACROSS EASTERN EUROPE were important not just for the individual problems and needs of **Chortkover** his chassidim but also for the running of the **Communities** Chassidus as a whole. After the First World War many communities were in a state of total disrepair, and people were despondent and worried about the future. The Rebbe's visits served to strengthen the many Chortkover communities and breathe new life into them.

Indeed, over the years, Chortkov made a name for itself with its model communities and flourishing *kehillos*. In a time and period when many were confused about the way ahead, Chortkov acted as a guide and beacon of light for other communities. Chortkover communities were to be found in many far-flung towns and cities across Eastern Europe and beyond. Even such cities as Budapest, Berlin and London had their own Chortkover shuls.

Following are descriptions of two Chortkover communities: the community of Lemberg and the community of Butatch.

In his book about life in Lemberg, Reb Zev Fisher, writes as follows:

> The Chortkover Chassidus in Lemberg deserves an extra mention for itself. Thousands of *Yidden* belonged to the Chortkover Chassidus and they would stream to their Rebbe to learn from him *daas* and *yiras Hashem*. Back in their hometowns the Chortkover chassidim stuck together in faith and

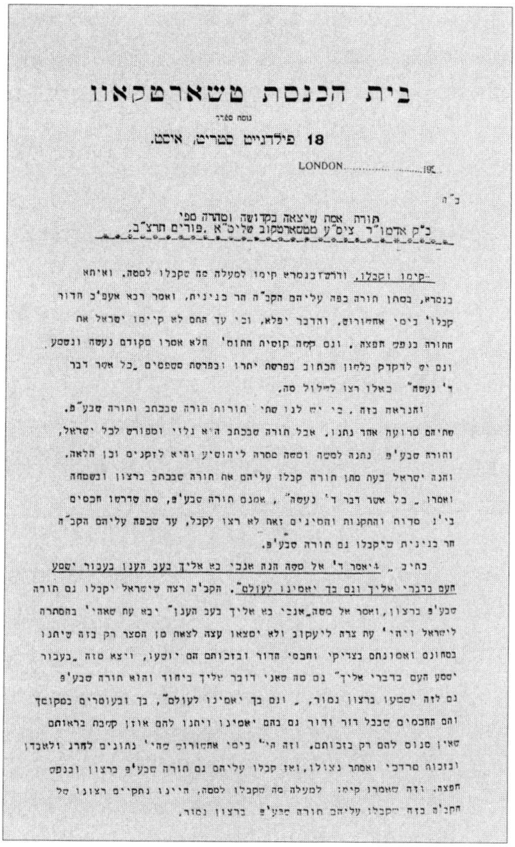

בית הכנסת טשארטקאוו

נוסח ספרד

18 פילדגייט סטריט, איסט.

LONDON..................... 192..

ב"ה

תורה אמת שיצאה בקדושה וטהרה מפי
כ"ק אדמו"ר זצ"ל מטשארטקוב שליט"א. פורים תרצ"ב.

קימו וקבלו. ודרשו בגמרא קימו למעלה מה שקבלו למטה. ואיתא
בגמרא, בשעת נתינת התורה כפה עליהם הקב"ה הר כגיגית, ואמר רבא אעפ"כ הדור
קבלוה בימי אחשורוש. והדבר יפלא, וכי עד אז לא קיימו ישראל את
התורה בנפש חפצה, וגם קשה קושית התוס' הלא אמרו מקודם נעשה ונשמע.
וגם יש לדקדק בלשון הכתוב בפרשת יתרו ובפרשת משפטים „כל אשר דבר
ד' נעשה" כאלו רצו לשלול מה.

והנראה בזה, כי יש לנו שתי תורות תורה שבכתב ותורה שבע"פ.
שתיהם מרועה אחד נתנו, אבל תורה שבכתב היא גלוי ומפורש לכל ישראל,
ותורה שבע"פ נתנה למשה ומשה מסרה ליהושע והיא לזקנים וכן הלאה.
והנה ישראל בעת מתן תורה קבלו עליהם את תורה שבכתב ברצון ובשמחה
ואמרו „ כל אשר דבר ד' נעשה" , אמנם תורה שבע"פ, מה שדרשו חכמים
בי"ג מדות והתקנות והסייגים זאת לא רצו לקבל, עד שכפה עליהם הקב"ה
הר כגיגית שיקבלו גם תורה שבע"פ.

כתיב „ ויאמר ד' אל משה הנה אנכי בא אליך בעב הענן בעבור ישמע
העם בדברי עמך וגם בך יאמינו לעולם". הקב"ה רצה שישראל יקבלו גם תורה
שבע"פ ברצון, ואמר אל משה „אנכי בא אליך בעב הענן" יבא עת שאהי' בהסתרה
לישראל ויהי' עת צרה ליעקב ולא ימצאו עצה לצאת מן המצר רק בזה שיתנו
בטחונם ואמונתם בצדיקי וחכמי הדור ובזכותם הם יושעו, ויצא מזה „בעבור
ישמע העם בדברי עמך" גם מה שאני דובר עמך ביחוד והוא תורה שבע"פ
גם לזה ישמעו ברצון גמור, „ וגם בך יאמינו לעולם", בך ובעוסקים במקומך
והם החכמים שבכל דור ודור גם בהם יאמינו ויתנו להם אוזן קשבת בראותם
שאין מנוס להם רק בזכותם. וזה הי' בימי אחשורוש שהי' נתונים להרג ולאבדן
ובזכות מרדכי ואסתר נצולו, ואז קבלו עליהם גם תורה שבע"פ ברצון ובנפש
חפצה. וזה שאמרו קימו למעלה מה שקבלו למטה, היינו נתקיים רצונו של
הקב"ה בזה שקבלו עליהם תורה שבע"פ ברצון גמור.

For over fifty years, until the Second World War, there was a Chortkover Kloiz in the East End of London

resolve. All over they maintained their own groups and erected *shteiblach* where they *davened* and learned. In addition, the *shteiblach* also hosted their many gatherings and *seudos* which were conducted in true chassidic spirit. The Chortkover *Kloiz* in Lemberg was no exception to this rule.

The large Chortkover *Kloiz* on Rapporport Street, opposite the Jewish hospital, was housed in a large building which was almost the size of a hall. The Chortkover chassidim had considerable influence in the city, and many of the chassidim occupied important positions. Especially in communal matters, their opinion carried great weight. In the field of *chinuch*, and regarding religious and social issues, they were able to introduce and push through many *takanos* and innovations. Their shul was a magnet for the youth; regular *shiurim* were organized for the *bochurim* day and night. Those who frequented the shul were known for their fine ways and *middos*.

The regular chassidic gatherings that took place inside the *kloiz* were noted for their joyful spirit. The words of the *pasuk*, *"Ivdu es Hashem besimchah,"* came to life in the *kloiz*. The chassidim sat in a state of *hislahavus* and longing for the *Shechinah*. The Rebbe's *divrei Torah* and his sayings were retold time and time again. Over a cup of *"bronfen"* rows of *ehrlicher talmidei chachamim* learned and delved into the meaning of their Rebbe's words. The stories about the Rebbe emphasized to the chassidim their own necessity to emulate his ways and overcome their own natural frailties. It was no wonder that from such an atmosphere of *d'veikus* and *aliyah*, the Chortkover chassidim were like one man with one heart.

The Chortkover *Kloiz* was also like a factory-line producing new generations of *frum askanim*. This point was deeply inbedded in the conscience of Chortkov — to feel an active responsibility for the rest of the community. The mark of *ahavas Yisroel* could be felt in every activity in which they participated. Such well-known *askanim* as Reb Reuven Winkler, Reb Moshe Hirshprung, Reb Berche Horn, Reb Alter Lipa and Reb Shmuel Nissenbaum were all products of the *kloiz*.

This *derech* that the Chortkover chassidim received from their great Rebbe left its mark on the town. They openly tried to be *mekarev* people and bring *Yiddishe* hearts closer together. They made efforts to draw near those who had strayed from the path of *Yiddishkeit* and to influence them to return. All their actions were carried out with the full consent of their Rebbe, with whom they maintained constant contact, either through regular messengers or through the post.

A second short description of a Chortkover community comes from a book about Jewish life in the town of Butatch, Galicia, written by one of the town's survivors. The author describes the many different groups and organizations in the town, and it is in this context that he refers to Chortkov as well:

> Not far from Butatch was the town of Chortkov. In the town lived one of the grandsons of the *tzaddik* of Rizhin, who became renowned as the Chortkover Rebbe. A number of people in Butatch followed his direction and they rented premises for a shul which observed the *minhagim* of Chortkov. Over the years their numbers increased until the rented accommodations became too small. They then built for themselves a shul. This was the Chortkover *Kloiz*, whose members were excep-

tional and whose ways were beautiful. Most of the Chortkover chassidim were learned and upright Jews. Their *tefillos* and their singing were pleasant to hear, as they issued from those who knew that they were in the presence of Hashem.

Just like their *tefillos* were pleasant, so was their speech pleasant, softly spoken and not in loud or harsh tones. During the week they engage in business and learn Torah, and on Shabbos and Yom Tov they make a *mishteh* in the *kloiz* with wine and nuts; they sing *zemiros* and relate stories about their Rebbe. When the *yahrtzeit* of one of their Rebbes arrives, they make a great *seudah* with meat and wine. The sounds of singing would attract outsiders who would come in to see what was going on. Newcomers were quickly ushered to a seat and within a short while a new member was enrolled.

During the long winter nights the *kloiz* was filled with people learning, and their voices could be heard right down the street. Passersby would peer through the windows and utter a heartfelt *berachah*, "If only my children would grow up to be like them."

The good wishes of the passersby, however, were not fulfilled. Over the years Butatch's shuls slowly but surely emptied of their *talmidim*. The new secular schools and colleges that had recently opened ripped a large hole across Butatch. There were still many *talmidei chachamim* who sat and learned, but the glory and honor of the Torah had disappeared, for the younger generation had deserted it.

This happened because many *Yidden* admired the cultural and modern achievements of the *goyim*. They thought that it wouldn't harm their children to know more about what was happening in the wider world. The result was that once the youth became acquainted with the wider world they no longer felt pulled by the confines of the *beis hamedrash*.

The chassidim, however, were better equipped to withstand the pull from the outside world. They had managed to insulate themselves, and most of their children remained faithful to their fathers. That was the reason why, in later

*Foundation scroll
of the Chortkover
Kloiz in Manchester*

years, they produced most of the *rabbanim, shochtim* and *melamdim* in the town.

Two or three times a year the chassidim would travel to Chortkov to consult with and to learn from their Rebbe. Often the trips resulted in new *shidduchim*, and new chassidim moved to the town. Over the years the *kloiz* became cramped, and if not for the war, they would have built a larger shul.

BESIDES HIS REGULAR VISITS TO CHORTKOV, THE REBBE also journeyed occasionally to Romania, Hungary, and even to

Blood Libel

Germany. During these trips the local *rabbanim* often took the opportunity to involve the Rebbe in the problems that were facing them and to seek his guidance. In his great *ahavas Yisroel*, the Rebbe rarely refused their requests for assistance. This was how the Rebbe became involved in the famous blood libel trial of Mendel Beilis.

In March 1911, the body of a young gentile boy was found in Kiev, and once again an ugly blood libel inflamed local passions. A Jewish resident of the area, Mendel Beilis, who was a factory worker, was arrested and charged, even though the real perpetrators were known to the police.

While the authorities sought to build a case against him, Beilis was imprisoned for two years before being brought to trial. By then, his plight had turned into a showcase for *Yidden* and *goyim* across the world. It wasn't just Mendel Beilis who was in the dock, all *Yidden* were also being accused of the centuries-old libel. The *Yidden* had to prove once and for all in a courtroom that the blood libel was a false and baseless accusation. Failure to do so was tantamount to admitting their own guilt and giving justification to the libel.

A lawyer was hired to defend Beilis in court, the renowned Oscar Gruzenberg. He knew that the prosecution would try to use the *gemara* and other scholarly volumes to prove its case. Therefore, the Chief Rabbi of Moscow, Rav Yaakov Mazeh, was chosen to lead a rabbinic advisory committee for the defense.

Before the trial the Rebbe discussed the Beilis case with Rav Mazeh at length and advised him how to proceed with the case. Although all the details of their conversations are not known, Rav Mazeh does disclose how the Rebbe became involved and one or two points that the Rebbe raised with him. Their discussion is presented here as written by Rav Mazeh in his memoirs:

> It was in 1913. After a difficult illness I was sent to recuperate in Marienbad. At that time the topic of the Beilis trial was on everyone's lips. While I was there I was informed that I had been chosen to lead the committee in defense of Mendel Beilis and therefore I had to cut short my stay in Marienbad. I started to pack my bags when I was disturbed by a knock on the door. A man stood in the doorway and said, "I came to Marienbad together with the Chortkover Rebbe, who is staying here in an apartment building on the ground floor. May *HaKadosh Baruch Hu* have mercy on him, for he has no peace, since the entire nation comes to him from morning to

night. He also feels great anguish over the Beilis case and it is regarding this matter that I have come to you.

"Our Rebbe heard that Rav Mazeh was called as an expert in religious matters, and he very much wanted to discuss with you privately the issues pertaining to this important case. However, because of our sins he is very weak and it is difficult for him to climb the stairs to the fourth floor. Perhaps the Rav will be kind enough to visit the Rebbe? That is why I was sent to you and I have done as I was bidden."

I willingly agreed to visit the Rebbe and later on I made my way to his apartment. Outside the flat stretched a long queue. Only once before had I seen a longer queue, at a non-Jewish event in the center of Moscow. A *gabbai* was on duty controlling the order and the decorum. I approached him and asked him for an audience with the Rebbe. "Not before next week Wednesday," the man replied. I explained to the man that the Rebbe had summoned me and was waiting to speak to me. The *gabbai* took my name and returned a few moments later. In a loud voice he called out: "Make way! Make way!" The crowds parted and suddenly I found myself in the Rebbe's room.

In front of me stood a man of more than 40 years (the Rebbe was then almost 50). He was of average height, his hair and beard a dark blond. His eyes expressed humility and a glimmer of trust sparkled from them. He stretched out his hand, asked me to sit and then he also sat. He stared silently into my face for a few moments and then turned his head away from me and began to speak.

"I read in the papers that the Rav (Rabbi Mazeh) was invited to serve as an expert in religious questions in the Beilis trial. We made some inquiries and we were told that you are a good speaker. Shlomo HaMelech tells us in *Mishlei*, '*Yesh yisron lebaal halashon* — The gifted orator has an advantage.'

"We also heard that you know Torah and are an expert in *halachah*. However, forgive us for asking, but we have no clear information of your knowledge and attitude toward

Chassidus. We wanted to hear what you have to say about this important matter and to tell you that if you *chalilah* don't defend the *derech* of Chassidus fully, then they will pin the blame on the chassidim. Afterwards they will proclaim outside the courtroom that all *Yidden* are chassidim. Therefore it is not just the defense of chassidim which is at stake, but the defense of all *Yidden*."

I explained to the Rebbe that even if I would find an aspect of Chassidus that is not to my liking, even then I would defend it with all my soul. Since I view myself as going out to war against our enemies, anyone who surrenders to the enemy even small vessels, items of lesser importance, is sentenced to death. Perhaps this is the secret our Sages revealed to us in the episode where Yaakov Avinu struggled with Eisav and risked his life for the sake of a few small vessels.

I had not yet finished speaking when the Rebbe looked at me with tears in his eyes and said, "Your precious words full of warmth are extremely pleasing and acceptable to us. Praise to *Hashem Yisbarach* who led me in the way of truth. With His help you will succeed in all you do. And what are we, who have no power but that of the mouth, to do? We will certainly *daven* for you as our fathers and *zeides* have taught us, for everything is from Hashem. If you need any *sefarim* in order to prepare your defense, just tell me which ones you want and we will certainly locate them."

I told the Rebbe, "The *sefarim* are '*Emek HaMelech*' and '*Ohr Yisroel*.'"

"When you return," the Rebbe added, "pass through Vienna and approach the Culture Gemeinde of the Viennese Jewish community. We will take care of everything. These volumes are certain to be in their libary, and if not then return to me and you will receive them from my own collection in Chortkov.

But do not put anything in writing, for I do not trust the governments, especially when a blood libel is involved. It is better not to write anything and this will be a sign that the *sefarim* were received, and if not, they will be sent by special messenger. Do not spare any expense when the blood of the nation is in danger." After this meeting I had another two sessions with the Rebbe during which we discussed the different aspects of the trial.

I returned to Moscow and from there went to Kiev. For six weeks I drank the cup of bitterness to its fullest. When Mendel Beilis was acquitted, I returned home. Upon my arrival a letter of gratitude and blessings greeted me; it was from the Rebbe of Chortkov. In the card he had written, "Blessed is Hashem Who did not allow us to become prey for their teeth. Hashem gave you wisdom and understanding to say the right thing at the right time. How good is your portion in this world and in the World to Come. You are called 'Mazeh' for you sprinkled (*hizah*) upon them the eternity of *Klal Yisroel* and have won for them. May my portion be with yours."

ALTHOUGH THE REBBE NEVER LEFT EUROPE, NEVERTHEless he was keenly attuned to developments affecting *Yidden* across **America** the globe. The Rebbe gave extra attention to the *Yidden* living in America, many of whom were in dire danger of being severed from their roots. In the decades before and after the First World War, hundreds of thousands of *Yidden* left Europe for America seeking a better and easier life. Once in America they soon realized that the harsh realities of life in the new and strange country were not as rosy as they had been led to believe.

The struggle for financial survival often caused them to compromise on their *Yiddishkeit* or to abandon it altogether. The Rebbe was aware of the trials and tribulations that the American immigrants faced and from the distance tried his best to help them.

Unlike many other *gedolim* who totally opposed any *Yidden* moving to the spiritual wastes of America, the Rebbe adopted a compromise position. On the one hand he forbade "economic migrants," those who were going there in search of a more prosperous future, while at the same time he encouraged *rabbanim* and *shochtim* to settle there.

Reb Yossel Halpern from Manchester would often relate a story that he had heard firsthand from the person involved:

> This person came to take leave of the Rebbe and to bid him farewell before moving to America. He had booked tickets for himself and his family, to travel on the inaugural voyage of the famous ship, the "Titanic" (which sank on its maiden voyage).
>
> "Send my regards to the American G-d," the Rebbe told the man. Rather startled by the Rebbe's unusual comment, he asked the Rebbe to explain what he meant. "I see that you think America has a different G-d than here in Europe," the Rebbe exclaimed. "Is Hashem not here in Europe that you have to go to America to find Him?"
>
> The man took heed of the Rebbe's words and canceled his tickets on the ship — thereby saving his life and that of his family.
>
> His children later opened a kosher food store in Manchester which bears the name "Titanic" in commemoration of their escape! (The stores still operates to this day.)

At the same time that the Rebbe tried to dissuade the masses from going to America he encouraged those involved in spreading Torah and *Yiddishkeit* to move there. The Rebbe realized that without local *rabbanim, melamdim* and *shochtim* to care for the immigrants, there was little hope of them remaining *frum* and raising a new generation that would be faithful to its heritage.

In this matter the Rebbe continued in the path of his father who had been among the first to actively send *rabbanim* to America.

Daily, letters had arrived in Chortkov asking the Alter Rebbe to send to America *shochtim, rabbanim* and teachers. Similarly, the Alter Rebbe was often called upon to solve problems that had cropped up in America and were awaiting his decision. In no small measure, a large portion of the credit for the beginnings of Orthodox *Yiddishkeit* in America can be laid on the Alter Rebbe's shoulders.

One example, typical of many, was the city of Galveston, Texas. Lacking an *ehrlicher shochet*, they turned in desperation to the Alter

The Boyaner Rebbe moved to America on the advice of the Rebbe

Rebbe to help them. The Rebbe called in one of his finest young chassidim, Reb Yaakov Geller, and instructed him to move to Texas. Although Rav Geller was not at all keen about leaving Galicia, he could not refuse the Rebbe's request. The Rebbe's *gabbai*, Reb Hershel Rapporport, gave the young scholar a letter in which he wrote: "At the request of our holy Rebbe, Reb Yaakov Geller is traveling abroad in order to save our fellow brothers from having to eat meat which was slaughtered through unreliable *shochtim*. Therefore, I was instructed by the holy Rebbe to give him this letter as proof so that when he arrives there, he should be properly cared for in order that he should be able to carry out his holy work with a clear mind." Rav Geller was indeed instrumental in strengthening *Yiddishkeit* in Texas until his *petirah* in 1930.

Included in the list of those whom the Rebbe persuaded to move to America was his nephew, the Boyaner Rebbe, Reb Mordechai Shlomo Friedman. Over the years many Chortkover and Rizhiner chassidim settled in America and the Rebbe worried greatly for their future. In 1925 the Boyaner Rebbe agreed to visit New York in order to be *mechazeik* the many Rizhiner chassidim living there, but he decided against settling there. He was worried that in America he would not be able to give a proper *chinuch* to his children. The Rebbe disagreed with his decision and advised him to move to New York, saying that he would be able to spread the observance of Torah and mitzvos, and raise the standards of *Yiddishkeit* in America. The Boyaner Rebbe accepted his uncle's decision and moved to New York in 1927.

Over the years and decades the Boyaner Rebbe emerged as one of the foremost Torah pioneers who was instrumental in establishing all that we now take for granted in America. He was also instrumental in rebuilding the Rizhiner Chassidus from the ashes of the Nazi inferno.

CHAPTER SEVENTEEN

Guiding His Chassidim

THE REBBE'S ROLE AS ONE OF THE FOREMOST LEAD-
ers of *Klal Yisroel* — who carried their heavy burden on his
shoulders — and his total involvement in all communal issues
of the day did not detract in any way from his main role in
life — to act as a Rebbe who teaches his followers how to ascend the
rungs of Torah and *yiras Hashem*. He felt a great responsibility toward his chassidim who looked to him to show them the way.

ALTHOUGH THE REBBE ACTED AS LEADER TO TENS OF
thousands of *Yidden,* he still was able to concentrate on the personal

**Individual
Care**

problems that faced each of his followers.

The following incident is an example of the
Rebbe's concern for every individual:

> When Reb Dovid Tierhoiz was a young boy, he had a daily
> learning session with a *chavrusa,* another boy of his age, in
> the Rebbe's *beis hamedrash* in Vienna. When one of the boys

became ill, the learning session was canceled for a few days. One evening, Reb Dovid's parents received a visitor in their house. The Rebbe's esteemed *gabbai*, Reb Yossel Sternberg, had come on an errand in the name of the Rebbe. The Rebbe had noticed that the two boys had stopped coming and he was concerned about them. Reb Yossel explained that the Rebbe had told him that he enjoyed listening to their learning and he wanted to know why they had stopped coming.

In a similar note, Reb Moshe Bude of London used to relate the following incident that he had witnessed while a young boy in Vienna:

Reb Moshe was standing next to a *Yid* who suffered from a variety of illnesses and misfortunes. While they were standing together the Rebbe happened to pass by. Seeing this unfortunate *Yid*, the Rebbe stopped and from an inner pocket he produced a *kvittel* that this *Yid* had given him some months earlier.

"You see how I care for you," the Rebbe told the hapless fellow. "I keep your *kvittel* on me wherever I go!" With that the Rebbe carried on his way, leaving the man beaming with joy.

IN HIS *SEFER "GINZEI YISROEL,"* THE REBBE WRITES:

A Spiritual Doctor "Just as there are diseases of the body so there are diseases of the soul, and just as Hashem has created medicines to treat the different bodily illnesses, so there are treatments for the spiritually ill. It is vital, however, to first diagnose the particular illness and to find its cause. Only then can one hope to cure the patient.

Once a diagnosis has been made a person is not yet healed. Now he has to follow the directives of a doctor as to which medicine he requires and what quantity to take, and how often to take it. Similarly, it is not enough for the spiri-

Title page of the first edition of
the Rebbe's sefer "Ginzei Yisroel"

tually sick just to receive a diagnosis of their condition. They still need the help of an expert Rav to administer the treatment. The Torah and mitzvos are the medicine but one must know how to absorb their properties. The Torah and mitzvos can only help him when they are done in the prescribed way: being performed *l'shem Shamayim* without any ulterior motives. Such directives can only be given by a doctor for spiritual illnesses, and those are the *tzaddikim* in every generation.

In a second *dvar Torah* the Rebbe writes:

> The main *avodah* of a *tzaddik* in this world is to teach the nation the *derech Hashem*. In order to ensure that the masses will flock to the *tzaddik*, Hashem has given *tzaddikim* the power, through their *tefillos*, to heal the sick and grant *parnassah* to those in need. When the masses hear that the *tzaddik* possesses the ability to help them they will stream to him from all corners of the earth. Once in the *tzaddik's* vicinity they build up a relationship with him and thus he will be able to draw them near to Hashem and show them the correct way.

In addition to acting as a guide for the masses, the Rebbe was also venerated by many *gedolim* who turned to him with their own problems and regarded him as their ultimate authority. Reb Binyamin Zev Jacobson from Germany was known as a distinguished Rav and educator. In one of his books he writes:

In the circle of *gedolei HaTorah* of our period, the Chortkover Rebbe stood out as one of the greatest in the group. Great in knowledge and deep in understanding, he did not hold back *halachah* from his *talmidim* and advice from his petitioners. "*Kol dichfin yeisei veyeichol* — All who were hungry could come and eat," both the individual and the public at large. He gave to all from his wellsprings of Torah. Everybody was free to pluck the fruits of this living *Eitz HaDaas* (Tree of Knowledge).

In the circle of gedolei HaTorah of our period the Chortkover Rebbe stood out as one of the greatest in the group

❧❧

IN AN ARTICLE WRITTEN TO MARK THE REBBE'S FIRST *yahrtzeit*, the *gaon* Reb Tzvi Hirshorn writes as follows:

D'veikus One of the main characteristics of that *tzaddik hador* who lit up the darkness in our lives with the burning light of his Torah and the flame of his *kedushah*, was his *middah* of *d'veikus*.

Those who were fortunate enough to be in the shadow of the *kedosh Yisroel*, those who had the *zechus* to smell the fragrance of Gan Eden that emanated from him and to feel the Rebbe's *kedushah*, they learned to understand the meaning of *d'veikus* which stems from the commandment to cling to Hashem.

The Rebbe taught us that *d'veikus* means to be connected to Hashem. This *d'veikus* comes about when a person perfects his *neshamah*, which comes from under the Heavenly Throne. The more a person purifies himself with a love for everything holy, and the more he develops inside his heart the longing for the *Shechinah*, the stronger the connection becomes.

The Rebbe taught us that true *d'veikus* is to gather together all one's abilities and inner powers and to focus on one point. The whole being must be concentrated on one central goal — the wish of the *Ribbono Shel Olam*.

The Rebbe taught us that a *tzaddik* who clings to Hashem, his mind is constantly in "Higher Worlds." And since his mind is there, his spirit and his soul are there too. This is the level of a true *tzaddik* who has elevated himself to the inner sanctuaries.

All the *tzaddikim* and sound of mind who came into contact with the holy Rebbe, spoke and testified about his level of *d'veikus*. All his actions were done only with the purest of intentions. From the holiest of acts right down to the most mundane, they were all done with the same measure of *d'veikus*, until they formed one long act of worship, connected together like a flame to the coal.

In the *beis hamedrash* of the Chortkover Rebbe we learned that *d'veikus* forms the backbone of *avodas Hashem*, which joins together all the various movements of a *tzaddik* from one end of the spectrum to the other.

*The Rebbe (center); on his left is his son, Reb Nuchem Mordechai;
on the Rebbe's right is the gabbai, Reb Yossel Sternberg*

Occasionly we might have been bothered with the question — when we saw the *tzaddik* wasting his time listening to the low and mundane problems of the masses — why is such an exalted person interested in such lowly matters?

Those, however, who looked with a clear vision and a deep understanding into the ways of the Rebbe, and observed his conduct while he listened and spoke to the crowds who beseiged him on all sides, have no room for such questions.

It was plainly obvious that even then, when he immersed himself into daily problems and heard the quarrels and squabbles, his mind was clinging to the "Higher Worlds." The *d'veikus* that we recognized in the Rebbe was not an abstention from life. It didn't consist of concealing himself in some hidden corner, removed from people and society. Those that seek to separate themselves, and cut themselves off from others, are running away from life and did not find favor in the Rebbe's eyes.

However, those who saw the Rebbe in action, leading and guiding the generation, whether before the war as founder of *Agudas HaChareidim* and fighter for new workshops in the *chareidi* curriculum, or after the war as active leader of Agudas Yisroel until his last day, came to the realization: In the *beis hamedrash* of this *tzaddik hador* we learned that *d'veikus* is to be found in the midst of the daily flow of life: a form of separation while being part of all that is going on. This type of separation longs for life and people and is full of the joys of life. It leaves its fiery stamp on all who come into its path, in order to underline and reveal the secret of life's existence — the Heavenly powers that control everything.

Indeed the Rebbe's pure actions earned him the unstinting praise of even the most outspoken and sharp of the *gedolim*. The famed Rav of Munkatch, Reb Chaim Elozor Shapiro, was known as one of the most zealous *tzaddikim* of his time. Even the greatest Rebbes and *rabbanim* did not escape his scathing rebuke. Always he stood on guard ready to battle against whatever he felt was the slightest breach or deviation from time-honored practices. It was very rare indeed to hear from him words of praise about one of his contemporaries. Yet, despite the fact that over the years many *gedolim* had fallen victim to his condemnations, the Rebbe remained unscathed.

Rav Avrohom Tzvi Weisz was a *dayan* in Satmar (and later a Rav in Bnei Brak) and a close *talmid* of the Munkatcher Rav. He would often relate in what esteem the Munkatcher Rav had held the Rebbe. The Rebbe once wrote to the Munkatcher Rav two letters about a certain matter. These letters were so precious to the Munkatcher Rav that he refused to keep them with all his other correspondence. Instead he put them in a special drawer where he kept all his other precious belongings. When Rav Weisz asked

ב"ה. יום א' י"ב לחודש מרחשון שנת תרח"ץ
פעיה"ק ירושלים ת"ו.

כבוד הרב מוה"ר **צבי טובי' הכהן
רוטינשטרייך** שיחי' מגזע קודש חכם צבי
זצ"ל בעל מחבר ספר דודי לצבי על ספר
תהילים מאמרים יקרים עפ"י אגדות חז"ל אשר
הסכימו עליו גאוני אה"ק גם גאוני חוץ לארץ
נבג"מ זי"ע, הביא לפני מחברתו חידושיו על
גפ"ת בחלק ההלכה בשם **הישר והטוב**
והנה עיינתי באיזה מקומות, וראיתי כי כשמו
כן הוא חידושים ישרים והערות נכונות טובים
להמעיין והנה בזה לעורר למוקירי תורה שיהיו
בעזרו להוציא לאור את ספרו כי זכות גדול
היא לחזק ולתמכו במילי דמיטב. גם יחד עם
ספרו ידפיס מאמרי אור תורה מקדוש עליון
האדמו"ר מטשארטקוב עטר ישראל
זצוקללה"ה זי"ע וראיתי בהם מעט והמה מאירים
ומעוררים לחיזוק התורה וי"ש ואהבת ה' וגם
אני אקח בל"נ את ספרו כשיצא לאור ותומכיו
יתברכו בכל חותמי ברכות.

כנפש הבעה"ח **איסר זלמן מלצר**
אב"ד ור"מ סלוצק
ר"מ ראשי להישיבה וראש המוסד הכללי עץ חיים
בעיה"ק ירושלים ת"ו.

*A haskamah from HaGaon
Reb Isser Zalman Meltzer in which
he praises highly the Rebbe and his divrei Torah*

him why he treasured the Rebbe's letters so highly, the Munkatcher Rav replied: "If there still is a *Yid* nowadays whose every action and movement is performed with *kavanah* and with totally pure intentions — it is the Rebbe of Chortkov!"

☙❧

THE REBBE LAID GREAT STRESS ON THE *DERECH* OF
"*kedoshim tihiyu.*" His whole outlook was governed by the principle

**Pure
Intentions**

that a person has to sanctify himself in all his mundane acts. He constantly repeated the Ramban's principle (*Parshas Kedoshim*) that it is quite possible for a person to keep all the 613 mitzvos and yet to remain devoid of all spirituality. The Ramban writes that in order for a person to acquire the level of *kedushah* he has to conduct himself in a way above and beyond the technical observance of the mitzvos.

The Rebbe constantly stressed that achieving the level of *kedushah* is not a simple task. It requires total devotion to Hashem's wish, so that nothing is done for any purpose except to fulfill the wishes of Hashem. In keeping with this the Rebbe regularly warned against the dangers of self-indulgence. Even those pleasures from which we are allowed to partake, should not become acts of mere physical enjoyment but should be performed in such an elevated way that they become acts of worship.

Chazal tell us that if someone eats without making a *berachah* it is as if he has stolen from Hashem. The Rebbe understood this to mean that a person must have more enjoyment from making the *berachah* than from the food itself, otherwise one has not given the value of what one has taken.

On one occasion, the Rebbe was asked by one of his close chassidim, HaGaon Reb Shmuel Halpern, how it was possible for a person to achieve such a high *madreigah*. "What's the problem?" the Rebbe answered. "Rebbi Yehudah HaNasi declared that he had never benefited from this world." "Who can compare to Rebbi Yehudah HaNasi?" asked Reb Shmuel.

"Why not? My *zeide* the Rizhiner made a similar declaration," said the Rebbe. Again, Reb Shmuel exclaimed, "Who can compare himself to the great Rizhiner?" The Rebbe, however, did not understand what Reb Shmuel found so difficult to understand and told him, "You should at least know that if you cannot achieve this *madreigah*, then you have not yet achieved anything!"

This statement echoed a similar remark by the Rebbe's father, the Alter Rebbe , who once said, "A person can live seventy years learning and *davening*, but if he hasn't learned how to eat properly, it's all worth nothing." The Rebbe lived by his father's words and constantly urged his chassidim to better themselves in all their mundane acts. It was his opinion that the only way to conquer the *yetzer hara* was by eating *l'shem Shamayim*.

It is in this vein that the Rebbe writes in his *sefer "Yismach Yisroel"*:

> Hashem has created a person with a body and a soul, a physical half and a spiritual half. A person's mission in this world is to ensure that the spiritual half of the body elevates the physical half until it also becomes a spiritual being.
>
> Still, we see people who learn Torah regularly and keep the mitzvos properly, and yet they are unable to elevate their bodies to follow the ways of the *neshamah*, and the *yetzer hara* attacks them constantly. The reason for this is because they have not learned to eat *l'shem Shamayim*, and they eat just for their own pleasure. Such eating feeds the *yetzer hara* and strengthens it in its fight against the *neshamah*. But if a person eats *l'shem Shamayim*, he nourishes his *neshamah*

The Rebbe wrote the divrei Torah that he delivered every week. Most of them, however, were lost during the war. Those that remained were later printed.

and not just his physical body, and the *yetzer hara* is left without any power.

ALL THE REBBE'S ACTIONS HAD ONLY ONE *KAVANAH*: *l'shem Shamayim*. The trait of *emes* and honesty also featured highly

Sincere Actions on the Rebbe's agenda. He demanded that a person behave in a truthful and upright manner. He disliked those who pretended to be acting *l'shem Shamayim* but whose real intention was just to further their own self-interests. When at a communal meeting he was confronted by behavior that seemed motivated by ulterior motives, the Rebbe made the following comment:

When the twelve stones argued over which one should have the honor of Yaakov Avinu resting his head on it, Hashem resolved their conflict by forging them together into one stone. "Why did Hashem leave them as a stone," questioned the Rebbe. "Since He was anyway performing a miracle, why not form them into a pillow? That way Yaakov would have been comfortable too!"

The Rebbe answered: "The stones did not really care whether Yaakov was comfortable or not. Each one just wanted to be able to lay claim to the honor that Yaakov had placed his head on it. That being the case Hashem did no more than resolve their dispute. He made them into one stone, thereby allowing them all the same share of honor. Hashem would not grant them the privilege of providing for the *tzaddik*'s comfort, something that they hadn't asked for or cared about.

"If we too wish to benefit from Hashem's assistance in our undertakings for *Klal Yisroel* we must make sure that our motives are pure. If we ask Hashem to help *Klal Yisroel* but in our hearts we are only trying to further our own personal agenda and are not sincere in our request on behalf of others, we cannot expect that from such a plea will emerge anything of substance for *Klal Yisroel*."

Indeed, this theme of serving Hashem with pure intentions, untainted by any thoughts of self-gain, appears again and again in many of the Rebbe's *divrei Torah*. It also formed the basis for many of his comments and advice to his chassidim. In his *sefer* "*Doreish Tov*," the Rebbe's son and successor, Reb Nuchem Mordechai, writes as follows:

The Rebbe with his son Reb Nuchem Mordechai

It was the way of my holy father to serve Hashem in all his actions. This was his aim and his ambition, that his every move and deed be only in the service of Hashem. It was also his hope and goal that the *klal* should also adopt this path, and sanctify their every action. He was of the opinion that a person has not fulfilled his obligation merely by setting aside time to *daven* and learn. He still has to ensure that all his other actions are also *l'shem Shamayim*, and do not cause him to become distanced from the *Shechinah*.

My father was especially stringent about those who do not have much time to learn and spend most of their day working. Since they are not occupied with the direct service of Hashem, they have an even greater obligation to make sure that at least whatever they are doing must be done with pure intentions and not just for greater personal gain and profit. He demanded of them to be extra careful that their businesses are conducted *l'shem Shamayim*, and to realize that a person's profits are already pre-ordained, and that to succeed one must put his trust in Hashem and be aware that a small amount of *hishtadlus* with *bitachon* will get him further than endless hours without *bitachon*.

Similarly my father demanded that a person must be careful in the way he acts toward others. He must know that the mitzvos *bein adam lechaveiro* are just as important to Hashem as other mitzvos. One should be sensitive to the feelings of others, and not oppress widows, orphans or any helpless person; nor may someone who lends money act as a creditor and embarrass the borrower. This was the way that my father expected all *Yidden* to follow.

Occasionally it happened that the Rebbe came across *talmidei chachamim* or *rabbanim* whose motives were not totally sincere. His opinion of one such person is illustrated by the following story:

> The Rebbe owned a large library, which contained many thousands of *sefarim*. It was the job of one of the *gabbaim* to see to its upkeep and to make sure all the *sefarim* were put back in their correct place. This *gabbai* once noticed that a particular *sefer* had been placed back to front in the bookcase so that the book's spine and name were concealed. Someone had used the *sefer* and put it back without due care.
>
> The *gabbai* replaced the *sefer* correctly with the spine facing outwards. The next day the *gabbai* noticed that the *sefer* had again been put back the wrong way. Once again he replaced the *sefer* the correct way, but to no avail. The following day he found the *sefer* back in its previous inverted position.
>
> The *gabbai* realized that this was no accident, and it must be the Rebbe's doing. At the first opportunity, he asked the Rebbe for an explanation. "The author of this *sefer* is a Rav in a large town," the Rebbe explained. "He gave me his *sefer* as a present. While he was here, he told me that he had intended to publish this *sefer* some years earlier but his wife had convinced him to wait. At the time he had not written much, and she said that it would not make a good impression if he gives out such a thin *sefer*. She advised him to wait until he has written more *chidushei Torah* and then publish a thick volume, which will make a better impression."
>
> The Rebbe finished his words and added, "That's the reason I placed the *sefer* the wrong way round."

This particular *gabbai* also once learned an additional lesson about how one's every movement must be done in the correct way. The Rebbe asked him to bring him a *Mishnayos* and also to bring him a cup of tea. Since the *gabbai* wanted to bring the Rebbe both items as quickly as possible, he came into the Rebbe's room carrying a tray with the tea in both hands and the *Mishnayos* tucked under his arm.

When the Rebbe saw him he became visibly upset and exclaimed, "Is that how one carries a *sefer*!" The Rebbe commanded the *gabbai* to go back out of the room and bring in the *Mishnayos* by itself. Afterwards he had to retrace his steps a second time and carry in the tray with the tea.

☙❧

THROUGHOUT HIS LIFE THE REBBE RAN AWAY FROM THE slightest hint of argument and *machlokes*. We already mentioned that

In Pursuit of Peace

it was due to his fear of provoking a *machlokes* that he scaled down his idea to introduce workshops in all *chadarim* and *Talmud Torahs*. The Rebbe's fear of causing argument can be seen from the following incident.

The Gerrer Rebbe held the Rebbe in great esteem and voiced his praises on many occasions. On one occasion when the Rebbe visited him, the Gerrer Rebbe even donned his Shabbos clothes out of respect. Such action was totally out of character for the Gerrer Rebbe who placed very little emphasis on external pomp and show, and it was the talk of chassidim far and wide.

The Gerrer Rebbe was in Vienna a number of times. Each time he would visit the Rebbe and afterwards the Rebbe paid him a return visit. During one of the Gerrer Rebbe's visits to the Rebbe, he told the Rebbe that he had a favor to ask of him, but he wanted the Rebbe to agree to the favor without knowing what it was.

The Rebbe thought for a moment and replied that he is unable to agree to the Gerrer Rebbe's request. While he is more than willing to do the Gerrer Rebbe a favor, he must first know what it entails before agreeing.

When the Gerrer Rebbe saw that the Rebbe would not give in, he told him what the favor was. He did not want to inconvenience the Rebbe and therefore he had wanted the Rebbe to agree not to pay him a return visit. Knowing that the Rebbe would never agree to such a thing he decided to ask the Rebbe for a blind favor.

The Gerrer Rebbe donned his Shabbos clothes out of respect for the Rebbe

When the Gerrer Rebbe had finished speaking, the Rebbe turned to those present and exclaimed. "How grateful I am to Hashem for having given me the *siyata d'Shmaya* to refuse the Gerrer Rebbe's request. If I don't pay the Gerrer Rebbe a return visit, everyone here would know the true reason. However, not all the many chassidim in their towns and villages would hear or believe the true reason. Some of them might start to think that we had had an argument and perhaps a rift had broken out between us. This in turn could cause friction between the chassidim. Therefore I am grateful that I didn't agree blindly to the request!"

Throughout his life the Rebbe longed to move to Eretz Yisroel; in his later years he often spoke about his wish and even started to make the necessary preparations for the move. In the end, however, his dream never materialized and the plans didn't come to fruition. One of the Rebbe's close chassidim once asked him why he had put his plans on hold. Surely whatever problem or difficulty had cropped up could be taken care of.

The Rebbe sighed and answered, "As you know a fierce *machlokes* has broken out in Yerushalayim between the Rav of Yerushalayim, Rav Sonnenfeld, and Rav Kook. If I move to Eretz Yisroel each side will try to involve me in the dispute and gain my support. To keep silent will not be possible; on the other hand, I don't want to get involved either. Therefore I have no option but to wait until such time as they have sorted out their differences." The hoped-for peace settlement never came during the Rebbe's lifetime, and therefore he remained in Vienna.

In his *sefer "Yismach Yisroel,"* the Rebbe writes as follows:

> One of the most important aims of the *derech* of Chassidus is the goal of true harmony and love among *Yidden.* The Baal Shem Tov and the Mezeritcher Maggid constantly stressed the need for all their *talmidim* to live together in *achdus.*
>
> In order to reach the level of *achdus* one must, however, acquire the trait of humility. As long as a person is proud and holds himself higher than others, he will remain unable to live together with them in harmony.

In a second *dvar Torah,* the Rebbe makes the following observation:

> The mitzvah of "loving your fellow Jew as yourself" is composed of two parts. The first half is to "love one's fellow Jew" and the second half is to love him "as oneself." It follows that someone who has a very inflated opinion of himself will find it difficult to honor his friends properly. He will never be able to love them "as himself," for he is convinced that he is far superior to them all.

THE REBBE'S HUMILITY WAS LEGENDARY. ALTHOUGH HE was descended from a house of royalty and he lived and acted as a **Humble** *Melech Yisroel,* he was still able to find opportunities to **as Hillel** forgo his own personal honor.

In Vienna there lived a *Yid* who was very vocal in his criticisms of anything that was not to his liking. The Rebbe's innovations in *chinuch* did not escape his scathing attacks and from time to time he would hurl verbal abuse on the Rebbe and his policies. One day, this *Yid* lost all his money and became a pauper overnight. Despite his long-standing antagonism to the Rebbe, in his hour of need he wasn't embarrassed to knock on the Rebbe's door and ask for a donation.

When this Yid arrived, the Rebbe received him very cordially and gave him a large donation. The gabbai who was standing in the background was aghast. Not only did the Rebbe not take the man to task for his unwarranted and hurtful attacks, but he even rewarded him with a handsome amount of money.

When the man had left the Rebbe's room, the gabbai was unable to contain himself any longer and he exclaimed, "How could the Rebbe give that man so much money? He is the one who always speaks against the Rebbe." The Rebbe, however, just replied simply, "Does that mean that I am exempt from the mitzvah of tzedakah?"

Despite the fact that the Rebbe was universally acknowledged as one of the great tzaddikim and talmidei chachamim of his time, this did not stop him from humbling himself in front of other talmidei chachamim. In the city of Cracow lived a great talmid chacham by the name of Reb Yosef Steinhardt. When he was still a young man he was already famous as a genius of the first order who was fluent in all sections of the Torah. Being a Chortkover chassid, he would often journey to the Rebbe. Despite Reb Yosef's youthful age, whenever he came into the Rebbe's room, the Rebbe would respectfully rise to his feet in his honor.

Although it was the norm that every chassid remained standing in the Rebbe's room, a great Rav or talmid chacham was offered a seat. However, not all those who were allowed to sit felt able to do so. Rav Yosef Mordechai Baumel remembers:

> Before I went into the Rebbe's room I felt so nervous that I was sure everyone could hear my heart thumping wildly. Once in the Rebbe's room, my knees would knock together with fright. Even if the Rebbe would have asked me to sit down, I don't think I would have been physically capable of doing so.

The Rebbe once asked a certain young talmid chacham to be seated. The young man felt unable to be seated in the Rebbe's presence and remained standing. "I am not going to sit while a talmid chacham stands," the Rebbe told him. With that he rose to his feet and conducted the conversation while they both stood!

In the Rebbe's later years, on one of his tours across Galicia, he happened to meet a local Rebbe from one of the nearby villages. They had never met before and neither of them recognized the other. When the Rebbe inquired about the local Rebbe, the latter introduced himself with his full title, "I am the So and so Rebbe." When this man asked in return who the Rebbe was, he answered him humbly, "I am the son of the Chortkover Rebbe."

Reb Dovid Moshe Spiegel related another story about the Rebbe's humility. In his booklet about the Rebbe called *"Pe'er Yisroel,"* Reb Dovid Moshe writes as follows:

> From the mouth of Reb Shimon Leitner of Strizov-Reisha I heard an interesting incident. Reb Shimon was a fiery Chortkover chassid and a *talmid chacham*. He enjoyed a close friendship with the Beitcher Rav, Reb Aharon Horowitz, who was a son-in-law of the Szanzer Rav. During a conversation Reb Aharon once remarked to Reb Shimon, "I want to tell you who your Rebbe really is …
>
> "I was in Marienbad, walking together with my cousin, Reb Avrohom Chaim Horowitz, the Plantcher Rav, when we were told that the Chortkover Rebbe was walking not far behind us.

> Since we knew that the Chortkover Rebbe was regarded as a great *gaon* we decided to wait for him and to engage him in a Talmudical debate.
>
> "We sat down on a bench and soon enough the Chortkover Rebbe caught up with us. He joined us on the bench and my cousin the Plantcher Rav launched himself right into a complicated Talmudical issue. I tried to rebuff his viewpoint and for three-quarters of an hour the two of us fiercely debated the various sides of the issue. Throughout this time the Chortkover Rebbe sat silently as if he hadn't heard a word of the debate around him.

The Beitcher Rav, Reb Aharon Horowitz

"When we had finished debating we got up and took leave of him. My mind, however, gave me no rest. How could the Chortkover Rebbe just sit there and take no part in the discussion of other *talmidei chachamim*? In a polite voice, I dared to ask him. 'Did the Chortkover Rebbe listen to our debate?' The Rebbe nodded his head slightly as a sign that he had heard our discussion. I then dared to ask him further, 'Does the Rebbe have anything to add to the debate?'

"'It would be worthwhile to look at the words of a certain *Tosafos*,' the Rebbe replied.

"I must admit that at the time I didn't grasp the relevance of that particular *Tosafos* to our discussion," Reb Aharon confessed to Reb Shimon. "Only later when my cousin and I examined the words of *Tosafos* carefully, did we understand what the Chortkover Rebbe meant. According to the logic put forward by *Tosafos*, the assumptions on which we had based our viewpoint had been totally refuted and disproved. The reason why the Rebbe had kept silent throughout our discussion was in order not to embarrass and shame us."

The Beitcher Rav finished his story and added, "The fact that the Chortkover Rebbe remembered a *Tosafos* that we had forgotten did not impress us. It can happen that a *talmid chacham* can overlook a particular comment from one of the *mefarshim*. But what did impress us greatly was his humility and his self-control. For almost an hour he sat next to us, knowing fully well that we had erred and yet he held himself back from telling us and embarrassing us!"

❧

ALTHOUGH THE REBBE DID NOT *DAVEN* TOGETHER WITH the rest of the congregation, and would *daven* in an adjacent side **Tefillah** room, as was the *minhag* of all the Rebbes of Rizhin,[1] there were enough opportunities for the chassidim to learn from him the importance of *tefillah*. Those who were present in the Rebbe's *beis hamedrash* at 4 o'clock every morning knew that if

---

1. See the *sefer* "*Iyunei Halachos*" by Rav Tzvi Rabinovitz for a lengthy halachic analysis of this *minhag*.

they stood quietly outside the Rebbe's room, they could often hear the sweetness of his voice as he recited *Tehillim* praising Hashem for His wondrous deeds.

It once happened that a Karliner chassid came to the Rebbe's *gabbai* in the middle of the week to ask if he would be able to *daven* in front of the *amud* on Shabbos, as he had *yahrtzeit* that Shabbos. The *gabbai* said that the Rebbe did not approve of the Karliner method of screaming and shouting during *davening* and therefore, if he wanted to lead the *tefillos* in the Rebbe's *minyan,* he would have to *daven* softly and in measured tones as was the *minhag* in Chortkov.

The Karliner chassid agreed to the condition, but when it came to Shabbos, he totally forgot about his promise and screamed and shouted all the way through *davening*. After *davening*, realizing his mistake, the man was hesitant to approach the Rebbe. The Rebbe, however, made no mention of the broken promise and thanked the man, adding that he had enjoyed his *davening*.

"But I thought the Rebbe doesn't like this type of *davening*?" the man queried confusedly. "I don't approve of a pre-ordained shout. If a man comes in the middle of the week and proclaims that when Shabbos comes he will *daven* in loud high tones, that's what I don't like. But if in the middle of *davening* he gets so carried away in the *tefillah* that subconsciously his voice starts to rise by itself, that is something else altogether," the Rebbe explained.

The Rebbe viewed *tefillah* not just as a way of procuring one's needs, but also as an end in itself. In his memoirs about the Rebbe, Reb Mordechai Gottfried writes as follows:

> I once visited the Rebbe in his residence in Vienna. During the discussion, which centered on the broader needs and requirements of the *Yidden*, the topic of *tefillah* came into the conversation.
>
> Suddenly the Rebbe became overcome with a fiery fervor and in the heat of the moment he exclaimed, "Through *tefillah* we are united with our Creator! Through *tefillah* we are united with the *neshamos* of all the *tzaddikim*! Can a person survive without *tefillah*? It is a wonder to me that there are people who live without *tefillah*. What can such a life be worth?"

It once happened that a large contingent of chassidim were in a hurry to present the Rebbe with their *kvitlach* before departing back home. Their train was soon leaving and the next one would only be the following day. The Rebbe, however, was not ready to see them; he was still busy finishing his *davening*. In desperation the chassidim requested that the *gabbai* ask the Rebbe if he could make a pause in his *davening*, in order to see them. The Rebbe, however, refused and said, "They will achieve more by allowing me to *daven* in peace than they will by disturbing my *davening* in order to read their *kvitlach*."

In his *sefer "Nezer Yisroel,"* the Rebbe portrays *tefillah* from a different perspective than it is generally perceived:

> *Chazal* have told us (*Devarim Rabbah* Ch. 88): "*Tefillah oseh mechzah — tefillah* achieves a half." These words of *Chazal* are very difficult to understand. Why does one accomplish only half one's requests through *tefillah* and not all one's needs? In *Chazal's* words, however, lie hidden another meaning. It is the wish of Hashem to help a *Yid* with all that he needs and to supply *Klal Yisroel* with only goodness and kindness. Not only does Hashem wish to do this, but He is also constantly waiting and hoping for the opportunity to do so. We, however, are not always deserving of this help, due to our many wrongdoings. This is the purpose of *tefillah* — to repair and rectify our half of the equation, to elevate ourselves that we be fitting to accept the goodness that Hashem is waiting to give to us. Hashem is always ready and willing to help us; we, however, must be ready and worthy of receiving the help. This is what *Chazal* meant when they said that *tefillah* achieves a half.

In the Rebbe's eyes, *emunah* and *tefillah* were closely intertwined, both of them serving the same purpose, to bring a person closer to Hashem. A *Yid* once asked the Rebbe to *daven* for him that he be helped in a particular problem. This problem weighed heavily on the *Yid's* mind and after a day or two he sent a reminder to the Rebbe to *daven* for him. When the Rebbe received the message, he remarked, "I see that this *Yid* has no *emunah* that Hashem will help him. I, however, do have *emunah* that Hashem will help him."

IN HIS *SEFER "TEKUFOS VE'ISHIM,"* REB SHABSI SHEINFELD recorded an interesting incident which is related to the theme of **The True** *emunah* and *tefillah*:

Tzaddik A *Yid* once came to the Rebbe in Vienna in desperation. His son had fallen ill with a fatal disease. The Rebbe gave the man his heartfelt *berachos* but the man wasn't appeased. He wanted the Rebbe to promise him that his son would recover. The Rebbe, however, refused to promise him anything. Hearing the Rebbe's words, the *Yid* could not contain himself and broke down in tears, crying and wailing. One of the prominent *rabbanim* in Vienna, Rav Hager, happened to be present at this scene. He approached the Rebbe and asked him why he had refused to promise the man's son a cure. Surely our Sages have taught us that a *tzaddik* has the power to overturn a bad decree and change it for the good. The Rebbe should decree that the man get better and Hashem will surely heal him!

Rav Hager's question did not sway the Rebbe and he answered simply, "And who says that I am a *tzaddik*?" At this, the unfortunate father of the ill man could contain himself no longer and he called out, "If the Rebbe is not a *tzaddik*, then who is a *tzaddik*?" "There are *tzaddikim*," the Rebbe answered him. "Please, Rebbe," begged the man, "Tell me where he lives so that I can approach him."

In a soft but serious voice the Rebbe answered the man. "I can give you the address of the true *tzaddik* — '*Tzaddik Hashem bechal derachav* — Hashem is a *tzaddik* in all His ways'" (*Tehillim* 145:17).

⁻⊃⊂⁻

THE REBBE USED TO SAY THAT THE ONLY MERIT HE had for asking Hashem to answer his *tefillos* was the mitzvah of

Helping the Poor *tzedakah*. The Rebbe distributed sizable sums of money each week to dozens of families. These families never found out from where the money came, and only when the Rebbe was *niftar* and the money stopped did they realize that it had come from the Rebbe. The Rebbe gave the money to a few messengers who would deliver it to the needy.

On one occasion, the Rebbetzin commented to one of the messengers about her own difficult financial position. There was no money even for basic health treatment that was needed. The messenger decided to relate the Rebbetzin's words to the Rebbe. The Rebbe listened to him in silence and did not comment, but from that day on the Rebbe did not ask him to distribute money anymore.

In an article about the Rebbe, Rav Moshe Leiter writes:

> Two *Yidden* once came to the Rebbe with a request that he impress upon a certain philanthropist to help a particular poor man. The Rebbe took out a hundred-ruble bill as his own donation and handed it to the men. The men refused to take the money and explained that it wasn't their intention to ask the Rebbe for money. All they wanted was that he should convince the philanthropist to give. "Such an important mitzvah has come my way!" the Rebbe exclaimed, "and I should not have a share in it?"

Reb Moshe ends off:

> I also know that the Rebbe once paid for a group of *talmidim* to holiday during the hot summer, in the cool air of the mountains. That year the Rebbe and his family stayed in Vienna and did not go away during the summer break, having spent the money on the *talmidim*.

Although there was no money for the day-to-day running of the household, the Rebbe was *makpid* to live in a palatial house. The Rebbe lived in fabulous luxury in keeping with his royal status. His house was decorated with the most costly furnishings. The most expensive woods and materials adorned the walls. But the Rebbe did not benefit at all from this luxury. Most of his day was spent in his private study, which was totally bare. Just a simple wooden chair stood on the plain stone floor. The luxury was just a show for the outside world.

EVEN THOUGH THOSE WHO HAD BEEN HELPED BY THE Rebbe deposited great sums of money in his hands, the Rebbe was

Unclean Money very careful never to use money received from non-kosher sources. This point is illustrated by the following story which was related by Reb Dovid Prever from Antwerp. Reb Dovid, who was a well-known Chortkover chassid, had lived in Berlin:

> One Friday night, Reb Dovid's doorbell rang. An assimilated Jew who had heard that Reb Dovid intended to visit his Rebbe in the near future, wanted to ask for a *berachah* for himself. The assimilated Jew took out a *kvittel* and some money and put them down on Reb Dovid's table, asking him to please hand them over to the Rebbe. Reb Dovid, aghast at this open display of *chillul Shabbos*, thought at first that he would not take the *kvittel* with him. On second thought, however, he decided that since he had been asked to carry out a mission, he would do so and whatever the Rebbe would do with the *kvittel* and *pidyon* was none of his business.
>
> When Reb Dovid entered the Rebbe's room he put the two sums of money down on the Rebbe's table, his and that of the other man. He made no mention of how the money from

The present Chortkover Kloiz in Antwerp, where Reb Dovid was one of the leading members

the other Jew had come into his hands. Normally the Rebbe never looked at the *pidyon*. He would ignore it, leaving it to the *gabbai* to clear away. This time, however, the Rebbe took the money which the assimilated Jew had sent, and put it in his breast pocket. Reb Dovid noticed this sudden change but said nothing. Reb Dovid's money remained lying on the table as usual, awaiting the *gabbai*.

After the conversation came to a close, the Rebbe told Reb Dovid that he had to go somewhere and that he wanted Reb Dovid to accompany him. On the way, a priest came over to the Rebbe and asked him for a donation for an orphanage that had just opened. The Rebbe put his hand into his breast pocket, took out the money that Reb Dovid had brought from the assimilated Jew, and handed it to the priest. Reb Dovid understood that the Rebbe had wanted to show him that he knew the money was not from a kosher source.

With his wisdom the Rebbe was able to solicit large donations even from people who were known as misers. Once, late at night, the Rebbe sent a summons to a rich man to appear before him. When the man arrived, the Rebbe asked him to finance the operation of an ill person whose treatment was being held up due to lack of money. The rich man had been under the impression that he was needed for an emergency that could not bear delay until the morning. He was rather taken aback to hear that he had been summoned just to donate some money. Surely the Rebbe could have waited until the morning to call him.

"I especially wanted to speak to you still tonight,"the Rebbe explained to the man. "I just heard that you made a very large profit today in your business. By tomorrow, you will already regard this money as your own and you won't be so willing to part with it. Tonight, however, it hasn't yet fully sunk into your mind that all this money is really yours. You are not yet used to the idea that this large sum now belongs to you. That's why I wanted to speak to you tonight. It is easier to give something away which you do not yet consider yours." The man did indeed give the entire sum that the Rebbe had requested!

In his *sefer "Ginzei Yisroel,"* the Rebbe gives an interesting perspective on how to sucessfully raise money for *tzedakah*:

> The *tzaddik* Reb Hirsh Leib Aliker used to comment on the phenomenon that wherever he went, people would give him large sums of money, while others who went to collect came home with far less. Reb Hirsh Leib was known as a *tzaddik* who despised money and riches. These feelings of his would penetrate the hearts of those who came into contact with him, thereby making it easier for them to part with their money.
>
> Those, however, who go collecting and try to impress on their listeners the importance of money and what they would accomplish with it if they only had the chance, wind up reinforcing the importance of money to their audience and therefore the potential giver hesitates to part with it.

The Rebbe derives a moral lesson from this story and he concludes:

> When a Yid attaches too much importance to gold and silver, he arouses the attention of the *yetzer hara* who is constantly seeking to strip the *Yidden* of all that is precious to them.
>
> If, however, the *Yidden* don't view gold and silver as a goal in themselves and realize that money has no value except to act as a tool in one's advance in Torah and mitzvos, the *yetzer hara* is unable to accuse the *Yidden* of partaking of undeserved luxuries. This is what the *pasuk* tells us, that in the time of Shlomo HaMelech money littered Yerushalayim like stones. Since he instilled into the hearts of *Yidden* that silver and gold have no value of their own and are like stones, the *yetzer hara* did not seek to take it away from them, and therefore it was in abundance like stones.

CHAPTER EIGHTEEN
In Agudas Yisroel

T HE GREAT LOVE THAT THE REBBE HAD FOR EACH and every member of *Klal Yisroel* knew no bounds. Constantly he was on the lookout, trying to help a fellow *Yid* in need, both physically and spiritually. Thus, when the idea was broached to found an international organization to help *Yidden* throughout the world, the Rebbe embraced the project wholeheartedly.

ON THE 11TH OF SIVAN 5672 (1912), AGUDAS YISROEL HELD its first meeting in the town of Kattowitz near the Polish-German

Kattowitz border. The conference took place just a few months after the Rebbe had founded and held the first meeting of his organization, *"Agudas HaChareidim,"* in Chernovitz.

The Rebbe was unable to be present at the inaugural meeting in Kattowitz and sent the Rav of Chortkov, Reb Yisroel Rapporport, as his representative. He also sent the delegates in Kattowitz a letter in which he wrote:

Your honorable letter reached me and my heart rejoiced to see that the *Ruach Hashem* has awakened the *ehrlicher Yidden* in Germany to unite under the banner of *Yiddishkeit*, in order to uplift the honor of the Torah and *emunah*, and to circle the holy Torah with a fortified wall which the foreign winds of the *maskilim* in Germany will not be able to penetrate.

How great is my joy to see that they wish to join forces with our fellow brothers in Galicia, to go hand in hand with them in strengthening the Torah. I also see that the *Ruach Hashem* has spread to *Yidden* in other countries who wish to unite and be like one man with a common aim. If only this spirit will remain in our hearts all the days.

Therefore I bless the organization in the Name of Hashem, that they succeed in accomplishing on behalf of the Torah and strengthen *Yiddishkeit*.

The holy idea to found an organization to help *Klal Yisroel* also occurred to me and to the other leaders of *Klal Yisroel* in our district. We saw that the major principles of our faith are beginning to weaken, and that the younger generation is no longer able to prevail in the difficult battles from inside and out. We therefore decided, myself and the *rabbanim* and *tzaddikim*, that it is not the time to keep quiet. To this end we came together during the previous Nissan to work out how to defeat the evil and to stop the storm enveloping the four corners of our religion.

And now, my fellow brothers, you can see which way we are heading and what our goal is. If you share the same worries and also the same ideas and solutions as we do, we will be prepared to join with you. Let us hope that our combined efforts will create a strong bond and we will indeed succeed in healing the wounds of the nation and uplifting the honor of Yisroel and the Torah.

After two days of deliberations the Kattowitz conference closed with the publication of the following resolution:

The representatives of observant Jews from all parts of the world, having met here in Kattowitz and having listened to various proposals hereby declare the founding of "Agudas Yisroel" and commit themselves to work for the growth of Agudas Yisroel with all their strength. Agudas Yisroel will take an active part in all matters relating to Jews and Judaism on the basis of the Torah without any political considerations.

The outbreak of the First World War in 1914 brought to a brutal end any plans of Agudas Yisroel. Even after the war's end in 1918, the terrible destruction left in its wake made it impossible for the Agudah to operate. Many of its founding members had been forced to flee their homes and were not in a position to be of much assistance. Thus it was only a few years after the war's end that the Agudah started to operate in earnest and accomplish its intended role. By then, a strong Agudas Yisroel was more of a necessity than ever. The years of neglect and destruction made the work of the Agudah even more vital.

WITH THE WAR'S END IN 1918, THE DECISION WAS MADE TO base Agudas Yisroel's world headquarters in Vienna. The city's

Under the Rebbe's Aura proximity to Poland, Lithuania, Germany and Romania made Vienna the obvious location. Thus the Agudah's very nerve centre was literally almost on the Rebbe's doorstep. The Rebbe assumed a very central role in all the Agudah's plans and activities and no decisions were taken without his prior knowledge and consent.

One of the founding members of Agudas Yisroel was Moreinu Reb Yaakov Rosenheim. In his book about Agudas Yisroel, he writes:

> Vienna, the capital city of Austria, emerged as an important base for the Agudah. According to the decision from the meeting in Pressburg, the central seat of Agudah and its main offices would be permanently based there. All the activities in Vienna were under the supervision of the Chortkover Rebbe, who was extremely dedicated to all the ideals of the Agudah and he bestowed on us his aura and spirit.

Although the central body of the Agudah was under the Rebbe's personal guidance, he nevertheless insisted that while general policy could be formulated on an international basis, only local *rabbanim* — who were familiar with the situation in their particular areas — could decide on how to implement the decisions.

The Rebbe made this condition explicitly clear in one of his many letters to the central offices of the Agudah:

> Since each country has its own methods and techniques for dealing with their own particular problems, it is therefore impossible to devise one single strategy for all countries. Each country must be run and structured according to its own unique needs and characteristics, according to the Moetzes Gedolei HaTorah in that country. The decisions of the *rabbanim* in one country must not be dependent on the opinions of the *rabbanim* in a second country.
>
> Similarly, the policies and actions that the Agudah intends to implement in the Holy Land, which is the heart of all countries and the joy of all *Yidden*, must be done only with the consent of the great *rabbanim* in the Holy Land.
>
> Through such steps, all *Yidden* faithful to the Torah can be confident that whatever action the Agudah embarks upon on behalf of *Klal Yisroel* will be according to the directives of the *gedolei harabbanim* and thereby the Agudah will go correctly and accurately in its way.

The Rebbe was dedicated to Agudas Yisroel with all his heart. A delegation from the Mizrachi movement once came to speak to the Rebbe. When they arrived they were upset to see that Reb Moshe Hirshprung from Lemberg, who was a well-known Agudas Yisroel activist, was also in the Rebbe's room. They asked the Rebbe to tell Reb Moshe to leave, as they would be uncomfortable speaking in the presence of a representative of Agudas Yisroel. Hearing their request, the Rebbe rose to his feet and said: "If that is the case, then I will also have to leave the room, because I am a member of Agudas Yisroel from the day it was founded!"

IN ORDER FOR THE AGUDAH TO ACHIEVE THE AIMS that its founders intended, it wasn't enough that the *gedolim* of the

Expansion

period had endorsed the actions of the Agudah. The average *Yid* in the street also had to join the movement and give his support and membership to make the dream turn

A letter from the Rebbe about the importance of Agudas Yisroel

into a reality. The Rebbe invested much strength and energy in spreading the ideals of the Agudah and trying to reach out to every single household across Europe. He publicized many letters in support of the Agudah in which he stressed that it was the duty of every *Yid* to become an active member of the Agudah. Presented here is part of one of those letters. In it, one can feel the Rebbe's immense love and concern for his people:

> *Klal Yisroel* can be likened to a ship far out at sea during a fierce and stormy gale. The ship is tossed from side to side without any sailor or captain to rescue it. A shattered and broken people cry and groan from the waves of sorrows that seek to engulf them. Enemies raise their hands and strangers heap scorn and even friends keep at a distance.
>
> If not for our belief that the Captain of the entire world watches our ship that threatens to disintegrate, and sends His *malach* to save us from the depths of the sea, our hearts would have melted and we would be like a man without hope. For not only are we surrounded by evil and wicked peoples who detest us intensely, but we have also fallen ill from the *galus* and the divisions and ruptures among us. We have become like a man without feeling or sensitivity, who remains oblivious to all that besets him.
>
> In times gone by, during the thousands of years of our *galus* and dispersion, we comforted ourselves with the knowledge that the *gedolei Yisroel*, the leaders of the nation, were on the lookout, watching our progress. They stood up for us in battle, both in *tefillah* — pouring out their hearts to Hashem to have pity on His people — and also they protected us against the schemes of mankind. Now, however, there is no one who is alert and arouses himself about the plight of his people.
>
> How great was my joy to hear that Agudas Yisroel, which was already founded before the war, is attempting again to strengthen itself. To its ranks have joined all the *tzaddikim* and *rabbanim* in Poland. Although the Agudah also has a large number of professional and academic members, we must not forget that for such a major task we still need many

more people and we need to develop a workforce that comprises all types of skills.

Therefore I plead with all faithful *Yidden* to listen to my words. Please take to your hearts the importance of the work that lies ahead of us in order to raise the *kavod* of Hashem and His Torah. Also realize the great responsibility that we bear if we fail and are lazy in our task.

To this end, how pleasant is the idea to unite and sit together as brothers in the Agudah, which has the Torah and *Yiddishkeit* engraved into its being and existence. Be strong and each man urge his fellow man to join the Agudah and serve in its ranks faithfully. Then, with the help of Heaven we will succeed and the garden we have planted will sprout forth. With this we shall merit to see the time when Hashem will reveal His mighty arm, and lead us back to our land speedily in our times.

The Rebbe had great aspirations for Agudas Yisroel. He placed much trust in the hope that the organization would indeed improve the lot of *Yidden* scattered throughout the world. These sentiments of the Rebbe and his dedication to the movement were highlighted by Reb Yitzchok Meir Levin in an article in the newspaper *"HaPeles."* Reb Yitzchok Meir was a son-in-law of the Gerrer Rebbe, the Imrei Emes, and a well-known figure in the Agudah. As such, during the course of his work, he met the Rebbe many times. These are his words as recorded in the newspaper:

> The Chortkover Rebbe was a rare and noble person. Someone who saw him even once could never forget him. He represented royalty in its true and literal sense. He was a person elevated over the nation whose *ahavas Yisroel* was beyond description.
>
> He was bound to the Agudah with his heart and soul. In order to enlarge and expand Agudas Yisroel he made contact and wrote letters to all the *gedolei Yisroel*, among them my father-in-law as well. He was always the first person and the main one to help and assist the Agudah in any of its

aims. From the Agudah's very inception he followed its every move and decision with great interest and concern.

The Chortkover Rebbe did not view the Agudah just as a joint platform to house all *frum Yidden*. He also did not view the Agudah just as a unified base for Jewish problems throughout the world. He also did not view the Agudah as just a single table where all *gedolei Yisroel* could gather together to discuss their actions.

Rather he also viewed the Agudah as a protective safehouse against the effects and influences of those anti-*frum* Jews who sought to poison the minds of the innocent. The joining together of all *frum Yidden* under one roof, united with their *gedolim*, turned the Agudah into a mighty force of fighters on behalf of our Holy Torah, a camp which would be strong enough to withstand all the foreign influences directed against it.

To this end, the Rebbe saw the Agudah's main objective being that of *chinuch*. During the many conversations that I had with him, he constantly stressed that Agudas Yisroel must concentrate on setting and achieving goals in the *chinuch* of the boys and girls. On this and only on this, he would say, does the *Beis Yisroel* have a future existence. He was also of the opinion that the Agudah must open technical schools where those who have finished their yeshivah studies can be taught a trade.

One particular incident sticks in my mind. In the year 1920, I visited the Rebbe in his home in Vienna. As usual he welcomed me in a very warm manner. After the conversation, he asked if I would come back again tomorrow and give a speech about the importance of the Agudah.

In his home he had assembled his entire family, men in one room and women in the other. The Rebbe rose to his feet and told his family, "I would like you all to listen to what this young man has to say about the Agudah." For a solid hour I spoke to them about the importance of Agudas Yisroel. Afterwards the Rebbe thanked me for my words.

The Chortkover Rebbe was not the only rare and noble person in his family. All the Rebbes of the Rizhiner Dynasty were unique. Their presence always added a special atmosphere to any meeting. At every Knessia Gedolah that they attended, they were a distinct unit in their own right. Their appearance at the meetings could be felt throughout the hall of the Knessia. Everybody could see and sense that they possessed unique regal qualities.

⁐⁐

The Knessia Gedolah

TEN YEARS AFTER ITS INCEPTION, AGUDAS YISROEL HELD its first major conference which became known as the "First Knessia Gedolah." The date was set for the 3rd of Elul 5683 (1923) and the venue was Vienna. The secular organizations and their newspapers ridiculed the forthcoming "*Shtreimel* Congress" and predicted that it would be a total failure. They were wrong. Over 900 delegates from across the world poured into Vienna. Many thousands of eager and curious *Yidden* also came to watch the historic occasion and merit meeting the many *gedolim* who came to participate in the seven-day conference. The most famous *gedolim* of the day assembled together in Vienna to publicly sanctify Hashem's Name. Not since the times of the *gemara* had such a great assembly gathered together. All in all, over 5,000 *Yidden* crammed themselves into the conference hall in the Cirkus Strasse.

From faraway Radin in Lithuania came the saintly sage, the Chofetz Chaim. Despite his frail condition, the elderly *tzaddik* had insisted on participating in person. The Gerrer Rebbe, who was the undisputed leader of Polish Jewry, arrived from Ger and the famed *gaon* Reb Chaim Ozer Grodzinski came from Vilna. Next to them sat table after table of other great luminaries, the *geonim* Reb Meir Arik, Reb Shlomo Zalman Breuer, Reb Moshe Mordechai Epstein, Reb Aharon Levin, Reb Isser Zalman Meltzer, Reb Meir Shapiro, Reb Elchonon Wasserman, Reb Menachem Ziemba and many others.

A view of the First Knessia Gedolah in Vienna, 1923

A holy and heavenly atmosphere could be felt in the vast hall where the Knessia Gedolah was taking place. Not a joyous atmosphere like on Simchas Torah but rather a serious and somber atmosphere similar to that of *Kol Nidrei* on Yom Kippur night. The Chofetz Chaim, who was also a Kohen, opened the proceedings with a short address and recited the *Birkas Kohanim*.

The Chofetz Chaim called to the assembled and said:

My beloved brothers! We have gathered here to find a cure for the weak body of the Jewish nation. A doctor was once treating a patient. Suddenly, in the middle of the treatment, the patient's heartbeat became weaker and weaker until it finally stopped. The doctor immediately stopped administering

The Chofetz Chaim declared that the purpose of the Knessia Gedolah was to find a cure for the weak body of the Jewish nation

his treatment and gave emergency first-aid in order to restart the man's heart. We have come here to save the heartbeat of the Jewish people. Our existence as a nation is in danger. Our first-aid is the Torah. We must rebuild the centers of Torah, the yeshivos, and the *Talmud Torahs*. Let the children be educated in the path of the Torah. This is the wish of Hashem, and if we acheive this, the glory of Hashem will be revealed upon us.

After the Chofetz Chaim had finished his address came the turn of the Chortkover Rebbe. Although the Rebbe was hardly a stranger in Vienna, still, like the Chofetz Chaim, his address was greeted with great anticipation and excitement. The Rebbe was not given to holding public speeches and only spoke in the confines of his own *beis hamedrash*. Thus his *derashah* marked a radical change from his time-honored practice and aroused much comment.

The newspapers of the day reported on the entire Knessia Gedolah, describing each day and each speaker in detail. In one of these papers, "*Dos Yiddishe Licht*," the Rebbe's entry to the hall and *derashah* are recorded as follows:

One of the personalities about whom the Agudah can and must be proud of, and who took a major role in the Knessia, is the Rebbe of Chortkov.

As is well known, the Chortkover Rebbe is considered one of the greatest *tzaddikim* of our generation. He is famous as a great and powerful Rebbe who commands many thousands of chassidim throughout the world. He is known as an outstanding *talmid chacham* who sits and learns throughout the day. While he is learning, no one is allowed to disturb him, no matter who he is. Therefore his appearance drew the interest of all present, chassidim and *misnagdim*. A special aura of *kedushah* could be felt as he spoke, which was one of the only occasions he has spoken in public.

The hall was jam packed with people. The main platform was filled with the many *gedolim*. Suddenly a whisper goes through the crowd, "The Chortkover Rebbe is coming." A beautiful yet awesome spectacle unravels in front of our eyes. All present rise quickly to their feet with a respect and reverence that one cannot describe. From the Rebbe's face shines a pure and brilliant light. Distinguished *gedolim* also get up from their seats on the top table and go forward to shake the Rebbe's hand.

Rav Aharon Levin from Sambour, who was chairman of the meeting, welcomed the Rebbe on behalf of all assembled. When he requested that the Rebbe address the gathering, the whole assembly respectfully rose again to their feet, and then sat down again. There was absolute silence in the vast hall. The Rebbe made his way to the central podium from where he delivered the following words:

"'MOSHE YEDABER VAHA'ELOKIM YAANENU BEKOL — Moshe spoke and Hashem responded to him with a voice.' The *Medrash* explains that Moshe became like 'a vessel full of words.'

Like a Gramophone

"Moshe Rabbeinu could be compared to a gramophone (or nowadays a tape recorder) which transmits to the listener the original recording without adding or subtracting even one word. Moshe Rabbeinu, who was the most humble person in the world, did not add his own message or interpretation into Hashem's words when he spoke to *Klal Yisroel*. That faithful shepherd transmitted Hashem's message to the *Yidden* without changing it in the slightest way.

"The Knessia Gedolah can be likened to the idea of '*Moshe yedaber*.' We do not seek to insert our own personal ideas or private agenda. Rather we are like a gramophone transmitting without change or deviation.

"The Knessia Gedolah is an event which is totally *hasgachah pratis*. To praise the Knessia is quite unnecessary. *Chazal* already praised the assembly when they declared, 'A gathering of *tzaddikim* is beneficial for them and beneficial for the world.'

"The central issues that need to be discussed during this Knessia are the following: The *chinuch* of boys and girls, strengthening the walls of *Yiddishkeit,* and Eretz Yisroel. We must not be complacent with our lot, with what has been achieved until now. Our voice must echo throughout the world. The *Mishkan,* which was the heart of the nation, did not remain rooted to one spot in the *Midbar.* It journeyed, bringing its values from one place to the next. The Knessia Gedolah is like the *Mishkan,* from which must radiate our message across the world.

"When Moshe Rabbeinu blessed *Klal Yisroel,* he blessed them that they should multiply like the stars in the sky. What did Moshe add with this *berachah*? Hashem had already blessed them that they multiply like the sand of the sea.

"Sand is comprised of many millions of tiny separate granules. They are not joined together and a wind can disperse the granules far apart. The stars in the sky, however, although far apart, are connected. The pull from the larger stars holds the smaller stars in orbit. Moshe Rabbeinu exhorted the *Yidden:*

The Rebbe's address to the Knessia Gedolah

When you enter Eretz Yisroel stay together like the stars in the sky. *Gedolei haTorah* are like large stars whose pull keeps the rest of the nation in the correct orbit.

"The *pasuk* says: *'Vayeired Moshe min hahar el haam* — And Moshe went down from the mountain (Sinai) to the people.' Moshe's greatness was that he was able to descend from his high level to understand the needs of the people. In a period where there is confusion and turmoil in the Jewish nation, the *gedolei haTorah* must be able to lower themselves 'from the mountain to the people.'

"In order for the Agudah to accomplish its goals, there must be true *achdus* between all its members. The people must know that they have to obey the instructions of the *gedolim*, and the *gedolim* must be able to listen to and understand the needs of the people. Then we will be able to look forward to the coming of the *geulah sheleimah* speedily in our times."

MAJOR ACHIEVEMENTS CAME OUT OF THE FIRST KNESSIA Gedolah. The Moetzes Gedolei HaTorah — the Council of Torah **With the** Sages — was formed. From now on, they were the supreme authority in all community issues, a body **Chofetz** that was the most powerful and respected collective **Chaim** voice of Torah in the world. Millions of *Yidden* looked to the Moetzes Gedolei HaTorah not just for help in dealing with the daily problems affecting them, but also for answers to questions affecting the future and destiny of *Klal Yisroel*.

The Moetzes Gedolei HaTorah was composed of some twenty *gedolim*, and was headed by four main members: the Chofetz Chaim, the Chortkover Rebbe, the Gerrer Rebbe and the *gaon* Reb Chaim Ozer Grodzinski. They were to form the inner cabinet of the Agudah, and had the last word on any decisions. They were appointed the presidents (*nesiim*) of the Agudah.

Reb Chaim Ozer was particular to stand up
every time the Rebbe entered the room

These *gedolim* were asked to sign a special document to commemorate the event. Being the oldest, the Chofetz Chaim was asked to sign first, but he refused and handed the document over to the Rebbe, insisting that he sign first. The Rebbe also refused to sign first and handed it back to the Chofetz Chaim saying, "The Chofetz Chaim is a Kohen and therefore according to the *halachah* he has to sign first." The Chofetz Chaim handed the document back to the Rebbe a second time and exclaimed, "The Rebbe is a *Melech Yisroel* and a king comes before even a Kohen Gadol." The Rebbe took out his pen and signed in the middle of the top line, leaving room for the Chofetz Chaim to still sign before him on the same line. The Chofetz Chaim, however, signed on the second line and the Gerrer Rebbe signed on the third line.

In the *sefer "Ish Chassid Hayah,"* the *tzaddik* Reb Elyah Rot from Yerushalayim related an interesting comment that he heard from the esteemed *gaon*, Reb Chaim Ozer Grodzinski, at the Knessia Gedolah:

> During the many meetings that took place during the week of the Knessia, it was noticed that Reb Chaim Ozer was particular to jump to his feet whenever the Rebbe came into the room, and to remain standing until after the Rebbe was seated. Although there were many other *gedolim* who were also constantly coming and going, Reb Chaim Ozer did not accord them the same respect as he gave to the Rebbe.
>
> When Reb Chaim Ozer was asked for an explanation as to why he had singled out the Rebbe for such honor, he answered as follows: "The Torah is divided into many different mitzvos and commandments. Yet there is one particular

mitzvah which is in a special league all by itself. This is the all-encompassing mitzvah of *ahavas Yisroel*. The Chortkover Rebbe possesses this all-encompassing quality of *ahavas Yisroel* and therefore deserves extra recognition and respect."

THE FORMATION OF THE MOETZES GEDOLEI HATORAH was not the only achievement of the Knessia Gedolah. The prestige

Resolutions

of Agudas Yisroel grew tremendously and the primacy of its *gedolim* was reaffirmed and its scope widened. A tired and weary *Klal Yisrael* found new hope in the Moetzes Gedolei HaTorah. From now on they had an address to which to turn — which was waiting to assist them in all their needs.

A new fund, called "Keren HaTorah," was founded to assist the building and refurbishing of yeshivos. The "Keren HaTorah" grew to become a strong and capable fund, which did indeed bring much relief to many. A second fund, called "Keren HaYishuv," was also established. It would assist those who decided to settle in Eretz

A proclamation of Moetzes Gedolei HaTorah after the Knessia Gedolah

The Rebbe examines an article in the Agudah newspaper, "The Togblatt," while a writer waits to hear the Rebbe's comment. The Rebbe's son, Reb Nuchem Mordechai, is next to him.

Yisroel. A plan was also drawn up to assist the new Bais Yaakov school network for girls and to further its scope, and it was agreed to start publishing a number of daily and weekly newspapers which would cater to the *frum* population. The Rebbe took an active role in supervising the style and content of the new newspapers and ensuring that they remain faithful to the task for which they were created.

BUT PERHAPS THE MOST FAMOUS DECISION OF THE Knessia Gedolah was the idea to launch the "Daf Yomi," which

Daf Yomi HaGaon Reb Meir Shapiro announced to the public for the first time from the podium of the hall. All over the world, *Yidden* should unite through learning the same *daf* of *gemara*.

"Just imagine," Reb Meir cried out. "A *Yid* is traveling on a ship from Eretz Yisroel to America. For two weeks he is on the ship and every day he learns a *blatt* of *gemara*. When he arrives in America, he enters a *beis hamedrash* in New York and finds to his surprise other

Yidden learning the same *blatt* of *gemara* that he is learning. They join each other and learn together and thereby Hashem's Name is sanctified. Not only will the Daf Yomi unite *Yidden* worldwide, it will also ensure that all the *masechtos* in *Shas* will be learned; no longer will some of the *masechtos* be 'orphaned,' only being learned by the elite."

The first *daf* of *gemara* was to be learned just under a month later, on Rosh Hashanah 5684 (1924). The new idea was greeted with extraordinary enthusiasm. Unlike many other ideas, which get off to a humble start and gradually gather momentum, Daf Yomi was eagerly learned by tens of thousands from its inception.

When Reb Meir Shapiro paid a visit some years later to the Chofetz Chaim in Radin, the Chofetz Chaim asked him how many *Yidden* were learning Daf Yomi. When Reb Meir answered him that over 150,000 *Yidden* had already joined the cycle, the Chofetz Chaim exclaimed, "I am envious of you, that you managed such a feat."

The Chofetz Chaim expressed his feelings that the learning of Daf Yomi would help to hasten the coming of Moshiach, and then he added, "People think that in the next world everyone will be called by their name — Reb Chaim, Reb Yankel, and so on. No, no, not at all, everyone will be referred to by the *masechtos* they have learned. This seat is reserved for those who learned *Berachos*, and the next seat is reserved for those who learned *Shabbos*, and so on. Until now many of those seats have remained empty and unoccupied. Now, however, thanks to the Daf Yomi all these empty seats will finally be filled."

A few days after Rosh Hashanah 5684 (1924), Reb Meir received a letter from his sister who lived in a small village in Bukovina. In her letter she wrote, "On the night of Rosh Hashanah I had a dream. In it I saw you in *Shamayim* surrounded by many *tzaddikim* with shining faces. You were standing among them and your face shone like the sun at midday. They were all smiling at you and were extremely happy with you. Please let me know the meaning of this dream to what it alludes." The sister had not been aware of the new idea that her brother had suggested and of the fact that on Rosh Hashanah the first *daf* had been learned worldwide.

CHAPTER NINETEEN

The Second Knessia Gedolah

KEEPING TOGETHER THE COALITION OF AGUDAS Yisroel did not always prove an easy task. Sometimes, discussions between the various *rabbanim* could turn rather heated, and one side or the other felt slighted or upset. Reb Tzvi Hirshorn, in the newspaper *"Dos Yiddishe Togblatt,"* recorded one particular occasion that directly involved the Rebbe:

AT A MEETING OF AGUDAS YISROEL, A CERTAIN RAV from Hungary contradicted the Rebbe's opinion in a rather disrespectful tone. At his words, the whole assembly was in an uproar. Among the *gedolim* who were present at the meeting was the Husyatiner Rebbe. When he heard this Rav's words, he got up from his place and went over to the podium and declared:

Just a Regular Member

"The Chortkover Rebbe is the epitome of goodness and he certainly forgives the Rav for his words. We, however, cannot

The Husyatiner Rebbe

and may not ignore what has been said. We have no right to remain silent when the honor of the Chortkover Rebbe has been slighted." The Husyatiner Rebbe finished his words and, as a mark of protest, immediately left the meeting.

After the Husyatiner Rebbe had left the hall, the Chortkover Rebbe mounted the podium and in a soft and pleasant tone addressed the assembled. "My dear friends! Perhaps someone could explain to me why everyone is so annoyed? Am I not just a regular member of the Agudah with my own private opinion? I don't seek to force my opinion on others and have my words adopted blindly. Although I am entitled to voice my opinion, if someone else disagrees with me, he is also entitled to say so and to voice his opinion. If such a disagreement occurs, the Agudah will debate the matter and adopt the opinion of the majority. If I am in the minority, I will change my own opinion to that of the majority. Is that not what the Agudah is all about? Therefore I really fail to comprehend why there was such an uproar because the Rav disagreed with me."

Due to this incident the Husyatiner Rebbe withdrew his membership from Agudas Yisroel. Before the Knessia Gedolah, the Rebbe visited the Husyatiner Rebbe and pleaded with him to return to the Agudah. The Husyatiner Rebbe, however, refused, and despite the Rebbe's pleas, he did not return to the Agudah, where his presence was sorely missed.

A proclamation signed by the Chofetz Chaim, the Rebbe, and the Gerrer Rebbe, to prepare for the Second Knessia Gedolah

Six years after the first Knessia, the *gedolim* reassembled at the Second Knessia Gedolah, and once again it was Vienna that merited hosting the event. The Second Knessia, which took place in Elul 5629 (1929), coincided with a worldwide fast on behalf of world Jewry. In Russia, *Yidden* were being persecuted terribly by the Communists who sought to destroy *Yiddishkeit* and all its adherents; and in Eretz Yisroel vicious Arab pogroms just weeks earlier had resulted in dozens of deaths. Yeshivah *bochurim* learning in Chevron had been hacked to death by blood-crazed gangs of Arabs.

Once again the greatest *tzaddikim* and *geonim* from across the globe assembled in Vienna to take part in the conference. The Chofetz Chaim, however, was unable to attend due to his advanced age, and therefore the Rebbe, as president of the Moetzes Gedolei HaTorah, was honored to give the first address.

When the Rebbe entered the hall, all present could not help but feel the seriousness of the hour. The air was heavy with sanctity, the Rebbe's every pace was slow and measured.

AT THE SIXTH KNESSIA GEDOLAH, WHICH TOOK PLACE IN
Yerushalayim in 1980, the Ponevezher *Rosh Yeshivah*, HaGaon Reb

Rav
Shach's
Fast

Eliezer Shach , commented to a close *talmid*, Reb
Chaim Braverman, that he was fasting. The *talmid*
protested to the elderly *Rosh Yeshivah* that he wasn't
looking after himself properly. How would he be able
to deliver a lengthy speech after having spent the whole day fasting? The *Rosh Yeshivah* answered him: "I know you are right, but
what can I do? I was present at the Knessia Gedolah in Vienna. I
saw how the Chortkover Rebbe entered the hall then, to give his
speech. I looked at his face and it was evident to me that he had
spent many hours readying himself for this moment. If even he felt
the need to prepare himself before the Knessia, the least I can do is
to fast for a few hours."

ANOTHER DESCRIPTION OF THE REBBE'S IMPACT AT THE
Knessia comes from the *Rosh Yeshivah* of Chevron, HaGaon Reb

Melech
Yisroel

Yechezkel Sarna, as recorded by Reb Dovid Moshe
Spiegel in the booklet *"Pe'er Yisroel"*:

> Whenever the Chevroner *Rosh Yeshivah* would reminisce
> about prewar *gedolim*, he would invariably end up mention-
> ing the impression that the Rebbe made on him at the
> Second Knessia Gedolah.
>
> Reb Yechezkel had come especially from Eretz Yisroel,
> together with his father-in-law, the *gaon* Reb Moshe

Mordechai Epstein, to attend the
Knessia. Reb Yechezkel would describe in detail the spell that the
Rebbe's appearance cast on the
crowds. How impressive and noble his princely features were, and
how all sat spellbound watching
and observing his every move
and gesture. His words were
drunk in thirstily by all, his voice
quiet but clear.

When the Rebbe mentioned the
recent pogroms in Eretz Yisroel and the young *korbanos* that
had fallen in Chevron, he started to weep and his whole being and posture suddenly changed. The Rebbe's straight and
erect figure became slumped and bent over. At his words, a
collective sigh escaped the lips of all present. After the Rebbe
left the hall, Reb Moshe Mordechai turned to those around
him, and in awe he exclaimed, "Now all we have to do is to
daven for the final *geulah*. We already have a king to lead us.
The Chortkover Rebbe is a true *Melech Yisroel*"!

This is part of the Rebbe's speech at the opening of the Knessia on
the 5th of Elul:

> Thanksgiving is to Hashem that we have merited to witness
> this special and exalted occasion. We *daven* to Hashem that
> the next Knessia Gedolah should take place in Eretz Yisroel,
> Hashem should bring us there in His mercy.
>
> The Knessia Gedolah is truly an event which is a "*simchah
> shel mitzvah.*" The heads of all sections of *Klal Yisroel* have gath-
> ered together for only one purpose: to honor Hashem and His
> Torah; this is a *simchah shel mitzvah*. A spiritual mitzvah is not
> like a physical pleasure which lasts for only a few moments

A picture of the Rebbe drawn using his derashah at the Knessia Gedolah

בעשריבען מיט זײַן רעדע אױף ב-כנס'הגדולה

and then is gone. The *simchah* derived from a mitzvah remains even after the completion of the mitzvah. The *simchah* from the first Knessia remained with us a long time after the Knessia had ended. We hope that this Knessia will also leave us with *simchah* for a long time.

We are obligated to remember the ruins of Yerushalayim at our *simchos*. Every head and every heart is pained and filled with anguish when we remember the holy *Yidden* whom we had in the Holy Land and are no longer. Every fiber in our heart is trembling and shaking at the events that have happened there. Woe is to the children that have been banished from their Father's table! Our Father in Heaven, Merciful Father! When will You return to Yerushalayim? Let us see You return to Zion with mercy!

From the *Beis HaMikdash*, all that is left is the *Kosel HaMaaravi*, from where the *Shechinah* has never departed. And now the foreign hands of the wicked spill Jewish blood like water.

THE HOLY ONES IN CHEVRON. *OY! OY!* IN CHEVRON, the town where the *Avos* are buried, murderers came and **Martyrs of Chevron** destroyed those precious *bochurim* who were toiling in Torah. We wanted to be able to comfort ourselves and to hope for better times. But our hopes have been dashed, our hearts are breaking from the constant stream of sorrows.

In Russia the situation is dreadful. It is a situation of *shmad*. Those caught teaching Torah are imprisoned for many years.

The pure Torah that emanates from the mouths of children, and upon which the world exists, is being silenced. In other lands *Yidden* are also suffering, both spiritually and physically. *Ribbono Shel Olam*! For how long can this go on? How long?

Nevertheless, we must be strong and believe with true faith that Hashem will help us. It is our duty to repent and to *daven* that the salvation should not be long in coming. Individuals have no ability on their own to help and succeed for the nation. Thus I regard the creation of Agudas Yisroel as a salvation from Hashem. Therefore it is the sacred duty of all *Yidden* to join the Agudah and support its work.

Time for Action

THERE ARE DIFFERENT STAGES DURING LIFE. THERE are times when it is important to speak and there are times when it is important to act. The First Knessia Gedolah was a time to speak. At the time the wider community did not yet know about Agudas Yisroel. We needed to speak and to explain in detail what our aims were and what needed to be done.

Now, however, what is needed is to act and to produce evidence of what has been achieved. At the previous Knessia, a fund called "Keren HaTorah" was created in order to support the institutions of learning. Unfortunately, due to lack of

A section of the top table at the Knessia: the Rebbe's son, Reb Dov Ber (1)
Reb Chaim Ozer Grodzinski (2) and Reb Yehudah Leib Tzirelzohn of Keshinov (3).

funds, they have not managed to accomplish as much as possible. We now have to rectify this and start on new projects.

First, we have to ensure that all children are being educated in *Talmud Torahs*. If a *kehillah* is unable to support its own *Talmud Torah*, Keren HaTorah must make the money available. We must support the existing yeshivos and also build new yeshivos.

The Bais Yaakov school network is very important in my eyes. Bais Yaakov educates the girls in the path of the Torah. In order to ensure the future of the Jewish home, we must have proper education for girls as we have for boys. This will also help issues of *"sholom bayis"* and safeguard the sancity of the Jewish family. Do we not entrust the future of our children into the hands of the mothers? Therefore it is vital to provide them with the correct *chinuch*.

We must also open workshops for those who are unable to continue learning in yeshivah. Not every *bochur* is able to become a Rav or teacher. We must worry for their future and not let them wander around aimlessly without any future. We must see to teach them a trade. If we fail to cater to them, and leave them to their own devices while they are still young, we might *chas vesholom* cause them to lose all that they have acquired during their years of learning.

No *Yid* has the right to remain outside our camp and ignore our demand to participate in building and strengthening the walls of the Torah. Only then will Hashem help us that Agudas Yisroel will succeed and we will be able to achieve the uplifting of the flag of the Torah with true *simchah*. Amen.

NO SOONER HAD THE KNESSIA FINISHED THAN THE REBBE took upon himself to put his words into action. If he expected others

Bais Yaakov

to heed his call for action, the Rebbe felt the need to make the first move and teach by example. The Rebbe decided to open a Bais Yaakov school in his hometown of Chortkov. Rather than collecting the large sum needed to acquire a building for the school, the Rebbe donated a wing of his home to be used as a school building. By giving away part of his own property for the school, the Rebbe had clearly demonstrated the importance of the Bais Yaakov movement and how precious the project was to him.

A women's committee was set up to oversee the running of the school and to ensure its success. A well-known educator from Kolomei by the name of Rebbetzin Rochel Fleker was brought in to lead the school and teach the girls.

One former pupil of the school recalled:

> Rebbetzin Fleker was not only concerned about teaching but also about the main objective of education — to instill in her pupils an appreciation and sense of duty for *Yiddishkeit*. To this end, she considered her visits to the girls' homes, her conversations with them, and the girls' social life more important than the hours that they spent studying at school. Rebbetzin Fleker gave her students the inspiration to continue their studies and to improve themselves.

IN HIS *SEFER "KOL YAAKOV,"* THE WELL-KNOWN RAV OF Queens (New York) and leader of the Agudah summer camp for

Lasting Impressions

many decades, Reb Avrohom Yaakov Teitelbaum, emphasized another vital achievement of the two Knessia Gedolahs. In a *hesped* for a Viennese *Yid*

he declared:

> What is this special bond that unites us together even twenty years after we fled from Vienna? What is it that makes us all feel like one family even after so many years? The answer is

that those who belonged to the ranks of Agudas Yisroel in Vienna did not only learn together but were also united in their struggle to uphold the honor of the Torah.

We were privileged to witness the two Knessia Gedolahs in which almost all of the *gedolim* of the period took part, and to hear their words. Those who heard and absorbed their words have remained with a clearly defined *derech* for the rest of their lives. All the winds in the world are unable to uproot the *hashkafos* that we received then in Vienna.

- As the spiritual leader of Camp Agudah for many decades, Rav Teitelbaum was instrumental in passing on to thousands of children the sights and impressions that he had absorbed in his youth. Many of America's finest *rabbanim*, educators and communal activists received their early guidance and *hashkafah* from Rav Teitelbaum at the Agudah camp.

CHAPTER TWENTY
Toward Eretz Yisroel

ALTHOUGH THE REBBE WAS TOTALLY INVOLVED IN rebuilding *Yiddishkeit* in Europe, as far as his own personal plans were concerned, this was only a passing phase. The Rebbe was not interested in staying in *chutz laAretz* longer than necessary. Like a person in need of air who desperately tries to extricate himself from a smoke-filled room and fill his lungs with fresh oxygen, so the Rebbe felt in *chutz laAretz*. He felt stifled by the *galus* air and he longed for the *kedushah* and the pure atmosphere of the Holy Land.

NOT ONLY DID HE REGARD MOVING TO ERETZ YISROEL AS his own personal goal, but he also encouraged *Yidden* as a whole

Supporting Aliyah
to move to Eretz Yisroel. This was one of the reasons the Rebbe refused to return to Chortkov after the First World War, and stayed in Vienna. "I have

Residents of Eretz Yisroel crown the Rebbi Nasi of Eretz Yisroel

already started on my journey to Eretz Yisroel," the Rebbe would say. "How can I turn around and go back to Chortkov?"

Throughout his life the Rebbe constantly talked about his wish to move to Eretz Yisroel and even made advance plans to go. Each time, however, they had to be canceled. Nevertheless, it remained his fervent hope and wish to be able to settle in Eretz Yisroel. The topic of Eretz Yisroel featured heavily in the Rebbe's *divrei Torah* and his letters. He often spoke about his longing for the land and its extra *kedushah*. Only in the Holy Land was a person truly able to perfect himself in the service of Hashem. Only there could one absorb a full measure of *kedushah*.

In a letter to one of his close chassidim, the *gaon* Reb Ephraim Zalman Halpern, the Rebbe wrote:

A newspaper headline declares: "Chortkover Tzaddik to travel to Eretz Yisroel to buy land"

I heard many times from my holy father that if half a million *frum Yidden* would settle in Eretz Yisroel, they would hasten the coming of the *geulah*.

The Satan also knew of this, and therefore he gathered a large crowd of empty people, with low morals, who are opposed to *Yiddishkeit*. The Satan instilled into these *Yidden* — who are bereft of all *Yiddishkeit* — a love of the Holy Land, and pushed them to ascend there and to work on the land and develop it.

The Satan was sucesssful in his plans and sent these people there. They profaned all that is holy, and thereby also deterred the *chareidim* from entering and developing the land. If, however, the *chareidim* come to Eretz Yisroel in large numbers and settle there, their own *kedushah* combined with the *kedushah* of the land will still be able to overcome the *tumah* of those whose *neshamos* are empty and bare, and return them back to the correct path.

Perhaps the greatest proof to the validity of the Rebbe's words was the burning passion which the Zionist Party invested in preventing *frum Yidden* from settling in Eretz Yisroel. Dr. Chaim Weizmann declared at the Zionist Congress in 1937: "The hope of millions of Jews is dependent on this congress. I seek to rescue two million of the youth. The old folk will perish, they must await their fate. They are like economic dust in a cruel world, only the youth can survive. The old people must step aside and make peace with this."

The principle behind the diplomacy of the Zionist movement was to gain control of the land and reserve it for those secular Jews who found favor in their eyes. This principle was further borne out when the administrator of the United Jewish Appeal sent the following refusal to a request to bring a shipload of refugees to Eretz Yisroel in 1940: "Many of the passengers are old men and women. They are not suited for such a voyage. Young people are needed who understand the essence of a Jewish homeland. It would be a terrible crime if the land were flooded with unproductive elements. They would undermine our efforts at establishing a state."

From the early 1920's the Zionist movement had managed to persuade the British government to refuse entry to those who did not fit the image laid down by the secular leadership. Of all the immigration certificates which England issued, 94 percent went to the Zionist movement. Agudas Yisroel received the remaining 6 percent, and this was only after waging a long and bitter battle, including many meetings with the British authorities. This terrible injustice continued even when the Zionist movement was unable to find enough immigrants to fill their quota and should have then allowed their unfilled places to go to the Agudah. Still they refused to increase the 6 percent quota. Better no Jews than *frum* Jews! These shameful facts have no logical explanation other than the words of the Rebbe. The Satan felt threatened by the arrival of so many *frum Yidden* in the Holy Land and wanted to stop them at all costs.

It was in this context that the Rebbe once issued a severe criticism of Zionism and the damage that it caused. The quote is in the *sefer* "*Likutei Amorim*," authored by the *gaon* Reb Shmuel Halpern, the first Rav of Zichron Meir:

> I heard from the holy Rebbe of Chortkov that a number of times the opportunity had arisen for *Klal Yisroel* to be redeemed and merit the *geulah*. Each time, however, the chance was ruined because of the sins of various people. Already in the time of the Second *Beis HaMikdash*, there was a possibility to merit the final *geulah*. That occasion was ruined by "*oso ha'ish*." The next occasion when the *geulah* was imminent was spoiled by Shabsai Tzvi. The third occasion was now, during our lifetime. There was a great *his'orerus* which could have brought us the Final Redemption. This opportunity was ruined by the Zionists.

This all-out effort of the Satan to prevent *frum Yidden* from settling in Eretz Yisroel was perhaps also the deeper reason why the Rebbe failed in his own many attempts to get to Eretz Yisroel. Over the centuries many *tzaddikim,* such as the Baal Shem Tov, the Vilna Gaon, the Alter Chortkover Rebbe and the Chofetz Chaim, failed to reach Eretz Yisroel despite their determined attempts to do so.

≈⸂

THE REBBE'S WISH TO IMMIGRATE TO ERETZ YISROEL MADE him of interest to the Zionists who thought that they could rely on

Rejecting Zionist Offers him as an ally. In the years before the British took power in Palestine, the Zionists were not yet a strong force on their own. At the time they were still a new and fledgling movement and they looked toward the *frum* community for help and support. The Zionist leaders took it for granted that the Rebbe would want to join forces with them and benefit from their organizations and connections. Through this they also hoped to gain legitimacy and recognition from the *frum* community. All their efforts, however, ended in failure.

Dr. Herzl himself also tried to enlist the Rebbe's support. In his diaries from the summer of 1896, Herzl writes of the considerable efforts he made to convince the Rebbe to support his ideas. Although Herzl never actually came to Chortkov, he did send a number of letters and even a delegation. At the time the Alter Rebbe was still alive and Herzl wanted the Alter Rebbe to agree to become the first "Chief Rabbi" of his future state.

In the book *"Dos Malchusdiker Chassidus,"* the author writes:

> Not many know about the efforts of Dr. Herzl and the time that he invested in attempting to convince the Alter Chortkover Rebbe to join the Zionist Party. He sent Dr. Bloch, who was the rabbi of Zemering and a member of the Austrian parliament, to persuade the Alter Rebbe to accept the post of president of the organization, and even offered that all the rabbinical posts in the state would be under his control.

The Alter Rebbe's son, Reb Yisroel, recognized right away whom he was dealing with, and when Dr. Bloch arrived with a delegation, he sent them away immediately, empty-handed.

When the Rebbe was once asked by Mr. Isserzohn, a leading Zionist figure, why he refused to support the Zionist movement, the Rebbe replied: "I have heard that many of your members live together in the fields and settlements without *chupah* and *kiddushin*. Do you really think I can support those who blatantly disregard the basic tenents of *Yiddishkeit* so publicly?"

Similar sentiments are quoted by Reb Yaakov Mazeh, the Chief Rabbi of Moscow, in his dairies. Rav Mazeh asked the Rebbe his opinion about the Zionist movement, when he visited him in Marienbad in 1913 during the Beilis Trial. The Rebbe replied:

"The plan for *Yidden* to settle in Eretz Yisroel is a very precious one. The Zionists, however, have ruined their movement through desecrating Shabbos and doing other *aveirahs*. The history of our people has proven that through sinful methods it is imposssible to achieve anything on behalf of *Klal Yisroel*."

In a *dvar Torah* given during Shabbos *Parshas Va'eschanan* in 1896, just weeks after having met with Herzl's delegation, the Rebbe said:

> The *Yidden* are not the only nation to be exiled from their country. Throughout history, other nations of the world have also been exiled from their countries. Yet there is a major difference between the exile of *Klal Yisroel* and that of other nations. Other nations might also have lost their land and their tranquility but they did not suffer a spiritual exile. It is the same to them if they are here or there. They serve their false gods, their molten idols, regardless of which country they reside in.
>
> Different, however, is the situation of the *Yidden*. Not only were they driven from their land, but they also lost the *Beis HaMikdash* and became cut off from Divine prophecy, which can occur only in Eretz Yisroel.
>
> Therefore, even if periodically people stand up and lead *Yidden* back to the Holy Land and restore hope to them that slowly *Yidden* are returning to their inheritance, still their

salvation will not be complete. They will not be able to restore the main aspects which we are lacking. Only when Hashem will redeem us will we merit both a spiritual and a physical redemption.

Although the Rebbe supported immigration to Eretz Yisroel, there was a fundamental difference between his view and that of the Zionists. They viewed *aliyah* as an end in itself. If *Yidden* had their own homeland, then the *galus* had effectively come to an end. The Rebbe, however, was of the opinion that even if all *Yidden* lived in Eretz Yisroel, they were still in *galus*. Nevertheless, the Rebbe still encouraged moving to Eretz Yisroel. Even in its destruction, the holiness of Eretz Yisroel remained, though in a weaker form. Its *kedushah* was still vastly superior to anything else the rest of the world had to offer.

∽∝

WITH THE FOUNDING OF AGUDAS YISROEL, THE REBBE demanded that the issue of Eretz Yisroel occupy a prominent place

The Balance of Power

in the Agudah's agenda. Some of the other *gedolim* felt that the Agudah should limit itself to problems in Europe and not seek to burden itself with more than it could manage. The Rebbe disagreed with this view. His heart and soul were bound up with Eretz Yisroel and its inhabitants. Under no circumstances was he willing to compromise on his position.

To the Radomsker Rebbe, Reb Shlomo HaKohen Rabinowitz, the Rebbe explained: "Forty years ago when *Yidden* started immigrating on mass to America, my father wanted to send *rabbanim* and *melamdim* and *shochtim* there, who would care for the population. No one was willing to listen to him then, and today the resulting tragedy is clear for all to see.

"Today the same problem is repeating itself, not in America but in Eretz Yisroel. Thousands of *Yidden* are arriving there without any *rabbanim* or leaders to guide them. If we don't send *rabbanim* to them, they will suffer the same fate as those in America."

At the turn of the 20th century, education and communal matters in Eretz Yisroel were firmly in the hands of the *rabbanim* in Yerushalayim. They had the ultimate word on any problems facing the community, and the ruling Turkish government also considered the *rabbanim* as the leaders of the Jewish community. In the wake of the British conquest of the Holy Land in 1917, new winds began to blow across Eretz Yisroel. No longer did the establishment view the *rabbanim* as the only spokesmen for the community. New secular voices were to be heard, and soon they achieved unprecedented influence. They established the "Vaad Leumi," or National Committee, as the self-governing body of the Yishuv. Their ultimate goal was the establishment of the State of Israel, and control over all Jewish affairs was their first step in this direction.

To further complicate the situation, a major *machlokes* had erupted between the Rav of Yerushalayim, Rav Yosef Chaim Sonnenfeld, and Rav Kook as to who was the legitimate head and ultimate spiritual authority in Eretz Yisroel. Rav Kook had been appointed by the new secular Vaad Leumi as the first Chief Rabbi of Eretz Yisroel. Yet, as far as the majority of *chareidim* were concerned, Rav Sonnenfeld was the true spiritual head and leader of the *frum kehillah*. Thus, the *frum* camp was further weakened, lacking even one joint leader who represented all strands of the community.

It was the Rebbe's aim to restore the balance of power in Eretz Yisroel right back to where it belonged — in the hands of those who represented Torah and mitzvos. The dispute between the Eidah Chareidis and the newly formed Rabbanut had created a power vacuum and in the meanwhile the Rebbe hoped to fill this vacuum through the influence of Agudas Yisroel.

The Rebbe often voiced his grievance that the Agudah had not involved itself earlier in the problems of Eretz Yisroel. "If Agudah would have been involved earlier," the Rebbe would say, "the British would have looked at us differently. They would have taken our words more seriously. It is a great pity we did not start earlier. Then we could still have influenced the British before they had formed their policies."

The Rebbe, together with his son,
Reb Nuchem Mordechai.
In the background is the gabbai,
Reb Yossel Sternberg.

DESPITE THE REBBE'S WARNINGS, THERE WERE MANY
rabbanim who remained oblivious to the problems in Eretz Yisroel.

**Not a
Second Paris**

Even after the sorrowful situation in the Holy
Land had become painfully clear for all to see,
they still preferred not to get involved.

In a newspaper article, Reb Alter Meir of Sonik writes:

> During a meeting of the Agudah in 1920, the question was
> raised whether to include Eretz Yisroel in the Agudah pro-
> gram or not. An elderly Rav from Hungary spoke up and
> said: "We don't need to get involved in Eretz Yisroel. The
> country has been overrun by the Zionists who are all *apikor-
> sim*. We cannot overthrow them and therefore we are best off
> staying out." At his words the Rebbe put his fingers in his
> ears and refused to listen to the rest of his *derashah*.
>
> Afterwards the Rebbe got up and said: "Instead of speak-
> ing against *Yidden* words which are better not to be said, let us
> rather speak in a positive fashion. I have a tradition in my
> family that dates back to the Baal Shem Tov, that if a person
> rectifies and perfects himself, automatically those around him
> will also be helped. When the level of *kedushah* is increased,
> automatically the level of *tumah* decreases. *Chas vesholom* to

leave Yerushalayim in the hands of the secular Jews. The light of the Torah comes to us via Yerushalayim. We may not allow others to transform Yerushalayim into a second 'Paris'! What type of Torah will we then have here in *galus*?"

A vote was taken and the Rebbe's opinion was accepted and so the issue was decided. Eretz Yisroel was entered into the program of the Agudah. A new office named Keren HaYishuv was opened. In the future it would be responsible for all Agudah operations on behalf of development in Eretz Yisroel. Based in Vienna, the new Keren HaYishuv office came directly under the control of the Rebbe, who spared no time and effort in promoting the new branch of Agudas Yisroel.

AFTER THE NEW OFFICE OPENED, A PROCLAMATION WAS issued by Agudas Yisroel under the heading: "Callup to work on

Responsibility for the Yidden in Eretz Yisroel

behalf of Eretz Yisroel." Signed by the Rebbe and also by a long list of famous Rebbes and *rabbanim*, the proclamation exhorted *Yidden* to come to the realization that they were obliged to worry about the welfare of Eretz Yisroel. This is part of the proclamation:

> *Sholom* and *berachah* to our fellow *Yidden*:
>
> Agudas Yisroel in Vienna has decided to widen its efforts on behalf of Eretz Yisroel — to build and develop there yeshivos and *Talmud Torahs*, and also to erect settlements and factories. Thereby *frum Yidden* will settle in Eretz Yisroel and the lifestyle there will be conducted in a *frum* manner.
>
> To this end Agudas Yisroel has opened a special center dedicated to matters pertaining to Eretz Yisroel. This office will bear the responsibility to explore all the different avenues needed to build the land in the spirit of Torah and religion.
>
> The office will also offer assistance and advice to those settling in the Holy Land. The office has already embarked on this aspect and is extremely busy helping those wishing to ascend.

The most pressing items on the office's agenda at present are the following: (1) to ensure the upkeep of *Talmud Torahs* and yeshivos; (2) to buy land and divide it into areas for settlements and factories in the spirit of the Torah.

Dear Brothers! We are all obligated to help our fellow brothers and sisters. Therefore we ask you to set aside 1 percent of your earnings to help build Eretz Yisroel. Through this let us merit witnessing the redemption of Zion and Yerushalayim.

In addition to the Agudah letter, the Rebbe also periodically issued his own letters in support of building Eretz Yisroel. In one such letter he wrote:

Our love for Eretz Yisroel obliges us to increase our work and our involvement in the Holy Land. We have to support those who are already living there and make it possible for others to follow them. This responsibility lies on those *Yidden* who wish to see Eretz Yisroel built on the foundations of Torah and *emunah*. Through supporting the efforts of Agudas Yisroel on behalf of Eretz Yisroel, you are helping the spiritual rebuilding of the Holy Land, increasing the light of Torah and erecting new *mosdos* of Torah for boys and girls.

Help save thousands of young *neshamos* who are being educated in secular schools devoid of Torah and *Yiddishkeit*. If the correct actions are taken, these children can still be transferred to institutions of Torah and *yiras Shamayim*. Help to rebuild the land in such a way that its *kedushah* will remain, its stones will declare its inner holiness and the *Shechinah* will not leave the land. Help protect the young so that no evil winds move them away and no evil people be able to uproot them.

WHEN THIS PROCLAMATION CAME INTO THE HANDS OF one of the prominent *rabbanim* of Lithuania, he told those around

No Time to Lose
him that he disagreed with the Rebbe's words. This Rav was not known to be an admirer of Agudas Yisroel and refused to be part of the movement or partake in

its programs. Nevertheless, when the Rebbe heard of this Rav's criticism, he wrote an uncharacteristically sharp letter.

In the letter, addressed to one of the Rav's confidants, the Rebbe writes:

> I write to you concerning the position of the Rav, who saw the *Kol Korei* and voiced his opposition without giving any clear reasons, and prefers rather to sit still and not take action.
>
> I ask you to please urge the Rav in this matter, for I have heard that he is from the *yirei Hashem* and a *chacham* who should be able to understand the situation, which has reached such proportions that the heart almost breaks to see the condition of the generation. There is not even time to allow for a meeting of all *gedolim* to decide on a course of action. If we take a back seat, the secular leaders will *chas vesholom* assume control, and then we will be powerless to act.
>
> Therefore, I ask you to urge the *gaon* to realize that there is no time to be wasted. If he has an objection to something in the *Kol Korei*, he should not bury the matter in his heart, rather he must explain clearly what bothers him so that his complaint can be assessed and judged. Similarly he should also express himself clearly in regard to his reservations about Agudas Yisroel. We are of the opinion that at this crucial hour it befits a man of great stature in Torah like the Rav, to be a *"chacham haroeh es hanolad* — a wise man who sees the future."

Who May Ascend

DUE TO THE DIFFICULT SPIRITUAL AND PHYSICAL CONDITIONS in Eretz Yisroel, the Rebbe did not automatically agree that anybody who wanted to move there should do so. Not all who asked him received his permission to ascend to the Holy Land. At a meeting of *gedolim* in Warsaw in Iyar 5684 (1924), the Rebbe clearly stated his opinion and said: "I am of the opinion that only three types of *Yidden* should be

encouraged to move to Eretz Yisroel: only a single person, or someone with a job in hand, or a well-to-do person may be encouraged to settle there. The financial situation in Eretz Yisroel is very precarious and a poor man with a wife and children will not be able to make ends meet. This will result in their going back to Europe and this gives a bad image to the Holy Land. They must rather wait here in *chutz laAretz* until such time as Hashem will have pity on them and enable them to leave."

One person who passed the Rebbe's criteria and succeeded in moving to Eretz Yisroel was Reb Dovid Moshe Spiegel. In his memoirs he writes as follows:

> From my youngest years a love of the Holy Land burned inside me and I longed to settle there. My parents agreed to my moving but insisted on first asking the Rebbe.
>
> In a letter to my father, the Rebbe replied: "Concerning the question about his son Dovid Moshe who wishes to ascend to Eretz Yisroel, it is a very worthy idea, for he is capable and suitable for a variety of jobs and tasks. Hashem should help him reach Eretz Yisroel without mishap and be successful."
>
> Another three friends of mine — Reb Shlomo Gelenski, Reb Shimon Begrophin and Reb Mordechai Korn — also decided to join me in my move. Finally, after a full year of waiting for our certificates, we left Poland on the 15th of Iyar 5686 (1926). We traveled via Vienna so as to take leave of the Rebbe as well.
>
> When we arrived in his *beis hamedrash*, the Rebbe walked a few steps toward us and warmly welcomed us. He put his right hand on his forehead and with his pure and sharp eyes he scanned us from top to toe. After he had scrutinized us,

the Rebbe proclaimed aloud: "These are the type of *bochurim* I want to go to Eretz Yisroel! You should all go on the correct *derech* and not be influenced by others."

Just months before we arrived, a major economic crisis erupted in Eretz Yisroel. Many people lost all their savings and their jobs. Large firms and factories declared bankruptcy and ceased trading. This sudden downturn of events sent many hundreds of new immigrants scuttling back to where they had come from. This mood of despair and depression greeted us as we disembarked the ship in Haifa. Instead of a cheery "*Shalom Aleichem*," the porters greeted us sighing, "New *korbanos* (sacrifices) are arriving …"

In Eretz Yisroel the four of us parted ways. Reb Shlomo and myself entered Sfas Emes Yeshivah in Yerushalayim. (Reb Shlomo became a well-known *talmid chacham* and author of *sefarim* on *Shas*.) Reb Shimon, who was a professional worker, found a job after a long search, and Reb Mordechai eventually found work doing hard physical labor.

After a time Reb Mordechai fell ill and as a result lost his job. He was an only child and wasn't used to the rough conditions and the hard labor. When his parents heard about his sorrowful state, they insisted that he return home. Their begging put Reb Mordechai in a quandary. Since he had come with the Rebbe's *berachah*, it was unthinkable to leave without the Rebbe's permission.

Reb Mordechai's father went to see the Rebbe and while telling the Rebbe of his son's travails, he burst into tears and begged the Rebbe to allow his son to return. He explained to the Rebbe that he had intended to follow in his son's footsteps and ascend to Eretz Yisroel. Now, however, due to the change in the economic situation this was no longer feasible. This being the case, he was desperate to be reunited with his son.

The Rebbe answered him that he is of the opinion that it is forbidden for someone living in Eretz Yisroel to leave for no reason, but since he cannot bear to see the father's tears he is allowing his son to return. When Reb Mordechai presented himself to the Rebbe on his return, the Rebbe told him: "You should know that I agreed to your leaving Eretz Yisroel only because I could not bear your father's crying. I have never yet advised someone that he would be better off leaving Eretz Yisroel!" (The boy and his family were killed during the war.)

⤚⤙

Throughout the 1920's the Rebbe concentrated on achieving his goal of ascending to Eretz Yisroel. When one of the Rebbe's rich chassidim, Reb Elimelech Backenrot, asked the Rebbe for a *berachah* for a large property investment that he had recently acquired, the Rebbe replied in a strict tone: "Why did you not consult me before you invested such a large sum? Nowadays, a *Yid* who possesses so much money must invest it in property in Eretz Yisroel and not in *chutz laAretz!*"

To one of his chassidim, Rav Moshe Leiter, the Rebbe confided: "It is my intention to soon move to Eretz Yisroel. But I don't wish to move there by myself. I want to arrive there with people who are well to do and in a financially strong position in order to build and breathe new life into the Yishuv. I want to make it economically feasible for dozens or even hundreds of families to be able to follow us later."

In a letter written in the winter of 1925, the Rebbe's *gabbai* publicized the Rebbe's wish to soon leave for Eretz Yisroel:

> With the help of Hashem, it is the wish of the holy Rebbe to travel to Eretz Yisroel immediately after Pesach, for a number of months.
>
> His intention is not simply to tour the country, rather his intention is to set in motion the necessary requirements to start building and developing the land. The Rebbe is unable to achieve such an accomplishment unless he has the full backing of those chassidim who have been blessed with wealth. If they accompany the Rebbe on his trip, together they will be able to buy fields and properties which will

bring returns to their owners. Besides which, they will also bring in desperately needed funds to the poor in Eretz Yisroel and to their *mosdos*.

Looking forward to meeting you in Eretz Yisroel with a joyous heart.

Tzvi Rapporport
Yosef Sternberg
(the *gabbaim*)

"Many are the thoughts in a man's heart, but in the end the council of Hashem will prevail" (*Mishlei* 19:21). The Rebbe's oldest son, Reb Chaim Aharon, fell deathly ill and the trip had to be canceled.

The Aron HaKodesh in the Chortkover shul in Yerushalayim, in memory of Reb Chaim Aharon

IN HIS ACTIONS ON BEHALF OF ERETZ YISROEL, THE REBBE received the full support of the Gerrer Rebbe, who was also of the

The Gerrer Rebbe's Support

same opinion as the Rebbe. He too yearned to live in Eretz Yisroel and did his utmost to convince his chassidim to move there.

In 1922 the Gerrer Rebbe decided to see for himself the situation in Eretz Yisroel. On his way he passed through Vienna, where the Rebbe attended a send-off in his honor. In addition, the Rebbe publicized an accompanying letter in the newspapers in which he made known his total support for all the Gerrer Rebbe's plans. This unusual step came about after the secular newspapers alleged that the Rebbe did not agree with the Gerrer Rebbe's ideas and had refused to sign a letter in support of the Gerrer Rebbe's trip.

In a letter printed in the Agudah paper "*Der Yid*," the Rebbe's *gab-bai*, Reb Tzvi Rapporport, strenuously denied the allegation.

> To the central office of Agudas Yisroel in Warsaw:
>
> Your honorable letter concerning the report in the news-paper "*HaSefirah*," number 115, that there is a difference of opinion between the holy Rebbe and the Gerrer Rebbe, reached the holy hands of the Rebbe.
>
> Although it is against his principles and almost an affront to his honor to answer and refute all the rumors and gossip that these cheap newspapers regularly churn out, neverthe-less, in order to bring a halt to all this small talk and wild accusations as to why the Rebbe didn't sign a letter in support of the Gerrer Rebbe, I have been commanded by the holy Rebbe to announce in his name the following declaration:
>
> "'Those *Yidden* who are faithful to the word of Hashem should know to ignore all the efforts of the secular press which seek to create a split and a division between the Rebbe and Agudas Yisroel. Likewise they should know that the Rebbe stands united together with the Gerrer Rebbe in regard to all aspects of Agudas Yisroel and especially so in regard to pushing forward work and development in the Holy Land. We hope that very soon their work will bear fruit and those that seek to spread false rumors and lies in order to discour-age others, will fall silent.'"

After his first visit in 1922 the Gerrer Rebbe wrote a long and de-tailed letter in which he described the impression the visit had made on him and his plans for the future of Eretz Yisroel. His opinions and views almost mirror those of the Chortkover Rebbe:

> I would like to inform you of my views about matters in the Holy Land. My heart overflowed with joy at seeing the splendor of the land. I visited the institutions and yeshivos that are maintained by the *chareidim* and found them all praiseworthy. However, they all need help and support from abroad to enable them to expand further. I was happy to see that it is possible to observe *Yiddishkeit* properly, without

hindrance. Someone who has been blessed with wealth would undoubtedly find there a *parnassah* without worry.

As for those who are not able or are unwilling to settle in Eretz Yisroel, they should at least help other *chareidim* to settle there, and set aside money to buy a piece of land, an investment which bears fruit in this world as well. I have joined a group that bought a plot of land in Jaffa on which will be built an apartment block. I ask that others follow my example and do likewise, for the time has come to put our plans into practice. I have also come up with several proposals for projects that can be carried out by Agudas Yisroel.

It would be a good idea to convene the Moetzes Gedolei HaTorah to discuss how to increase settlement in the Holy Land. You no doubt know that the Moetzes Gedolei HaTorah already decided that the Agudah become involved in further building the Holy Land regardless of the changing political climate. I really do believe that the mitzvah of living in Eretz Yisroel is not dependent on time but on the physical possibility of doing so. We therefore have to use our maximum strength to do all we can to achieve that goal, for the more *chareidim* that will live there, the greater will be their influence and this in turn will guard the *kedushah* of the land. No one, however, should set out hastily — but only after due deliberation and planning and after he knows how he will earn his living there and how much money he will need.

On his return home to Poland the Gerrer Rebbe did his utmost to try to coax people into moving or at least investing their money in Eretz Yisroel. "If 500 rich *frum* families will settle there, then Eretz Yisroel will be ours both physically and spiritually," the Gerrer Rebbe once said.

Due to the efforts of the two Rebbes, many people did move to Eretz Yisroel, but the vast majority of people failed to understand their words or didn't have the means to do so. Had the Rebbes been listened to then, the whole situation that the *chareidim* face nowadays in Eretz Yisroel might well have been totally different!

On his way back home to Ger, the Gerrer Rebbe passed through Vienna, where he briefed the Rebbe about his trip. The Rebbe listened with excitement to the Gerrer Rebbe's words and afterwards he said: "If only I would be able to move there already. Things, however, are not yet in place for such a move."

"Why don't you go now for a visit?" the Gerrer Rebbe asked. "Later on when you are finally ready you can move there."

"I have the strength to travel there," the Rebbe answered with a sigh. "I just don't know from where I will find the strength to leave."

≈⌒

ALTHOUGH THE REBBE NEVER ENDED UP MOVING OR EVEN visiting Eretz Yisroel, he did manage to send groups of his chas-

Chortkover Settlements sidim to settle there. One such group was called "Chevras Nachlas Krakow" and it comprised 120 families. The Chevrah sent two representatives, Reb Chaim Bulbaum and Reb Benzion Grossfeld, to buy a plot of land on their behalf. They bought a 2,000-dunam plot of land near Haifa for 12,000 liros. The land was to be developed and gotten ready for its new inhabitants, who would arrive once the houses had been built.

The Satan, however, did not allow the plan to materialize. Halfway through the work, the company that was in charge of the land went bankrupt and the project came to an abrupt halt. Only a few of the 120 families finally arrived.

Nevertheless, there were other groups of chassidim that did succeed in moving to Eretz Yisroel. In a letter to one such group the Rebbe wrote:

> How happy I was to hear that a group of our chassidim have decided to settle in Eretz Yisroel and to live there a life of holiness. They seek to acquire a plot of land from Agudas Yisroel and to work the land and plant the fields and vineyards, according to the *halachos* pertaining to the land. They have decided to call their group "Beis Dovid."

Let my portion be with you to take part in your settlement, for which my soul and being longs. Let Hashem allow my desire and your desire to succeed.

Together with you is my friend who is great in Torah, the chassid Reb Shmuel Halpern, whose heart is also alert to developing the country, and he will help you to achieve this goal with faith and haste.

In addition Agudas Yisroel has a number of honorable representatives who will also inflame your desires in pursuit of the holy goal of settling in Eretz Yisroel. It is my opinion that working on the land in Eretz Yisroel is conducive in helping a person to learn Torah. That is why our holy forefathers and Moshe Rabbeinu chose to be shepherds.

This land, whose *kedushah* still hovers over it, has the ability to reignite in those who work it, the belief that the whole world belongs to Hashem, and we are mere laborers who have to keep the laws and rules of our Master. This land on which princes and holy *tzaddikim* carved and left their imprint, can restore *emunah* back into its inhabitants.

Therefore be strong in bringing the project to its conclusion and through our efforts may Hashem be aroused to have pity on us and bring us all back to Zion with joy.

Over the years a number of Chortkover shuls were opened in Eretz Yisroel. Yerushalayim itself hosted two shuls, one in the Old City and one in Meah Shearim. Similarly, Haifa also was home to two Chortkover shuls. In Tzefas, Teveriah and Tel Aviv additional branches also sprouted. Two of the shuls, one in Meah Shearim and the other in Tzefas, still function to this day.

Through the Rebbe's efforts and those of Agudas Yisroel, great achievements were accomplished in Eretz Yisroel. One such example was the founding of the settlement Machanei Yisroel in the Lower Galilee. Bought from its Arab owners by Agudas Yisroel in 1925, it comprised an area of

Stamp of the Chortkover Yeshivah in Yerushalayim

30,000 dunams. When Rav Yosef Chaim Sonnenfeld visited the settlement he could not contain his joy, and he recorded his feelings:

> Machanei Yisroel has been founded, with Hashem's help, by Agudas Yisroel. The heart warms to see this "Camp of Hashem" established by *frum* settlers. The settlers and workers are all G-d-fearing *bnei Torah* who have left their homes in the Diaspora to come to the Holy Land to rebuild its ruins and restore the Holy Land to its former glory.
>
> They have come here to build not only the Jewish body but also the pure and unblemished Jewish soul. May this be the first of a whole series of *frum* settlements founded by Agudas Yisroel. All our brothers who desire the rebuilding of our Holy Land support the efforts of the Agudas Yisroel. May Hashem grant success to their efforts and may they continue performing great deeds and hasten the *geulah* in our time.

In another letter, Rav Sonnenfeld made clear his great appreciation to Agudas Yisroel for their efforts on behalf of Eretz Yisroel:

> Agudas Yisroel has accepted upon itself the task of spiritually and materially providing for our religious brothers in the Holy Land. Its leaders have dedicated themselves to this high ideal and have laid the cornerstone for many developments in the Holy Land. They have worked with great sacrifice and *baruch Hashem* they have succeeded in all areas.
>
> They have established *mosdos* true to the Torah and *yiras Shamayim*. They have reinforced many yeshivos that were on the point of collapse. They have helped farmers to keep *Shemittah*. Just recently they bought a large area of land on which many *frum* people will settle and keep the Torah's agricultural laws.
>
> We have seen firsthand the violations of the Torah by the settling in Eretz Yisroel of those disloyal to *Yiddishkeit*. We, who grieve over the work of those who spread *apikorsus* through their schools, appreciate the work of Agudas Yisroel even more deeply. We raise our hands in thanksgiving to Hashem Who has not denied a redeemer to His people and land.

CHAPTER TWENTY-ONE

The Rebbe and His Faithful Chassid, Reb Meir Shapiro

CHORTKOV HAD ALWAYS SERVED AS A MAGNET FOR many *gedolei Yisroel*. Among the masses that flocked to the Rebbe were some of the most famous and greatest Rebbes and *rabbanim* of the generation. Literally dozens of great *tzaddikim* considered themselves to be faithful chassidim of Chortkov and regularly traveled to seek the Rebbe's guidance and *berachah*. The Rebbes of Slonim, Radomsk, and Amshinov were all faithful chassidim of the Rebbe, as were the great *geonim*: Reb Sholom Schwadron, the Maharsham; Reb Dov Berish Weidenfeld, the Tchebiner Rav; Reb Velvel Nissenbaum, Rav of Drohibisht; and Reb Meshullam Rot of Chernovitz.

THE REBBE WAS ALWAYS EXTREMELY CAREFUL TO GIVE THE proper respect due to these *tzaddikim*, who were acclaimed *gedolim*

A Magnet for Gedolei Yisroel

in their own right. Thus, for example, the Rebbe insisted that all these illustrious guests must receive an *aliyah* to the Torah on

Shabbos. Although this meant adding quite a few extra *aliyahs*, which was a burden on the rest of the *minyan*, the Rebbe refused to stop the practice. "This is the Torah's honor," he would say. "I cannot overlook *kavod haTorah*."

Often the Rebbe went out of his way to show his esteem to his venerated chassidim. The Rav of Tarnov, Reb Meir Arik, was acclaimed as one of the greatest *poskim* of his day. Yet this did not deter him in any way from being a faithful chassid of the Chortkover Rebbe. He traveled many times a year to bask in the Rebbe's presence and learn his ways.

Reb Meir Arik greeting his Rebbe was a sight worth seeing. Moments before he came face to face with the Rebbe, hot tears trickled down his cheeks as he stood waiting in anticipation of seeing his beloved Rebbe.

Yet, just as it was worth seeing Reb Meir greeting his Rebbe, so it was worth seeing the Rebbe greeting his chassid. When the Rebbe was informed that Reb Meir Arik was waiting outside to see him, he hurried to the door. "It's good that you came," the Rebbe once said humbly. "A number of difficult questions on the Rambam

A letter from the Rebbe to Reb Meir Arik

have accumulated since your last visit. I have been waiting for you to answer them."

⥼⥽

YET, FROM ALL THE *GEDOLIM* WHO TRAVELED TO CHORTKOV, one particular *tzaddik* stood out. The relationship that the Rebbe en-

My Urim VeTumim
joyed with Reb Meir Shapiro, the Lubliner Rav, far surpassed his relationship with any of the other *gedolim*. The bond between the Rebbe and his great chassid was already considered to be a legend during their lifetime. From Reb Meir's youngest years, the Rebbe had carefully nurtured him and watched his progress until he eventually blossomed into a *gadol* in his own right.

Even then, when Reb Meir was renowned across the world as one of the foremost leaders and thinkers in *Klal Yisroel*, he still considered himself a humble chassid of his Rebbe. In his last years he was heard to say, "The Rebbe is my *Urim VeTumim*. From my earliest years I have never lifted a hand or foot before I consulted him."

The *mashgiach* of the Lubliner Yeshivah, Rav Shimon Zhelichover, used to say that if one wanted to see what true Chassidus is, he should watch how Reb Meir trembled in the presence of his Rebbe. Once, at a *tisch* in Chortkov, Reb Meir didn't have a seat. The Rebbe noticed that the Lubliner Rav was standing and said to him, "Meir'l sit down." Immediately Reb Meir crouched down. He remained in a sitting position until a chair could be passed through the crowds.

Reb Meir's awe for his Rebbe knew no bounds. The Potiker Rav related that he was once present when Reb Meir was walking together with a group of his

Reb Meir Shapiro declared that from his earliest years he has never undertaken anything without first consulting the Rebbe

talmidim. Reb Meir was expounding about the greatness and the *kedushah* of *tzaddikim* when he suddenly stopped walking and, raising his voice, he exclaimed: "How can I adequately describe to you the true extent of the Chortkover Rebbe's *kedushah*? The holy *Zohar* says that a person's fingernails possess a *tumah* and therefore need to be constantly cut. Yet, by the Rebbe, even the fingernails are *kodshei kodashim* (holy of holies)!"

Some of the elder *rabbanim* felt slightly displeased and uneasy at the unusual status that Reb Meir enjoyed in Chortkov. Here was a junior Rav hardly over 30 years of age, and yet each time he came, they had to make room for him and offer him first place. Sensing their displeasure, the Rebbe explained:

> When a *talmid chacham* comes to see me, I honor him so as to honor the Torah that he possesses. When a rich man comes to me I honor him in keeping with the custom of Rebbi Yehudah HaNasi who used to honor the wealthy. When a person who possesses *yiras Hashem* comes to see me, I honor him in reverence for the *Shechinah* of which this man is constantly aware. When a person who is descended from a distinguished family comes to see me, I honor him in recognition of his great ancestors. If an *askan* (a communal worker) comes to see me I honor him in the merit of the community that he represents. Now this being the case, how can I not give special honor to Reb Meir Shapiro? He contains all these good qualities in himself. Is it possible not to welcome him?

❦

Reb Meir Shapiro was born on the 7th of Adar 5647 (1887) to Reb Yaakov Shimshon who lived in the town Shotz, Bukovina. From his youngest years it was apparent that he was no ordinary child. When he turned bar mitzvah his teacher told Reb Yaakov Shimshon that he had exhausted his stores of knowledge; the young Reb Meir by now knew more than he did.

Reb Meir was sent to study under his grandfather, the *gaon* Reb Shmuel Yitzchok Shorr, author of *"Minchas Shai"* on *Tanach*. For three years Reb Meir sat at the feet of his grandfather, who prepared him to become a leader of *Klal Yisroel*. The Minchas Shai was an illustrious chassid of the Chortkover Rebbe, and Reb Meir absorbed the teachings of Chortkov under his grandfather's direction.

At the age of 19 Reb Meir married the daughter of Reb Yaakov Breitman, a well-known and influential businessman from Tarnopol, Galicia. Reb Meir settled in his wife's hometown and was soon besieged by young men wishing to be his *talmidim*. Although he held no official position, his reputation and his personality drew throngs of people who came to learn from him and bask in his presence.

As the years went by and Reb Meir's name spread ever further, people could not understand why he didn't emerge from behind his *sefarim* and start to lead a *kehillah*. Reb Meir was opposed to the idea, as were his parents-in-law. He wanted only to learn in peace and to climb ever higher in Torah rather than have to burden himself with the problems of others — at least not for several years. His *talmidim* and his followers refused to accept his decision and pressured him and his family that he accept a position, hoping they would finally give in.

BEING A CHORTKOVER CHASSID, REB MEIR NATURALLY turned to the Rebbe for advice and counsel and was ready to accept **Near** whatever the Rebbe would decide about the question of his future. When the Rebbe heard that people were **Lemberg** already waiting for Reb Meir to assume a position, he ruled that Reb Meir should use his talent for the benefit of *Klal Yisroel* and take up the *Rabbanus*.

Reb Meir's *shver*, however, wasn't able to come to terms with the decree and told the Rebbe, "But my son-in-law is really not interested in the *Rabbanus*."

The Rebbe turned to Reb Meir and asked him, "Meir'l, why don't you want to become a Rav?"

"I really don't need it," Reb Meir replied. "I am happy as I am."

"If you don't need the position, then you are needed even more."

"Who needs me so desperately?" Reb Meir asked. "Is the city of

Lemberg waiting for me?" The Rebbe listened to his words and then answered him. "If that is what you want, you will be near Lemberg."

Hardly had a week gone by when a delegation arrived in Tarnopol from the town of Galina, which was situated next to Lemberg. The delegation wanted Reb Meir to become their Rav. Seeing that the words of the Rebbe had been fulfilled, Reb Meir agreed immediately to their request. And so, at the tender age of 24, Reb Meir Shapiro assumed the *Rabbanus* of Galina.

Despite his youth, he already then exerted great authority. His mere presence commanded respect and honor. In a letter written at the time, the new Rav stated:

> It is impossible to describe the honor that the town gives me. All sections of the community, from the highest to the lowest, seek my counsel. Without my advice no one does anything. Blessed be the One Who has given me the wisdom to know how to answer them all. Many new decrees have been enacted since I arrived here; the place has taken on a new look. Hashem should continue His blessing to me, that my words be heeded in His service all the days.

≈◠

IN 1922, A MEETING OF AGUDAS YISROEL TOOK PLACE IN Warsaw, attended by hundreds of *rabbanim* and lay leaders. The meeting was convened to try to work out a uni-

President of Agudah

form strategy to strengthen Torah in Poland and Galicia. Although Reb Meir Shapiro was only 35 years old at the time, his personality and his brilliant speech at the convention electrified the audience.

His voice rolling across the hall, Reb Meir cried out:

> The honor of the Torah and its *rabbanim* have been thrust to the ground. Any proud and haughty individual is free to open his mouth and deride and belittle us. It is not enough just to repair the broken fences. We must take upon ourselves to start from scratch, to totally rebuild. In years to

come people are going to look back and examine our actions to see what we have achieved. How ashamed we will be! The history books will be full of blank pages.

Reb Meir's fiery *derashah* left a great impact on all who heard it. He was indeed correct! Someone must be found who could stand up in battle and would be able not just to protect but to build and strengthen *Yiddishkeit* in Poland. After deliberation, the *rabbanim* of the Agudah came to the conclusion that there was no candidate more suitable for the job than Reb Meir Shapiro himself. And so the young Rav came to be the president of Agudas Yisroel in Poland.

The Gerrer Rebbe gave his full support to the appointment. "There are those," he said, "who conjure up stories that Agudas Yisroel is controlled by Ger. Therefore I am especially happy that Reb Meir Shapiro, who is known to be an unswerving chassid of the Chortkover Rebbe, has been elected president!"

Reb Meir's entry into such a high position served to further elevate the prestige of his Rebbe in the eyes of the masses. Reb Binyamin Zev Jacobson from Germany was known as a distinguished Rav and educator. In one of his books he writes:

> In front of our eyes still stands a glorious picture, a beautiful and magnificent picture. It is the image of the Rebbe of

> Chortkov as we saw him the last time, not long before his *petirah*, and as we saw him the first time many years ago: the inner beauty, the beauty whose source is from the soul and spreads over the whole body. At the Knessia Gedolah the Rebbe stood, and in a soft and gentle voice blessed the assembled. Next to him stood Reb Meir Shapiro. The young and dynamic Reb Meir stood listening to his Rebbe, swallowing every word that left the

In front of our eyes still stands the glorious image of the Rebbe of Chortkov

Rebbe's mouth. The scene symbolizes the Rebbe's strength, a symbol of his inner strength over his chassidim.

His thousands of chassidim respected him like a *malach* from heaven; the whole world regarded him as the prince of our people. The leaders of our nation stood before him in awe and fear; even those who had fallen by the wayside realized their insignificance in his presence. The Rebbe, however, walked in humility in front of his Creator; the more the people honored him, the more he humbled himself.

Despite his youth, Reb Meir was already then considered by all to be one of the Torah giants of his period. Testimony to his standing among the *gedolim* can be seen from a letter written to him at the time by the Chofetz Chaim, who was old enough to be his grandfather. In his letter the Chofetz Chaim wrote:

> To the great *gaon* who is famed for his *geonus*, who is *yirei Elokim beemes*, Reb Meir Shapiro, Rav of Sonik. I received the pure letter of his honor with his comments on my *sefer* "Likutei Halachos," for which I thank him, and I was overjoyed to see that great men like himself look into my *sefer*, which will be a *zechus* for me.

The Chofetz Chaim ends his letter with a *berachah* to Reb Meir that he be able to carry on serving *Klal Yisroel*, "for who else will help them if not the great leaders of our time."

⁀⌒

REB MEIR'S SPECIAL STATUS AMONG ALL SECTIONS OF Jewry made him uniquely suitable for tasks that other *gedolim* were
Daf Yomi hesitant to undertake. Although it is commonly accepted by all that the idea of Daf Yomi was Reb Meir Shapiro's brainchild, there are those who dispute this fact. Among a few of the elite Chortkover chassidim there was a closely guarded secret that in reality the Daf Yomi was not Reb Meir's own idea but that of his mentor, the Chortkover Rebbe.

Two of the great *rabbanim* of the previous generation, the Potiker Rav HaGaon Reb Shlomo Zalman Horowitz, and HaGaon Reb Fishel Harling (he was a nephew of Reb Meir Shapiro), were both privy to this secret. They both revealed that Reb Meir had told them on separate occasions that in truth the idea of Daf Yomi was not really his own invention.

Reb Meir told them that in reality Daf Yomi was the Rebbe's idea but he had commanded Reb Meir to present it as his own brainchild. "I know fully well," the Rebbe explained, "that if I broach the idea it will not be greeted with the same enthusiasm as it would be if Reb Meir launches it. There are many people who are under the misconception that a Rebbe's ideas and decrees are intended only for his immediate circle of chassidim and followers. Reb Meir, however, was regarded by all as a neutral figure and as such the idea had more chance of being accepted."

Therefore, in order to increase its chances of success, the Rebbe insisted that Reb Meir pass off the idea as his own and the Rebbe's name was not to be mentioned at all in connection with the Daf Yomi.

As long as the Daf Yomi was still in its teething stage and had not yet become a worldwide success, these *rabbanim* kept the secret to themselves in keeping with the Rebbe's instructions. It was only in their later years, after the Daf Yomi had achieved international recognition and acceptance, that they finally divulged what Reb Meir had revealed to them.

Besides the testimony of these two great *rabbanim* who were respected by all as truthful and G-d-fearing Jews, their words can be backed up by circumstantial evidence (or rather the lack of it). The Rebbe wrote countless letters and proclamations concerning and promoting the many projects that his faithful chassid undertook. There is, however, one blatant exception to this list.

Although the Rebbe constantly exhorted his chassidim both in writing and verbally to support every idea his beloved Reb Meir innovated, there is not a single mention anywhere about Daf Yomi. There is not even one letter or comment from the Rebbe in support of Daf Yomi. Similarly he never issued a request to his chassidim encouraging them to learn Daf Yomi or to take part in any event linked to it. It was almost as if he seemed to be trying to distance himself from Daf Yomi as much as possible. This glaring omission cannot be explained or reconciled in any other logical way, and is in itself the biggest proof that the Rebbe himself was involved in its formation and therefore sought to distance himself from any connection that might link him with the Daf Yomi!

≈⌐

Reb Meir used to say, "The *gemara* says, 'In times of danger one takes the *Sefer Torah* out of the *beis hamedrash* to the street.' We must take the Torah out of the *beis hamedrash* and spread it to the masses. We are obligated to reach every far-flung corner, to penetrate into every home."

To this end Reb Meir traveled up and down Poland, speaking and meeting the local people. Wherever he went hundreds of people came to hear his fiery words and to learn what was expected of them. His words of promise and hope gave new strength to the many weary souls that he encountered. He urged his listeners to cast off their yoke of despair and start to take pride in themselves and their religion. In an article he wrote, "This is my life's aim, to see a strong and organized generation, fighting with all its strength for its values and its religion."

In 1923 Reb Meir was asked to become a member of the Polish parliament, the Sejm. Agudas Yisroel needed someone who would be able to defend *Yiddishkeit* from the lawmakers. This time, however, Reb Meir refused. It was one thing to sacrifice his time and energy to help guide *Yidden*, but to sit surrounded by Polish anti-Semites was too much for him.

Nonetheless, in the end Reb Meir gave in to the pleas of Agudas Yisroel and against his will he took his place in the parliament. Although he had not wanted the position, once he was elected, Reb Meir threw himself fully into the task and proved himself to be a formidable politician who was feared and respected by all the various factions in the parliament.

When Reb Meir was once interviewed together with one of the members of the Zionist Party, Yitzchok Greenbaum, the journalist later wrote:

> Although Reb Meir Shapiro is totally immersed in his learning and concerns himself with the problems of the *chareidim*, he is still extremely well versed in the political situation in Poland and beyond. His ideas and his opinions are well thought out with all the implications and the connecting problems. The fact that Rabbi Shapiro is an outstanding Talmudic scholar and a great politician is evident to all. But if Greenbaum is also able to explain a difficult *Rambam*, that is very doubtful indeed.

IN 1928 ELECTIONS TOOK PLACE IN POLAND AND REB MEIR decided that the time had come for him to finally step down. Reb Meir consulted his Rebbe, the Chortkover Rebbe, and asked him for

A Person's Mission in This World

his permission to leave the job. The Rebbe's answer wasn't long in coming.

In a letter to Reb Meir the Rebbe wrote:

> Every person has a mission in this world which Hashem requires him to fulfill. A person can work out what his mission is according to the talents and abilities that Hashem has given him. Hashem has given his honor a sharp mind to delve into the sea of Talmud and to teach those who flock to him from the well of life, and indeed very special *yungerleit* have already emerged from his *beis hamedrash*. On the other hand, his honor could do much good for the *klal* and bring a blessing to them as well. Therefore my advice is as follows: His honor should not make any effort to remain in the parliament. If, however, the committee of the Agudah should assert pressure that his honor run for a second term, then he should not refuse. Hashem should help His honor to go on the correct way and to sit and learn and teach as he wishes, and as I wish for him.

Much to his surprise and delight, Reb Meir was indeed freed from the yoke of the Sejm and was allowed to return to his *sefarim* and his *talmidim* as his Rebbe had blessed him.

≈⌒

For a number of years Reb Meir had been walking around with a plan that gave him no peace. The time had come, he felt, to build a modern yeshivah with all the facilities that were required so that *bochurim* would be able to learn in the way which befitted the holy Torah. No longer would they have to beg for a bed to sleep on or for a piece of bread from the community. Not only would such a yeshivah improve the standard of their learning, it would also have a second vital role. It would uplift the honor of the Torah and its scholars across Poland and beyond.

Reb Meir envisioned a yeshivah that would be like no other:

> I see in my dreams a yeshivah the likes of which has never been, not in size nor in splendor. No longer will *talmidim* sleep in dark damp cellars and look for food like beggars. I will build for them a yeshivah like a palace! In the yeshivah every *bochur* will have a comfortable bed with clean linen and room for all his needs. He will eat his meals in a special dining room where he will feel as if he is at home. No longer will he be looked down upon and be derided for being a yeshivah *bochur*. The yeshivah will house the best and the brightest heads of the Jewish people. The yeshivah will become a center for Torah like Neharde'a and Pumbedisa in Bavel, a production line for the great *neshamos* of *Klal Yisroel*. People will exclaim about every *talmid* that learned in the yeshivah, "*Ashrei yoladeto* — Fortunate is the one who gave birth to such a son."

Reb Meir Shapiro was fully aware of what such an undertaking entailed. He knew that for many years he would have no day or night, he would have to sacrifice his every last second to make such a dream become a reality. But in his great love of the Torah, Reb Meir was willing to make such a sacrifice.

THE IDEA OF BUILDING SUCH A LARGE AND GRAND
yeshivah had its origins firmly rooted in Reb Meir's inner spiritual

An Inner Connection
bond to the Rebbe and the majestic *derech* of Chortkov. In his biography about Reb Meir Shapiro, his close *talmid* Reb Yehoshua Baumol wrote:

> There was one path of Chassidus to which Reb Meir felt drawn from his earliest years, the way that was derived from the Kabbalistic concept of *"Hod She'b'tiferes* — Glory in Majesty."
>
> Reb Meir felt attached to the revered Rebbe of Chortkov who followed this path, and from when Reb Meir first met him, he recognized that this is where he belonged. Under his Rebbe's influence, Reb Meir's inner ideas and visions of majesty began to take shape.
>
> From our earliest years we had heard fantastic stories about the Chortkover Rebbe's *zeide*, the Rebbe of Rizhin: amazing tales about how he lived in a palace surrounded with gold and diamonds, with a crown studded with precious stones on his head. We heard how he was revered as a Jewish monarch and people would bow down to him. This was the world that Reb Meir grew up in and absorbed in

> Chortkov, and when he related to us these stories, he instilled in us awe toward the chassidic dynasty of Rizhin.
>
> In Reb Meir's later years, the *derech* of Rizhin was evident in him for all to see, glowing brightly inside him. These feelings gathered force inside his mind and being, until they finally emerged in the guise of Yeshivas Chachmei Lublin, a true Torah palace of majesty.
>
> Once, during a visit to the yeshivah by the Sadigerer

A golden crown that belonged to the Rebbe of Rizhin

The Rebbe speaks at the Even HaPinah ceremony

Rebbe, who was also descended from the Rebbe of Rizhin, Reb Meir took the opportunity to spell out clearly the link between the Chassidus of Rizhin and the yeshivah.

"It is well known," he said, "that the *derech* of Chassidus is itself comprised of a number of different pathways. The path of Rizhin is that of splendor and majesty. Its goal is to beautify the Torah and the mitzvos. Just as a diamond needs the correct setting to bring out its qualities, so each mitzvah needs its own special place and setting.

"The Rizhiner also demanded that not only must the outer external trappings of the mitzvah be beautiful and glorified, but the inner thoughts and intentions of the mitzvah must also be performed to perfection.

"This is also the *derech* of our yeshivah, whose source is rooted in this *derech* of majesty and whose purpose is to show the true splendor of our holy Torah."

This inner connection between the Rebbe and Reb Meir's yeshivah was also stressed by Rav Tzvi Hirshorn in an article in the mass circulation daily, "*Dos Yiddishe Togblatt*":

He who has a deep understanding of the holy path of the Chassidus of Chortkov, where the Torah is housed in halls of

The palatial building of Yeshivas Chachmei Lublin

luxury positioned in royal palaces, and once spent time in the glorious palace that is the Chortkover Rebbe's court, and felt the sudden fear of Heaven that aroused all who entered its confines, he can attempt to appreciate the meaning of a *"Mikdash Me'at"* and try to imagine the beauty of our destroyed *Beis HaMikdash*.

He who once went in the Rebbe's glorious garden in the shadow of hundreds of tall erect trees and beautiful flowers and saw the fish swimming in the pond, and at the same time watched the Chortkover Rebbe walking in the garden, almost bent over to the ground under the weight of the daily sorrows of *Yidden*; he who saw the Rebbe with his *Tehillim* in his hand, and there between the trees saw him pouring out his heart over the long *galus* and the sorrows of *Yidden*; or those who saw his actions as he learned a paragraph from the holy *Zohar* — they knew that in this wonderful garden were broken hearts of stone, and that even frozen *neshamos* were instilled with a fear and love of Hashem.

He who saw the holy Torah weeping in its royal palace, he was the one who could understand the inner connection that bonded the Rebbe's court in Chortkov with the palatial mansion of Torah and *yirah* that is the yeshivah of Lublin. He could appreciate why, despite his failing health and the long journey involved, the Chortkover Rebbe made such an effort to attend the cornerstone-laying ceremony of the yeshivah.

Indeed the Rebbe took an unusual interest in every aspect of the building of the yeshivah and everything connected to it. A number of times he stressed that he wanted to be totally involved in the work and he expected to be kept up to date with developments. From its very inception he was active in promoting the yeshivah and raising money and support for the building.

$$\backsim\!\!\frown$$

The first stage of Reb Meir's grand plan ran quite smoothly. During a visit to the town of Lublin in Cheshvan 5684 (1924), Reb Meir was shown around by one of its wealthy inhabitants, Reb Shmuel Eichenbaum. During the trip Reb Shmuel showed Reb Meir a large plot of land in the center of the town that he had bought some years earlier. Despite its prime location the land lay empty and Reb Shmuel did not know what to do with it.

Reb Meir thought for a moment and said, "Reb Shmuel, I'm going to offer you a business deal which far surpasses any deal you have ever been offered until now." Wondering what Reb Meir could possibly be referring to, Reb Shmuel told him that he was willing to listen.

"I want part of this plot," Reb Meir replied. "It would be just right for a yeshivah." Reb Shmuel's face shone with joy at the idea and he immediately promised Reb Meir the land.

$$\backsim\!\!\frown$$

Building Starts

ON LAG BA'OMER 5684 (1924), LUBLIN WAS FLOODED WITH tens of thousands of *Yidden* who came to take part in the *hanachas even hapinah*. Among the vast crowds stood out the many *geonim* and *tzaddikim* who had come from all over to take part in the celebrations, which were headed by the Rebbes of Chortkov and Ger.

In a letter one participant described the celebration:

> Praise be to Hashem, I returned from Lublin full and satisfied with spiritual joy, having seen for the first time in my life such a public demonstration of *kavod haTorah*. Approximately 50,000 *Yidden* took part, including all the major *rabbanim* of Poland. When the Chortkover Rebbe arrived, a royal division of police mounted on horses surrounded his carriage. They escorted him to the platform where he spoke to the assembled crowds.
>
> After he had finished speaking, the Gerrer Rebbe also spoke and then the Chortkover Rebbe laid the first stone. It is impossible to describe the atmosphere that prevailed here in Lublin; all the windows in the town were decorated and festooned. No one remembers such a great rejoicing as there was here this week.

Once the celebrations had finished and the crowds had gone back home, Reb Meir went back to work making his dream come true. The first part had been much easier than he had anticipated, but the main job still lay ahead. Reb Meir took to the road traveling the length and breadth of Poland. Wherever he went, he delivered passionate speeches begging people to have pity on themselves and their children and to help him to raise the huge sums of money needed.

After almost two years of hard labor, Reb Meir succeeded in raising over $30,000. Although it was a tremendous amount of money, it was less than a third of the required sum. Reb Meir grew despondent and began to wonder if he had indeed taken upon himself the impossible. He would simply have abandoned the whole idea but he knew that if he did, it would be a terrible *chillul Hashem*, not to speak of the great disappointment that *Yidden* all over would feel. A letter written by the Chortkover Rebbe to his chassidim in America, asking them for help, spells out clearly the predicament in which Reb Meir found himself:

> The yeshivah whose cornerstone we laid two years ago is not yet completed. Thousands of *Yidden* are waiting desperately

for the day that light will shine forth from its windows to dispel the darkness of the times, and to ease the heavy burden of raising their children in the way of the Torah, before they are influenced by the foreign winds that seek to topple them. The donations that the *Yidden* in Poland have contributed have already been used up, causing the *askanim* to give up their work in despair. We can already hear the voices of our opponents, who are mocking us and the Torah. They are saying that for secular studies there is plenty of money but when it comes to strengthening the walls of the Torah, we are not able to raise the required sum.

At first when we saw the great joy on the faces of everyone at the cornerstone-laying, our hearts were full of hope that we would manage to complete the work from the contributions of those who reside here. But much to our dismay, times have changed and many have lost their wealth. *Yidden* have become poverty stricken and all work on the yeshivah has ceased.

Therefore I request of you: not once and not twice have you assisted your brothers here, please assist them now again by helping my friend, the *gaon* Reb Meir Shapiro, to erect these great stones and to engrave upon them the words of the Torah. Let the gates of the yeshivah be opened already and gather in it the holy flock who are thirsting to taste its waters, before they are contaminated by other sources. The *zechus* of the Torah and its students should protect and shower upon all of us the goodness that Hashem has promised us.

In Teves 5689 (1929) the building of Yeshivas Chachmei Lublin was finally finished, almost six years after work had first started. The building had room for 1,000 *bochurim* to learn and dormitory facilities for 500. The yeshivah also had a large library, which contained over 30,000 *sefarim*. The modern dining room and adjacent kitchen were also a novelty; each table was covered with a white tablecloth and set with plates and cutlery. A sick room and dentistry were also on the premises in case a *bochur* needed medical treatment. And the yeshivah also had its own launderette so that the *bochurim* would not have to waste time washing their clothes.

Even before the yeshivah opened its doors, long lines of hopeful candidates formed, hoping to be admitted to its ranks. But Reb Meir had one strict condition on which he wasn't willing to compromise: Every *bachur* must be tested on at least 200 *blatt gemara*, which he had to know by heart. Through this condition Reb Meir insured that only the best and the elite would learn in the yeshivah. His plan was for the yeshivah to produce the future *gedolim* of *Klal Yisroel*. Here the greatest and the brightest *bochurim* would be groomed and prepared to lead their people.

THE 28TH OF SIVAN 5690 (1930) WAS A DATE THAT MILLIONS of *Yidden* throughout Poland and beyond were impatiently await-

The Yeshivah Is Opened

ing. On that day the yeshivah would be officially opened and Reb Meir would be crowned its *Rosh Yeshivah* and the Rav of Lublin. As the date grew nearer, the suspense and excitement built to a peak. Never before in the history of Poland had such a massive public demonstration of *kavod haTorah* taken place.

Two days before the grand opening, Reb Meir arrived in Lublin on a train from Pietrikov. Thousands assembled at the station to greet him and accompany him to his new home in the yeshivah building. The following day the same scene repeated itself when the Chortkover Rebbe arrived on a train from Vienna.

Reb Meir with the entire yeshivah went to the station to greet the Rebbe. Before the train pulled into the station Reb Meir begged his *talmidim* not to push when the Rebbe arrived. Such conduct was not the way to greet a *Melech Yisroel*. Rather, they should form two long rows and allow the Rebbe to pass through the center. In their eagerness to see the Rebbe many of the *talmidim* forgot their Rebbe's request and started to run and to push in order to gain a better view of the Chortkover Rebbe. Reb Meir was visibly upset by their conduct and in front of the thousands present, he humbly begged forgiveness from his Rebbe for the disorder.

The Rebbe, with his two sons on the right and Reb Meir Shapiro on the left

At 3 o'clock on the following day, the proceedings began as the choir started to sing "*Mizmor Shir Chanukas HaBayis.*" Soon the vast crowd joined in the singing. The sound of 100,000 voices joined together with praise to Hashem moved even the policemen watching the proceedings.

As the song came to an end, a respectful silence fell on the assembled. Reb Meir Shapiro had made his appearance, flanked by the Rebbe of Chortkov on one side and the Rebbe of Ger on the other. Behind them came a long procession of many of the *gedolim* and *tzaddikim* of the time.

From a platform Reb Meir blessed the assembled in an emotional voice:

> Six years ago I greeted you all on an empty and desolate plot of land. Now, however, I bless you all from the *beis Hashem*, from this magnificent building which stands completed in all its splendor. Anyone who looked with a bit of his heart was able to see the terrible situation that young *bochurim* find themselves in. The "*pas bamelach*" that the Mishnah prescribes was a luxury for many who used to go hungry. The young Torah scholar was abused and ridiculed. Even if there

The Rebbe speaks from the balcony of the yeshivah building;
next to him can be seen the Gerrer Rebbe and Reb Moshe of Boyan-Cracow

were those who tried to help their physical situation, nothing had been done to elevate their social and emotional standing, and this is the novelty and the revolution of Yeshivas Chachmei Lublin.

After Reb Meir had finished his *derashah*, the Rebbe also addressed the crowds:

> The *gemara* tells us that the *simchah* of the consecration of the *Mishkan* was like the *simchah* of a *kallah* under the *chupah*. The *simchah* of marriage does not finish with the end of the *chasunah*. Rather the ending of the *chasunah* heralds the beginning of a long new existence for the couple. Similarly, when the *Mishkan* was erected the *simchah* wasn't limited to the completion of the building but rather to the *avodah* which could now start to take place within its walls.
>
> Today the very Torah is rejoicing with its new home! With the completion of the building the Torah can take up its new residence. The start of the spiritual building can now begin.
>
> *Chazal* tell us that Bezalel who built the *Mishkan* knew how to combine the holy letters of Hashem's Name with

which the heaven and
earth were created.
After the *Yidden* had
sinned with the Golden
Calf, the *Shechinah* in
heaven became dis-
tanced from the earth.
Bezalel used his wisdom to construct the *Mishkan* in such a
way that the earth regained its former *kedushah* and the
Shechinah in heaven returned back to the earth.

We are living nowadays in times of great spiritual darkness. I hope and *daven* that through this *simchah* the heavens
will once again be reunited with the earth.

After the Rebbe had finished speaking, the Gerrer Rebbe also delivered his short blessing after which came the great moment for
which everyone had been waiting. Reb Meir took a *mezuzah* out of
his pocket and handed it to the Chortkover Rebbe. In front of 10,000
pairs of eyes the Chortkover Rebbe took the *mezuzah* and fixed it to
the front doorpost of the yeshivah. The yeshivah doors were opened
with a specially made golden key and a beaming Reb Meir called
out, "Just as the gates of the yeshivah were opened, similarly may
Hashem open the gates of salvation for the *Yidden*."

At the opening ceremony, the Rebbe met Reb Shmuel
Eichenbaum, the person who had donated the plot of land on which
the yeshivah was built. When the Rebbe saw him, he said, "I am not
jealous of the mitzvah that you did by donating this land. It was a
mitzvah that was done in the public eye and you are receiving a lot
of honor as a result. *Chazal* tell us that one mitzvah brings another
(*mitzvah goreres mitzvah*). I do envy the precious mitzvah that you
did in private that has brought you this mitzvah."

The Rebbe stayed in Lublin for four days. During those four days
not one person died in Lublin. The *chevrah kadisha* attributed this to

the *zechus* of the Rebbe. Lublin had 40,000 *Yidden* and there was never a day without at least one *levayah*. Four days without a *levayah* was literally a miracle. No one could find any other explanation except that it had been in the Rebbe's *zechus*.

∾⌣

IT DID NOT TAKE LONG FOR THE YESHIVAH TO MAKE A name for itself; many of the *bochurim* were accomplished *talmidei chachamim* before they had even joined the yeshivah. **Yeshivas** The task of the yeshivah was to teach them and to **Chachmei** show them how to use their knowledge to the fullest, **Lublin** to train them how to properly analyze what they had learned and draw the correct conclusions.

Reb Meir formed a program of *limud* that was divided into three sections. Each section would take two years to complete. The first two years would be spent learning the *masechtos* of *Berachos, Shabbos, Pesachim* and *Beitzah* with the relevant *halachos* in *Shulchan Aruch*. The *bochurim* would also have to know all the various *midrashim* connected to the topics they were learning plus the commentaries of the classic *mefarshim* on the Torah. Besides all the above-mentioned *masechtos*, the *talmidim* also had to learn *masechtos Yoma, Tamid*, and *Middos* with all the relevant *halachos* in the Rambam.

During the second stage of the yeshivah program, the *bochurim* would learn for *semichah*. They had to acquire a deep knowledge of all the necessary parts of *Yoreh De'ah*, which was learned together with *Chullin* and *Bechoros*. In addition, they also had to be fluent in *hilchos challah* and *hilchos mikvaos* and the *halachos* pertaining to the *kashrus* of *Sifrei Torah, tefillin* and *mezuzah*s.

The final stage in the yeshivah program was intended for those who would take up positions as *rabbanim*. During these last two years, the *bochurim* learned *hilchos gittin, chalitzah*, and *takanos agunos*, which was followed by *Seder Chosen Mishpat*, which deals with all the various complicated monetary *sha'alos*. The *talmid* also had to review the whole of *Seder Nashim* and *Nezikin* with the commentary of the *Rosh*. At the end of the six-year course, the *talmid* was ready to assume a position as a Rav or *Rosh Yeshivah*.

Haskamah from Reb Meir Shapiro to his talmid, the bochur Yosef Boim

Looking at this unbelievable *seder halimud*, it is clear why the yeshivah was intended only for *iluyim*. Such a heavy and exhaustive program could only be tackled by the elite. Reb Meir's *talmidim* did not let him down, and many of them completed the program without a problem.

The *bochurim* from the yeshivah became known as true *geonim*, despite their youth. Many of them were fluent in all of *Shas*. When one of the *bochurim* — Reb Yosef Boim — published a *sefer* of his own *chiddushim* on the Rambam, Reb Meir gave him a *haskamah* in which he wrote, "These lines serve to testify about the great Rav and *baki* Reb Yosef Boim from Itbitza. From when he arrived in the yeshivah he has mastered a thorough knowledge of the whole *Talmud Bavli* and *Yerushalmi* and the many commentaries on them. He is like a well overflowing with *chiddushim*, and in our generation is a rare and precious wonder."

Reb Yosef Boim wasn't the only one in his league. There were many others like him too. They would no doubt have been among the *gedolim* of *Klal Yisroel* had the accursed Germans not destroyed them all.

⇒⇐

The Chortkover chassidim were a distinct group in their own right in the yeshivah

EVERY FEW MONTHS, REB MEIR WOULD LEAVE THE
yeshivah in order to spend a Shabbos in the company of the Rebbe.

**On the Way
to Chortkov**
Each time Reb Meir would take along with him a
group of his *talmidim* so that they could taste for
themselves the meaning of a Shabbos in Chortkov.

A description of one such trip was highlighted in the paper *"Dos
Yiddishe Togblatt"* by one of the participants:

Reb Meir on his way to meet the Rebbe, accompanied by his talmidim

The Shabbos after Shavous 5691 (1931) is engraved in my mind as one of the most memorable Shabbosim of my yeshivah life. The Chortkover Rebbe had come from his home in Vienna to his court in Chortkov, and our *Rosh Yeshivah*, the Lubliner Rav, Reb Meir Shapiro, was taking fifteen *talmidim* along with him to see the Rebbe.

We left the yeshivah in high spirits and made our way to the train station. Very soon the train was on its way toward Chortkov. The Rav launched into a conversation about the topic of the day, namely *divrei Torah* and stories that centered on the Rebbe of Chortkov. His voice full of awe and respect, the Rav related each story with such reverence that it evoked in him new feelings of wonder and veneration toward his Rebbe. Only now did we finally begin to understand the concept of a "true chassid."

So the journey continued while we sat open-mouthed, hungrily devouring every word that left the Rav's mouth. From time to time the Rav switched topics and reverted back to the *gemara* we were learning. One *pilpul* followed another and then he suddenly changed the conversation back to Chortkov again and then back to the *gemara* and so on.

Throughout the journey the Rav kept us captivated and enthralled; one minute he was speaking as the "humble chassid," the next minute as the "great *Rosh Yeshivah*."

We arrived in Chortkov refreshed and invigorated. After a short rest we went to the Rebbe's home to greet him. One cannot describe the great joy with which the Rebbe and the Rav greeted each other. The Rav introduced us to the Rebbe with the words, "I have brought the Rebbe *maaser* (a tithe)!" (At that point 150 boys were learning in the yeshivah.) The Rebbe showed great interest in us and inquired about conditions in the yeshivah. Even the minutest details were of concern to him.

Friday night after *davening*, the Rebbe recited *Kiddush* in front of his chassidim. The whole assembly stood transfixed, watching the Rebbe's every move and action. We felt elevated — almost like in another world. This was especially true of the Rav. Throughout the *tisch* he did not remove his gaze from the Rebbe. His normally confident posture was replaced with one of humility, as he absorbed his Rebbe's every nuance.

After the Rebbe had recited *Kiddush* and given a *dvar Torah*, the short *tisch* ended. The Rav accompanied by his *talmidim* returned to his accommodations where a joyous *seudah* soon got underway. During the course of the night many other chassidim came in to join the Rav and hear his *divrei Torah* and stories. The sounds of the *zemiros* and singing carried on until the early hours of the morning.

Shabbos morning we were granted a special privilege: to enter the Rebbe's private room and wish him a "Gut Shabbos." This privilege was normally reserved only for *rabbanim*. That Shabbos the Rebbe requested that we also be admitted, and he explained, "With Hashem's help they will also one day be *rabbanim*."

It was long after midnight on Motza'ei Shabbos when we were ushered into the Rebbe's room to take leave before returning home to Lublin. The Rebbe had recently undergone an operation on one of his eyes and was therefore not allowed to strain his vision. Due to this, he had refrained for some weeks from reading his chassidim's *kvitlach* and had let the *gabbai* read them to him. Nevertheless, the Rebbe insisted on personally reading all our *kvitlach*. "They exert and strain themselves all year round to learn the holy Torah," the Rebbe exclaimed. "I can strain myself to see their requests!" The Rebbe did not leave our notes on the table for the *gabbai* to clear away. Instead he placed them in his pocket and said to us: "You see how I treasure your notes."

⁌⁍

JUST AS IN HIS LIFETIME REB MEIR WAS REGARDED BY ALL as unique, so was his death regarded as a unique culmination to such **To Prepare the Way** a special life. And just as during his lifetime Reb Meir was totally bound to the Rebbe, so in death did he remain inextricably linked to his Rebbe.

As the end of the Elul 5693 (1933) *z'man* drew to a close and the *bochurim* were looking forward to going home, Reb Meir suddenly announced that *bein hazmanim* had been canceled. He wanted the yeshivah to stay with him over Succos. Although many were puzzled by this unusual move, who could have realized that very soon their beloved *Rosh Yeshivah* would no longer be with them.

In his last weeks Reb Meir, who was normally very joyous, became very somber and spent much of the day by himself in his study. At the time no one could fathom what was going on. Only later would they all understand. At his annual *Kol Nidrei derashah* to the *kehillah* in Lublin, he urged them to tear their hearts in *teshuvah*; otherwise they might have to tear *keriah* on their clothes.

Another unusual occurrence that everyone noticed was when Reb Meir suddenly announced his intention to move to Eretz Yisroel. In fulfillment of this wish, Reb Meir started to deliver a daily *shiur* concerning the *halachos* of Eretz Yisroel. He kept on repeating to his *talmidim* that "very soon I am going to move to Eretz Yisroel to prepare the way for my Rebbe, the Rebbe of Chortkov, in fulfillment of the *pasuk:* 'And he sent Yehudah before him.'" (Reb Meir's full name was Reb Yehudah Meir.)

When Reb Meir was *niftar*, the family of the Chortkover Rebbe refused to let him know for fear that it would affect his poor health. The Rebbe, however, had felt by himself that his faithful chassid was no longer alive and he also quoted the same *pasuk*: "*Ve'es Yehudah shalach lefanav* — And he sent Yehudah before him," and said that Reb Meir had gone ahead to prepare the way for him. And, indeed, just five weeks later the Chortkover Rebbe was also *niftar*!

On Hoshana Rabbah, the *yahrtzeit* of the first Chortkover Rebbe, Reb Dovid Moshe, Reb Meir revealed to his *talmidim* a dream he had had that night. Although the *talmidim* were quite taken aback by the dream's message, Reb Meir retold the dream in a calm and accepting tone. In his dream he found himself face to face with the Alter Chortkover Rebbe, Reb Dovid Moshe, and his son Reb Yisroel, the present Rebbe. The Rebbe introduced Reb Meir to his father and recounted his many praises. "If he really is so great and so capable," the Alter Rebbe responded, "we should summon him here in Heaven." Reb Yisroel of Chortkov tried to intercede on behalf of Reb Meir and asked that he be spared, for he was still needed in this world. Nonetheless, two weeks later the dream became a reality.

❧❧

ON TUESDAY THE 4TH OF CHESHVAN 5695 (1934) THE *bochurim* were rather surprised when Reb Meir did not show up on time for the early morning *shiur*. Normally, he was the first one there. As the minutes ticked by they realized that something must have happened. When Reb Meir did not appear for *Shacharis* either, the *bochurim* went to his home to see where he was. Reb Meir was lying in bed with a bad cold. The doctor who was by his bedside said that there was no cause for worry. The *Rosh Yeshivah* simply had a bout of flu.

Only With Joy

The following day Reb Meir's condition worsened; a swelling had developed in his throat making it difficult for him to breathe.

Other doctors were summoned to his bedside but they also said that there was no cause for worry and in a few days he would be better again. By Thursday, Reb Meir had no strength left to even talk; as the hours ticked by, he grew gradually weaker but still the doctors remained unperturbed.

In a *kvittel* written by the yeshivah *menahel*, to be sent to the Chorkover Rebbe, it was stated, "Please mention to the Rebbe that the *Rosh Yeshivah* is very weak. It is difficult for him to breathe and he is not able to swallow even a glass of water." Reb Meir, however, refused to allow the *kvittel* to be sent. The Chortkover Rebbe was then seriously ill and Reb Meir didn't want to upset him.

Late Thursday night it became clear that Reb Meir's remaining minutes were limited. On a piece of paper he wrote an instruction to the *talmidim* around his bed, "Everyone should drink *l'chaim*." In a flash a bottle and cups were produced and the *bochurim* drank *l'chaim*.

Reb Meir stretched out his hand and shook the hand of each and every *bochur*. After this, Reb Meir made a sign that they should sing one of his *niggunim* to the words "*Becha batchu avoseinu*." In the middle of the song he beckoned to them to form a circle around his bed, and then on a scrap of paper he wrote his final two words, "*Rak b'simchah* — Only with joy."

The *bochurim* danced around his bed singing and crying while in the middle lay Reb Meir, his face shining like a *malach*. With his hand he beckoned to them to go faster, to sing louder, until suddenly Reb Meir's holy *neshamah* flew upwards to meet the *Tannaim* and *Amoraim* who were waiting to greet him.

CHAPTER TWENTY-TWO
The Last Months

I N THE REBBE'S LAST MONTHS, A NEW THREAT STARTED to loom on the horizon. In Germany, the ugly specter of Nazism had begun to raise its head. At the time people were confident that it was only a passing phase, and things would soon return to normal. The death threats that Hitler (*yemach shemo*) issued upon world Jewry were ignored by many and dismissed as the ranting of a crazed lunatic who would soon disappear from the public arena.

THE REBBE, HOWEVER, DIDN'T SHARE THIS OPTIMISTIC forecast. To his chassidim he said, "In Egypt the *Yidden* assimilated

The Nazi Rise to Power into the ways and culture of the Egyptians. This brought upon them the wrath of Hashem, as it is written in *Tehillim* (108: 25): 'Hashem changed the hearts of the Egyptians to do evil to His servants.' Now also, assimilation has reached terrible proportions. If we don't stop the tide of assimilation, I am worried that this *rasha* might take over the whole world!"

*The last picture of the Rebbe,
just two months before his petirah*

ALREADY SOME TIME BEFORE the Nazi rise to power, the Rebbe

Black Clouds in Europe

had given broad hints of difficult times ahead for European Jewry. The Rebbe advised many of his chassidim to leave Europe, even to head for the spiritual wastes of America. To one *Yid* who complained to the Rebbe that life as a *frum Yid* in America was not easy, the Rebbe sighed and answered, "What can I do? I see black clouds here in Europe."

During a visit to Germany in 1925, the Rebbe said: "We must do our best to help the German economy. If the German currency loses its value, the *Yidden* will become the scapegoats!" This comment later on proved to be prophetic. In order to gain public support for his policies against the *Yidden*, Hitler used the economic difficulties as an excuse to blame the *Yidden* for Germany's problems.

During a visit to Galicia some years before his *petirah*, the Rebbe was greeted at the train station by a large crowd of enthusiastic chassidim. The Rebbe turned to one of his close chassidim, the *gaon* Reb Nuchem Leiberzohn (he survived the war and later lived in Eretz Yisroel), and said to him: "There will soon come a time when all this won't exist anymore. One will only be able to cheer oneself up with a *blatt gemara!*"

As the months went by, the situation in Germany worsened and it became apparent that Hitler was intent on keeping all his threats to the full. The Chortkover chassidim in Berlin sent a delegation to the Rebbe to apprise him of the situation and to seek his *berachah* that no harm befall them.

The delegation explained to the Rebbe the fears of *Yidden* in Germany and asked the Rebbe for a message of hope and comfort that they could bring back with them to the panic-stricken *Yidden* in

Germany. The Rebbe granted the chassidim a regular *berachah* and that was it. The delegation explained that they were waiting for a message of hope and reassurance about the future, they could not return home just with a regular *berachah*.

THE REBBE ANSWERED, "LET ME TELL YOU A STORY":

May Hashem Help the Survivors

There were once two powerful kings; each of them had fought and conquered many other nations. Eventually these two kings each ruled half the world. Yet neither of them was satisfied, each one wanted to be the sole ruler of the world. Only the danger of losing deterred them from launching an all-out war to achieve their aim. One day, an adviser to one of the kings hit upon a peaceful plan to solve the question of who would be the sole ruler in the world. One of the kings had a son and the other a daughter. Let them marry and the child born to them would one day rule the whole world.

Both kings agreed to the idea and the wedding took place. Alas, the great expectations pinned on the young couple failed to materialize: the couple was childless. Although many years had passed from their marriage, the long awaited child did not arrive. The best doctors were summoned but they were unable to help. Eventually, one doctor promised a cure that would enable them to have a child. However, the doctor warned the couple that the life of the mother might be in danger due to complications which would occur during the pregnancy.

The royal couple agreed to undergo the risk, for this was the whole point of their marriage. Indeed the whole world was waiting impatiently for this child. During the course of her pregnancy the woman did indeed become seriously ill a number of times. Each time, however, the doctor was able to deal with the crisis and keep everything in check. When the woman entered the ninth month, her pains increased until they became almost unbearable. In a panic, she called the doctor and begged him to alleviate her pains as he had done previously. This time the doctor said there was nothing he could do. These were different pains than the previous ones; she was now experiencing the pains of childbirth. Only with the birth of the child would the pains go away. She would just have to bear them until the baby is born.

The Rebbe finished his story and with a sigh told the delegation:

You understand the message! We are experiencing the birth pangs of Moshiach. May Hashem help and look after those who survive.

The Last Seudah in Berlin

AN INTERESTING INCIDENT IS RECORDED IN THE RIZHINER journal "*Tiferes Yisroel*" (issue 49) about how, in the Rebbe's *zechus*, many of the Chortkover chassidim in Berlin did indeed merit a miraculous escape from the Nazis. Berlin had a sizable Chortkover shul, which was destroyed shortly after Kristallnacht (November 9, 1938). Only a few days before the shul was destroyed the whole community gathered together on the night of the 13th of Kislev for a *seudah* to commemorate the Rebbe's *yahrtzeit*. This was done at great personal risk, for the Nazis had strictly forbidden the gathering of Jews under any circumstances. This *seudah* did indeed prove to be their last occasion together.

One of the *Yidden* who participated in that last *seudah* in Berlin was the chassid Reb Elozor Teicher (later of New York).

While the *seudah* was in progress, a *Yid* came into the shul and frantically banged on the table and desperately urged that no one go home that night. Word had came through that the Nazis had swooped down on the Jewish area and were systematically checking all the houses and deporting all men with Polish passports to the concentration camps. Most of the chassidim fell into this category, having arrived in Germany from Poland after the First World War. Despite the man's warning, a few of the chassidim present decided to leave the shul and return to their families. Most of the men, however, decided that it would be safer to remain in the shul. Later on it emerged that all those who had returned home were never heard from again, while those who remained were saved!

Reb Elozor was one of those who heeded the man's advice and did not return home. For the rest of his life he attributed his survival to the kindness of Hashem and to the miracle that had happened in the Chortkover *Kloiz*. He felt that his close ties to the Rebbe had been instrumental in saving his life.

❧

FOR EIGHTY YEARS THE REBBE'S INNER LIGHT SHONE forth, illuminating the way for thousands of *Yidden* across the globe.

The Last Succos

While the Rebbe was still in his element, his guiding hand being sought ever more, signs began to appear that the sun was starting to set.

Two months before his *petirah*, during Succos 5694 (1933), the first signs emerged that the Rebbe's strength was leaving him. At the end of the Yom Tov, the Rebbe recited the customary *tefillah* said upon leaving the *succah* and then stood up to leave. Normally, the Rebbe walked out of the *succah* briskly. This time, however, he stood for a long time deep in thought. Finally, after a few minutes he slowly made his way out of the *succah*. Hardly had he left when he retraced his steps and went back into the *succah* one last time. Never before had he ever reentered the *succah* after bidding it farewell! For a few moments the Rebbe stood inside the *succah* deep in thought as he bade one more final farewell.

The following morning came the next deviation. Suddenly, during the *hakafos* the Rebbe felt ill and was unable to dance as usual with the *Sefer Torah*. He spent most of the *hakafos* seated in his place. His white and unusually pale complexion betrayed the seriousness of his condition to his concerned chassidim. Although the Rebbe had been in poor health for some time, until then it had not really been noticeable to the wider public. Only now did it become apparent to all that the Rebbe was seriously ill. The rest of Simchas Torah was conducted in a subdued and sober manner.

❧

The newspapers raise alarm about the Rebbe's health

TWO WEEKS AFTER SIMCHAS TORAH, ON THE 7TH OF Cheshvan, the day the Lubliner Rav was *niftar*, the Rebbe's condi-

Thanking Hashem for the Bad

tion worsened and he was admitted to the hospital. The doctors diagnosed that the Rebbe was suffering from a complicated illness of the stomach. The Rebbe underwent an operation to ease his ailment and within a few days was back home again. For close to a month the Rebbe was able to resume his daily schedule almost as normal.

With the onset of the month of Kislev, the Rebbe's condition took a turn for the worse. The doctors who examined him decided to operate again and on Monday the 9th of Kislev the Rebbe was readmitted to the hospital.

Every Erev Shabbos before candlelighting, the Rebbe would count all the money in his possession and then faithfully give away a tenth to *tzedakah*. When the Rebbe was informed that he had to go to the hospital, he did not wait until Erev Shabbos to distribute the *tzedakah* money. That Monday, before his departure to the hospital, the Rebbe counted his money and then gave it away to *tzedakah*.

Afterwards he summoned his family to his side and instructed them all to be *b'simchah*. He commanded each one of them to say aloud "*Baruch Hashem*" and then he himself said: "*Baruch Hashem! K'shem she'mevarchim al hatov kach mevarchim al hara* — Just as one must thank Hashem for the good so one must thank Hashem for the bad."

The news of the Rebbe's hospitalization spread like wildfire across the world. The columns of many newspapers reported on the Rebbe's condition, day by day. In the mass circulation daily "*Dos Yiddishe Togblatt*," we read:

"The Chortkover Rebbe is seriously ill; all are asked to daven for his well-being"

News has just arrived by telephone from Vienna that the
Rebbe of Chortkov is dangerously ill. For some weeks the
Rebbe has not been well but in recent days his condition has
worsened. The Rebbe of Chortkov is suffering from a disease
of the stomach and is unable to eat anything. The community
is asked to *daven* for the Rebbe — Yisroel ben Feiga.

The day before the Rebbe's entry to the hospital he held his last
public engagement. Despite his weak and ill state the Rebbe gave a
short *tisch* in honor of the *yahrtzeit* of his grandfather, Reb Aharon of
Chernobyl. At the *tisch* the Rebbe gave a brief address in which he
gave a clear hint of his imminent *petirah*. His entire speech centered
on the topic of the *petirah* of *tzaddikim*. The Rebbe finished with the
words: "My *zeide*, the *tzaddik* Reb Nuchem of Chernobyl, used to say
that if a *Yid* can feel that his life is coming to its end, he should try
with all his strength to keep going until Friday afternoon after midday." Little did the listeners know that the Rebbe's words were
directed at none other than himself, and that on that very Friday
right after midday he would depart from their midst.

After two days in the hospital the Rebbe had a second operation. The newspaper "*Dos Yiddishe Togblatt*" wrote:

> "For some time the Rebbe of Chortkov has been suffering
> from an illness of the stomach. At first it did not seem that it
> was a serious illness and the Rebbe went around in his house
> as normal. Today (Wednesday), however, his doctors de-
> cided that the Rebbe needs another operation. They say that

it is a simple procedure and they do not anticipate any complications. Now, at 12 o'clock, while these lines are being written, hundreds of people have gathered to ask for mercy for the elder of the *tzaddikim*, the Rebbe of Chortkov. The operation is due to be carried out at 12:30 and all are asked to *daven* for the well-being of the *tzaddik*, Reb Yisroel ben Feiga.

The doctors proclaimed the operation a success and remained confident that the Rebbe would recover and soon be allowed home. The Rebbe, however, did not share their optimism. His first words upon waking from the operation were: "They did not achieve anything. They merely opened and closed me again." When his sons inquired about his well-being, the Rebbe answered them: "First thank Hashem that you still have a father to greet!" Only after they had done so did he answer their question.

Despite the doctors' promising reports, the Rebbe's condition suddenly deteriorated on Thursday evening, the 13th of Kislev, and his temperature spiraled out of control. Throughout the night the Rebbe did not sleep and his family remained around his bed. Early Friday morning it became apparent that the Rebbe's hours were numbered. A few hours before his *petirah*, the Rebbe closed his eyes and started to hum to himself the tunes that he would sing at a *tisch*. From time to time, he raised his voice and those present could hear the words of *tefillah* that he was *davening*.

Finally, just after 12 o'clock, the Rebbe opened his eyes and stared at those in the room around him. Not a word passed from the Rebbe's lips but it was evident to all that he was bidding them farewell. The Rebbe looked for a long time into the eyes of each and every person present and then, closing his eyes, his holy *neshamah* departed this world. *Zechuso yagein aleinu.*

DUE TO THE FACT THAT ONLY A FEW HOURS REMAINED until the onset of Shabbos, it was decided to postpone the *levayah* un-

The Levayah til Sunday. In the short time remaining it would be impossible to give him a *levayah* according to his

*The Rebbe's petirah was widely
reported in many newspapers*

honor and therefore the *halachah* permitted postponing the *levayah*.
Even though it was close to the onset of Shabbos, hundreds of people gathered outside the hospital in order to escort the Rebbe's coffin
to his home where it was to lie for the duration of Shabbos.

Despite it being Shabbos, a palpable feeling of sadness descended
on Vienna. After *davening* ended in the Chortkover *beis hamedrash*, the
entire congregation, with the Rebbe's sons at their head, silently filed
past the Rebbe's *aron*. Throughout the day people came to walk past
the Rebbe's *aron* and spend one last Shabbos in the Rebbe's presence.
Occasionally those filing past broke down in tears and it became necessary to remind them that it is forbidden to cry on Shabbos.

The Rebbe's *levayah* took place on Sunday, the 15th of Kislev.
Already from the early hours of the morning thousands of *Yidden*

The Rebbe's levayah

had been arriving in Vienna in order to participate in the *levayah*. Specially chartered trains of chassidim arrived from across Poland, Galicia, Hungary and Romania. Over 100 extra policemen were drafted to control Vienna's largest-ever funeral procession. Close to 200,000 *Yidden* lived in Vienna and although most of them were not *frum*, nevertheless the Rebbe's name and personality were revered by all. Even those who were far removed from the path of Torah were not willing to forgo paying their last respects to the most famous Rabbi in their midst. This was also demonstrated by the unusual press coverage given to the Rebbe's funeral. Even the non-Jewish daily newspapers devoted their entire front pages to the story, and on details of the Rebbe's life and death. The public outpouring of grief especially fascinated them and many of the newspapers tried to understand why the Rebbe's death had caused such widespread mourning.

Early Sunday morning the *taharah* was performed. Only the closest relatives of the Rebbe were permitted to be present: the Rebbes of Husyatin, Sadiger and Rimanov.

After the *taharah* was completed, the Rebbe's two sons called out in voices choked in tears: "*Heiliger Tatte*! You are going in front of the

The paper reports:
"Gigantic levayah of the Chortkover Rebbe in Vienna —
Many thousands attended —
Over 100 policemen keep order —
Rebbes, rabbanim and delegations from
Austria, Hungary, Czechoslovakia and Poland —
A special train from Cracow"

Heavenly Throne! Plead for us that the *geulah* come already! *Yidden* cannot manage any longer! Let your *tefillos* pierce the very Heavens!" At their words the entire crowd broke down in tears and wept and a number of people fainted. Afterwards, the brother of Reb Meir Shapiro, the Lubliner Rav, also called out: "*Heiliger* Rebbe! Every year my brother would come to you for Chanukah, this year you are going to him."

At 12 o'clock the *levayah* finally got underway. The newspapers reported the procession as follows:

Throughout the morning thousands of people assembled outside the Rebbe's *beis hamedrash* on the Heinestrasse learning *Mishnayos* and saying *Tehillim*. The crying and weeping of the crowd was spine-chilling. According to the *minhag* in Rizhin no *hespedim* were said. Especially moving was the scene next to the Rebbe's *aron*. The almost continuous crying was enough to melt even the hardest of hearts. Throughout the morning, a constant stream of people who had fainted had to be removed and carried out from the packed hall.

At 11:30 the Rebbe's *aron* was brought into his *beis hamedrash* one last time. *Tehillim* were recited and then at 12 o'clock the *levayah* finally got underway. It was only with great difficulty that it was possible to forge a pathway through the densely packed masses. Although the plan had been to carry the *aron* the whole way by hand, in the end the idea had to be abandoned. The police insisted that it would be too dangerous to allow the *levayah* to proceed by foot. Instead, special trams were used to transport the waiting crowds to the cemetery, and the Rebbe's *aron* was taken by car.

At the cemetery additional thousands were waiting to greet and escort the Rebbe's *aron*. At 1 o'clock the Rebbe's holy body was finally lowered into his *kever* accompanied by the hysterical crying of the thousands present. Afterwards the Rebbe's sons said *Kaddish*, and then *Tehillim* was again recited. After the *levayah* had ended many continued to mill around, unable to accept the fact that the Rebbe had finally departed.

≈≈

The Kever as a Makom Tefillah

JUST AS DURING HIS LIFETIME THE REBBE WAS A SOURCE of comfort and solace, so after his *petirah* his *kever* has become a place of comfort and solace for many. The Rebbe's *kever* has remained a *makom tefillah* until this very day. Many travel especially to Vienna in order to *daven* at his grave. The Manchester *Rosh Yeshivah*, Reb Yehudah Zev Segal, was a regular visitor at the

The Rebbe's kever and ohel in the fourth section of the cemetery in Vienna

Rebbe's *kever* on his yearly holiday trip to Zemering in Austria. When the *Rosh Yeshivah* was asked what drew him to the Rebbe's *kever* more than to the many other *gedolim* who were buried in the cemetery, he answered as follows:

Although I never knew the Chortkover Rebbe, one particular story that I heard about him made a deep impression on me.

I heard that the Chortkover Rebbe was once sitting on a park bench deep in conversation with another Rebbe, when a non-Jewish woman came and sat herself down at the other end of the bench. The other Rebbe wanted to jump up immediately but the Chortkover Rebbe held his hand, restraining him. After a minute or two the Rebbe looked at his watch and exclaimed loudly in German: "Oh, it is already very late, we have to be on our way." The Rebbe had not wanted to insult the woman's feelings by getting up the second she sat down!

Such sensitivity shows exemplary character. The fact that the Rebbe worried about the feelings of some unknown gentile woman to such a degree indicates what level he had

The Manchester Rosh Yeshivah felt that it was worthwhile to daven at the Rebbe's kever

reached in perfecting his own *middos*. Such a person is worthy and capable of helping others even after his *petirah* and therefore it is worthwhile *davening* at his *kever*.

In this context, it is worth mentioning a powerful story that was recorded by Reb Tzvi Hirshorn in one of his articles:

The Rebbe was once visiting a certain Rav, when he apologized that he had to rush away because a large crowd of chassidim was waiting to see him. "I understand," the Rav said. "Business is business and one can't afford to keep one's customers waiting!"

When the Rebbe heard these words his face turned a ghostly white. Rising from his chair he exclaimed: "*Chas vesholom*. With me this is not a business! Hashem knows the truth that I don't need any of them. It is they who need me!"

Many are the stories that abound of those who were helped as a result of a visit to the Rebbe's *kever*. We will suffice with one such story that took place sixty years after the Rebbe's *petirah*:

A couple in Eretz Yisroel was already married many years but they had not been blessed with children. They had almost exhausted every possible avenue of help, both medical and otherwise. One day, the young man's mother advised him to travel to Vienna and *daven* at the Rebbe's *kever*. They were descended from Chortkover chassidim and therefore she felt it was only correct that after having asked so many other famous *tzaddikim* for a *berachah*, her son should at least *daven* by the grave of their own Rebbe.

At first the young man was reluctant to make the long and costly journey, but eventually he agreed to the trip. He waited for the Rebbe's *yahrtzeit,* and on the 13th of Kislev he arrived in Vienna, where he *daven*ed at the Rebbe's *kever.* The following year on the 13th of Kislev the man's wife gave birth to a healthy baby boy, their first of many children!

So important is the Rebbe's *kever* that it has even become a standard feature in many books about places of Jewish interest worth visiting. In the book "Travels In Jewish Europe" (printed 1981), we read as follows:

> Rabbi Israel Friedman, the Rebbe of Chortkov, had a very great following throughout Galicia; he lived in Chortkov where he had a veritable palace. When the Russians invaded Galicia during the First World War he fled to Vienna, where he remained until his death in 1933. Large masses turned out to attend his funeral, which was one of the biggest ever witnessed by Viennese Jewry.
>
> I was especially interested in going to the grave of the Rebbe of Chortkov, which I heard is visited by chassidim from all over the world. While walking among the graves I met two women, a mother and daughter, recent immigrants from Russia, who were temporarily staying in Vienna. When I asked them where the grave of the Chortkover Rebbe was, they told me to follow them. The mother visits the *kever* every Sunday.
>
> "We don't know Hebrew and so we don't know how to pray. Would you please *daven* for us," the mother asked me in Yiddish as we reached the *kever* of the Rebbe. I was glad to do so and also lit the candles they gave me. An *ohel* has been erected over the grave of the Rebbe; his wife and son are also buried there.
>
> "I come here often," the woman explained. "I have heard that many people have been healed by the intercession of this Rabbi. He is a miracle worker; please say a Hebrew prayer for my daughter's health. I hope she will soon be reunited with her husband who is still in the Soviet Union."

~⊙~

The Rav of Slonim, Reb Yehudah Leib Fein

JUST AS DURING HIS LIFETIME THE REBBE WAS A SOURCE
of advice and help for all, so after his *petirah* did he remain a source

**Revelations
After His Petirah**

of help for others. Many are the stories told
of how after his *petirah* the Rebbe would appear in dreams to various people and
advise them how to act.

One of the most famous stories was recorded by one of the great
rabbanim before the Second World War, the Rav of Slonim, HaGaon
Reb Yehudah Leib Fein. The dream centered upon a *din Torah* in
which Rav Fein was involved:

> The Rav of the general *kehillah* in Vienna was an acclaimed
> *gaon* by the name of Rav Meirzohn. Due to his strict stance
> on all matters of *halachah*, he had many opponents in the
> wider, more secular, community. In 1931 when Rav
> Meirzohn turned 70, these opponents seized their oppor-
> tunity and forced his retirement, claiming that according
> to Austrian law he was no longer allowed to work. His po-
> sition was assumed by the *gaon* Reb Yosef Babad from
> Tarnopol.

Rav Meirzohn of Vienna

Rav Meirzohn challenged Rav Babad's right to take his place and took him to a special *beis din* convened to judge the case. The three judges were the Chofetz Chaim, the *gaon* Reb Chaim Ozer Grodzinski of Vilna and Rav Fein, whom the Rebbe selected as the third judge.

The case was long and complicated and it was only after the Rebbe's *petirah* that the proceedings finally wound up. Although the case had finished early in 1934, Rav Fein adamantly refused to issue the final ruling as to who was right. Major pressure was brought to bear on Rav Fein to reveal the outcome of the case but he refused to comply. In addition, he also refused to reveal his reasons for not divulging the final *psak*, much to the annoyance of all concerned. No one was more exasperated than Rav Meirzohn, who was convinced that he would win the case and he did all he could in trying to get Rav Fein to issue a ruling, but to no avail. Finally, in Iyar 5696 (1936), Rav Fein issued his ruling.

A year later, on the 25th of Iyar 5697 (1937), Rav Fein wrote the following letter to the Rebbe's son and successor, Reb Nuchem Mordechai. The contents of his letter speak for themselves:

"To his Glory, the Pride of Israel, the Leader and Teacher of Chasidei Chortkov:

"It is already over three years since I was called to Vienna to act as a judge upon the advice of his holy father, after which I withheld the *psak din* a further two years. This time last year, I finally issued my ruling and that was only under much pressure and coercion. Many were taken aback by my refusal to divulge the *psak* and unable to understand or accept my behavior, which I had been unable to reveal until now.

"At the time, after I had finished my work in Vienna and was preparing to leave for home, your holy father appeared to me in a dream at night in a most amazing vision, and warned me not to release my *psak din*. He said that if I were to reveal the *psak*, Rav Meirzohn would not live more than twelve months from the day the *psak* was delivered.

"I was very frightened by this warning and decided to listen to the dream. I also decided that I would not tell anyone about the dream and its contents. I was worried that they would not believe me and say that it is merely an excuse not to issue a ruling.

"This is the reason I delayed issuing the *psak* for a full two years. Last year I was summoned by the Agudas HaRabbanim in Warsaw and was told in no uncertain terms that I must issue the *psak*. They pressured me a lot and said that my non-compliance was playing into the hands of those who seek to undermine the Torah and increase *machlokes*. Under these conditions I felt unable to hold myself back any longer and decided to release my verdict. I based my decision on the words of *Chazal* that dreams are not to be relied upon.

"The night before I issued my ruling, your holy father appeared to me again in a dream and warned me a second time not to release my verdict, otherwise Rav Meirzohn would die within twelve months. Just recently I have heard that Rav Meirzohn has died (he died on the 3rd of Nissan 5697 (1937), eleven months after the *psak* was issued) and it has frightened me greatly and my conscience gives me no rest."

Rav Fein continues in his letter to ask for guidance to help him atone for any wrongdoing and also asks if it will be worthwhile to publicize the incident in order to strengthen people's *emunah*. Rav Fein ends off his letter with the words:

"Although I am almost sure that I need to ask for forgiveness, but in my confusion from this whole issue I am unable to come to any clear course of action. *Nafshi b'she'eilasi* that the Rebbe should go to his holy father's resting place and ask for forgiveness on my behalf, Yehudah Leib ben Feiga, that I did not listen to his father's words. If I have found favor in his eyes may I also request that he make a special visit to his father's *kever* just for this one particular matter."

Another amazing incident in which the Rebbe helped someone after his *petirah* through a dream was related by Reb Avrohom Gerstler from Manchester:

> Prior to the war, Reb Avrohom lived in Vienna where he was a regular in the Rebbe's *beis hamedrash*. With the Nazi takeover of Austria in 1938, Reb Avrohom tried desperately to obtain a visa to travel out of the country, but to no avail.
>
> One night the Rebbe appeared to Reb Avrohom in a dream and instructed him to leave Austria the following day. "But I have no visa," Reb Avrohom answered. "They won't let me out the country without one."
>
> "Don't worry," the Rebbe answered him. "Your name is Avrohom, I will be your shield, a *Magein Avrohom*! Tomorrow you shall take a train out of the country."
>
> The next day Reb Avrohom boarded a train heading to France. When they arrived at the border, Nazi troops entered and started to scrupulously examine everyone's papers. The Germans knew that some *Yidden* would in desperation try to use false papers and therefore they carried out a careful and methodical examination. One

The tombstone of Reb Avrohom Gerstler on which is engraved that the Rebbe's berachah "Magein Avrohom" saved him during the Holocaust

Yid on the train did indeed have forged papers. In a fit of rage the soldiers hauled him off the train and he was beaten unconscious by the German beasts. The poor man was never heard of again.

Although the Nazis combed the train meticulously, demanding that every *Yid* show his visa papers, Reb Avrohom was not asked. As the Nazi troops came to where he was sitting, one of the soldiers looked at him and exclaimed: "*Er hat keine Judishe nase!* — He does not have a Jewish nose." With that the soldiers continued on to the next row without even bothering to ask him any further questions or to see his papers.

A third recent amazing event is recorded in the "*Meoros Daf Yomi*" newsletter (issue 100):

In 1995 Reb Alter Schwebel of Bnei Brak needed to undergo a serious eight-hour heart operation. It was a difficult operation and it was only by a miracle that Reb Alter made it to tell the tale. When Reb Alter woke up after the operation, he found by his bedside Professor Sekolorovsky, head of the Heart Institute of the Rabin Medical Center in Petach Tikva.

The professor was waiting desperately to ask Reb Alter a question. "I have carried out many operations," the man said. "Never before have I seen a patient who reacted as you did. Always, once the anesthetic has been administered, the patient lies on the table motionless as if he were dead. You, however, during the operation suddenly started to contort your face and it appeared that something exciting was going on in your mind. I have never before heard of a patient under anesthetic displaying signs of life and mental activity like you did. Do you perhaps recollect anything?"

"During the surgery," Reb Alter related, "I felt that I was being severed from this world. A tremendous brilliance greeted me and I was standing before the Gates of Death. Against my will I was slowly being forced inside and I started to scream. At that moment the Rebbe of Chortkov appeared and he repeated to me a blessing that he had given me when I was in Chortkov in my youth: 'May you live a long life!' He then escorted me away from the Gates of Death back down to this world."

These are just three stories of how the Rebbe's merit continues to help people even many years after his passing from this world. This is the concept that is mentioned in the *gemara*: "*Mah kan omeid u'me'shamesh af sham omeid u'me'shamesh* — *Tzaddikim* continue to procure help for *Yidden* even after their passing from this world."

Zechuso yagein aleinu!

PART FOUR

The Continuation of the Dynasty

CHAPTER TWENTY-THREE
Joint Leadership

AFTER THE *PETIRAH* OF THE CHORTKOVER REBBE, Reb Yisroel, his chassidim took it for granted that the Rebbe's two sons, Reb Nuchem Mordechai and Reb Dov Ber, would assume their father's position. Both of them were well known to the chassidim and esteemed by all. Reb Nuchem Mordechai, the older brother, was born in 1874. During his sixty years he had succeeded in perfecting himself until all who came into contact with him could testify that he was a holy person. He married his first cousin, the Rebbetzin Chava Leah, daughter of his uncle, Reb Shlomo of Sadiger.

THE YOUNGER SON REB DOV BER WAS BORN IN 1882 AND was greatly respected for his vast Torah knowledge and his deep **Reb Nuchem Mordechai and Reb Dov Ber** and penetrating views and knowledge on any topic or problem about which he was asked.

He also married his first cousin, the Rebbetzin Miriam, daughter of the Boyaner Rebbe, the Pachad Yitzchok.

YET DESPITE THEIR GREATNESS AND THEIR SUITABILITY TO assume the *Rabbanus*, both of them adamantly refused to even con-

Refusal to Be Anointed Rebbes

template such a move. Great was the chassidim's shock when they heard that the two brothers would not hear of the idea, and were both steadfast in their refusal to become Rebbes. When the chassidim approached them, they each answered with the same excuse, "I am not worthy of sitting in my holy father's place." In a letter sent at the time to the Chortkover chassidim in Eretz Yisroel by Reb Shmuel Halpern (who was a Rav in Amsterdam and a close chassid of the Chortkover Rebbe), he wrote:

> After the terrible calamity that has befallen us and the whole of *Klal Yisroel*, it has become known to the chassidim in Vienna that the sons of the Rebbe have declared that they do not intend to accept the yoke of the *Rabbanus*. Therefore, I was asked to come to Vienna and attempt to convince them to change their minds.
>
> I told the chassidim that the terrible calamity has left me in a very weak state and I am confined to my bed. But when they told me that until now none of the chassidim who had arrived from Galicia had managed to convince the Rebbe's sons to change their minds, and perhaps I would succeed, I was forced to leave my bed and journey to Vienna.

Reb Shmuel Halpern

I arrived there on Thursday, and on Motza'ei Shabbos I spoke to them for about four hours, and after all my pleading and begging, I wasn't able to achieve anything. Only on Monday, after much additional pleading and with the help of the holy Reb Dov Ber, did we finally succeed that at least his older brother would start to accept *kvitlach*. Reb Dov Ber, however, refuses to be Rebbe under any circumstances. He did agree to help his brother read the post and to answer and advise the chassidim with their problems. He also said that he would like to lead the chassidim as a friend, not as a Rebbe.

On Shabbos Chanukah, the two brothers sat together at the head of the table. The older brother said that he had no intention of saying Torah, and Reb Dov Ber said that if he would be told from the Heavens what to say, he would not hold himself back. Reb Dov Ber is very strong in his opinion, and he told us that he does not agree to this *minhag* that when a *tzaddik* dies all his sons automatically become Rebbes, for it causes *machlokes* among the chassidim and splits the family in two. And, indeed, the love between the holy brothers is so great that nothing in the world would entice them to move apart.

Believe me, during the two weeks that I was there, I spoke and dealt with them a lot, and I was amazed by their *kedushah* and their humility. I haven't seen their equal anywhere else, especially when it comes to matters concerning *emes*. Every move of theirs is *emes*. I can almost testify about them that even when they blink their eyelids, it is only *l'shem Shamayim*!

When I argued with them concerning their *parnassah*, they answered that they had learned from their father the *middah* of *bitachon*, and they were not worried for their future, and they looked at me in amazement, wondering at my anxiety.

I cannot write any further, and I hope I have written enough to explain the situation. Hashem should help us through the hands of the holy *tzaddikim*, in honor of His Name.

In a newspaper article written after Reb Dov Ber's *petirah* in 1936, Reb Shabsi Sheinfeld also refers to this period and to the brothers' refusal to become Rebbes:

> For over fifteen years I have enjoyed a close and intimate relationship with the great *niftar*. I was *zocheh* to stand next to him when he busied himself with matters of *Klal Yisroel*, and I also saw how he conducted himself in his own private affairs. Every point and every action of his was stamped with the seal of *emes*. It is easy to utter the word *emes*, but how many leaders live a life of falsehood when they are supposed to symbolize the truth …
>
> The extent of his *emes* can be seen by the fact that after the *petirah* of his father, the Rebbe, Reb Yisroel of Chortkov, the senior chassidim gathered in Vienna in order to crown both sons Rebbes. It had not occurred to anyone that Reb Dov Ber would refuse the offer! All the efforts of the entire family plus the elder chassidim produced no results. Despite all their pleas Reb Dov Ber refused to be swayed. Once he had come to the conclusion that he was not worthy of assuming the position, all the arguments in the world could not move him.
>
> When he was asked the reasons for his refusal he answered: "Let me tell you who my father was. Nine years after we arrived in Vienna from Chortkov, my father suddenly looked at the furniture in the room and asked when it had arrived. The furniture had been sent a few months after we had arrived and the first half a year we had borrowed furniture from others." Reb Dov Ber added: "Do you appreciate what it means for a person to be so absorbed in Heavenly matters that he simply failed to notice his daily surroundings for nine years? And you want me to sit on his place and assume his position?!"

*Reb Dov Ber (l.) and
Reb Nuchem Mordechai (r.)
being greeted by chassidim
while passing through Cracow in 1934*

THE MATTER ENDED WHEN their mother decreed *b'toras kib-bud eim* that they **Brotherly Love** must accept the position. Against their will the two brothers became Rebbes, leading their chassidim together. The chassidim were awestruck by the love and *achdus* between the two brothers. It was a living *mussar sefer* to watch how each one honored the other, neither of them doing anything without the prior consent of the other one. Even when a chassid went in with a *kvittel*, both brothers sat together and each one would read the *kvittel* and then give his own *berachah*. A chassid who wanted to seek advice had always to ask both brothers and together they issued a joint answer. Similarly, any letters or other public proclamations were written in the plural with the signatures of both brothers adorning the letter. Any letter that was addressed to them also had to be written in the plural and addressed to both brothers, otherwise they refused to answer.

Although the chassidim were very impressed by the *achdus* between the two brothers, they felt that in the long run it would be detrimental for the Chassidus. Both brothers shied away from making any of the decisions that were necessary for the running of a large Chassidus. Each one relied on the other to make the decisions, each thinking in his humility that really only the other one was suited to be Rebbe.

The chassidim tried to convince Reb Dov Ber to move to Shtefanesht in Romania to be Rebbe to the thousands of Shtefaneshter chassidim who were left without a Rebbe after the *petirah* of the Shtefaneshter Rebbe. He, however, refused to leave his

מברך הסכמה מאלמורי"ם אחים הקרושים תרי צנתרי דדהבא בו"ק ממשאארטקוב שליט"א הררים
כמה בוויען יצ"ו:

ב"ה ה' דחנוכה תרצ"ו וין.

אל כבוד ידידנו החסיד הרב הגאון התריף ובקי עצום סעוו ומבדיל כס"ת מו"ה יהושע ווידערקעהר
ראבד"ק פרעמיסלא יצ"ו:

אחרשה"ט. הקוונטרסים מחיבורו חידושי מהרו"יי על הס"ע או"ח הי' לנגד עינינו ושבענו רב פונג לראות כי פלה
לו בכסיפהא די פמיא להוליא לאור ספר חמוד יקר מרך אשר בע"ה יתקבל לרצון בין הלומדים ויבלשוהו
כככרה בפרם קין. כי בכקילות נפלא ובהגין יפר הפלה פניגים יקרים ואהני הן המשמחים חת הלב, וכל בי הני מילי
מפליימא יתאחרו כבי מרדפא. ומהראהו שכל אוהב תורה יחיאהו לביחו להחוק כידי מחברו, וייחוד אנו מקום אשר
אנ"ם יזליו לפללאות את חובתם מול איש סובס וברייתם אשר חסה מעותו בכל האמור"ר ז"ל ונם בכל אחוומ"ר ז"ל
צאלות ואחזולא, וכל יהיי יגב ופמל בתולה. ויקנו את הספר בכסף מלא לאמק חודה והכרה, וד' יוכתו לעסוק בתורה
כהראהא הלוא לאסוק שמחתהא אליבא דהלכחא להגדיל חורה ולהאדיריה:
והננו הדורשים שלומו ופובתו כל היחים הטלפים לישועה.

נחום מרדכי בחוהר"ך ישראל זללה"ה.   דובער בחוהר"ך ישראל זללה"ה.

A joint haskamah from both brothers

brother's side and Reb Nuchem Mordechai also refused to listen to any suggestions in the matter.

When a delegation of Shtefanshter chassidim arrived with a *ksav Rabbanus* signed by hundreds of *Yidden*, Reb Dov Ber still refused to give in. When a *Yid* told him that the *Rabbanus* would also include financial security — which was not something to be dismissed out of hand in those times — Reb Dov Ber answered: "Where is it written that I have to live in comfort? Unfortunately, there are so many *Yidden* who are struggling for a *parnassah*. I can join them too."

Reb Dov Ber's Life and Service

ALTHOUGH REB DOV BER refused to accept upon himself the title of Rebbe, he did not hold himself back from assuming other duties and holding other posts in the public service. Already many years before the *petirah* of the Chortkover Rebbe, Reb Dov Ber had been his right-hand man, busy representing his father at various communal affairs. His father held very highly of him and on one

For many years Reb Dov Ber had been his father's right-hand man. Reb Dov Ber is seen here with his father.

occasion exclaimed, "My son is fit to be a Rebbe of Rebbes!" On another occasion Reb Dov Ber once entered his father's room and whispered something in his father's ear. In an unprecedented show of affection for his son, the Rebbe rose to his feet and in front of his many chassidim, kissed his son on his forehead!

Reb Dov Ber was especially active in Agudas Yisroel, becoming one of the main decision makers on its Vaad HaPoel. He appeared at many of its conferences and meetings where he often spoke to the assembled. Reb Dov Ber did not suffice himself with merely repeating well-known ideas and concepts. His speeches often contained in them some new viewpoint or alternative strategy on which he wanted the Agudah to experiment. Typical of his outlook were the following comments of his recorded at a conference of the Agudah in Warsaw in 1932:

> The program of Agudas Yisroel is the handling and solving of all problems according to the dictates and ways of the Torah. This program is fixed and not given to change, but the ways to achieve this aim are many and varied and subject to change according to the place and time.

Reb Dov Ber of Chortkov

Unfortunately, until today the Agudah has failed to understand this. It continues to employ only one method of action. It is true that from time to time people do put forward new ideas, but still the basic strategy has remained the same. We are living in difficult times, both physically and spiritually, and we must find new ways of dealing with the ever-changing challenges that face us.

One of Reb Dov Ber's fellow co-Agudists from those days was Reb Yitzchok Meir Levin. In an article, he recounted his memories of Reb Dov Ber's involvement in the Agudah:

I enjoyed a special relationship with the *tzaddik* Reb Dov Ber, a friendship that I will never forget. We had an inner deep bond that united us. As members of the Vaad HaPoel we often spent many hours together in discussion. His *derech* was the way of splendor and glory. He never gave up hope on anyone, no *Yid* was ever beyond help or had strayed beyond the point of no return. He always acted carefully and only after due deliberation, with *yishuv hadaas* which was fueled by the great love for *Klal Yisroel* that burned inside him. In his eyes, there was no problem which could not be solved through patience and love.

≈≈

In his great *ahavas Yisroel*, Reb Dov Ber sacrificed most of his time and energy for others. When a large orphanage opened in Vienna, Reb Dov Ber agreed to be its *menahel*. Not only did he see to its financial situation, he also took time to speak to the children, lifting their spirits.

Reb Dov Ber's real *mesiras nefesh* came to light through the mitzvah of *bikur cholim*. He took upon himself to visit those lying in hospitals, and to see to their needs. Vienna had some of the best doctors and hospitals in Europe, and as a result *Yidden* came from all over Europe to receive treatment. Many of them did not have any family in Vienna to look after them and Reb Dov Ber was their only lifeline. He made a special point of visiting people ill with contagious diseases, completely ignoring the risk to himself.

Reb Dov Ber also opened a free-loan fund to help the many that were not able to make ends meet. A lot of them were not able to repay their loans but Reb Dov Ber did not have the heart to demand that they repay the money. Instead he accepted the losses himself. As one can imagine, it wasn't too long before the *gemach* closed down.

Reb Dov Ber was once traveling on a bus when he noticed an old *Yid* on the street carrying a heavy load. In order that the man should not realize that Reb Dov Ber had gotten off especially to help him, Reb Dov Ber stayed on the bus until it turned the corner, and then he hurried back to help the man, taking his heavy load from him.

Besides being famed for his great *ahavas Yisroel*, Reb Dov Ber was also known as a great *talmid chacham*. Renowned as a genius of the first order, he was thoroughly familiar with every section of the Torah. One of the great *talmidei chachamim* of the previous generation, HaGaon Reb Yisroel Yitzchok Piekarski of New York, was privileged to spend a whole night together with Reb Dov Ber when he was a young man. For hours they spoke together in learning, unraveling the secrets of the Torah. Until the end of his days, Rav Piekarski would reminisce about those hours they had spent together, and the *geonus* that Reb Dov Ber had demonstrated. He would say that although he had been a *talmid* of Yeshivas Chachmei Lublin and had been *zocheh* to learn from many of the great *geonim* in Poland, such *geonus* as he saw in Reb Dov Ber he had never seen anywhere else!

Concerning the same visit Rav Piekarski also told of the *ruach ha-kodesh* that he had witnessed:

> Before he left Vienna, he went to bid farewell to Reb Dov Ber. When he entered Reb Dov Ber's room he saw that Reb Nuchem Mordechai was also sitting there, next to his brother. In his humility, Reb Dov Ber moved down a place, seating Rav Piekarski between them. Rav Piekarski told them that he had come to say good-bye and was leaving soon on a certain flight. Hearing that he was going to travel by plane, Reb Dov Ber told him that he must postpone his trip until the following day. Rav Piekarski explained to Reb Dov Ber that he could not delay his journey and he had to catch that particular flight. Hearing his reply, Reb Dov Ber turned to his brother and asked him to forbid Rav Piekarski from taking that plane. After Reb Nuchem Mordechai had echoed his brother's words, Rav Piekarski reluctantly agreed to wait until the following day.
>
> That particular flight ended in tragedy. The plane crashed and all on board were killed. When Rav Piekarski heard of the plane crash, he rushed to Reb Dov Ber to thank him for

saving his life. When he saw him coming, Reb Dov Ber told him, "I don't know why you have come to me, it was my brother who forbade you to fly."

His Premature Passing and Loss

ALTHOUGH REB DOV BER FINALLY AGREED TO BECOME a Rebbe, his days in his father's place were numbered. Only two years after his father's *petirah*, Reb Dov Ber fell ill with a fatal disease. When the illness was first diagnosed, the doctor did not want to tell him that he had only a short time to live. When Reb Dov Ber left the room for a moment, the doctor took the opportunity to tell Reb Dov Ber's son, Reb Dovid Moshe, that his father was gravely ill and his days were numbered. Reb Dovid Moshe did not tell his father what the doctor had said, but his face must have betrayed him. As they went home, Reb Ber told his son, "If a person cannot be told something without being able to conceal what he has heard from others, it is better that he shouldn't have heard it in the first place."

When the doctor told Reb Dov Ber that he would not be able to fast on Yom Kippur, he became very upset and told his son, "If I can't fast on Yom Kippur, I don't want to have any association with this year's Yomim Noraim." And so it was; on the 24th day of Elul 5696 (1936), the first day of *Selichos*, he was *niftar*. He was only 54 years old.

In his last few hours he spoke to his only son, giving him guidance for the way ahead. Among the many things he told him was this: "If there ever comes a time when you feel that Agudas Yisroel is not living up to their standards, you must not oppose them or fight against them. Instead just withdraw your membership and sit quietly on the side, but you must not harm them in any way, under any circumstances!" After Reb Dov Ber finished speaking, his holy *neshamah* went to join the *neshamos* of his *zeides* in the Next World.

Reb Dov Ber's loss was greatly mourned not only by Chortkover chassidim but also in the wider community. In an article in the Viennese newspaper "*Die Judishe Presse*," one of the leading *rabbanim* from Germany, Reb Binyamin Zev Jacobson wrote:

נפטר געווארען הרה"צ רבי בּעריניו פרידמאן זצ"ל אין וויען

The newspapers report Reb Dov Ber's petirah

We cried for Reb Dov Ber in the same way that *Klal Yisroel* cried for Moshe Rabbeinu. When he saw in our midst even the slightest blemish, he right away stood up in battle, giving rebuke with his words of gold, words which came from the depth of his pure and holy heart and entered deep into all our hearts.

We cried for him in the same way that *Klal Yisroel* cried for Aharon HaKohen, for he was full of love for everybody, young and old alike. Even when he was ill, stricken with painful wounds, he still worried for *taharas hamishpachah* and the sanctity of the Jewish home.

We cried for him in the same way that *Klal Yisroel* cried for Reb Yehudah HaNasi. For just like Reb Yehudah HaNasi cared for *limud haTorah*, so he also cared for *limud haTorah*. Constantly he urged us to do more, to improve the *chadarim*, to build more *Talmud Torahs* and yeshivos.

Now that he has gone from us, we must remember his last words to us all. We hear him say, "All my days I occupied myself with increasing light in the world. I constantly stressed that the youth are our future and the yeshivos are our lifeline." We hear him say, "Don't forget what I always said, if there is no flour, there is no Torah. We must ensure that after the *bochurim* leave yeshivah they will have a job with which to support themselves." We hear him say, "Your camp shall be holy, to sanctify the Jewish home. Only through *taharah* can the *Shechinah* dwell among us."

L'shem Shamayim! That was his life. From it stemmed his *dikduk* in his ways, his love for others and his stringency on himself. We all loved this pure person, we loved him with deep, deep respect.

In Warsaw, the Agudah newspaper, *"Dos Yiddishe Togblatt,"* gave the following obituary:

> From Vienna has come the news that the *tzaddik* Reb Dov Ber Friedman was *niftar*. HaRav HaTzaddik Reb Dov Ber is no longer! The legendary Agudah leader whose whole being belonged to the Agudah, who constantly worried and thought about the movement, is no more! This is a difficult and major loss for all *chareidim*.
>
> We have lost that legendary figure who bestowed on us his light at every Agudah convention. Everybody was always overawed by his noble and royal conduct, which was steeped in the wondrous path of Rizhin. Always we waited to hear from him something new, some novel idea which would ignite everyone's heart and instill in our minds the obligation to strive ever higher.
>
> In the Agudah world, where Reb Dov Ber was recognized as a deep thinker and a man responsible for his actions, great hopes were pinned on him. Everyone was convinced that

Reb Dov Ber's tombstone

from this man would emerge strong words that would shake *frum Yidden* across the world to the core. In his few years he had dedicated himself to *Klal Yisroel* and it had been hoped that *Klal Yisroel* would still benefit from his service for many long years to come.

Throughout the wider community and especially within the Chortkover circles his passing has brought a deep mourning. People are undertaking an accounting of their actions, for a great prince has been taken from our midst. Great and deep is the pain that this tragedy has caused us. We can only try to emulate his special ways and wondrous personality. He will always remain an example to us all. May his memory be blessed!

CHAPTER TWENTY-FOUR

In the Shadow of War

AS LONG AS REB DOV BER WAS ALIVE, HIS BROTHER Reb Nuchem Mordechai didn't fully reveal himself. He had hoped that Reb Dov Ber would see to the running of the Chassidus, thus leaving him free to serve Hashem in total privacy. Although Reb Nuchem Mordechai was almost 60 years old when he became Rebbe, almost nothing was known about him. From his younger years he had succeeded in totally concealing his actions from the public eye. His *zeide*, Reb Dovid Moshe, would refer to him as "my holy *einikel*."

THE LAST TIME THE LUBLINER RAV, REB MEIR SHAPIRO, was in Vienna before his *petirah*, the Chortkover Rebbe, Reb Yisroel,

A True Servant of Hashem told him that before he returns to Lublin he should not forget to take leave of his sons. Reb Meir Shapiro wondered greatly at the Rebbe's words, for he visited the Rebbe's sons every time he was in Vienna.

Reb Nuchem Mordechai of Chortkov

When he came to Reb Nuchem Mordechai's house, Reb Nuchem Mordechai engaged him in a deep Talmudic discussion. For hours, the two of them unraveled the depths of Torah from one end of the *gemara* to the other. When Reb Meir Shapiro arrived back in Lublin, he called together his *talmidim* and told them, "Reb Nuchem Mordechai is famous as a holy person, a *tzaddik* who has perfected himself. I have known him for many years and yet it never occurred to me that he was so great in Torah. If he has managed to hide his Torah learning for so many decades, it proves that he learns Torah *l'shem Shamayim* and is a true servant of Hashem."

In keeping with his unassuming *derech*, Reb Nuchem Mordechai never regarded himself as being able to tell others what to do. When one of his chassidim requested that he write a letter commanding somebody to carry out a certain job, the Rebbe answered him, "I can't command, I can only ask."

The Rebbe's son-in-law, Reb Yaakov Heschel, once asked his mother-in-law why Reb Nuchem Mordechai occasionally took a key out of his pocket and placed it on the table in the middle of a meal. She explained to him that in his humility the Rebbe never interrupted a conversation even if he didn't like the topic being spoken about. Instead he placed the key on the table as a sign to change the subject.

Typical of his simple way were the words that he uttered during one of his first *tischen*. The Rebbe spoke at length about the greatness of his father and finished by saying: "My father was totally spiritual and therefore it was no wonder that he was able to do miracles. But me, one has to take as I am." In a subsequent *dvar Torah* he added: "I am not on the *madreigah* of my father and *zeide* but I ask that their merits accompany me, that the *berachos* I give should be fulfilled."

It once happened that the Rebbe was asked a complicated technical question by one of his chassidim who owned an oil refinery in the town of Drohibisht in Galicia. Part of the machinery had broken down and the *Yid* wanted to know if he should replace it, or first invest money to try and locate the fault and repair it.

"I'll tell you the truth," the Rebbe told the *Yid*. "I am not an expert in such matters and I am unable to offer you any advice. But no doubt similar occurrences happened in the past and you then consulted my holy father."

The *Yid* told the Rebbe that the last time he had consulted his father, he had advised him not to change the machinery but to see if they could detect the problem. Although such a process could often take many weeks, miraculously they had found the problem almost immediately and he was thereby saved from great loss.

Hearing his words, the Rebbe instructed the *Yid* to carry out the same inspection again and added: "Just as my father's *berachah* helped you then, so it should help you now again." And, indeed, once again the fault was located right away and repaired without the need to replace all the machinery.

~⁂~

Reb Nuchem Mordechai recites a berachah on the challah (Chol HaMoed Succos). On the right (standing) is Reb Shmuel Melamed, a respected Chortkover chassid.

LIKE HIS FATHER BEFORE HIM, THE REBBE WAS UTTERLY committed to the service of Agudas Yisroel. One of his first steps as

In His Father's Footsteps

Rebbe was to issue a joint proclamation with his brother Reb Dov Ber, in support of the movement. The two brothers publicized a letter to their chassidim a few weeks after their father's *petirah* in which they wrote: "When we visited Galicia after the terrible tragedy that has befallen us, we were comforted to see the realization of our father's plan, which is the only way to raise a new generation which will be faithful to the Torah and *avodah* and will be able to protect *Yiddishkeit*. This is the way which has always been our father's hope and wish — that everyone be united under the banner of Agudas Yisroel."

At the Third Knessia Gedolah of Agudas Yisroel in 1937, the Rebbe was elected to sit on the Moetzes Gedolei HaTorah of Agudas Yisroel. In his address to the Knessia the Rebbe told the assembled, "It wasn't easy for me to agree to join the Moetzes Gedolei HaTorah. *"Bemakom gedolim al taamod,"* and especially in the place of my holy father who was known for his total dedication and loyalty to the Agudah."

An eyewitness at the Knessia Gedolah recorded his impressions of Reb Nuchem Mordechai's participation in Marienbad:

> Like his holy father who was one of the founders of the Agudah and one of its central pillars, so was Reb Nuchem Mordechai. In his public appearances and his speeches he acted royally and with majesty. His appearance was like that of a *"Melech Yisroel,"* and when he spoke an awed hush fell on all those assembled. His words and ideas were clear and explicit and were presented with great wisdom. The Rebbe himself once said, "I am sure of the *derech* I have taken, because I did not invent a new path but just continued the way my holy *zeides* already started."

At the Knessia the Rebbe emerged as one of the Agudah's major spokesmen and pathfinders. Many of the points he raised during his address are still relevant nowadays. These are some of them:

Our main concern is the *chinuch* of the next generation. Agudas Yisroel took upon itself the task of educating the girls. One only needs to remind oneself how little the girls used to know about *Yiddishkeit* and the tragic consequences thereof, to realize what an important undertaking this was. Today, *baruch Hashem*, the education of our girls stands at a high level and the seminars produce *frum* girls who are faithful to the Torah.

Why, however, is the *chinuch* of the boys so neglected? Many of the *Talmud Torahs* employ teachers who are not qualified. The teachers are often those who have lost their jobs and they resort to being *melamdim* to earn a living. The truth is, however, that to be a teacher is a special skill and not everybody is suitable for the job.

We also have to open more workshops for those who want to work, and to create jobs for those who are not suited to pursue further studies in yeshivah. Once people were embarrassed to admit that they were working and not learning, but such an approach is totally incorrect. A businessman works hard for his *parnassah* and adheres to the *pasuk*, "You should eat the labor of your hands and it shall be good for you." The workshops must be run under *frum* supervision so that those who want to learn a trade should not need to compromise on their *Yiddishkeit*. All these issues have to be discussed and resolved during this Knessia.

After the Knessia Gedolah was over the Rebbe publicized a letter in which he wrote:

During these turbulent times in which strong winds threaten to uproot the pillars of our faith and the foundation of Chassidus, it is vital to gather together and to be *mechazeik* each other. Through joining and working together one can bring about great and wondrous achievements, especially in the field of *chinuch*, which is so vital. A group can supervise the progress of every individual so that he will not stray from the source of life, and ensure that all will raise a generation who are *yirei Hashem*. To this end we must safeguard and fight for the well-being of the *kehillah*, so that it be run in the spirit of the Torah and be an honor to Hashem and His Torah.

With the clouds of war gathering over Europe, the Rebbe also actively campaigned for *Yidden* to leave Poland for Eretz Yisroel. He said, "I support very strongly the idea of *Yidden* moving to Eretz Yisroel. The more *frum Yidden* there are in Eretz Yisroel the better it will be for *Yiddishkeit* there. In addition, if we look at the sorrowful state of *Yidden* here in Poland and the rest of Europe, we must realize that this is the direction we must take, that as many as possible should immigrate to Eretz Yisroel."

Concerning the founding of a Jewish state, the Rebbe said, "I don't view a Jewish state as the beginning of our redemption. We are waiting for Moshiach and he will be the one who will bring us the final *geulah*. But we must ask that the state encompass the whole of Eretz Yisroel, Yerushalayim and all the other holy places. We want Eretz Yisroel according to the definitions and the borders that were given to us in the Torah."

⊃⊂

WITH THE ENTRY OF THE NAZIS INTO VIENNA IN 1938, the Rebbe suffered the pains and agonies of his fellow Jews. His

Under Nazi Tyranny

only son Reb Shlomo was sent to Dachau concentration camp, and only through a miracle came back alive. The Rebbe himself was hauled out of his home into the street and forced to scrub the road in front of hundreds of jeering *goyim*. A number of times his house was raided by sadistic German thugs who took the opportunity to molest and injure the Rebbe.

Chortkover chassidim the world over made tremendous efforts to obtain a visa in order to extricate the Rebbe and his family from the Nazis' clutches. In a letter sent from Vienna to Eretz Yisroel at the time by one of the prominent chassidim, Reb Dovid Zeideman, he writes:

I want to inform you of the situation here during the last few days in order that you appreciate the urgency to obtain a visa for the Rebbe as soon as possible. It has become too dangerous to *daven* in the Rebbe's home. Instead we have been *davening* in the home of Reb Hershele. This last Thursday the Germans forced thousands of people from their homes. Throughout the night they pulled *Yidden* from their beds, young and old alike. Those who were taken by the local police and imprisoned were the lucky ones. The others who fell into the hands of the German troops were beaten and humiliated in the most terrible ways. In addition, all their money and personal belongings were confiscated. The Rebbe was also forced from his house and made to walk in the pouring rain without a coat. *Baruch Hashem* they later released him after midnight. The rest of his family was only released Friday afternoon. Throughout this time they were forbidden to sit down and were not even given a bit of water to drink. Praise to Hashem that the Rebbe's nephew, Reb Dovid Moshe, his mother and sister were not taken. May Hashem protect us all.

Please do all you can to ensure that the visas arrive as quickly as possible for we cannot tell what the future holds for us.

Escape to Eretz Yisroel

AFTER TREMENDOUS EFFORTS, IN THE SPRING OF 1939 a visa for Eretz Yisroel was finally procured for the Rebbe and his family. The Rebbe left Vienna a week before Purim 1939. On his last Shabbos in Vienna, he gave a short *tisch* during which he said as follows:

Once, on Rosh Hashanah, the Berdichever Rav was standing with his *shofar* in hand ready to blow the *tekios*. The whole shul was waiting patiently but the Berdichever Rav just stood there. Eventually the Rav turned to his *kehillah* and explained to them. "Outside is sitting a *Yid* who was never taught how to *daven*. When he saw us all *davening* with such fervor, he became very envious; he also longed to *daven* to

Hashem, but he does not know how. He started to cry and pleaded to Hashem, 'Please Hashem, You know all the *tefillos* and all the words and meanings that go into them. But I don't know how to *daven*. All I know is how to say the *aleph-beis*. I will say all the letters of the *aleph-beis* and You, Hashem, will form the letters into the correct order to make the right words and meanings.'

"Now," explained the Berdichever Rav, "Hashem is busy forming all the letters into words and therefore we have to wait!"

The Rebbe finished the story and added:

We, who are suffering so much in this *galus*, have to *daven* to Hashem that He forgive us for all our sins. If, however, there comes a time when we are no longer able even to *daven*, we have to beg Hashem in the way the Berdichever Rav explained — that at least He should accept our *aleph-beis* and convert them into *tefillos* on our behalf and have pity on us to redeem us soon with the final *geulah*.

From Vienna the Rebbe journeyed one last time to Chortkov to take leave of his chassidim, and from there he continued on to Eretz Yisroel. Over 2,000 chassidim converged on Chortkov to bid farewell to their beloved Rebbe. The Rebbe knew and the chassidim also realized and felt that this was the last Shabbos they would ever spend together. On the first day of Nissan, the Rebbe parted from Chortkov for the last time. With tears streaming down his cheeks, the Rebbe stood in front of the *aron hakodesh* as he said good-bye to his chassidim for the last time. In a voice choked with tears his parting words were: "May it be the will of Hashem that we all meet again in Eretz Yisroel."

The Destruction of Chortkov

DURING THE SECOND WORLD WAR THE CHORTKOVER Chassidus was almost totally decimated. Across Poland and Galicia all the Chortkover *kehillos* and institutions were destroyed and their members cruelly murdered. Almost the entire *Yiddishe* population of the town of Chortkov was killed. From the many thousands who lived there before the war, only some thirty *Yidden* survived the massacres. The Nazis entered Chortkov on the 6th of June 1941. Just three days later, these sadistic German animals started their murder of the pure and righteous *Yidden* of Chortkov. Over 300 *Yidden* were rounded up and shot to death in the courtyard of the town's prison. Two weeks later, on the 28th of June, the exercise was repeated; this time 150 *Yidden* were murdered. In April 1942, a ghetto was set up in a small area of Chortkov and the entire Jewish community was restricted to its narrow confines. Over the next few months hundreds died from disease and malnutrition.

Half a year later, in August 1942, the Nazis finally destroyed the last vestiges of the once proud and great *kehillah* of Chortkov. On the 28th of August the Nazis entered the ghetto and rounded up some 2,000 *Yidden*. They were the first of many transports to be sent in cattle cars from Chortkov to the Belzec death camp, where they were gassed to death. After the ghetto was emptied of its inhabitants, it was blown up in order to eliminate any last Jews who may have been there. Chortkov was then declared "Judenrein!" The holy and legendary *kehillah* of Chortkov, which had been mentioned in awe and respect across the world, was no longer.

≈≈

The Enemy's Mistake

THE REBBE ARRIVED IN ERETZ YISROEL A BROKEN AND SICK man. The suffering of his fellow Jews lay heavily on his heart. Yet although the Rebbe had succeeded in escaping from Europe he was not yet safe from Nazi hands. In 1941 the situation in Eretz Yisroel was critical. The Germans had already conquered most of Europe, Egypt was under German control, and they were threatening to invade Eretz Yisroel any day. When the situation deteriorated even further the Chortkover chassidim in Eretz Yisroel came to plead with the Rebbe to *daven* for them. They explained the situation, adding that short of a miracle nothing could save them.

Reb Nuchem Mordechai of Chortkov;
in the background is Reb Dovid Moshe Spiegel

In his memoirs, Reb Dovid Moshe Spiegel describes the event:

I remember that serious and emotional meeting. The Rebbe sat, his holy heart overflowing with mercy, his eyes aglow, listening to the words of his chassidim as they entreated him to save them. He sat deep in thought and then he said, "It is well known that in order to perform a miracle which does not infringe on the boundaries of nature, it is enough if one has just a few *zechusim*. It seems, however, that the strength of the enemy is very great. He has destroyed many strong and powerful nations with the greatest of ease. Normal warfare against him is useless. Therefore we need a supernatural miracle to annul the evil decrees against us, to silence the enemy. To perform such a miracle is, however, very difficult, and so we have to find a method of defeating the enemy through natural means. We must *daven* that they should make a mistake, for anybody is capable of miscalculating and making a mistake. Let us *daven* that the enemy makes a fatal mistake that will cost them the war and bring about their defeat."

And so it was; the Germans made a fatal mistake by attacking Russia. Winston Churchill wrote in his book "The Second World War": "The German invasion of Russia changed the course of the war and its outcome. The Russians were far stronger than the Germans had thought and this caused their downfall."

Although Yerushalayim boasted two Chortkover shuls and a Chortkover yeshivah, the Rebbe refused to settle there and instead

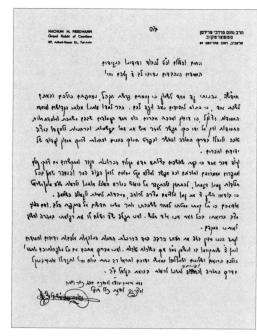

Letter of chizuk written
by the Rebbe to his
chassidim during the war

chose to live in Tel Aviv. When his father Reb Yisroel of Chortkov was contemplating moving to Eretz Yisroel, he said that he was unable to live in Yerushalayim due to the raging *machlokes* which had broken out between various groups and *rabbanim* in the city. "To live there and ignore the *machlokes* — I am unable," Reb Yisroel explained. "And to become involved, I don't want to either." When Reb Nuchem Mordechai arrived in Eretz Yisroel, he told his chassidim, "The reason that prevented my father from living in Yerushalayim applies to me as well!"

Indeed, throughout his life the Rebbe tried his hardest to ensure that only peace and harmony reigned among *Yidden*. Many of his Torahs and his speeches centered around this theme. In a letter written to his chassidim during those difficult times, he urged them to make an extra effort to be kind and friendly to each other and he added:

> When we sit together and remember the days gone by and the *tzaddikim* and their Torah and their ways, we can find a small measure of comfort in these bitter and terrible times which have no comparison in all the history of our people. Thus we can also be *mechazeik* each other and overcome the terrible despair that is eating away at all of us and thereby ensure that *Klal Yisroel* not stay orphaned. We must have faith that Hashem will definitely save His people and take them out of slavery to freedom and the final *geulah*.

For the Rebbe to live in Tel Aviv was not an easy undertaking. It pained him terribly to see the *chillul Shabbos* around him, and the secular spirit of the city. The Rebbe was *makpid* not to go out of his house on Shabbos in order that he should not have to see the desecration of the holy Shabbos. Occasionally the Rebbe would spend a Shabbos in Yerushalayim in order to inspire his many chassidim there. Large crowds would come to spend Shabbos in the Rebbe's company and bask in his *kedushah*. Among those present could sometimes be seen the future Gerrer Rebbe, the Beis Yisroel. When the Rebbe would recite *Shalom Aleichem* and then *Kiddush*, the Beis Yisroel would suddenly appear and stand in the next room, from where he would listen to the Rebbe's *avodah*. Hardly had the Rebbe ended reciting *Kiddush* than the Beis Yisroel would disappear.

Just as in Vienna the Rebbe had occupied an important position on all matters concerning *Yidden*, so in Eretz Yisroel he continued to stand in the forefront on behalf of *Klal Yisroel*. He constantly urged all *Yidden* to put aside their differences and unite. Only through such action would they succeed in rebuilding what had been destroyed and overcoming their adversaries.

In his address to the National Convention of Agudas Yisroel in Petach Tikva in 1944, he said:

> "*Morai VeRabbosai*! At the Knessia Gedolah my holy father said that in the near future the Knessia Gedolah of the Agudah would take place in Eretz Yisroel. His words have been fulfilled and we have gathered here today in the Holy Land. But to our sorrow, it has not taken place in the way he envisioned, and we are all here today with broken hearts. Hashem in His mercy should have pity on us and redeem us soon.

The Rebbe then again reiterated his plea for all *Yidden* to be united in brotherly love:

> Reb Yochanan ben Zakkai instructed his *talmidim:* "Go out and see what is the best *derech* a person should adopt." Reb Yochanan ben Zakkai lived in the generation immediately after the destruction of the *Beis HaMikdash*. He saw for himself the reasons that had caused the *churban*, the needless hatred

*Reb Nuchem Mordechai
in his last years*

between *Yidden* and the lack of Torah learning. Therefore when he wanted to start to repair and rectify the situation he told his *talmidim*: "Go out and see" — look and see what has caused the *churban*.

Similarly, we who have gathered here today also have to say "Go out and see." We have to see and feel for ourselves the terrible *churban* that has occurred. Reb Yochanan ben Zakkai told his *talmidim* that the *middah* that is most encompassing is *lev tov*, a good heart. We also have to join together in unity to have one heart to be good natured and friendly to all *Yidden* and our hearts should only be filled with good. Through such behavior we shall merit the *geulah*, as we find that Hashem told Yirmiyahu HaNavi, "And I will give them one heart and one *derech* so that they fear Me all the days and it will be good for them and their children after them."

Besides Agudas Yisroel, the Rebbe was also active in other public arenas. He appeared at a large rally in Tel Aviv in support of Shabbos. The Rebbe did not enjoy attending such demonstrations. In his address to the crowds the Rebbe gave a deep sigh and said: "The truth is that the mere fact that we have to hold such a rally to promote the observance of Shabbos is an embarrassment and a humiliation. The *gemara* tells us that Shabbos is a special present that Hashem gave to *Klal Yisroel*. What can be a bigger disgrace than a son wantonly smashing the present his father gave him? Is a bigger insult possible? Therefore, when we see *chillul Shabbos* how we can we possibly remain silent?"

Although the Rebbe did not hesitate to speak out when he saw the need to, it was only on rare occasions that he did so. Especially during the terrible war years, he would say that one must be extra careful not to be *mekatreig* (make accusations) against *Yidden*. Indeed, many of the *divrei Torah* that he delivered during those dark times are full of *limud zechus* on *Yidden*. Constantly he begged Hashem to have mercy on them and to save them from their oppressors. Typical of this approach is the following story that he once related:

> A *Yid* once asked my holy father for a *berachah* for success in business. My father blessed him that he should be a *yirei Shamayim*. "Rebbe!" the *Yid* exclaimed. "I ask you for a *berachah* for my business and you bless me with *yiras Shamayim*?"
>
> My father answered the *Yid*, "It is written in *Tehillim*, 'Your wife will be like a fruitful vine in your house, your sons like clusters of olives around your table, for so is blessed a person who is a *yirei Shamayim*.' Therefore if I bless you with *yiras Shamayim* then automatically all your other needs will be fulfilled as well."

The Rebbe then added:

> Although such an approach was fine years ago, nowadays, however, which is a period of suffering, *Yidden* are simply unable to serve Hashem in their current situation. First we must beg Hashem to remove the terrible decrees and grant us the ability to live normal lives. Only then will we be able to develop into true *ehrlicher Yidden*. The *pasuk* that my father quoted can also be understood in this vein. "For so is blessed a person who is a *yirei Shamayim*" — somebody who is so blessed, he can be a *yirei Shamayim*. First we must have the *berachos* and then we can become *yirei Hashem*, but in our present condition *Yidden* are unable to accomplish anything.

⁂

IN HIS LAST YEARS, THE REBBE BECAME WEAKER AND weaker. On his 70th birthday on the 17th of Shevat 1944, he told

Reb Nuchem Mordechai's Last Years

those around him in a tear-choked voice: "*Harei ani k'ven shivim shanah velo zachisi* — I am already 70 years old and I haven't yet been *zocheh* to do *teshuvah*. Please *daven* for me that I should mend my ways and serve Hashem from now on with a whole heart."

When the terrible news arrived in Eretz Yisroel of the true extent of the Holocaust, the Rebbe's soft heart broke totally. He took to his bed and his health deteriorated. During his *tischen* when he spoke about the state of *Klal Yisroel*, deep sighs and sobs often accompanied his words. His face a ghostly white, his body racked with an inner emotional pain over the loss of his fellow *Yidden*, the Rebbe could not hold himself back from mentioning the terrible loss at every speech and occasion. As a result of this mental agony, the Rebbe's temperature often rose and spiraled out of control whenever he mentioned the suffering of *Klal Yisroel* during the Holocaust, and by the end of a *tisch*, a doctor had to be summoned.

Even though the Rebbe suffered from a variety of painful ailments, he never complained about them. When one of his chassidim saw the Rebbe's calm face and remarked, "It seems that the Rebbe is *baruch Hashem* feeling better," the Rebbe answered him, "*Baruch Hashem* I am feeling a little bit worse."

On the 18th of Adar 1946, the Rebbe's holy *neshamah* ascended upwards. He was only 72 years old. Before his *petirah* he gave voice to his great pain over the Holocaust, crying bitter tears over the loss of his fellow *Yidden*. The *gemara* in *Kesubos* relates that before Reb Yehudah HaNasi was *niftar* he also cried bitter tears. His *talmid*, Reb Chiya, asked his rebbi in surprise, "Rebbi, why are you crying, have we not learned that if someone dies with a smile, it is a good sign for him?"

Reb Yehudah HaNasi answered him, "I am not crying for myself, but for the Torah and mitzvos."

Similarly, the Rebbe also shed tears before his *petirah*, not for himself, but for his fellow *Yidden* and the *kavod* of the *Shechinah*. He died from a broken heart, unable to withstand the terrible decrees that had afflicted his people. The Rebbe's holy body was laid to rest on Har HaZeisim, in an honorable place overlooking the Har HaBayis.

The Rebbe's matzeivah on Har HaZeisim

CHAPTER TWENTY-FIVE

Fourth Generation of the Dynasty

AFTER THE REBBE'S *PETIRAH*, THE ORPHANED chassidim looked up to the Rebbe's one and only son, Reb Shlomo, to fill his father's place and become the new Chortkover Rebbe. Like his father before him, he too had succeeded in hiding himself from public scrutiny. Although he was already 52 years old when he became Rebbe, Reb Shlomo was hardly known to the wider community. He had rarely appeared in public and most of his time was spent secluded with his *sefarim*.

DESPITE HIS RETICENCE, REB SHLOMO WAS WELL KNOWN to the inner circle of Chortkover chassidim. There, among the elite

The New Flag Bearer
and senior chassidim, he mixed freely and easily. In this limited circle he allowed these elder *Yidden* to gain access to his true greatness. Indeed, his father Reb Nuchem Mordechai would occasionally tell some of the elder chassidim that they should seek the counsel of Reb Shlomo. In his

Reb Shlomo of Chortkov

memoirs the chassid Reb Dovid Moshe Spiegel wrote that the Rebbe said to him:

My son is a hidden *tzaddik* and he has concealed his true *madreigah* in accordance with the way of Rizhin. Only those who possess a deeper sense and understanding know who he really is. I can testify that he is a true *yirei Shamayim*. My holy father held him in high esteem and praised him often.

In the last months of his life, the Rebbe, Reb Nuchem Mordechai, often instructed his chassidim to go to his son with their problems. In this way he showed that he approved of Reb Shlomo becoming his successor.

Although most of the Chortkover chassidim had been murdered in the war, nevertheless a small group of chassidim had survived, numbering perhaps some 300 people or more. (Over 200 names are listed in the first edition of Reb Nuchem Mordechai's *sefer*, "*Doresh Tov*," printed in 1964.) Some of the chassidim had arrived in Eretz Yisroel before the war and a few came afterwards. In America, a similar number of surviving chassidim also resided. Among them numbered quite a few great and distinguished *rabbanim* such as the *geonim* Reb Zev Wolf Leiter of Petersburg, Reb Mordechai Harling of New York, Reb Shlomo Zalman Horowitz of Potik, Reb Pinchos Hirshprung of Montreal and Reb Avrohom Shapiro of Toyest.

These chassidim now crowned Reb Shlomo as their new Rebbe. Five of the most senior chassidim in Tel Aviv, the *geonim* and *rabbanim* Reb Shmuel Halpern, Reb Yisroel Rapporport, Reb Yisroel Meizel, Reb Meir Melamed and Reb Dovid Zeideman issued the following proclamation:

Baruch Hashem, Tel Aviv 24th of Adar 5706 (1946)

To our honorable beloved chassidim and friends, partners in our grief, Chassidei Chortkov, may Hashem look after them:

Woe is to us, we have lost our crown. Rabbeinu, the holy and pure one, has been taken from us. We have become like orphans for he was like a father to us all. Our pain was his pain and he made himself ill over our problems. When the afflictions of our people increased he took ill and could not be cured.

During his illness he suffered greatly but he accepted his lot with love, in a manner which amazed all around him until even the doctors were moved. Throughout his life he concealed himself, but now his true greatness has become revealed in all its glory. Great is our loss and who will comfort us.

But a small comfort has remained for us: the Rebbe's only son, the Rav and *tzaddik* Reb Shlomo. He will carry our flag — the flag of Chortkov that has been sanctified through three generations, may their merit protect us. Through their teachings and their influence, Chassidus Chortkov has developed its own *derech* and outlook and its own special qualities.

We are going to guard this *derech* that it does not become spoiled and we are going to guard these special qualities that they do not become dulled. United under the flag of Chortkov we will ensure that the tree does not wither or become uprooted. The Rebbe will carry our flag with pride and honor in the merit of his holy forefathers. Our covenant will not be annulled and the link will not be broken. We shall continue the holy dynasty until the coming of Moshiach.

Today, Wednesday the 24th of Adar, we gathered in Yerushalayim at the *kever* of our holy Rebbe and there we crowned his son, the Rav and *tzaddik* Reb Shlomo, and we proclaimed that he will comfort us from our sadness.

This will be for sure a *nachas* for our holy Rebbes in Gan Eden and thus we will merit their help and their comfort.

May Hashem turn our sadness to joy and our mourning to happiness and send us the Moshiach soon in our days.

From those who speak in honor of our holy Rebbes, may their *zechus* protect us and all of *Klal Yisroel*.

Shmuel Halpern from Amsterdam
Yisroel Rapporport
Yisroel Meizel
Meir Shmuel Melamed, head *shochet* of Tel Aviv
Dovid Zeideman

~)(~

Although many of the senior chassidim were much older than Reb Shlomo, they all accepted his authority without any discontent or hesitation. The only one who was not happy about the new appointment was the Rebbe himself. Although he accepted the position without a fight, he made sure to show the chassidim that he did not regard himself as his father's successor. To this end, Reb Shlomo adamantly refused to use his father's chair. Also, he refused to sit in his father's place at the head of the table, rather he would sit in the middle of the table. His father's chair remained in its original position at the head of the table, empty and forlorn. Thus he demonstrated to his chassidim that although he was Rebbe, he did not view himself as his father's successor. That position remained unfilled!

Reb Shlomo assumed the mantle of leadership in a difficult period for Chortkover Chassidus. This once great Chassidus which had numbered tens of thousands of chassidim, including many *gedolim,* was no longer. Its numerous *kehillos* and shuls lay destroyed across Europe. Wherever one turned, all one found was despair and anguish. In these trying times Reb Shlomo ascended to the challenge.

ONE OF THE REBBE'S FIRST STEPS WAS TO REOPEN THE Chortkover yeshivah in Yerushalayim called "Or Yisroel." This

The Chortkover Yeshivah yeshivah had first opened its doors some ten years earlier in 1937. During the war years, the yeshivah had been forced to close and now the time had come for it to reopen.

הישיבה הקדושה „אור ישראל"
בעיה"ק ירושלים ת"ו

קול קורא לאחינו אנ"ש די בכל אתר ואתר ד' עליהם יחיו

הוות ביום כ"ד אלול תרצ"א בהלולא ראשונה של כ"ק ציס"ע דוכר"ד וצ"ל התאספו כל טובי וזקני חסידי טשארטקוב והתליטו ליסד ישיבה בירושלם עיה"ק ת"ו בשם „אור ישראל" עיש אדמו"ר הגאון הקדוש רשכבה"ג רבינו ישראל זצוק"ל להגציה את זכרן הזקרוש במפעל שהי יתקיים לדורות. כי ירעו למדי גורל הבינותו לישיבות ועד כמה החשיב והעגין ביסוד ישיבות נוספות ובפרט בארצנו הקדושה חמרת לבבו...

(גוף הכרוז בכתב קטן)

כברכת חברי ההנהלה

שמואל הורביץ הלוי
אברהם יחיאל ווילבר
דוד משה שפיגל

Address: Jeshivath „Or Jsrael" Jerusalem, Meah Shearim, Palestine

A proclamation on behalf of the Chortkover Yeshivah in Yerushalayim

A brief history of the yeshivah is contained in a public letter written by the *hanhalah* of the yeshivah in 1947:

> On the 24th of Elul 5697 (1937), the first *yahrtzeit* of the holy *tzaddik* and *kadosh*, Reb Dov Ber, all the elders and the finest of the Chortkover chassidim gathered together to found a yeshivah in Yerushalayim.
>
> The yeshivah was named "Or Yisroel" in memory of our master Rabbeinu Yisroel and to perpetuate his holy legacy in a project which was his life's work and aim. His great love for yeshivos is well known, how he stressed the importance of additional yeshivos, and especially here in the Holy Land.
>
> It is also well known how he desperately longed to come to live in Eretz Yisroel, but from Heaven it was decided otherwise. Therefore the founding of a yeshivah in Yerushalayim in his name will surely be a *nachas* for him in Gan Eden and he will act there on our behalf.

The idea received an enthusiastic response from the Rebbe, Reb Nuchem Mordechai, who wrote as follows:

> It was pleasing to hear about a new organization whose aim is to unite all Chortkover chassidim into one group so that no individual becomes distanced from the Chassidus and is left to drift without an anchor.
>
> Especially delightful is the news that you are opening a yeshivah in Yerushalayim. It is to be called "Or Yisroel," in the name of my holy father and teacher. Any new Torah institution that opens arouses in me feelings of joy and I do my utmost to give it my support. All the more so when the institution concerned is a yeshivah in the holy city of Yerushalayim and is being run by our chassidim, and my father's ways and teachings are to be its guiding force. I will surely give the yeshivah my total and full support as much as I am physically able. I also expect all our chassidim throughout Eretz Yisroel and *chutz laAretz* to do likewise so that the yeshivah will prosper and grow and develop in a glorious way.

The yeshivah got off to a good start and attracted a number of promising young men. This in itself was no small feat. At the time Eretz Yisroel was suffering a severe financial crisis and there was very little money to be had for starting new *mosdos*. Thus the opening of the yeshivah was heralded as a great achievement and something that was long overdue.

A well-known *talmid chacham* and Chortkover chassid, Reb Shmuel Horowitz, was appointed as *Rosh Yeshivah*. In addition, a second *maggid shiur,* Reb Yechiel Vilner, was also appointed. The treasurer and secretary of the yeshivah was Reb Dovid Moshe Spiegel.

Although the yeshivah got off to a bright start, it soon fell victim to the war. The yeshivah had depended almost entirely on the support of the chassidim in Europe. Once this avenue dried up, the yeshivah was no longer able to survive and reluctantly had to close its doors four years after its inception.

The yeshivah remained closed until after Reb Nuchem Mordechai's *petirah*. After the war's end, the survivors started to arrive in Eretz Yisroel. Among them numbered young boys and men who were in dire need of a yeshivah where they could learn and once again put into practice the ways that they had absorbed in their homes before the war. Thus the reopening of the yeshivah took on an added urgency — to cater to and look after the war-shattered orphans. In addition, the reopening of the yeshivah would greatly contribute toward rebuilding the Chortkover Chassidus, which had so recently suffered the double loss of its Rebbe and the masses of its chassidim.

Thus one of Reb Shlomo's first actions as Rebbe was to reopen the yeshivah and call for all to support it. In a letter he wrote:

> I have derived great satisfaction to hear that the yeshivah "Or Yisroel" has started again its holy work and is to be enlarged and widened. Be strong and courageous and do not be deterred from this holy and important task. The *zechus* of my father, who cared so much for this *mosad,* and the *zechus* of my *zeide,* whose name the yeshivah carries, should help you all to succeed so that the yeshivah shall prosper and be worthy of its namesake. No doubt all our chassidim will

understand their duty to help the yeshivah and will give it their full support.

IN 1953, FIVE YEARS AFTER THE YESHIVAH'S REOPENING, the Boyaner Rebbe, Reb Mordechai Shlomo Friedman, came to visit Eretz Yisroel. During his visit he proposed that the time had come to open a new yeshivah which would serve all Rizhiner chassidim and would perpetuate the Rizhiner *derech* for generations to come. The Boyaner Rebbe broached his idea to the other Rebbes of the Rizhiner Dynasty, and all gave him their enthusiastic support. The Chortkover Rebbe, Reb Shlomo, also lent his full support to the idea. From now on all Rizhiner chassidim would learn in one central yeshivah under the joint guidance and leadership of all the Rebbes of the Rizhiner Dynasty.

The Rizhiner Yeshivah

In his letter on behalf of the yeshivah, the Chortkover Rebbe wrote:

> In Yerushalayim a yeshivah has been founded called "Tiferes Yisroel," in the name of my holy *zeide*, the Rebbe of Rizhin.
>
> Its aim is to spread the knowledge of Torah among the young in the spirit of Chassidus and pure *yiras Shamayim*. Dozens of diligent boys have already joined the yeshivah's ranks and are learning with *hasmadah*.
>
> Therefore it is our duty to help the yeshivah and support it. An extra duty lies upon the Rizhiner chassidim to ensure the success of this *mosad* whose aim is to teach Torah together with the unique values of Rizhin. These are the values of *emes*, modesty, and acting in a way which brings glory to the mitzvos and glory to the Creator.
>
> Each and every one is obligated to make an extra effort to help as much as possible that the yeshivah achieve its aims so that our "well does not run dry and our tree does not become uprooted."

Chortkover chassidim heeded the call of their Rebbe, and until today have played a major role in caring for the Rizhiner Yeshivah's success and continued financial stability.

Reb Shlomo of Chortkov speaking at a meeting on behalf of Chinuch Atzmai

The Rizhiner Yeshivah has indeed lived up to the high goals set for it by its founders. Under the tutelage of its great *Rosh Yeshivah*, the *gaon* Reb Yehoshua Brim, countless *talmidim* have been educated in its *beis hamedrash*, and until this day the yeshivah continues to produce *talmidei chachamim* steeped in the unique *derech* of Rizhin.

SUPPORTING THE GROWTH OF TORAH AND *CHINUCH* WAS a major goal in the Rebbe's itinerary. He did not limit himself just to **Chinuch Atzmai** helping those in his own camp or Chassidus. Wherever and whenever some new plan or idea was broached, the Rebbe was invariably involved. The great importance that he put into *chinuch* can be seen from his fiery words at a fundraising convention on behalf of *Chinuch Atzmai*:

> *Morai VeRabbosai!* Arouse yourselves and listen to my words!
> If you were to be asked to contribute toward building the future *Beis HaMikdash*, one can imagine with what excitement and eagerness everyone would run to bring their money and valuables. You would do so with joy and *simchah*. All the more so now that you are being asked to contribute toward something that is even more important —

the building of *mosdos* for our children. *Chazal* have told us that the Torah learning of children is so important that it even takes precedence over building the *Beis HaMikdash*!

Therefore I urge you all to contribute with joy and to run eagerly to perform this great mitzvah before others complete the mitzvah. Don't allow yourselves to fall into the trap of the *Nesiim* who due to their complacency almost missed out on the opportunity to contribute toward the *Mishkan*.

∽◠

ALTHOUGH THE REBBE WAS AN ACTIVE MEMBER OF Agudas Yisroel and many other communal bodies, he refused to

Sins of the Righteous

take a central role and get involved in many of the burning issues of the day. Like his *zeides* before him, Reb Shlomo's soft and warm *neshamah* was reviled by *machlokes*. Any sharp statements or inflammatory language was enough to cause him to withdraw from the most important of organizations.

It is in this vein that the Rebbe wrote the following comments in his *sefer "Divrei Shlomo"*:

> It is well known that the task of the *yetzer hara* is to cause people to sin. The *yetzer hara* has many different ways and strategies to achieve its goal. It even found a way to cause *tzaddikim* to sin. How is this possible? How can people who have perfected themselves to such a degree that their minds never wander from the service of Hashem, possibly sin?
>
> The *yetzer hara* devised a plan. It will show the *tzaddikim* the low and evil deeds of the wicked and impress upon these *tzaddikim* that the *reshaim* have fallen so low that they are beyond help and can no longer be rescued. Therefore, argues the *yetzer hara*, it is a mitzvah to despise and curse these *reshaim*!
>
> This is indeed a serious sin, as we find that Yeshayah HaNavi was rebuked for proclaiming that *Klal Yisroel* had become defiled. It is our duty to continue to *daven* and hope

that the wicked repent their ways and that no bad befalls them. This is the way that my holy *zeides* instructed us to follow. They constantly sought to help all sections of *Klal Yisroel* and beseeched Hashem on behalf of all *Yidden*.

If nowadays we are faced with the sad and distressing phenomenon of *Yidden* who have left the path of the Torah, we must make an even greater effort that at least all the *chareidim* must perfect themselves and unite as one with *mesiras nefesh*. Then we can hope that these distanced souls will want to come near and accept the Torah and its mitzvos.

Reb Shlomo practiced what he preached. Every *Yid* who came to see him was received with a warm welcome and words of encouragement. Even when it was necessary to rebuke someone for a wrongdoing, it was always said in a soft and gentle tone, almost apologetically. On one occasion, after the Rebbe had used harsher language than usual, he sent the person a letter of appeasement in which he sought to justify his harsh tones.

⇌

An Early Demise

DESPITE ALL THE REBBE'S EFFORTS TO REBUILD THE shattered Chassidus and restore it to its former glory, in Heaven things were decided otherwise. Only a few years after Reb Shlomo became Rebbe, he fell ill with a life-threatening disease. Although at first he was able to conceal his illness from the wider public, he was unable to hide the seriousness of his condition from his close circle of chassidim. Frequently he was forced to take to his bed and cancel his daily schedule.

As his condition deteriorated and the Rebbe needed to be hospitalized, he could no longer keep his illness a secret. Yet, between his painful treatments and frequent hospital stays, the Rebbe somehow managed to still see his eager chassidim, and despite his agony, to greet them in a warm and cheerful manner.

The Rebbe's last public appearance was at *Kol Nidrei* 5719 (1959). The next morning the Rebbe was too weak to attend the *davening*. The Rebbe spent Succos lying in bed critically ill. When one of his chassidim wanted to inform the Rebbe of worldly developments, he refused to listen and said, "I no longer have any connection with this world."

The Shabbos before the Rebbe's *petirah*, an *aufruf* of one of the Rebbe's closest and most devoted chassidim took place in the Rebbe's *beis hamedrash*. After the *davening* had ended the *chasan* went into the Rebbe's bedroom to ask for a *berachah*, as is customary.

Instead of granting the boy the usual *berachah* the Rebbe said to him. "A *chasan* has the power to

The Rebbe's matzeivah in the Nachlas Yitzchok cemetery in Tel Aviv

bless others. Please *daven* that I don't disrupt your *simchah*."

The *chasunah* took place Tuesday evening. A few hours later, early Wednesday morning, the 15th of Cheshvan 5719 (1959), the Rebbe was *niftar*.

≈

Part of the crowds at the levayah

Sitting in the succah: Reb Nuchem Mordechai (l.) and Reb Tzvi Aryeh of Zlatipol (r.)

WITH THE REBBE'S *PETIRAH* THE CHASSIDIM WERE LEFT orphaned without any leader. Reb Shlomo left behind him only one daughter and she also had only one daughter. Yet all was not yet lost. In Tel Aviv lived the *tzaddik* Reb Zvi Aryeh Twersky, or Reb Hershele, as he was fondly known.

Reb Hershele Zlatipoler

Reb Hershele was the son-in-law of the Chortkover Rebbe, Reb Yisroel, and he was revered by all. Although not actually a descendant of the Chortkover Dynasty, Reb Hershele nevertheless conducted himself according to the ways and *minhagim* of his *shver,* the Chortkover Rebbe. Now, in their moment of need, it was not surprising that the chassidim were content to offer him the position.

Over twenty years earlier the Chortkover chassidim in Eretz Yisroel had approached Reb Hershele with a request to come and live in Eretz Yisroel. At the time, in 1935, the chassidim wanted a member of the Chortkover family to live in their midst and help build and establish a strong community. Reb Hershele, however, refused their offer and remained in Vienna. He was happy to keep a low profile and not to be thrust into the limelight. Now, however, Reb Hershele understood that he no longer had the right to deny the chassidim a guide and Rebbe.

Already as a young man Reb Hershele had earned the highest praises from his *shver*. When someone once commented to Reb Yisroel Chortkover that his son-in-law Reb Hershele was not very tall, the Rebbe remarked. "He might be physically short but spiritually he is very tall. He possesses a high and lofty *neshamah*!"

In the Rebbe's last years he asked Reb Hershele to write a *sefer* to guide people in the correct path and values of the Torah. In his introduction Reb Hershele explains the goal of his *sefer*, "HaTov VeHaTachlis," as follows:

> The aim of this *sefer* is to make clear what the purpose of a person is in this world. What is the truth and what is the real good? These are topics that are buried deep in the conscience of every thoughtful individual, but nevertheless many have been unable to sift through the matter clearly in their own minds, or have never taken the opportunity to study the matter properly.
>
> The clear objective of this *sefer* is to sift through and separate the fruit from the peel, the truth from fiction, the good from bad. Only through careful and honest deliberation can a person arrive at the truth and afterwards achieve his goal in this world.

During the terrible and dark period of the Second World War, Reb Hershele wrote a second *sefer*, this time on the topic of *emunah*. Reb Hershele was famed for his deep *emunah* and trust in Hashem. When he was once asked by a concerned chassid where the Rebbe would find *parnassah* in those difficult and turbulent times, he answered: "I am not worried. We have been commanded to place our trust in Hashem, as it is written, '*Tamim tihiye im Hashem Elokecha*.' *Chazal* explain this to mean that we should not worry unnecessarily about the future. If so, there is no need to be concerned."

⇒⇐

Already before Reb Hershele was appointed as Chortkover Rebbe, he held a position as a Rebbe. Reb Hershele was a son of

Reb Hershele Zlatipoler

the Zlatipoler Rebbe (part of the Chernobyler Dynasty) and after his father's *petirah* he assumed his father's place and was known as Reb Hershele Zlatipoler. Thus, for Reb Hershele to assume a second position was rather out of the ordinary and something of a novelty. Indeed, Reb Hershele already had his own *beis hamedrash* in Tel Aviv, which was known as the Zlatipoler shul. Nevertheless, he somehow managed to divide his time between the Zlatipoler and Chortkover shuls and serve as Rebbe in both positions. In his last years Reb Hershele was asked to become Rebbe for the Karliner chassidim, who had also become orphaned of their Rebbe. This time Reb Hershele refused. He explained to the Karliner chassidim: "A person can wear one hat very easily and comfortably. It is even possible for a person to put on two hats at the same time. If, however, a person would try to put on three hats simultaneously, all three would fall off and the person would be left without anything!"

It was not for nothing that many chassidim ran after Reb Hershele and begged him to be their Rebbe. It was enough to spend just a few minutes in his presence to make you realize that you were in the presence of a true *yirei Shamayim*. A typical story of his great *ehrlichkeit* is the following incident:

> Reb Hershele lived in Tel Aviv in a small flat without any air conditioning or any other type of cooling system. During the hot summer months, the flat, which suffered from poor ventilation, became almost unbearable.
>
> In his later years, when Reb Hershele was already quite weak, the chassidim begged him to take a holiday in the Swiss Alps. They said it was important for his health to take the trip. Reluctantly, Reb Hershele agreed to go.

Upon his return a delegation of chassidim visited Reb Hershele and welcomed him home again. That day there was a heat wave in Eretz Yisroel and as a result the humidity in the flat was almost unbearable. During the visit one of the chassidim asked Reb Hershele if he had enjoyed the trip — people say it is so beautiful there and the air in the Alps is so pleasant.

When Reb Hershele heard the question he jumped up from his place and exclaimed: "Who is interested in what people say? Does the Torah not tell us that Hashem is constantly watching Eretz Yisroel? What could be better than to be in the place which is constantly under Hashem's gaze? Hashem should help me that next year I should not give in so easily to your ideas to leave Eretz Yisroel!"

The chassidim left Reb Hershele's house in a daze. Here in an airless and totally unbearable flat sits a *Yid* who feels as if he is sitting in the most beautiful airy palace. He does not notice the difficult climate; all he feels is the pleasantness of Hashem's presence!

Although Reb Hershele needed nothing for himself, when it came to others he was always very forthcoming. He used to keep money in his breast pocket. When he was once asked the reason for this, he replied, "It takes less time to take out my money from there than from another pocket. When a poor man is waiting for a donation, one must try to put him out of his misery as quickly as possible. Therefore every second counts!"

For almost a decade Reb Hershele guided the Chortkover chassidim, until his *petirah* in his 75th year. On his last day, the 18th of Menachem Av 5728 (1968), he told those next to him with tears in his eyes: "Only a thin curtain is left that still separates us from the coming of Moshiach. How upsetting it is to have to depart this world just now, on the eve of his arrival."

⁀⁀

Reb Hershele left no sons after him to assume his place. His only daughter, the Rebbetzin Malka, married Rav Pinchos Biberfeld, a

Reb Chaim Michoel Biberfeld shlita,
together with Reb Dov Ber Friedman (l.) and Reb Yitzchok Halpern (r.)

prominent *talmid chacham* in Tel Aviv. After Reb Hershele's *petirah*, his son-in-law opened a *kollel* in Tel Aviv for outstanding *avreichim* in memory of Reb Hershele. The Zlatipol-Chortkov *kollel* still functions to this day and continues to produce *talmidei chachamim* of high caliber. Reb Pinchos assumed the post of *rosh kollel* and for many years delivered *shiurim* there. In addition, Reb Pinchos served as the founder and editor of the famous Torah journal "*HaNeeman*" for over thirty years. Published under the auspices of the *kollel*, this Torah journal was famed throughout the world. Many leading *gedolim* chose to use the journal as a platform from which to issue their *divrei Torah* and thoughts.

Reb Pinchos was *niftar* on the 5th of Shevat 5759 (1999). His son, Rav Chaim Michoel, who is a well-known Rav in the Stamford Hill community in London, survives him.

CHAPTER TWENTY-SIX

A Rebbe in Disguise

AFTER REB HERSHELE'S *PETIRAH*, THE CHASSIDIM SET their eyes on Reb Dovid Moshe Friedman, the only son of Reb Dov Ber, and the only surviving grandson of Reb Yisroel of Chortkov.

THREE WEEKS AFTER REB HERSHELE'S *PETIRAH* ALL THE Chortkover chassidim gathered together and unanimously agreed to appoint Reb Dovid Moshe as the new Chortkover Rebbe. A specially drafted letter was sent to Reb Dovid Moshe, signed by the chassidim, accepting him as their Rebbe. Presented here is a translation of their proclamation:

Reb Dovid Moshe Friedman Crowned as Rebbe

> Abundant peace and blessings of a good and long life to our holy crown, a man who encompasses in him all great qualities, a son of *tzaddikim*, Reb Dovid Moshe Friedman, from Chortkov.

שלום רב וברכת חיים טובים וארוכים וכתיבה וחתימה טובה לקדושת עטרת ראשנו,
איש האשכולות בנן של קדושי עולם, רבי דוד משה פריעדמן שליט"א מטשארטקוב.

בעזרת השי"ת היוצר והבורא ועושה הכל, התאספו אנשי שלומינו חסידי
טשארטקוב מארצינו הקדושה ביום י"א אלול תשכ"ח, בבית הרבנית הצדקת מרת
רחל תחי' מטשארטקוב. בכדי לתנות צרותינו אחרי שנשארנו בלי מנהיג ופטרון,
ולבשא את דאגתנו לעתיד-שנעשינו הפקר כצאן אשר אין להם רועה ועל גבינו חרשו
חורשים כאוות רצונם. בנינו עוזבים אותנו ואין לאל ידינו לעזור, אלא הולכים ודלים
יום יום לבושתנו ולבושת כל בית טשארטקוב.

אי לזאת נתקבלה החלטה פה אחד למנות את כבוד הוד קדשו לאדמו"ר
לחסידי בית טשארטקוב ולהתקשר אליו בכל נימי הנפש וידריך עדתנו במקובל
מאבותיו הקדושים והטהורים נ"ע, בדרך התום, האמת ואמונה ובאהבת עולם.

ולעדות זאת באנו וה"ח ומתחייבים לקבל את מרותו ולסמוך אליו כמו
לאבותיו הקוה"ט זי"ע, ואין אנו מבקשים מכ"ת שום תנאים מוקדמים וכן לא דנני על
כל תכלית איך לבצע את המשימה הקשה -אלא מתוך הנחרצות בדבר הסכמנו בדעה
אחת להכתיר את כ"ק בכתר האדמורות, ואנו חזקים בדעה כי כ"ת לא ישיב פנינו
ריקם. כי חוב קדוש מוטל עליו לא פחות מעלינו. לאגן לטובת בית טשארטקוב שלא
תכבה הנחלת ובפרט לגבי ענין סמטות בכבוד אבותיו תלויה בו השייר גם לאחר
פטירתם, במאמר חז"ל קידושין לא: וכך נפסק ביו"ד סי' ר"מ ס"ח ט'.

ובכן, ברכתנו שטוחה לפני כ"ק שיאריך ימים על ממלכתו וזכות אבותיו
מסייעתו, ואנו תפלה לה' כי בימיו תיוושע יהודה וישראל ישבון לבטח ובא לציון
גואל בב"א.

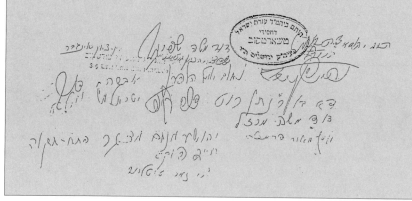

A letter signed by Chortkover chassidim crowning Reb Dovid Moshe as Chortkover Rebbe

With the help of Hashem, Creator and Designer of everything, the chassidim of the Chortkover Chassidus in Eretz
Yisroel have gathered together on the 11th of Elul 5628
(1968) in order to examine our sorrowful state and voice our
concern for the future. We have become left without a leader
and without someone who will care for us.

Therefore we have come to a unanimous decision with one
voice, to appoint his holy honor as the new Rebbe for the
chassidim of the House of Chortkov and to bind ourselves to

him with all the fibers in our bodies. The Rebbe will lead his flock in the way he has been guided by his holy and pure *zeides* in the *derech* of *temimus*, *emes*, *emunah* and *ahavah*.

We attach our signatures as testimony that we hereby obligate ourselves to accept his rule and to listen to and obey him as we did to his *zeides* without any prior conditions.

We are sure that his honor will not reject us and leave us empty-handed, for like us, he too is obligated to worry for the welfare of the House of Chortkov and ensure that its spark is not extinguished.

Therefore it remains for us only to place our blessings before the Rebbe, that he will have a long life on his throne and the *zechus* of his *zeides* shall assist him. We pray to Hashem that in his days Yehudah will be saved and Yisroel will live in peace and tranquility with the coming of the final *geulah* speedily in our times. Amen.

This letter, accompanied by pages of signatures, was sent to London to Reb Dovid Moshe. Yet despite all the pleas of the chassidim, Reb Dovid Moshe refused to hear of the idea and adamantly rejected the notion of being Rebbe. The chassidim, however, also remained steadfast in their desire that Reb Dovid Moshe become their Rebbe and decided to treat him as their leader regardless of whether he consented or not. Over the years they constantly begged him and sent many delegations and distinguished *rabbanim* to try and make him change his mind. But it was all to no avail. This tug of war continued for many years until, eventually, the chassidim realized with a heavy heart that they would just have to accept and respect Reb Dovid Moshe's decision. Nevertheless, although Reb Dovid Moshe was unwilling to act as the official Rebbe of Chortkov, he was willing to act and guide the chassidim in an unofficial capacity. Thus, from then on, Reb Dovid Moshe was regarded and acknowledged as the spiritual leader and head of the Chortkover Chassidus, even though he refused to be known by the title of Rebbe.

The home of the Boyaner Rebbe, where Reb Dovid Moshe was born

IN ORDER TO UNDERSTAND AND APPRECIATE WHY REB
Dovid Moshe refused the position to which he was so suited, a
A Hidden   fuller picture of Reb Dovid Moshe's life and character
Tzaddik   is necessary.

    In every generation there are hidden *tzaddikim*.
Some of them are famous as *tzaddikim*, but even so they are still considered hidden *tzaddikim*, for their true *tzidkus* is hidden from view,
their real greatness being far greater than people think. Others are
literally "hidden" *tzaddikim*, people who pass themselves off as simple and ignorant, while inside them burns a holy *neshamah* carrying
out its lofty task far away from prying eyes.

    Many people considered Reb Dovid Moshe Friedman to be one of
these hidden *tzaddikim*. Even those who thought that they knew him
well did not know him at all. During his lifetime he served his
Creator with *mesiras nefesh* under all conditions. Reb Dovid Moshe
hardly ever mentioned a word about his illustrious past and his life,
and indeed all that is known about him is what people discovered
by accident, through circumstances beyond his control.

    Born on the 28th of Tammuz 5674 (1914) in Boyan to his father, Reb
Dov Ber of Chortkov, Reb Dovid Moshe's arrival in this world was
in itself a miracle. Some years earlier his mother had had a miscarriage with serious complications. As a result of the damage wrought
through the miscarriage, the doctor told her she would not be able to

The only known picture of the Boyaner Rebbe, the Pachad Yitzchok

have any more children. A few years went by and the Rebbetzin Miriam remained childless; it appeared that the doctor's prognosis was indeed true. The Rebbetzin pleaded with her father, the Pachad Yitzchok of Boyan, to promise her a child. The Boyaner Rebbe did indeed promise her a child, telling her, "You will have one more child, it will be a boy, and you will have *nachas* from him!"

Not long after Reb Dovid Moshe was born, the First World War broke out in all its fury. Although the Boyaner Rebbe advised his chassidim to flee to Vienna, he himself refused to leave Boyan. When the Sadigerer Rebbe, Reb Avrohom Yaakov, asked him why he did not also flee to Vienna, the Boyaner Rebbe told him that he was worried that in Vienna they wouldn't find a *frum* lady to nurse his new grandchild, and he was very concerned that his *einikel* should not receive his nourishment from a non-*frum* source. Only after an *erlicher* woman was found to take care of Reb Dovid Moshe, did the Boyaner Rebbe agree to leave Boyan for Vienna.

IN VIENNA, REB DOVID MOSHE BECAME VERY CLOSE TO HIS other grandfather, the Chortkover Rebbe. His *zeide* showed him un-

Under His Zeide's Direction usual love and affection, taking Reb Dovid Moshe with him wherever he went. Although the Chortkover Rebbe was very particular to eat in total solitude, not even allowing his own sons to eat with him, for Reb Dovid Moshe he made an exception. From the time he was just a toddler, he joined his grandfather for all the meals, every Shabbos and Yom Tov.

When Reb Dovid Moshe turned 6 he fell ill with appendicitis. The doctors examined him and decided that he needed an operation.

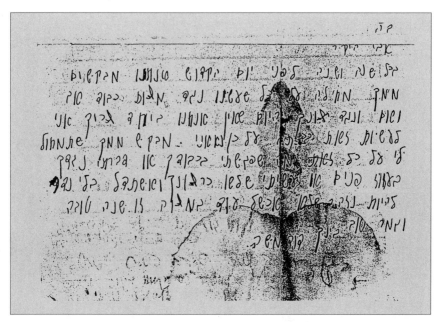

A letter written by Reb Dovid Moshe to his father when he was 6 years old

When the family told the Chortkover Rebbe of his grandson's condition, the Rebbe told them that he wanted to visit his sick *einikel*. His visit caused a big sensation among his chassidim, for in the twenty years that the Rebbe had lived in Vienna, it was the only time that he had stepped foot inside the house of his son, Reb Dov Ber.

Although a chair had been prepared next to Reb Dovid Moshe's bed, the Rebbe chose to sit on the end of the bed — a sign of his great affection for his grandson. Looking at Reb Dovid Moshe, the Rebbe exclaimed, "He hasn't got appendicitis and he never will have." And indeed he recovered without an operation.

The great love the Rebbe had for his grandson manifested itself every year on Pesach at the Seder. During the Seder, the Rebbe sat on a beautiful golden chair, which he had inherited from the Rizhiner and was one of his most treasured possessions. The Rebbe was particular that no one else should sit on the chair, and even he only used it once a year, during the Seder.

Being very wide, the chair really had room for two people, and from when Reb Dovid Moshe was a small child until the Rebbe's last year, the Rebbe would request that his grandson come and sit next to him on this priceless chair.

Reb Dovid Moshe was educated to follow in the footsteps of his ancestors. He never learned in a school or yeshivah but was educated at home by private *melamdim*. The best *talmidei chachamim* in Vienna were selected to teach him, his two main *rebbeim* being Reb Dovid Ochs (who was later *Av Beis Din* of Toronto) and Reb Hershel Schmerler (who was later *Rosh Yeshivah* of Chaye Olam in

Reb Dovid Moshe as a young boy

Yerushalayim). Under their careful tutelage, Reb Dovid Moshe made steady progress and by the age of 20 he was already fluent in most parts of *Shas* by heart!

Many of the great *talmidei chachamim* who came to see the Chortkover Rebbe would take the opportunity to engage Reb Dovid Moshe in a Talmudical discussion. He became especially close to the Lubliner Rav, Reb Meir Shapiro, who foretold a great future for the young boy. The extent of Reb Meir Shapiro's esteem for Reb Dovid Moshe is illustrated by the following story that was related by Reb Bershe Shapiro (a nephew of Reb Meir):

> When Reb Meir Shapiro opened Yeshivas Chachmei Lublin in 1930, the Chortkover Rebbe together with his whole family traveled to Lublin for the event. Reb Dovid Moshe had also been intending to go along, but a few days before they were scheduled to leave, a telegram arrived from Reb Meir Shapiro. In the telegram he wrote that Reb Dovid Moshe shouldn't come to Lublin because Reb Meir recognized his great potential, that every minute he spent learning was irreplaceable, and therefore he couldn't accept responsibility for his *bitul Torah*.

In addition to his demanding schedule, Reb Dovid Moshe had a daily *chavrusa* with his *zeide*, the Chortkover Rebbe, who handed over to him the special *derech* of Beis Rizhin. When the Chortkover Rebbe was *niftar* on the 13th of Kislev (5694) 1934, Reb Dovid Moshe was heartbroken. His *zeide* had been more like a father to him than a grandfather. Two and a half years later tragedy struck again when his father, Reb Dov Ber, was *niftar* after a serious illness.

Reb Dovid Moshe did not despair and tried to carry on like normal. He started to give regular *shiurim* in the *beis hamedrash* underneath the Shiff Shul, which was the main center of Torah and *Yiddishkeit* in Vienna. He also became active in Agudas Yisroel, continuing the projects and programs that his father had started.

WITH THE GERMAN TAKEOVER OF AUSTRIA IN 1938, hardship and suffering became the lot of the Viennese Jews. Many

The War Years *Yidden* were rounded up and sent to the Dachau concentration camp. The Germans took special pleasure in terrorizing Rebbes, *rabbanim* and their families. Even so, Reb Dovid Moshe was not molested, and although much of his family had been tormented, he himself was left untouched.

One day, as Reb Dovid Moshe's older sister was walking along the road, she was approached by a very high-ranking German officer who stopped her and told her, "Until now I have been watching over your younger brother so that no one should harm him. Now, however, I am being transferred to a different city and I won't be able to look after him any longer," and with these words the officer strode away. Who this officer was and why he wanted to protect Reb Dovid Moshe remains a mystery to this very day.

Reb Dovid Moshe went into hiding to evade capture, but after a time he was caught. The Germans proceeded to beat him with such fury that a river of blood flowed from his body. Only when he fell to the ground unconscious did the accursed Germans leave, thinking that they had succeeded in killing him.

Finally, in 1939, just two months before the outbreak of the Second World War, Reb Dovid Moshe succeeded, through the help of Dr. Schonfeld of London, to leave Vienna for England together with his mother and sister. In England he was interned on the Isle of

Man together with thousands of refugees. The refugee camp became very overcrowded and the British authorities decided to send some of the refugees to Australia. Reb Dovid Moshe managed to remain in England by volunteering to join the British Army. Although the British did not accept any refugees for fear that there might be German spies among them, they accepted him, because in Vienna Reb Dovid Moshe had not had the status of an Austrian but of a foreigner.

Reb Dovid Moshe joined the anti-aircraft gunners a few days before Shavuos. Their task was to shoot down enemy warplanes. In a panic he realized that he would have to work on Yom Tov even if there was no immediate threat of an enemy raid. He decided to pretend to be ill and was given a letter by the doctor exempting him for a few days. When Motza'ei Yom Tov came, Reb Dovid Moshe climbed out of bed and went to his commanding officer to report for duty. Now that Yom Tov was over he felt that he had no right to evade his duty.

When the officer saw Reb Dovid Moshe he exclaimed, "This is the first time that a soldier exempt from serving has reported back for duty because he now feels better and is capable of resuming his task," and with that he told Reb Dovid Moshe, "I see that you are a very truthful person. From now on whenever you need to take a day off you may do so without having to first ask for permission."

From then on Reb Dovid Moshe took off every Shabbos and Yom Tov, and during the four years that he was in the army, it never happened that he had to be *mechallel Shabbos*. Reb Dovid Moshe often related this story to show that a person gets further by telling the truth, and it is not as people think, that one achieves more through lies and deceit.

Hidden From the Public

AFTER THE WAR'S END, REB DOVID MOSHE MOVED TO Hampstead where he lived with his mother. When she was *niftar* in 1956 he decided to leave Hampstead and move to Edgware, in the suburbs of London, where his cousin Reb Yaakov Heschel was the Rav of the Adass *kehillah*. At that time Edgware was still a very small and undeveloped community, which was just ideal for Reb Dovid Moshe; here he could serve Hashem far away from the public eye, sitting and learning without interruption.

Although he was very careful not to tell anyone that he came from a very important family and that he was well versed in Torah, it was impossible not to notice his refined speech and his deep and penetrating comments on any topic about which he was asked.

If Reb Dovid Moshe had hoped to escape from his many followers by hiding himself in Edgware, it was not to be. People constantly phoned him or came to ask his advice and receive his *berachah*. A well-known *askan* in Eretz Yisroel, Reb Yaakov Katz, published an article about Reb Dovid Moshe in which he wrote:

> I was delighted to meet Reb Dovid Moshe Friedman, the son of Reb Dov Ber from Chortkov, in London. A great *talmid chacham* and extremely learned is the young Rav Friedman, who continues in his father's ways. I remember him from the days of the Knessia Gedolah in Marienbad in 1937 when he came there on behalf of Agudas Yisroel. His speech and manner are refined as befits somebody from such a family. He sits and immerses himself in the Torah in total concealment.

Reb Dovid Moshe's knowledge left everyone to whom he spoke breathless. During a visit to Eretz Yisroel he became acquainted with Reb Nota Zheinwirt, one of the foremost *rabbanim* in Yerushalayim. They entered into a deep discussion on *Hilchos Shabbos* (in which Reb Nota was considered an expert). Reb Nota later said that during their conversation he couldn't "find his hands and feet" to answer Reb Dovid Moshe's *geonus*. Similar sentiments were heard from Reb Shmelke Pinter from London who used to say that one could ask Reb Dovid Moshe a question on any *Tosafos* in *Shas* and he would answer it. On one of the rare occasions that Reb Dovid Moshe mentioned something about himself, he said that in a few *masechtos* he even knew *Rashi* by heart, word for word!

In worldly matters Reb Dovid Moshe was equally knowledgeable. Once he met a top heart specialist. Reb Dovid Moshe spoke with him at length about the way the heart works. The specialist was dumbfounded by Reb Dovid Moshe's vast understanding and asked him if he was a doctor, for he was convinced that Reb Dovid Moshe must have studied medicine for years. When Reb Dovid

Moshe told him that he had never studied medicine the specialist refused to believe him.

In politics and economics he was considered to be one of the top experts in the country. His knowledge earned him a job in the Treasury in Whitehall, which is responsible for organizing the government's spending programs and budget. His work was top secret so he never elaborated on exactly what his job was, and until this day it remains a secret.

Reb Dovid Moshe made his way to work every day by subway (London Underground). Each way took about three-quarters of an hour. During the journey Reb Dovid Moshe would sit with his eyes tightly shut. Even when he was accompanied by his children he would not converse with them but would continue his practice of sitting with his eyes shut.

ALTHOUGH REB DOVID MOSHE WAS CONSIDERED BY MANY to be worthy of becoming Chortkover Rebbe, and after the position

Unworthy to Be Rebbe
became vacant there were constant delegations who came to plead with him to take over the mantle and lead his chassidim, he always answered them in his great humility that he does not feel he is worthy of doing so.

It hurt Reb Dovid Moshe very much that people thought that he was fitting to be Rebbe. This point can be illustrated by the following story:

> Every year, on Simchas Torah, Reb Dovid Moshe would dance the *hakafos* with great joy. One could see on his face the happiness that he had in dancing with the Torah. One year, however, Reb Dovid Moshe appeared to be very upset and it was noticeable that something was bothering him greatly. When he was asked what caused his change of mood, he answered that when the *gabbai* had called him up to dance with the Torah he had called him, "Reb Dovid Moshe, the Chortkover Rebbe," and he felt that this was an insult to his *zeide*s, and therefore he was not able to dance properly!

The Bohusher Rebbe leaves
Reb Dovid Moshe's house

Even though Reb Dovid Moshe never agreed to become Rebbe, he did not stop his many followers — who regarded him as their Rebbe and leader — from coming to him. Many people came to him for his *berachos* and to ask his advice. The *Rosh Yeshivah* of the Rizhiner Yeshivah in Yerushalayim, Reb Yehoshua Brim, was a fervent chassid of Reb Dovid Moshe. He often said that it was a pity that Reb Dovid Moshe did not agree to become Rebbe, for if he had accepted the title, everyone would have seen immediately that he was one of the true Rebbes of his generation. On another occasion Reb Yehoshua exclaimed, "I am ready to go through fire and water for Reb Dovid Moshe!"

Another of Reb Dovid Moshe's great admirers was the Bohusher Rebbe, Reb Yitzchok Friedman, from Tel Aviv. He constantly spoke about Reb Dovid Moshe, saying that people did not realize who he was. He often said that Reb Dovid Moshe was one of the true *tzaddikim* of the generation and he would tell people to go to him with their problems. When the Bohusher Rebbe came to London he gave Reb Dovid Moshe a *kvittel* and indeed, whenever he spoke to Reb Dovid Moshe, he did not call him by name, but referred to him as the Chortkover Rebbe.

≈≈

A *YUNGERMAN* WHO HAD BEEN MARRIED FOR MANY YEARS without children often went to the Bohusher Rebbe to ask for a *berachah*

Our Signatures Bear Witness Forever

for children. After a number of years had passed and he still hadn't been *zocheh* to children, he asked the Rebbe to promise him a child. Hearing his request, the Rebbe became very serious and after a moment's thought he told him to go and ask the Chortkover

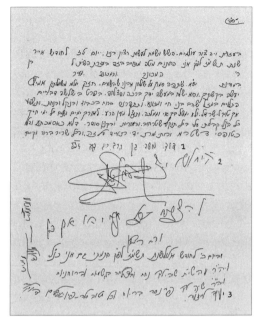

A letter promising someone children. The letter is signed by
1. Reb Dovid Moshe
2. the Bohusher Rebbe
3. the Pshevorsker Rebbe

Rebbe in London, and if he agreed to promise him a child and was ready to sign on it, the Bohusher Rebbe would agree as well.

The *yungerman* did as instructed and prepared a text for Reb Dovid Moshe to sign. The text read as follows:

> We who have signed below promise to Mr. So and So from such and such a country that Hashem will send him *berachah* and *hatzlachah* in his work and especially in the following three things: children, health and wealth. He should have *parnassah* without difficulty and with *kavod*, and foreign peoples should not rule over him and he should be saved from *ayin hara* for many long years. All this we have accepted on ourselves with total responsibility, our signatures bearing witness forever.

Reb Dovid Moshe signed the text and underneath him signed the Bohusher Rebbe.[1] Just over nine months later the man's wife gave birth to a healthy baby!

---

1. A few months later the *yungerman* went to see the Pshevorsker Rebbe, Reb Yaakov Leiser. The Rebbe was very impressed by the letter and said that he also wanted to give the man his *berachah,* and with that he added his signature to the letter.

PEOPLE NEVER FAILED TO BE AMAZED AT REB DOVID
Moshe's *middas ha'emes*. On one of the few occasions that he spoke

Only the Truth about himself he said that he could testify that he had never said a lie in his life! It happened quite a few times that he decided he would go to a certain place the following day but the next day it had become inconvenient or the weather had turned bad. Even so he refused to postpone the trip since he had said that he would go on that day and therefore he did not want to go back on his word.

On one occasion Reb Dovid Moshe was approached by a well-known *askan* who wanted Reb Dovid Moshe to influence a certain philanthropist to give money to a particular yeshivah. The *askan* added that it would help if Reb Dovid Moshe would exaggerate a little the number of *bochurim* learning in the yeshivah. Reb Dovid Moshe looked at the *askan* in disbelief — as if he had just asked him to commit the most terrible crime imaginable — and told him, "I would rather throw myself from the top of the Eiffel Tower than tell a lie!"

When it came to *lashon hara* he was equally strict. It did not matter that the person telling the story hadn't even mentioned anyone's name. If he heard someone relating a bad story about *Yidden* he immediately interrupted the person, telling him, "One may not speak badly about *Yidden*." Reb Dovid Moshe was once at a meeting during which the participants heaped scorn on a particular person, saying that he did not behave in a correct and civilized fashion. Hearing their words, Reb Dovid Moshe asked them to refrain from speaking badly about this person, adding that this person was not fully accountable for his actions because he wasn't mentally stable.

A few days later Reb Dovid Moshe wrote a letter to the person in whose house the meeting had taken place. In the letter he wrote:

> After I left your house last week, I realized that I had transgressed the *aveirah* of *lashon hara* through my words when I said that this person isn't mentally stable. And even though

my intention was to protect his honor, by showing that his behavior is not a result of his bad *middos*, even so, it wasn't correct of me to say that he was not in control of himself. I therefore ask of you to contact all those who were at the meeting and to tell them that I retract my words and I regret having spoken them in the first place and I ask that they should not pass on what I have said to others. Hashem in His mercy should accept my *teshuvah* and have pity on me together with the rest of *Klal Yisroel*.

Reb Dovid Moshe's feeling for Hashem's creations did not include only people. It once happened that a bird became trapped in the chimney of his house. Unable to escape, it chirped loudly in despair. Reb Dovid Moshe took a ladder, climbed into the dark and dirty chimney, and set the bird free.

Reb Dovid Moshe was very careful to give the proper respect to the Torah. In a local shul not far from his home a non-Jewish caretaker would put back the *siddurim* and *Chumashim* after they had been used on Shabbos. Not being able to read Hebrew, he would put many of them away upside down. Reb Dovid Moshe would go himself every week and take them all out and replace them in the correct way. This he did for many years, even when he was already very ill and the most minor tasks were difficult for him.

HIS WHOLE LIFE REB DOVID MOSHE RAN AWAY FROM *kavod* and honor, shunning any public position. On one occasion, af-

Lofty Kavanos ter one of the influential Chortkover chassidim, Reb Zalman Hocherman of Yerushalayim, tried to convince Reb Dovid Moshe to change his mind and become Rebbe, Reb Dovid Moshe told him, "The reason I don't grow a beard (he was clean shaven) is so that people shouldn't mistake me for a *chashuva* person … If I would become Rebbe, then I would have cut my beard for nothing all these years and that I don't want!" When Reb Zalman would tell over Reb Dovid Moshe's words he would add, "Even though it is written in *sifrei* Kabbalah that there are lofty *kavanos* for having a beard, Reb Dovid Moshe had even more lofty *kavanos* for not having one!"

Reb Dovid Moshe

Indeed, although most of his neighbors and friends didn't know who or what he was, they knew he was different. His mere presence had a great effect on his surroundings. Although he hardly ever raised his voice during *davening*, sometimes, from great concentration, he forgot himself and said parts out loud. Every day in *Maariv*, when he came to the words, *"ki beyadcha nafshos hachayim ve-hameisim asher beyado nefesh kol chai veruach kol besar ish, beyadcha afkid ruchi,"* he would say them very loudly, until they were audible throughout the whole shul, and those who heard him were deeply moved at how he entrusted himself in the hands of Hashem.

Later in life he agreed to give a private *gemara shiur* to a group of *baalei battim* in Golders Green. For thirteen years he delivered the *shiur*, during which time they covered much of *Shas*. When a Rizhiner *shteibel* was opened in Stamford Hill he was overjoyed and would make the long journey from Edgware to participate in the *seudos* on the *yahrtzeiten* of his *zeides*. During the *seudos* he would address the gathering, saying Torah in the *derech* he had received from his *zeides*.

SIX YEARS BEFORE HE WAS *NIFTAR*, REB DOVID MOSHE fell seriously ill. During these years he was faithfully nursed by his

His Last Years wife, Rebbetzin Leah, who took care of all his needs. They had been married in 1968 in Switzerland, where his parents-in-law lived. His *shver*, Reb Shimon Noson Gut, had been Rav of the Eitz Chaim *kehillah* in Johannesburg. In his later years he retired to Switzerland where he was *menahel* of the Jewish old age home in Lengnau. A senior teacher in the Bais Yaakov grammar school of London for over twenty years, Rebbetzin Friedman has had a major impact on the *chinuch* of the many hundreds of girls who have passed through her classes.

Despite his illness, Reb Dovid Moshe struggled with his last strength to carry on as normal. On the last night of Chanukah 1988,

At the engagement of Reb Dov Ber, the oldest son of Reb Dovid Moshe.
From left to right: The Sadigerer Rebbe, the Bohusher Rebbe, the chasan, the Boyaner Rebbe.

he went to Golders Green to deliver his *shiur* as usual. When he arrived home he collapsed. The following night, Friday night, his condition became critical and he had to be rushed to the hospital.

That Friday night the Bohusher Rebbe was sitting with his family around the Shabbos table in his house in Tel Aviv. Suddenly, in the middle of the meal, the Shabbos *lecht* fell on the floor and went out. The Bohusher Rebbe became very upset and told his family, "I see that things are not as they should be with Reb Dovid Moshe, we must say *Tehillim* for him."

Although his condition was desperate and the doctors needed to know how he was feeling in order to treat him, Reb Dovid Moshe refused to speak a word. When he was asked if he was making a *taanis dibbur* he nodded his head. After three weeks he agreed to answer the doctors' questions, with a "yes" or "no," but besides these few words he refused to speak at all.

During the few weeks that Reb Dovid Moshe was lying critically ill in the hospital, the Bohusher Rebbe didn't stop *davening* for his recovery (together with many others around the world). Before every mitzvah that he performed he said that the *zechus* of this mitzvah should help Reb Dovid Moshe. Finally, on the night of the 27th of

Reb Dovid Moshe's passing was greatly mourned by many

Shevat 5748 (1988), the Bohusher Rebbe suddenly exclaimed, "*Oy vey*! Reb Dovid Moshe has left us, we have lost our crown, his passing is a terrible loss for the generation." Hearing how the Rebbe was speaking, his daughter said to him, "*Tatte*! What are you saying? He is still alive!" The Bohusher Rebbe didn't answer her and burst into tears; the next morning the sad news arrived that Reb Dovid Moshe had been *niftar*.

AT THE LARGE *LEVAYAH*, THE RAV OF LONDON, RAV Henoch Padwa, was *maspid*. He said that Reb Dovid Moshe had

A Sleepless Night been a *gaon* in *nigleh* and a *gaon* in *nistar*. (They had learned together *b'chavrusa* as *bochurim* in Vienna.) Another *maspid*, HaGaon Reb Chuna

Halpern, told the assembled that he would like to tell them the following story from which they would be able to see who Reb Dovid Moshe really was:

R. DOVID MOSHE FRIEDMAN ז״ל

ON SUNDAY night, after a long and serious illness, Rabbi Moshe Dovid Friedman of Edgware passed away. He was a son of Rav Dov Ber ztl, a son of Rav Yisroel ztl Rebbe of Czortkov.

The levayo started from the Ruzhiner Beis Hamedrash in Stamford Hill where hespedim were made by the Moro D'Assro, Rabbi H B Padwa and Rabbi S Pinter. Both spoke of his outstanding *midas ha'emes* and his hidden *geonus.*

In Edgware the Rav of the Adass Rabbi R Kahan delivered a hesped and from there the levayo went on to the Enfield Cemetery where the *niftar* was accompanied by a crowd of hundreds. At the *Beis Olom* hespedim were made by Rabbi Elchonon Halpern, Rabbi Gershon Hager, Rabbi Biberfeld from Munich and Rabbi Yisroel Moshe Friedman, son of the Rebbe of Sadigur.

Report of the levayah

One day, very early in the morning, Reb Chuna's phone rang. Reb Dovid Moshe was on the other end. He sounded very distraught and told Reb Chuna that he was very upset and hadn't been able to sleep the entire night. The previous day he had been at a *chupah*, where he had agreed to be one of the witnesses. After he had left the *chupah*, he felt terrible that he had agreed to be a witness. *Chazal* tell us that in order for the *chupah* to be valid, the witnesses must be *frum, erlicher Yidden*. Reb Dovid Moshe was worried that perhaps he didn't qualify, and therefore the *chupah* hadn't been valid. It was only with the greatest difficulty that Reb Chuna managed to convince him that he was indeed a kosher witness.

Reb Chuna finished his *hesped*, saying that he very much doubted that there was another *Yid* in the world who was *medakdek* on himself to such a degree. *Zechuso yagein aleinu.*

Reb Dovid Moshe is survived by his wife, three children and grandchildren. His oldest son, Reb Dov Ber, is a leading figure in the Chortkover shul in Antwerp; the second son is the writer of these lines; and his daughter Miriam is married to Reb Yitzchok Halpern, son of the Vasloier Rebbe from Bnei Brak.

Glossary

A

achdus – unity

ahavas Yisroel – loving one's fellow Jews

aleph-beis – the 22 letters of the Hebrew alphabet

aliyah – (1) call to the Torah at the public reading of the Torah; (2) immigration to Israel

Amoraim – Jewish scholars whose teachings are quoted in the *gemara*

amud – podium where the leader of the prayer service stands

apikorsim – heretics

apikorsus – heresy

aron – coffin

aron hakodesh – ark in the synagogue where the Torah scrolls are kept

askan (pl. askanim) – communal worker; activist

aufruf – special *aliyah* for a groom on the Shabbos before his wedding

aveirah (pl. aveiros) – sin; transgression

avodas Hashem – service of G-d

avreichim – students in a yeshivah or *kollel*

B

baal habayis (pl. baalei battim) – layman; householder

baal teshuvah – a penitent returnee to Jewish observance

bechirah – free will; one's ability to make choices to do good or bad

bein hazmanim – break between semesters in yeshivah

beis din – rabbinical court of law

beis hamedrash – communal synagogue or house of study

Beis HaMikdash – the Holy Temple

bekeshe – long satin frock coat

berachah (pl. berachos) – (1) blessing recited before performing a mitzvah; (2) an invocation of Divine favor, as in a blessing given by a Rebbe

bikur cholim – the mitzvah of visiting the sick

bimah – table in synagogue from which the Torah is read

bitachon – trust in G-d

bitul Torah – wasting time from Torah study

blatt – folio page (of Talmud)

bli neder – without intending to take an oath

bnei Torah – (1) those who study and observe the teachings of the Torah; (2) yeshivah students

bochur (pl. bochurim) – unmarried young man, esp. yeshivah student

bris milah – circumcision

bronfen – liquor

C

chacham (pl. chachamim) – sage; scholar; wise person

chalilah – Heaven forbid

chareidim – those who are rigorously observant

chas vesholom – Heaven forbid

chasan (pl. chasanim) – bridegroom

chasunah – wedding

chavrusa – study partner

Chazal – our Sages, of blessed memory

chazzan – leader of prayer services

cheder (pl. chadarim) – elementary school (for religious studies)

cheshbon hanefesh – soul-searching; self-examination

chevrah kadisha – burial society

chiddush (pl. chiddushim) – original Torah insight

chillul Shabbos – desecration of the Sabbath

chinuch – Jewish education

chizuk – encouragement

chochmah – wisdom

chodesh – month

chupah – canopy under which marriage ceremony takes place, or the ceremony itself

churban – destruction

chutz laAretz – the world outside the land of Israel

D

d'veikus – the ecstatic state of cleaving to Hashem

daf – page (of Talmud)

daven – pray

dayan – a judge in a *beis din*

derashah (pl. derashos) – sermon or discourse

derech – way; path; appraoch

din – judgment

dvar Torah (pl. divrei Torah) – a Torah thought or exposition

E-F

ehrlich – sincerely religious; honest

einikel – grandchild

emes – truth

emunah – faith; belief in G-d

even hapinah – cornerstone

frum – religious

G

gabbai (pl. gabbaim) – attendant of a Rebbe

gadol (pl. gedolim) – great Torah personality; outstanding Torah scholar

gadol hador – prime Torah leader of the generation

galus – exile; Diaspora

gaon (pl. geonim) – brilliant Torah scholar; genius

gartel – belt worn during prayer

gedolei Torah – outstanding Torah scholars

gemach – fund providing interest-free loans (or other items)

gemara – loosely, a synonym for the Talmud as a whole

gematria – numerical values of the Hebrew alphabet

geonus – brilliance

get – a bill of divorce

geulah – redemption

goy (pl. goyim) – gentile; non-Jew

H

hachanah – preparation

haftorah – portion of Scripture read following the public Torah reading

HaKadosh Baruch Hu – the Holy One, Blessed is He

hakafos – the dancing (while carrying the Torah) on Simchas Torah

halachah (halachos) – Jewish law

halachah lemaaseh – the practical application of Jewish law

hanachas even hapinah – laying the cornerstone

hanhalah – administration

hashkafah – ideology; outlook

haskamah – letter of approbation recommending the publication of a book

hasmadah – diligence in Torah study

Havdalah – ceremony marking the end of Sabbath and holidays

Heiliger Rachamim – Holy Compassionate One

Heiliger Tatte – Holy Father

hesped (pl. hespedim) – eulogy

his'orerus – (spiritual) awakening

hishtadlus – effort

hislahavus – enthusiasm

I

iluyim – geniuses

issur – that which is forbidden

issur d'rabbanan – that which is forbidden by rabbinic decree

K

Kaddish – prayer sanctifying G-d's Name, often recited by mourners

kallah – bride

kapparah – atonement

kavanah (pl. kavanos) – intent; concentration; thought or intention

kavod haTorah – honor for the Torah or for a Torah scholar

kedushah – holiness; sanctity

kehillah (pl. kehillos) – community; congregation

keriah – tearing one's clothes in mourning

kever – grave

kevod Shamayim – honor of Heaven

kibbud av – honoring one's father

Kiddush – blessing recited over wine expressing the sanctity of Sabbath and festivals

Kiddush Levanah – sanctification of the moon

kiddushin – marriage

kisvei HaArizal – the writings of the Arizal

Klal Yisroel – the community of Israel; Jewish people in general

kloiz – synagogue

kol haTorah – the sound of Torah being learned

Kol Nidrei – prayer which begins the Yom Kippur service

kollel – academy of higher Jewish learning, usually for married men

korban (pl. korbanos) – sacrifice; offering

Kosel HaMaaravi – the Western Wall of the Temple

krias haTorah – reading of the Torah in the synagogue

Krias Shema – prayer in which one accepts upon himself the yoke of the Kingdom of Heaven

kvittel (pl. kvitlach) – a written note to a Rebbe containing a special request

L

l'chaim – "To Life!"; traditional toast

l'ilui nishmas – to cause an elevation of the *neshamah* of a deceased person

l'shem Shamayim – for the sake of Heaven

lamdan – a Talmudic scholar

lashon hara – speaking evil of others

lecht bentching – candle-lighting

levayah – funeral

limud – learning

limud haTorah – learning of Torah

limudei kodesh – sacred learning

lishmah – for the sake of the Torah itself, or for the sake of Heaven, without ulterior motives

M

Maariv – evening prayer service

machlokes – dispute; divisiveness

machzor – prayerbook for the festivals and high holy days

madreigah (pl. madreigos) – level; status

maggid – preacher

magidei shiur – Torah lectures

makom tefillah – a place for prayer

makpid – careful; strict

malach – angel

manhig – leader

masechtos – tractates of Talmud

mashal – analogy; parable

mashgiach – spiritual guide in a yeshivah

maskil (pl. maskilim) – adherent of the Haskalah movement, which sought to uproot traditional values and practices

masmid – an exceptionally diligent Torah student

matzeivah – tombstone

mechallel Shabbos – person who desecrates the Sabbath

mechazeik – to support

mechilah – forgiveness

mechutan – the father of one's son-in-law or daughter-in-law

medakdek – careful; punctilious

medrash (pl. medrashim) – homiletical teaching on the Torah

mefarshim – commentaries

mekarev – to bring close to Torah observance

mekubal (pl. mekubalim) – one who is well versed in Kabbalah

melamed (pl. melamdim) – a Torah teacher, esp. of young children

melamed zechus – to seek the merits in someone or something

Melech HaOlam – King of the World

Melech Yisroel – King of Israel

menahel – principal; supervisor of an institution

mesiras nefesh – physical or spiritual self-sacrifice

mezuzah – parchment scroll affixed to doorpost, to serve as a constant reminder of G-d's presence

middah (pl. middos) – character trait

or attribute

middas ha'emes – the trait of honesty

mikveh – body of water used for ritual immersion

Minchah – afternoon prayer service

minhag (pl. minhagim) – custom

minyan – quorum of ten men necessary for conducting a prayer service

mishmaros – watches

Mishnayos – the teachings of the Tanaaim which form the basis of the Talmud

mofes (pl. mofsim) – miracle

mosad (pl. mosdos) – institution

muktzeh – items forbidden to be moved on the Sabbath and festivals

Mussaf – additional prayer recited on Sabbath, festivals, and Rosh Chodesh

mussar – ethical and religious teachings

mussar sefer – book containing ethical and religious teachings

N

nachas – spiritual pleasure or satisfaction

navi – prophet

Neilah – the concluding prayer service on Yom Kippur

ner tamid – eternal flame

neshamah (pl. neshamos) – soul

niftar – deceased

niggun (pl. niggunim) – tune; melody

nigleh – the revealed part of Torah

nistar – the hidden part of Torah

nusach – version, esp. relating to prayers

P

pachad Hashem – the fear of G-d

parnassah – livelihood

parshiyos – the handwritten parchments contained in the *tefillin*

pasken sha'alos – to issue rulings on halachic questions

pasuk (pl. pesukim) – a verse of Scripture

payos – earlocks

petirah – demise

pidyon nefesh – the contribution for charity which accompanies a request to a Rebbe

pikuach nefesh – a matter of life and death

pilpul – a discourse weaving together various statements of the Talmud

poritz – local landowner (squire) in Eastern Europe

posek (pl. poskim) – halachic decisor or authority

psak din – decision of Torah law

pshat – the plain sense and meaning of a text

R

rabbanim – rabbis

Rabbanus – the Rabbinate

rasha – wicked person

Ribbono Shel Olam – Master of the World

rosh kollel – head of a *kollel*

Rosh Yeshivah – head of a Torah institution

ruach hakodesh – Divine spirit or inspiration

ruchniyus – spirituality

S

sefer (pl. sefarim) – book, esp. on a learned topic

Sefer Torah – Torah scroll

Selichos – penitential prayers recited before and after Rosh Hashanah

semichah – ordination of scholars

seudah – meal, esp. a festive meal

Shacharis – the morning prayer service

Shalom Aleichem – (1) traditional greeting; lit. peace be on you; (2) prayer recited on Friday night

Shamayim – Heaven

Shas – the Talmud as a whole

she'elah (pl. sha'alos) – question on Jewish law

Shechinah – Divine Presence

sheliach – emissary; messenger

sheliach tzibbur – lit. representative of the congregation; chazzan

Shemittah – the Sabbatical year when agricultural work is forbidden in Israel

Shemoneh Esrei – the 18 blessings that are the main feature of the three daily prayer services shiur (pl. shiurim) – lecture on Torah subject

shivah – seven-day period of mourning

shmad – religious persecution

shochet (pl. shochtim) – person who slaughters animals in accordance with Torah law

shteibel (pl. shteiblach) – synagogue

shtreimel – fur-trimmed hat worn by male chassidim on Sabbath and festivals

Shulchan Aruch – Code of Jewish Law

shver – father-in-law

siddur – prayerbook

simchah – joyous occasion; celebration

siyata d'Shmaya – help from Above (Heaven)

T

taanis – fast day

taanis dibbur – abstaining from speaking

taharah – (1) ritual purity; (2) ritual purification of a body in preparation for burial

takanos – ordinances; rules and regulations

tallis – prayer shawl

talmid (pl. talmidim) – student

talmid chacham (pl. talmidei chachamim) – Torah scholar

Talmud Torah – school for Torah studies

Tanach – acronym for Torah, Neviim, Kesuvim; the 24 Books of the Bible

Tannaim – sages of the Mishnah

techiyas hameisim – resurrection of the dead

tefillah (pl. tefillos) – prayer

tefillin – phylacteries

Tehillim – the Biblical Book of Psalms

tekios – one of the sounds of the shofar

temimus – wholeheartedness

teshuvah – repentance

tisch – a chassidic gathering around a Rebbe's Shabbos or festival table during which the Rebbe expounds on Torah and leads his disciples in songs of praise to G-d

toivel – immerse oneself for purification

treif – term used to describe anything not kosher

tumah – ritual impurity

tzaddik (pl. tzaddikim) – (1) saintly individual; (2) chassidic Rebbe

tzaddik hador – the righteous person of the generation

tzadekes – a very righteous woman

tzedakah – charity

tzitzis – fringed garment worn by Jewish men and boys

U

Urim VeTumim – stones which lit up on the Kohen Gadol's breastplate, i.e. a source of Divine inspiration

V

Vidui – the confession recited on Yom Kippur and before death

Y

yachid – unique individual

yahrtzeit – anniversary of a person's passing

yemach shemo – may his name be obliterated

yeshuah – salvation

yetzer hara – evil inclination

yetzer hatov – good inclination

yichus – distinguished lineage

Yid (pl. Yidden) – Jew

Yiddishkeit – the Jewish way of life

yirah – fear; reverence

yiras Shamayim – fear of Heaven

yirei Hashem – G-d fearing

yishuv hadaas – a state of tranquility

Yomim Noraim – High Holy Days

yungerleit – young married men

Z

z'man – semester

zechus (pl. zechusim) – merit

zechuso yagein aleinu – may his merit protect us

zeide – grandfather

zemiros – songs sung at Sabbath and festival meals

zocheh – to merit; to be worthy

Zohar – the basic work of Kabbalah

This volume is part of
THE ARTSCROLL SERIES®
an ongoing project of
translations, commentaries and expositions
on Scripture, Mishnah, Talmud, Halachah,
liturgy, history, the classic Rabbinic writings,
biographies and thought.

For a brochure of current publications
visit your local Hebrew bookseller
or contact the publisher:

Mesorah Publications, ltd

4401 Second Avenue
Brooklyn, New York 11232
(718) 921-9000
www.artscroll.com